The University of Law
incorporating The College of Law

Insurance Law Handbook

Insurance Law Handbook

Fourth edition

Barlow Lyde & Gilbert LLP

Tottel
publishing

Published by
Tottel Publishing Ltd
Maxwelton House
41–43 Boltro Road
Haywards Heath
West Sussex
RH16 1BJ

ISBN 978 1 84766 093 0
© Tottel Publishing Ltd 2008
Formerly published by LexisNexis Butterwoths Tolleys
Fourth edition published by Tottel Publishing Ltd 2008

M03576

British Library Cataloguing-in-Publication Data
A catalogue record for this book is available from the British Library

Typeset by Kerrypress Ltd., Luton, Bedfordshire
Printed and bound in Great Britain by
CPI Antony Rowe Limited, Chippenham, Wiltshire

Preface

This 4th edition marks the continued development of Professor Robert Merkin's original work and seeks to maintain his aim of providing a concise and practical statement of insurance law for the benefit of both practitioners and students of the subject.

We have considered most major business classes and reflected upon how the essential principles of insurance law relate to them.

For this new edition of the book we have re-organised the chapter structure into four parts – which we hope will enable the reader to gain a sound and joined-up understanding of the subject. First, it looks first at the legal principles relevant to the creation of insurance contracts. Second, it considers the various parties who may be involved in the creation and operation of an insurance contract and how they go about their business and are regulated. Third, it considers the legal principles applicable to the making of claims. Fourth, it looks at the question of how insurance contract disputes can be resolved. Fifth, it looks at the various types of insurance that are available in the market, from motor to space. Finally, it considers two separate regulatory topics, namely the regulation of sales of insurance products and insurance business transfers under the *FSMA 2000*.

Among the legal and regulatory developments which are covered in this new edition are the impact of the Gambling Act 2005 on the requirement of insurable interest; the cases of *ERC Frankona Reinsurance v American National Insurance Co (2006)* and *North Star Shipping Ltd v Sphere Drake Insurance plc (2005)* – both of which deal with the assured's duty of utmost good faith disclosure; *Bonner v Cox (2006)* which deals with the reinsured's duty of care in respect of his writing and ceding of business to his excess of loss reinsurers; the recently imposed industry-wide requirement of contract certainty; and the new FSA regulatory regime to which brokers are subject.

We hope that the reader will find this revised work continues to satisfy the criteria originally set down by Professor Merkin, namely to provide the reader with a basic understanding of insurance law in an easy to follow, logical format.

Barlow Lyde & Gilbert LLP
London
May 2008

List of contributors

David Abbott
Tracey Anderson
Jennifer Ball
Gawaine Batchelor
Michael Benguigui
Kevin Bitmead
Chris Brennan
Jason Bright
Elliot Bromley
Tina Collier
James Cooper
Simon Cooper
Adrian Cottam
Tanguy de Schwarz
Patrick Foss
Ben Gold
John Hanson
Lyall Hickson
Douglas Howie
Simon Jackson
Yvonne Jefferies
Joanne Jolly
Giles Kavanagh

Francis Kean
Marc Kish
Simon Konsta
Janet Lambert
Ian Mason
William Norris
Clive O'Connell
John Palmer
James Parker
Patrick Perry
Ian Plumley
Toby Rogers
Jennifer Salmon
Antony Sassi
Victoria Sherratt
Danielle Singer
Kiran Soar
Aidan Thomson
Denis Whelan
Leigh Williams
Katy-Marie Wilson
Jon Yorke

Contents

Preface	v
Contributors	vii
Table of statutes	xxiii
Table of statutory instruments	xxvii
Table of directives	xxix
Table of treaties	xxxi
Table of cases	xxxiii

Part 1   The Insurance Contract

Chapter 1: Contract of insurance	**3**
General definition of insurance	3
Premiums	3
The benefit payable to the insured	4
Uncertain events	4
Contract formation	4
The offer	5
The proposal form	5
The cover note	6
The acceptance	7
Intention to create legal relations	9
Consideration	9
Formation of a contract at Lloyd's	9
The slip	9
LMP/MR Slip	10
The policy	12
Insurance company policies	12
Lloyd's policies	12
Contract certainty	13
Chapter 2: Terms in insurance contracts	**15**
Classification of terms	15
Warranties	15
Conditions precedent	16
Suspensive conditions	17
Exclusion clauses	17
Mere conditions	17
Innominate terms	18
Construction of terms	18
The intention of the parties must prevail	18

Words should be given their ordinary and natural meaning 18
Technical or trade meaning 19
Meaning may be limited by the context 19
Surrounding words 20
Business-like interpretation 20
Resolution of ambiguity 21
Implied term 21
Extrinsic evidence 22

Chapter 3: Duration of insurance contracts 25
Duration of cover 25
When does cover commence? 25
Termination of cover 25
Expiry of cover 25
Renewal of cover 26
Early termination 27
The effect of termination on claims 27

Chapter 4: Insurable interest 29
Introduction 29
Definition 30
The requirement of an insurable interest 30
The distinction between indemnity and non indemnity insurance 31
Non-indemnity insurance and insurable interest 31
Indemnity insurance and insurable interest 32
Marine insurance 33
Non-marine insurance 33
Marine insurance 33
Non-marine indemnity insurance: illustrations of insurable interest 34
The indemnity principle 36

Chapter 5: Premiums 37
Definition 37
Amount of premium 37
Payment of premium 38
Renewal of premium 39
Life insurance 39
Indemnity insurance 40
The role of brokers 40
General principles 40
Lloyd's policies and contracts of marine insurance 40
Return of premium 42
Indivisibility of premium and total failure of consideration 42
Application of the law 42

Chapter 6: Policyholder duties 45
Duty of utmost good faith 45
Continuing duty of utmost good faith 46
Disclosure 46
The nature of the obligation to disclose 47
Innocent non-disclosure 48
The use of agents 49

Materiality and inducement 49
A presumption of inducement 50
Illustrations of material facts 51
Limitations on the duty of disclosure 53
Waiver of the duty to disclose 54
Waiver or affirmation 55
Duration of duty of disclosure 55
Superfluity 56
The insurer's remedies for breach of duty to disclose 56
Misrepresentation 57
Materiality and inducement 57
The construction of statements made by the insured 58
The insurer's remedies for misrepresentation 59
Fraud 60
The definition of fraud 60
The effect of fraudulent statements 60
Materiality and inducement 61
Fraudulent claims 61
Agents of the insured 61
Criminal liability for fraudulent statements 62
Minimising loss and alteration in the risk 62
Increase in hazard clauses 63
Continuing warranties 63
Reasonable care clauses 63
Fire protection clauses 64
Duty on the insurer 64

Chapter 7: Policyholder protection **65**
Introduction 65
Liability of insolvent insurers to policyholders 65
Valuing claims 66
The Financial Services Compensation Scheme 66
Powers 66
Funding of the Financial Services Compensation Scheme's
  obligations 67
Amounts payable under the Financial Services Compensation Scheme 68
Compulsory insurances 69
General insurance other than compulsory insurance policies 69
The FSCS's liability in relation to long-term policies 69
Insolvent insurance intermediaries 70
Summary 70

Chapter 8: Global insurance programmes **71**
Introduction 71
Obstacles to a single global policy 71
Retaining risk 72
Vertical contractual chains 72
'Difference in conditions' cover 73
Problems with global programmes 73
Jurisdiction and choice of law 73
Inconsistency between the local and master policy 73
Controlling claims 74

Contractual inconsistency 74
Captive insolvency 74
Summary 74

Part 2   The Parties

Chapter 9: Brokers **77**
Brokers and agency law 77
The broker as the insured's agent 77
Practical difficulties 77
Authority 79
The regulation of brokers 79
Other amendments to the FSA Handbook 86
The rights of brokers 87
Commission 87
Lien 88
The duties of brokers 88
Nature of the duties 88
Finding insurance 88
Completing the proposal form 89
Payment of the premium 90
Post-formation duties 90
Claims 91
The liabilities of brokers 92
Contract and tort 92
Limitation of actions 93
Measures of damages 93
Persons to whom duties are owed 94

Chapter 10: Underwriting agencies **97**
Nature of underwriting agencies 97
Definition 97
Authorisation 97
Underwriting agencies and Lloyd's 99
Underwriting agencies and reinsurance pools 100
Underwriting agent's authority 101
Underwriting agent's duties 101

Chapter 11: Lloyd's **103**
History and structure 103
Regulation of Lloyd's 104
Challenging the imposition of fines or suspension 106
The course of business at Lloyd's 106
The Lloyd's slip 106
Binding nature of a slip 106
Oversubscription 107
Effect of the issue of the policy 107
Payment obligations at Lloyd's 108
Premiums 108
Losses 109

Chapter 12: Insurance companies   111
The authorisation requirement   111
Regulated activities   112
Defining what constitutes a contract of insurance   112
     Characteristics of an insurance contract   114
Consequences of conducting unauthorised insurance business   115
Legal and procedural requirements for authorisation by the FSA   116
Ongoing supervision   117

Part 3 The Claim

Chapter 13: Causation   121
Proximate cause   121
Sequential causes of loss   121
     Unbroken chain of events   122
     Broken chain of events   122
     Linked events   122
Concurrent causes of loss   123
Mitigation   124
Insured's negligence   124
Alternative policy formations   126

Chapter 14: Claims   127
Notification of claims   127
     Time for giving notice   128
Proof of loss   128
     Waiver of breach of condition precedent   129
     Burden of proof   129
     Proof of loss by an insured peril   130
Fraudulent claims   131
     Proof of fraud   132
Limitation   132
     The Limitation Act 1980   132
     Contractual limitation periods   133
     The insurer's obligation to pay   133
     Payments in respect of assigned policies   133
     Payments in respect of policies under trust   134

Chapter 15: Valuation of Loss   135
Loss   135
     General meaning of 'loss'   135
     Loss of possession of property   135
     The defrauded insured   137
Indemnity   137
Valued policies   138
     Valuation   138
     Total loss under a valued policy   139
     Partial loss under a valued policy   139
     Valued policy not subject to average   139
     Valued policy subject to average   140
Unvalued policies   140

Valuation   140
Total loss under an unvalued policy   140
Partial loss under an unvalued policy   143
Consequential loss   143
Insurance on a 'reinstatement' basis   144
Late payment by the insurer   144
Damages for breach of contract   144
Interest   145
Restrictions on recovery   146
Betterment   146
Contractual limitations   146
A series of losses   147
Settlements between insurer and insured   148
The insurer's right of salvage   150
Reinstatement   151
Definition   151
Reinstatement under the policy   152
Statutory reinstatement   153

Chapter 16: Subrogation and Assignment   **155**
Nature of subrogation   155
Role of subrogation   155
Practical operation of subrogation   156
Assignment as an alternative to subrogation   157
Scope of the right of subrogation   157
Indemnity contract   157
Insured must have a cause of action   158
Loss of cause of action by the insured   160
Waiver of subrogation rights by the insurer   160
Indemnification of the insured   160
Actual payment by the insurer   160
The insurer's liability to indemnify the insured   161
Rights of the insurer prior to payment   161
Loss exceeding the sum insured   162
Actions against the emergency services   163
Procedural aspects of subrogation actions   164
Sums recovered by way of subrogation   165
Ownership   165
Allocation   165
Assignment   166
Assignment of the policy   167
General prohibition   167
Consent of the insurer   167
Formalities   168
Marine policies   169
Life policies   169
Consequences of assignment of a policy   170
Assignment of the proceeds of the policy   171
Principles governing assignment   171
Sale of land   172

Chapter 17: Co-insurance   **173**
Introduction   173
Joint insurance   173
Composite insurance   174
      Definition and significance   174
      Creation of composite insurance   175
Co-insured subrogation immunity   177
Insurance for the benefit of another   178

Chapter 18: Double insurance and contribution   **181**
Introduction   181
Double insurance   181
      The insured's rights   181
      Variation by contract   182
Double insurance and contribution   182
      Definition of contribution   183
      The conditions for contribution   184
      The amount of contribution   185

Chapter 19: Average   **187**
Average defined   187
Policies subject to average   188

Chapter 20: Third Parties (Rights Against Insurers) Act 1930   **189**
Background   189
Conditions for the operation of the 1930 Act   190
      The insured's insolvency   190
      Proof of the insured's liability   190
      Dissolved companies   190
Compliance with policy terms   191
Agreements between the insurer and the insured   191
Limitation periods   191
The third party's right to information   192
Problems with the operation of the 1930 Act   192
Proposals for reform   193

Part 4   Dispute Resolution

Chapter 21: Arbitration   **197**
The arbitration agreement and arbitration clause   197
The scope of arbitration   198
Procedure governing arbitrations   198
Confidentiality   198
Honourable engagement clause   199
Right to appeal   200

Chapter 22: Court proceedings   **201**
Civil Procedure Rules   201
The overriding objective   201
The court's case management powers   202
Pre-action protocols   203
The three 'tracks' to litigation   203

Part 36 offers   204
Disclosure   205
Expert evidence   205
Summary   205

Chapter 23: Alternative dispute resolution   **207**
Mediation   207
Executive tribunal (or 'mini trial')   208
Expert determination   208
Early neutral evaluation   209

Part 5   Specific Types of Insurance

Chapter 24: All risks insurance   **213**
Nature of all risks insurance   213
Effect of the policy being all risks   213

Chapter 25: Aviation Insurance   **215**
Introduction   215
Aircraft operators' insurance   216
    Loss of or damage to aircraft   216
    Liability of operators to passengers   217
    Liability to third parties other than passengers   218
    General exclusions to cover   218
    Conditions precedent to liability under the policy   219
    Liability for loss of or damage to cargo   219
    Standard exclusion clauses   220
Airport owners' and operators' liability insurance   222
    Premises liability   222
    Hangar keeper's liability   224
    Products liability   224
    Exclusions applicable to all sections of the policy   225
    General conditions   225
Spares cover   225
Products liability   226

Chapter 26: Bloodstock insurance   **227**
Veterinary certificates and declarations of health   227
Common clauses   227
    All risks mortality   227
    Loss of use   228
    Theft and unlawful removal   228
    Public liability   228
Moral hazard and fraud   229

Chapter 27: Buildings and property insurance   **231**
Introduction   231
Types of building and property insurance   231
    Specified perils v All Risks   231
    Trigger of cover   232
    Disclosure of risk   232
Exclusions   233

The University of Law
Moorgate Campus Library

Issue Summary

Natural peril exclusions 233
Industrial perils 234
Computer systems 234
War and allied perils exclusions 235
Theft and fraud exclusions 235
Inevitable loss 236
Other exclusions 237
Typical conditions 237
Extensions to buildings and property insurance 238
Business interruption 238
Denial of access 239
Debris removal 239
Increased cost of construction 240

Chapter 28: Construction risks insurance **241**
Risk issues 241
Project insurance 241
Insurance under the JCT construction contracts 242
Insurance against injury to persons or property 242
Insurance against damage to the works 243
Insurance for employer's loss of liquidated damages 243
Issues arising from the operation of Contractors' All Risks insurance 243
Coverage 243
Risks excluded 243
Latent defects insurance 244

Chapter 29: Directors and officers liability **245**
The nature and scope of directors and officers insurance 245
Background 245
Permutations of cover 245
Common sources of liability for directors 246
Duties to the company 246
Other statutory liabilities 248

Chapter 30: Employers' liability insurance **249**
Introduction 249
Compulsory insurance for injuries at work 250
The obligation to insure 250
Contents of the policy 251
Liabilities faced by an employer 251
Common law liability 251
Liability arising under statute 253
Who is the employee? 255
An 'employee' 255
Residence in Great Britain 255
Relatives 255
Specific exceptions 255
Transfer of liabilities 256
Enforcement 256
Sanctions 256
Certificates 257

Chapter 31: Environmental insurance   **259**
Sources of environmental liability   259
      Common law   259
      Statute   259
Insurance against environmental liability   260
      Public liability policies   260
      Environmental insurance policies   261

Chapter 32: Goods in transit insurance   **263**
Goods in transit insurance in context   263
Goods in transit and carrier's liability distinguished   264
Coverage under goods in transit policies   265
      Commencement and termination   265
      Transit   265
      Storage   265
Exclusions and conditions   266
      Loss   267
The Marine Institute Cargo Clauses   267
      Commencement and duration of cover 267
      Scope of cover   268
      Change in the course of transit   269

Chapter 33: Legal expenses insurance   **271**
Forms of cover   271
      Before the event insurance   271
      After the event insurance   272
Relationship with conditional fee agreements   272
Regulation   273

Chapter 34: Marine Insurance   **275**
Marine insurance defined   275
      The Marine Insurance Act 1906   275
      Nature of marine insurance   276
      Policies covering mixed sea and land risks   276
General principles   276
      The duty of good faith   276
      Insurable interest   277
      Assignment   277
      The policy   277
Types of marine policy   278
      Voyage and time policies   278
      Valued and unvalued policies   278
      Floating policies and open covers   279
The premium   280
Warranties   280
      What is a warranty?   280
      Marine insurance warranties   281
      Implied warranty of seaworthiness for vessels   281
      Seaworthiness of goods   282
      Warranty of legality   282
      Warranty of neutrality   282
      Warranty of nationality   282

Warranty of good safety 283
Currency of the voyage 283
Commencement of risk 283
The performance of the voyage 283
Marine risks: hulls and freight policies 285
General considerations 285
Summary of cover 285
Perils of the seas 286
Piracy 288
Machinery damage 288
Barratry 288
Negligence 289
Marine risks: cargo policies 289
Summary of cover 289
Exclusions from marine cover 289
War and strikes risks 289
Wilful misconduct 289
Delay 290
Inherent vice and related perils 290
Marine losses 290
Forms of loss 290
Actual total loss 291
Constructive total loss 291
Partial loss 293
General average 293
Measure of indemnity 294
General introduction 294
Loss of or damage to the vessel 294
Loss of or damage to cargo 295
Loss of freight 295
Suing and labouring 296
Rights of insurers 297

Chapter 35: Motor vehicle insurance **299**
Nature of motor vehicle insurance 299
The contract 299
Utmost good faith 299
Warranties 300
Policy conditions 300
Driver extension clauses 302
First party cover 302
Compulsory insurance scheme 303
Compulsory insurance requirement 303
Scope of the compulsory insurance 304
Obligation for insurer 305
The victim's direct action against the insurer 306
Motor Insurers' Bureau 306
Compensation of victims of uninsured drivers 306
MIB's obligation to satisfy compensation claims 306
Exceptions 307
Conditions precedent to the MIB's obligation 307

Limitations on MIB's liability 308
Untraced drivers 308

Chapter 36: Product liability insurance **309**
Introduction 309
The risk insured 309
Compensation or damages 310
Financial loss 310
Accidental injury and damage 310
Territorial and jurisdiction restrictions 311
Claims occurring or claims made 311
Claims occurring 311
Claims made 312
Exclusions 312
Injury to insured's employee and damage to insured's property 312
Contractual liability assumed by insured 313
Damage to a product, lack of fitness for purpose, repair, replacement,
recall and disposal of defective goods 313
The giving of advice, design and specification for a fee 313
Other exclusions 314
Conditions 314
Reasonable precautions 314

Chapter 37: Professional indemnity insurance **315**
Sources of professional liability 315
Compulsion to insure 315
Basis of cover 316
Scope of cover 316
Extensions to the basic insuring agreement 317
Exclusions 317
Conditions 318
Dispute resolution 318

Chapter 38: Reinsurance **319**
Nature of reinsurance 319
General definition 320
Separate contract 320
Forms of reinsurance 321
Formation of reinsurance agreements 322
Reinsurance in advance of insurance 322
Reinsurance pools 322
Misrepresentation and non-disclosure 323
Facultative agreements 323
Treaties 323
What is 'material'? 325
Remedies for misrepresentation or non-disclosure 326
Terms of reinsurance agreements 326
Duration 326
Incorporation by reference 326
Inspection of records clauses 327
Arbitration clauses 328
Losses and claims 329

Loss settlements clauses   329
Claims co-operation and control provisions   331
Choice of law problems   332

Chapter 39: Space insurance   **333**
Introduction   333
Terminology   334
General   334
The risks   334
The legal framework   335
    Treaty on Principles Governing the Activities of States in the
        Exploration and Use of Outer Space, Including the Moon and
        Other Celestial Bodies   335
    The Convention on International Liability for Damage Caused by
        Space Objects 1972 ('the Liability Convention')   335
Industry practice   336
Types of coverage   336
    Loss or damage to the space object   336
    Partial loss   337
    Liability   338
    Transponder coverage   338
    Delay   338
    Political risks   338
    Re-launch guarantee   338
And finally …   339

Chapter 40: War risks and related perils   **341**
The insurability of war risks   341
    The market   341
    Commercial insurance in time of war   341
Particular war risks   342
    War   342
    Civil war   342
    Rebellion and revolution   343
    Insurrection   343
    Civil commotion   343
    Riot   343
    Hostile acts by or against a belligerent power   344
    Derelict weapons of war   344
Proximate cause   344
Perils related to war risks   345
    Other causation tests   345
Strikes   346
Terrorism and political risks   346
    Political risks exclusions   346
    Terrorism risks and commercial buildings   346

Part 6   Regulatory Matters

Chapter 41: Regulation of sales of insurance products   **351**
Regulation of insurance intermediaries   351
    Implementation of the IMD   351

Contents

What insurance intermediation activities are regulated?   352
    Qualifying contracts of insurance   353
    By way of business   353
    Exclusions   354
    Appointed representatives   355
Authorisation and ongoing supervision   355
    Insurance: Conduct of Business Sourcebook (ICOB)   355
    General Rules   356
    Financial promotion   357
    Advising and selling standards   357
    Status disclosure   357
    Product disclosure   358
    Cancellation   358
    Claims handling   359
    Specific rules in connection with distance non-investment mediation
        contracts with retail customers   359
    The ICOB Review   359

**Chapter 42: Insurance Business Transfers under the Financial Services
    and Markets Act 2000**   **361**
Introduction   361
Use of insurance business transfers   362
Law and practice   362
Meaning of 'transfer'   363
The court's jurisdiction   363
Procedure   364
    The role of the Financial Services Authority   364
    Policyholders in EEA states   365
    Independent expert and scheme report   366
    Notification to policyholders and others, and access to
        documentation   366
    The court application   367
    Final hearing   368
Effect of court's order   369
UK taxation   370

Index   **371**

Table of statutes

PARA

Access to Justice Act 1999
s 29 .... 33.02
Animals Act 1971
s 2(2)(b) 26.06
Arbitration Act 1996 .... 21.01, 21.04
s 7 .... 21.02
s 46(1) 21.06
s 46(1)(b) **21.06,** 38.17
s 69 .... 21.07
Companies Act 1985
s 651 .... 20.04
Companies Act 1989 .... 20.04
Companies Act 2006
part 31
ch 3 .... 20.04
s 170(1) 29.03
s 170(3) **29.03**
s 170(4) **29.03**
ss 171–177 .... 29.03
s 233 .... 29.01
s 260(4) 29.03
s 1030 .... 20.04
**Company Directors
Disqualification Act 1986** 29.05
**Contracts (Rights of Third
Parties) Act 1999** 15.30, 17.05,
38.03
**Employers' Liability
(Compulsory Insurance)
Act 1969** 30.01, 30.13
s 1 .... 7.07
s 1(1) 30.02
s 1(2) 30.03
s 1(3)(a) 30.02
s 1(3)(b) 30.02
s 2(1) 30.09
s 2(2)(a) 30.11
s 3 .... 30.01
s 3(1)(a) 30.12
s 3(1)(b) 30.12
s 3(2) 30.12
s 5 .... 30.14, 30.15
**Employers' Liability (Defective
Equipment) Act 1969** 30.08
**Environmental Protection
Act 1990**
s 73(6) 31.04
s 78E 31.04
Factories Act 1961 .... 30.05

PARA

**Financial Services and Markets
Act 2000** .. 7.14, 10.02, 11.02, 38.01
part I 42.07
part VII 42.01, 42.03
part XIX 11.02
s 19 .... 12.01
s 20(2) 12.05
s 22(1) 12.02
ss 23–24 .... 10.02
s 24 .... 12.01
s 26 .... 12.05
ss 26–28 .... 10.02
s 31 .... 12.01
s 38 .... 12.01
s 41(2) 12.06
s 42(6) 12.06
s 43(1) 12.06
s 90 .... 29.05
s 105 .... 42.02, 42.05
s 109 .... 42.07, 42.09
s 110 .... 42.07
s 112 .... 42.13
s 112(2)(a) 42.13
ss 212–224 .... 7.01
ss 314–324 .... 11.02
s 316(1) 10.02
s 397 .... 6.32
s 418 .... 12.01, 42.05
sch 1
para 6(1) 12.07
sch 3 .... 12.01
sch 4 .... 12.01
sch 6 .... 12.06
sch 12 .... 42.03, 42.07, **42.08**
**Fires Prevention (Metropolis)
Act 1774**
s 83 .... 15.11, 15.30, 15.34, 17.08
Fraud Act 2006
s 2 .... 6.32
s 3 .... 6.32
Friendly Societies Act 1992
s 99 .... 4.05
Gambling Act 2005 ..... 4.01, 4.03, 4.05,
4.07, 4.08, 4.14
Gaming Act 1845 .... 4.03, 4.08
**Health and Safety at Work etc.
Act 1974** 30.08
Insolvency Act 1986
s 214 .... 29.05

PARA

Insurance Companies Act 1982 ... 33.04
  sch 2C 42.03
Landlord and Tenant Act 1985
  s 42(2) 17.08
  sch 3
    para 7 .... 17.08
Landlord and Tenant Act 1987 .... 17.08
Latent Damage Act 1986 .... 9.36
Law of Property Act 1925 .... 16.27
  s 47 .... 16.31
  s 136 ...... 14.13, **16.23**, 16.25, 16.29,
                          16.30
Law Reform (Contributory
  Negligence) Act 1945 .... 9.37
Life Assurance Act 1774
  s 1 .... 5.12
Life Assurances Act 1774 .... 4.05
  s 1 .... 4.05
Limitation Act 1980 .... 14.10
  s 2 .... 9.36
  s 5 .... 9.36
  s 14A 9.36
Lloyd's Act 1982 .... 11.02
  s 14 .... 11.01
Marine and Aviation Insurance
  (War Risks) Act 1952 .... 40.02
Marine Insurance Act 1906 .... 4.07,
                         15.17, 34.01
  s 1 .... 34.02
  s 2 .... 34.03
  s 2(2) 34.03
  s 3 .... 34.02
  s 4(1) 34.05
  s 4(2)(b) 34.05
  s 5 .... 4.02, 34.05
  s 6 .... 34.05
  ss 7–14 .... 34.05
  s 9(2) 38.03
  s 15 .... 16.23, 34.06
  s 16 .... 34.09, 34.50
  s 17 .... **6.01**, 6.02, 34.04
  s 18 .... 6.01, 9.02
  ss 18–19 .... 34.04
  s 18(1) 6.04, 6.07, 6.19, 6.31
  s 18(2) 6.04, 6.07
  s 18(3) 6.12
  s 18(3)(a) 6.13
  s 18(3)(b) 6.14
  s 18(3)(c) 6.15
  s 18(3)(d) 6.16, 6.20
  s 19 .... 6.01, 6.06, 9.02
  s 19(1) 6.05
  s 20 .... 6.01, 6.04, 34.04
  s 20(2) 6.23
  s 20(3)(5) 6.24
  s 20(4) 6.22
  s 21 .... **1.21**, 34.07

PARA

Marine Insurance Act 1906 – *contd*
  s 22 .... 1.05, 5.03, 34.07
  s 23 .... 34.07
  s 24 .... 34.07
  s 25 .... 34.08
  s 26 .... 34.07
  s 27 .... 34.09
  s 27(3) 15.05, 34.09, 34.50
  s 29(1) 34.10
  s 29(3) 34.10
  s 31 .... 34.11
  s 31(1) 5.02
  s 31(2) 5.02
  s 32 .... 34.57
  s 32(2) 18.02
  s 33 .... **2.01**
  s 33(1) 34.12
  s 33(3) **2.01**, 34.12
  s 34 .... 34.12
  s 34(3) **2.01**
  s 36(1) 34.21, 34.23
  s 36(2) 34.21
  s 38 .... 34.22
  s 39 .... 34.14
  s 39(1) 13.06, 34.15, 34.32
  s 39(1–4) 34.08
  s 39(2) 34.15
  s 39(3) 34.15
  s 39(4) 34.15
  s 39(5) 13.06, 34.08, 34.16, 34.32
  s 40(1) 34.18
  s 40(2) 34.18
  s 41 .... 34.19
  s 42 .... 34.08
  ss 42–49 .... 34.08
  s 42(1) 34.24, 34.25
  s 42(2) 34.24
  s 43 .... 34.08, 34.24
  s 44 .... 34.08, 34.24
  s 45 .... 34.08, 34.26
  s 45(2) 34.26
  s 46 .... 34.08, 34.27
  s 46(1)(3) 34.27
  s 47 .... 34.27
  s 48 .... 34.08, 34.27
  s 49 .... 34.08, 34.27
  s 50(1) 16.24, 34.06
  s 50(2) **16.24**, 16.29
  s 50(3) **16.24**
  s 52 .... 5.03
  ss 52–54 .... 34.11
  s 53 .... 9.27
  s 53(1) 5.09, 9.31, 11.08
  s 53(2) 11.08
  s 54 .... 5.09
  s 55(2) 13.08
  s 55(2)(a) .. **13.01**, 34.36, 34.39, 34.55

PARA

Marine Insurance Act 1906 – *contd*
s 55(2)(c) 34.40
s 56 .... 34.42
s 56(3) 34.42
s 57 .... 34.43
s 57(2) 34.46
s 58 .... 34.43
s 60(1) 34.44
s 60(2)(i)(a) 34.44
s 60(2)(i)(b) 34.44
s 60(2)(ii) 34.44
s 60(2)(iii) 34.44
s 61 .... 34.45
s 61(2) 34.49
s 62(1) 34.46
s 62(2) 34.46
s 62(3) 34.46
s 62(5) 34.46
s 62(6) 34.46
s 62(7) 34.46
s 62(8) 34.46
s 63(1) 34.47
s 63(2) 34.47
s 64 .... 34.48
s 65 .... 34.48, 34.56
s 66(1) 34.49
s 66(3) 34.49
s 66(4) 34.49
s 66(5) 34.49
s 67(2) 19.02
s 68(1) 34.51, 34.52
s 68(2) 34.51, 34.52
s 69(1) 34.51
s 69(2) 34.51
s 69(3) 34.51
s 70 .... 34.53
s 71(1) 34.52
s 71(2) 34.52
s 71(3) 34.52
s 71(4) 34.52
s 73 .... 34.49
s 76 .... 34.42
s 77 .... 15.22
s 78(1) 34.55
s 78(2) 34.56
s 78(3) 34.55
s 78(4) 34.55
s 79 .... 16.01
s 80 .... 34.57
s 81 .... 19.01, 19.02, 34.50
ss 82–84 .... 34.11
s 84(1) 6.28
s 84(3)(a) 5.15
s 84(3)(b) 5.13
s 84(3)(c) 5.12
s 84(3)(d) 5.12
s 84(3)(e) 5.18

Marine Insurance Act 1906 – *contd*
s 84(3)(f) 5.18, 18.02
s 91(2) 34.01
sch 1 .... 40.09
  para 7 .... 34.30
  para 8 .... 34.33
  para 9 .... 34.29
  para 11 .... 34.35
**Marine Insurance (Gambling
  Policies) Act 1909** 4.07
**Married Women's Property
  Act 1882**
s 11 .... 4.05
Misrepresentation Act 1967
s 2(1) 6.25
s 2(2) 6.21, 6.25, 38.13
Nuclear Installations Act 1965
s 19 .... 7.07
Occupiers Liability Act 1957 ...... 28.01
Occupiers Liability Act 1984 ...... 28.01
Policies of Assurance Act 1867 .... 14.13,
                                    16.25, 16.26
s 2 .... 16.29
**Policyholders Protection
  Act 1975** 7.01
**Policyholders Protection
  Act 1997** 7.01
Public Order Act 1986
s 1 .... 40.09
s 1(1) **40.09**
s 1(2)–(5) 40.09
s 10(2) 40.09
**Rehabilitation of Offenders
  Act 1974** 6.11
**Reinsurance (Acts of Terrorism)
  Act 1993** 40.17
s 2(3) 40.17
Riding Establishments Act 1964
s 1(4A)(d) 7.07
Road Traffic Act 1988 ...... 20.01, 30.01,
                                    30.04
part VI 7.07, 35.21
s 143 .... 35.05, 35.08
s 144 .... 35.21
s 145(2) 35.13
s 145(3)(a) 35.13
s 145(3)(b) 35.13
s 145(5)–(6) 35.13
s 148 .... 35.04
s 148(1)–(2) 35.04
s 148(3)–(5) 35.04
s 148(5) 35.04
s 148(7) 35.05
s 149 .... 35.13
s 151 .... 35.14
s 151(1) 35.14
s 151(1)(a) 35.14

PARA

Road Traffic Act 1988 – *contd*
s 151(1)(b) 35.15
s 151(4) 35.15
ss 157–159 .... 35.13
s 170 .... 35.16
s 185 .... 35.08
s 192 .... 35.08
**Road Traffic (NHS) Charges
Act 1999** 35.13
Sale of Goods Act 1979
s 18 .... 27.11
**Supply of Goods and Services
Act 1982**
s 13 .... 37.01
s 16 .... 37.01

PARA

Supreme Court Act 1981
s 35A 15.18
Theft Act 1968 .... 27.11
s 2(1) 2.10
**Third Parties (Rights Against
Insurers) Act 1930** 9.38, 20.01,
20.03, 20.04, 20.09,
20.10, 30.01
s 1 .... 20.02, 20.05
s 2 .... 20.08
s 3 .... 20.06
Vehicle (Excise) Act 1971 .... 35.04
War Damage Act 1943 .... 40.02
War Risks Insurance Act 1939 .... 40.02
Water Resources Act 1991 .... 31.05
s 161A 31.04

Table of statutory instruments

	PARA
Civil Procedure Rules 1998 (SI 1998/3132)	22.01
part 1	22.02
part 3	22.03
part 24	22.03
part 31	22.07
part 35	22.08
part 36	22.06
r 1.1(2)	22.02
r 1.4	**22.02**
r 3.3	22.03
r 3.4(2)(a)	**22.03**
r 26.6–26.9	22.05
r 31.16	22.04
r 44.3	22.03
Conditional Fee Agreement Regulations 2000 (SI 2000/692)	33.02
Conditional Fee Agreement (Revocation) Regulations (SI 2005/2905)	33.02
County Court Rules (SI 1981/1687)	22.01
Employers' Liability (Compulsory Insurance) Exemption Regulations 1971 (SI 1971/1933)	30.12
Employers' Liability (Compulsory Insurance) Exemption (Amendment) Regulations 1992 (SI 1992/3172)	30.04, 30.12
Employers' Liability (Compulsory Insurance) General Regulations 1998 (SI 1998/2573)	30.10
reg 2(1)	30.05
reg 2(2)	30.05
reg 3	30.03
reg 5	30.15
reg 6	30.15
reg 7	30.15
reg 8	30.15
European Communities (Rights against Insurers) Regulation 2002 (SI 2002/3061)	35.17
Financial Services and Markets Act 2000 (Control of Business Transfers)(Requirements on Applicants) Regulations 2001 (SI 2001/3625)	42.03
reg 3	42.10
reg 3(4)	42.10
Financial Services and Markets Act 2000 (Regulated Activities) Order 2001 (SI 2001/544)	33.04, 41.01
Insurance Companies (Legal Expenses Insurance) Regulations 1990 (SI 1990/1159)	33.01, 33.04
reg 3	33.04
reg 4	33.04
reg 5	33.04
reg 6	33.04
reg 8	33.04
Insurance Companies (Legal Expenses Insurance)(Application for Authorisation) Regulations 1990 (SI 1990/1160)	33.04
Insurance Companies (Winding Up) Rules 1985 (SI 1985/95)	7.03

Table of statutory instruments

PARA

Insurers (Winding Up) Rules 2001 (SI 2001/3635) 7.03
  r 6 .... 7.03
  sch 1 .... 7.03
Management of Health and Safety at Work Regulations 1992 (SI 1992/2051) 30.08
Management of Health and Safety at Work (Amendment) Regulations 2006
  (SI 2006/438) 30.08
Manual Handling Operation Regulations 1992 (SI 1992/2793) 30.08
Motor Vehicles (Compulsory Insurance) Regulations 1992 (SI 1992/2036) 30.04
Motor Vehicles (Compulsory Insurance) Regulations 2000 (SI 2000/726) 35.08
Personal Protective Equipment Regulations 1992 (SI 1992/2966) 30.08
Provision and Use of Work Equipment Regulations 1992 (SI 1992/2932)
  reg 6(1) 30.08
Rules of the Supreme Court (SI 1965/1776) 22.01
Transfer of Undertakings (Protection of Employment) Regulations 1981
  (SI 1981/1794) 30.13
Work at Height Regulations 2005 (SI 2005/735) 30.08
Workplace (Health, Safety and Welfare) Regulations 1992 (SI 1992/3004) 30.08

Table of directives

PARA

85/374/EEC (Product Liability Directive) 36.06
87/344/EEC (Legal Expenses Directive) 33.04
92/49/EEC (Third Non-Life Directive) 41.09
2000/26/EC (Fourth Motor Insurance Directive) 41.09
2001/17/EC (Reorganisation and Winding-up of Insurance Undertakings
    Directive) 7.03
2002/65/EC (Distance Marketing Directive) 41.09
2002/83/EC (Consolidated Life Directive) 41.09
2002/92/EC (Insurance Mediation Directive) 9.04, 41.01–41.02

Table of treaties

	PARA
Montreal Convention 1999	32.02
Outer Space Treaty 1967	39.06
Space Liability Convention 1972	39.07
Warsaw Convention 1929	25.04
Montreal Additional Protocol No. 4 1975	32.02
York-Antwerp Rules 1974	34.50

Table of cases

PARA

A Company, Re (No 0013734 of 1991) [1992] 2 Lloyd's Rep 415 .... 38.18
AB Exportkredit v New Hampshire Insurance, unreported, 1998 .... 16.13
Abbey National plc v Solicitors Indemnity Fund, [1997] PNLR 306 .... 2.10
Abrahams v Mediterranean Insurance and Reinsurance Co Ltd
    [1991] 1 Lloyd's Rep 216 .... 2.14
Ackman and Scher v PPB [1992] 2 Lloyd's Rep 321 .... 7.03
Agapitos v Agnew [2002] 3 WLR 616 .... 16.01
Alfred McAlpine plc v BAI (Run-Off) Ltd [2000] 1 Lloyd's Rep 437 (CA) . 2.06, 35.04
Allen v Robles [1969] 3 All ER 154 .... 14.04
Amey Properties Limited v Cornhill Insurance plc [1996] LR LR 259 .... 35.04
Anders & Kern UK Ltd v CGU Insurance plc [2007] EWHC 377 (Comm) 27.14
Anderson v Commercial Union Assurance Co [1885] 55 LJQB 146 .... 15.33
Andreas Lemos, The [1982] 2 Lloyds Rep 483; [1983] 1 All ER 590 .... 34.33, 40.09
Aneco Reinsurance Underwriting Ltd v Johnson & Higgins Ltd
    [1998] 1 Lloyd's Rep 565; [2002] Lloyd's Rep IR 91 .... 9.37, 11.05
Anonyme d'Intermediaries Luxembourgeois v Farex GIE [1995] LRLR 116 .... 6.16
Arbuthnot v Feltrim [1994] 2 Lloyd's Rep 468 .... 11.01
Arbuthnott v Fagan: Deeny v Gooda Walker Ltd, [1996] LRLR 135 .... 2.11
Ashmore v Corporation of Lloyd's (No 2) [1992] 2 Lloyd's Rep 620 .... 11.01
Assicurazioni Generali SpA v Arab Insurance Group [2003] 1 WLR 577 ...... 6.07, 6.08
Assicurazioni Generali SpA v CGU International Insurance plc and Others
    [2003] Lloyd's Rep 1R 725; [2004] EWCA Civ 429 .... 38.22
Athens Maritime Enterprise Corporation v Hellenic Mutual War Risks Ass.
    (Bermuda) (The Andreas Lemos) [1982] 2 Lloyds Rep; [1983] 1 All ER
    590 483 .... 34.33, 40.09
Axa Equity & Law Life Assurance Society plc and Axa Sun Life plc, Re
    [2001] 1 All ER 1010 .... 42.12
AXA General Insurance Ltd v Gottlieb [2005] Lloyd's Rep IR 369 .... 6.30
AXA Reinsurance (UK) plc v Field [1996] 2 Lloyd's Rep 233 .... 38.03
Balfour v Beaumont [1982] 2 Lloyd's Reports 493 .... 1.17
Ballantine v Employer's Insurance Co of Great Britain [1893] 21 R 305 .... 14.03
Bamburi, The [1982] 1 Lloyds Rep 312 .... 34.44
Bank Leumi Le Israel BM v British National Insurance Co Ltd
    [1988] 1 Lloyd's Rep 71 .... 11.05
Bank Of America National Trust & Savings Association v Christmas (The
    Kyriaki) [1993] 1 Lloyd's Rep 137 .... 14.10, 34.46
Bank of Nova Scotia v Helenic Mutual War Risks Association 2.01
Barker, ex parte Gorely, Re [1864] 4 De G J&Sm 477 .... 15.34
Barnett & Block v National Parcels Insurance Co Ltd (1942) 73 Ll LR 17 .... 32.05
Barrett v London General Insurance Co [1934] 50 LI LR 99 .... 35.04
Bartlett & Partners Ltd v Meller [1961] 1 Lloyd's Rep 487 .... 32.03
Bartoline Ltd v (1) Royal & SunAlliance Insurance plc (2) Heath
    Lambert Ltd 31.05
Baugh v Crago [1975] RTR 453 .... 35.11
Bayview Motors Ltd v Mitsui Marine & Fire Insurance Co Ltd
    [2002] 1 Lloyd's Rep 652 .... 34.55
Beacon Carpets Ltd v Kirby [1984] 2 All ER 726 .... 15.33
Beckensdale v Harvey (1859) 4 H&N 445 .... 6.33

PARA

Becker v Marshall [1922] Ll L Rep 413 .... 6.11
Berger v Pollock [1973] 2 Lloyd's Rep 442 .... 6.19
Bernadone v Pall Mall Services Group [2000] (CA) 30.13
Berriman v Rose Thomson Young (Underwriting) Ltd [1996] 5 Re LR 117 .... 9.29
Blackburn, Low & Co v Vigors (1887) 12 at APP Cas 531 .... 6.05
Board of Trustees of the Tate Gallery v Duffy Construction [2007] EWHC
    361 (TCC) 27.07
Boggan v Motor Union Insurance Co [1923] 26 Ll LR 64 .... 40.13
Bonner v Cox Dedicated Corporate Member Ltd [2006] 2 Lloyd's Rep 152 .... 38.08,
    38.16
Boobyer v David Holman & Co Ltd (No 2) [1993] 1 Lloyd's Rep 96 .... 11.01
Boss v Kingston [1962] 2 Lloyd's Rep 431 .... 16.22
Bradley v Eagle Star Insurance Company [1989] 2 WLR 568 .... 20.04
Bradley v Essex and Suffolk Accident Indemnity Society [1912] 1 KB 415 .... 2.02
British and Foreign Marine Insurance Co Ltd v Gaunt [1921] 2 AC 41 .... 24.02
British and Foreign Marine Insurance Co Ltd v Wilson Shipping Co Ltd
    [1921] 1 AC 188 .... 15.23
British Equitable Insurance Co v Musgrave (1887) 3 TLR 630 .... 6.28
Broad v Waland [1942] 75 Ll LR 263 .... 35.02
Bromley LBC v Ellis [1971] 1 Lloyd's Rep 97 .... 9.38
Brotherton v Aseguradora Colseguros (No 2) [2003] Lloyd's Rep IR 758 .... 6.11
Broughton Park Textiles (Salford) Ltd v Commercial Union Assurance Co Ltd
    [1987] 1 Lloyd's Rep 194 .... 14.09
Brown v KMR Services Ltd [1995] 2 Lloyd's Rep 513 .... 11.01
Brownsville Holdings Ltd v Adamjee Insurance Co Ltd [2000] 2 Lloyd's Rep
    458 .... 34.39
Buckland v Palmer [1984] 3 All ER 554 .... 16.14
Bucks Printing Press Ltd v Prudential Assurance [2000] CLY 880 .... 14.08
Caledonian North Sea v London Bridge Engineering [2002] UKHL 4 .... 16.08
Canning v Farquhar (1886) 16 LR QBD 727 .... 1.14
Caparo v Dickman [1990] 2 AC 605 .... 37.01
Cape plc v Iron Trades Employers Association [2004] Lloyd's Rep IR 75 .... 6.14
Capital and Counties plc and Digital v Hampshire County Council and Others
    [1997] 2 Lloyd's Rep 161 .... 16.16
Carreras Ltd v Cunard Steamship Co [1918] 1 K.B. 118 .... 19.02
Carter v Boehm (1766) 3 Burr 1905 .... 6.01
Cassel v Lancashire & Yorkshire Insurance Co (1885) 1 TLR 495 .... 14.02
Castellain v Preston (1883) 11 QBD 380 .... 16.02
Cater Allen Ltd, Re (30 April 2002, unreported) 42.13
Chapman v Fraser [193] Marshall on Marine Insurances (4th Ed) 525 .... 6.28
Charles v Altin (1854) 15 CB 46 .... 9.37
Charman v Guardian Royal Exchange Assurance plc [1992] 2 Lloyd's Rep
    607 .... 38.21, 38.22
Charter Reinsurance Co Ltd v Fagan [1996] 2 Lloyd's Rep 113 .... 38.18
Cherry Ltd v Allied Insurance Brokers Ltd [1978] 1 Lloyd's Rep 274 .... 9.32
Chippendale v Holt [1895] 1 Com Cas 197 .... 38.20, 38.21
Citadel Insurance Co v Atlantic Union Insurance Co [1982] 2 Lloyd's Rep
    543 .... 38.08
Clark v National Insurance [1964] 1 Lloyds Rep 199 .... 35.04
CNA International Reinsurance Co Ltd v Companhia de Seguros
    Tranquilidade SA [1999] CLC 140 .... 1.09
Co-operative Retail Services Ltd v Taylor Young Partnership Ltd
    [2002] 1 WLR 1419 .... 17.07
Cobb v Williams [1973] RTR 113 .... 35.10
Coleman's Depositories Ltd, Re [1907] 2 KB 798 .... 1.13
Collingridge v Royal Exchange Assurance Corpn (1877) 3 QBD 173 .... 4.12
Commercial Union Assurance Co Ltd v Hayden [1977] QB 804 .... 18.08

Commercial Union Assurance Co plc v Sun Alliance Insurance Group plc
[1992] 1 Lloyd's Rep 475 .... 3.3, 38.14
Commercial Union Assurance Co v Lister (1874) 9 Ch App 483 .... 16.14
Compania Maritima San Basilio SA v The Oceanus Mutual Underwriting
Association (Bermuda) Ltd (The Eurysthenes) [1976] 2 Lloyd's Rep 171 ..... 34.17
Conn v Westminster Motor Insurance [1966] 1 Lloyds Rep 407 .... 35.04
Connecticut Mutual Life Insurance Co of Hertford v Moore (1881) 6 App Cas
644 .... 6.24
Continental Illinois National Bank and Trust Co of Chicago v Bathurst [1985]
1 Lloyds Rep 625 .... 34.02
Coolee v Wing Heath & Co (1930) 47 TLR 78 .... 9.32
Corcos v de Rougemont [1925] 23 L1 LR 164 .... 35.02
Cornfoot v Royal Exchange Assurance Corporation [1904] 1 KB 40 .... 3.1, 3.2
Costain-Blankenvoort (UK) Ltd v Davenport, (The Nassau Bay)
[1979] 1 Lloyd's Rep 395 .... 40.11
Cox v Orion Insurance Co Ltd [1982] RTR 1 .... 14.08
Coxe v Employers' Liability Assurance Corporation Ltd [1916] 2 KB 629 .... 13.09
Crow's Transport Ltd v Phoenix Assurance Co Ltd [1965] 1 WLR 383 .... 32.03
CTI v Oceanus [1984] 1 Lloyd's Rep 476 .... 6.04, 6.07, 6.18
Curtis & Sons v Matthews [1918] 2 KB 825 .... 40.04
Cutter v Eagle Star Insurance Company Limited, Clarke v Kato
[1998] 4 All ER 417 .... 35.08
Davidson v Guardian Royal Exchange Assurance [1979] 1 Lloyd's Rep 406 .... 15.32
Davitt v Titcumb [1989] 3 All ER 417 .... 17.03
Dawsons Ltd v Bonnin [1922] 2 AC 413 HL 1.08
De Maurier (Jewels) Ltd v Bastion Insurance [1967] 2 Lloyd's Rep 550 .... 32.06
Delver v Barnes (1807) 1 Taunt 48 .... 38.02
Dent v Blackmore [1927] 29 L1 LR 9 .... 35.02
Department of Trade and Industry v St Christopher Motorists Association Ltd
[1974] 1 All ER 395 .... 1.03, 12.04
Derry v Peek (1889) 14 App Cas 337 .... 6.27
Desouza v Waterlow [1999] RTR 71 .... 35.14
Deutsche Genossenschaftsbank v Bunhope [1993] 2 Lloyd's Rep 518 .... 27.11
Devco Holder and Burrows & Paine v Legal & General Assurance Society
[1993] 2 Lloyd's Rep 567 .... 13.08
Dibbens, E & Sons (In Liquidation), Re [1990] BCLC 577 .... 4.13
Dickinson v Dodds [1976] 2 ChD 463 .... 1.07
Dixon v London Fire and Civil Defence Authority, The Times, 22 February
1993 .... 30.06
Dobson v General Accident Fire and Life Corporation plc [1989] 3 All ER
927; [1990] 1 QB 274 .... 15.03, 27.11
Dodson v Peter H Dodson Insurance Services [2001] Lloyd's Rep IR 278 .... 16.22
Dominion Mosaics and Tile Co Ltd v Trafalgar Trucking Co Ltd
[1990] 2 All ER 246 .... 15.12
Dora, The [1989] 1 Lloyd's Rep 69 .... 6.13, 15.05
DPP v McArthy [1988] RTR 323 .... 35.14
DR Insurance Co v Seguros American Banamex [1993] 1 Lloyd's Rep 120 .... 10.02
Drake Insurance plc v Provident Insurance plc [2003] EWCA Civ 1834;
[2004] 1 Lloyd's Rep 268 .... 6.38, 18.06
Dunbar v A&B Painters Ltd [1986] 2 Lloyd's Rep 38 .... 9.32
Dunthorne v Bentley [1996] PIQR 323 .... 35.13
E Dibbens & Sons (In Liquidation), Re [1990] BCLC 577 .... 4.13
Eagle Star Co Ltd v Provincial Insurance plc [1993] 3 All ER 1 .... 18.06
Eagle Star Insurance Co Ltd v Games Video Co (GVC) SA (The Game Boy)
[2004] 1 Lloyd's Rep 238 .... 15.05
Eagle Star Insurance Co v Spratt [1971] 2 Lloyd's Rep 116 .... 11.07
Earl of Egmont's Trusts, Lefroy, Re v Earl of Egmont [1908] 1 Ch 821 .... 15.12

PARA

Earle v Rowcroft (1806) 8 East 126 .... 34.35

Economides v Commercial Union Assurance Co plc [1998] Lloyd's Rep IR 9;
    [1998] 1 QB 587 .... 6.22, 15.05

Edgington v Fitzmaurice (1885) 29 Ch D 459 .... 6.22

Edmunds v Lloyd Italico e L'Ancora Cia di Assicurazioni e
    Riassicurazioni SpA and Another [1986] 2 All ER 249 .... 15.18

Edwards v Skyways Ltd [1964] 1 WLR 349 .... 38.22

Eide UK Ltd v Lowndes Lambert Group Ltd [1998] 1 Lloyd's Rep 389 .... 9.27

Eisinger v General Accident Fire and Life Corporation Limited
    [1955] 2 All ER 897 .... 15.03

Elcock v Thomson [1949] 2 KB 755 .... 15.08

Electro Motion Ltd v Maritime Insurance Co Ltd [1956] 1 Lloyd's Rep 420 .... 32.09

England v Guardian Insurance Ltd [1999] All ER (Comm) 481 .... 16.01

Equitable Fire and Accident Office Ltd v Ching [1907] AC 96 .... 18.04

ERC Frankona Reinsurance v American National Insurance Co [2006] Lloyd's
    Rep IR 157 .... 6.05

Ernest Scragg & Sons Ltd v Perseverance Banking and Trust Co Ltd
    [1973] 2 Lloyd's Rep 101 .... 10.04

Euro-Diam Ltd v Bathurst [1988] 2 All ER 23 .... 34.19

Eurodale Mfg Ltd v Ecclesiatical Insurance Office plc [2003] EWCA Civ
    203 .... 32.03

Eurysthenes, The [1976] 2 Lloyd's Rep 171 .... 34.17

Everett v Hogg, Robinson and Gardner Mountain (Insurance) Ltd
    [1973] 2 Lloyd's Rep 217 .... 9.37

Exchange Theatre Ltd v Iron Trades Mutual Insurance Co Ltd
    [1983] 1 Lloyd's Rep 674; [1984] 1 Lloyd's Rep 149 .... 6.34, 15.11

Faircharm Investments Ltd v Citibank International plc, The Times,
    20 February 1998 .... 16.13

Farnham v Royal Insurance (1976) 2 Lloyd's Rep 437 .... 6.34

Farra v Hetherington [1931] 40 LL LR 132 .... 35.02

Feasey v Sun Life Assurance Co of Canada [2003] Lloyd's Rep. IR 637 ...... 4.02, 4.05

Felicie, The [1990] 2 Lloyd's Rep 21 .... 20.07

Fenton Insurance Co Limited v Gothaer Versicherungsbank V Vag
    [1991] 1 Lloyd's Rep 172 .... 5.03

Fifth Liverpool Starr-Bowkett Building Society v Travellers Accident
    Insurance [1893] 9 TLR 22119.02

Figre Ltd v Mander [1999] Lloyd's Rep IR 193 .... 5.03

Firmin & Collins Ltd v Allied Shippers Ltd [1967] 1 Lloyd's Rep 633 .... 32.05

First National Tricity Finance Ltd v OT Computers Ltd (in Administration)
    [2004] EWCA Civ 653 .... 20.08

Forsikringsaktieselskapet Vesta v Butcher [1989] AC 852; [1989] 1 All ER
    402 .... 9.29, 38.03, 38.15, 38.24

Fraser Shipping Ltd v Cotton [1997] 1 Lloyd's Rep 586 .... 34.43

Fraser v BN Furman (Productions) Limited [1967] 1 WLR 898 ;
    [1967] 2 Lloyd's Rep 1 .... 2.13, 6.36

Fytche v Wincanton Logistics plc [2004] 4 All ER 221 .... 30.08

Game Boy, The [2004] 1 Lloyd's Rep 238 .... 15.05

Gan Insurance Company Limited v Tai Ping Insurance Company Limited
    (No 2) [2001] Lloyd's Rep IR 291 .... 38.23

Garrett v Halton Borough Council [2006] EWCA Civ 1017 .... 33.03

GE Reinsurance Corp v New Hampshire Insurance Co and Willis Ltd (Pt 20
    defendant) [2003] EWHC 302 .... 9.37

Geismar v Sun Alliance and London Insurance Ltd [1978] QB 383 .... 4.11

General Accident Fire and Life Assurance Corporation Ltd and Drysdale v
    Midland Bank Ltd [1940] 2 KB 388 .... 17.02, 17.03

General Accident Fire and Life Assurance Corporation Ltd v Tanter (The
    Zephyr) [1985] 2 Lloyd's Rep 529 .... 1.17, 9.38, 11.06, 38.05

PARA

General Accident Insurance Corporation v Cronk [1901] 17 TLR 233 .... 1.14
General Reinsurance Corporation v Forsakringsaktiebolaget Fennia Patria
  [1983] 2 Lloyd's Rep 287   .... 1.17, 11.05
Giles v Thompson, The Times, 1 June 1993 .... 16.02
Glasgow Assurance Corporation Ltd v William Symondson [1911] 104 LT
  254   .... 6.19, 38.08
Glasgow Training Group Ltd v Lombard Continental plc (1988) Times,
  21 November 27.07
Glencore International AG v Ryan [2001] 2 Lloyd's Rep 608, 613 .... 34.10
Glengate v Norwich Union [1996] All ER 487 .... 27.15
Godfrey Davis v Culling and Hecht [1962] 2 Lloyd's Rep 349 .... 15.32
Good Luck, The [1992] 1 AC 233 .... 2.01, 2.02
Gould v Curtis [1913] 3 KB 84 .... 1.04
Grace v Leslie & Godwin Financial Services Ltd [1995] LRLR 472 .... 9.32
Grant v Reliance Insurance Company (1879) 44 UCR 229 .... 1.13
Great North Eastern Railway Ltd v Avon Insurance plc [2001] 2 Lloyd's Rep
  649   .... 9.32
Grecia Express, The [2002] 2 Lloyd's Rep 88 .... 6.11, 34.09, 34.39, 38.16
Griffiths v Fleming [1909] 1 K.B. 805 .... 4.05
Groupama Navigation et Transports v Catatumbo CA Seguros
  [2000] 2 Lloyd's Rep 350   .... 38.03, 38.24
Guardian Assurance v Sutherland [1939] 63 L1 LR 220 .... 35.02
Gunns v PA Insurance Brokers [1997] 1 Lloyd's Rep 173 .... 6.36
Hair v The Prudential Assurance Co Ltd [1983] 2 Lloyd's Rep 667 .... 6.15
Halford v Kymer (1830) 10 B & C 724 .... 4.05
Halsey v Milton Keynes General NHS Trust [2004] EWCA Civ 576 .... 23.02
Harbutt's 'Plasticine' Ltd v Wayne Tank & Pump Co Ltd [1970] 1 QB 447 .... 15.18
Harrington Motor Insurance Co Ltd, Re [1928] Ch 105 .... 20.01
Harris v Poland [1941] 1 KB 462 .... 13.08
Harse v Pearl Life Assurance Co [1904] 1 KB 558 .... 5.12
Hatton v Hall [1997] RTR 212 .... 35.10
Hawke v Niagara District Mutual Fire Insurance Company (1876) 23 Gr 139 .... 1.13
Hawkes v Southwark LBC, unreported, 1998 (CA) 30.08
Hayler v Chapman [1989] 1 Lloyd's Rep 490 .... 16.14
Hayter v Nelson [1990] 2 Lloyd's Rep 265 .... 38.22
Hayward v Norwich Union Insurance Ltd [2000] 1 CL 270 .... 35.04
Hebdon v West (1863) 3 B. & S. 579 .... 4.05
Hedley Byrne & Co Ltd v Heller & Partners Ltd [1964] AC 465 .... 37.01
Heinrich Hirdes GmbH v Edmund (The Kiel) [1991] 2 Lloyd's Rep 546 .... 3.2
Henderson v Merrett [1995] 2 AC 145 .... 37.01
Highlands Insurance Co v Continental Insurance Co [1987] 1 Lloyd's Rep
  109   .... 6.25, 38.13
HIH Casualty and General Insurance Ltd v Chase Manhattan Bank
  [2001] Lloyd's Rep IR 191; [2001] Lloyd's Rep IR 703; [2003] 2 Lloyd's
  Rep 61   .... 6.06, 6.15, 6.22, 6.25, 9.02, 38.08
HIH Casualty and General Insurance Ltd v New Hampshire Insurance
  [2001] 2 Lloyd's Rep 161; [2001] LRIR 244   .... 1.21, 2.16, 11.07
Hill v Mercantile & General Reinsurance Company plc [1996] 1 WLR 1239 ...... 38.19
Hiscox v Outhwaite (No3) [1991] 2 Lloyd's Rep 524 .... 38.17
Hobbs v Marlowe [1978] AC 16 .... 16.15
Holland v Russell (1863) 4 B&S 14 .... 9.34
Holmes v Payne [1930] 2 KB 301 .... 15.02
Home & Overseas Insurance Co Ltd v Mentor Insurance Co (UK) Ltd
  [1989] 1 Lloyd's Rep 473   .... 21.06, 38.17, 38.18
Home Insurance Co of New York v Gavel [1928] 30 Ll LR 139 .... 18.04
Home Insurance Co of New York v Victoria-Montreal Fire Insurance
  Company [1907] AC 59   .... 38.15

PARA

Hopewell Project Management Ltd v Ewbank Preece Ltd (1998) 1 Lloyd's
  Rep 448 .... 17.05
Horry v Tate & Lyle Refineries Ltd [1982] 2 Lloyd's Rep 416 .... 15.28
Houghton v Trafalgar Insurance [1953] 2 Lloyds Rep 503 .... 35.04
Howard v Refuge Friendly Society (1886) 54 L. T. (N.S.) 644 .... 4.05
Hugh Allen & Co Ltd v Holmes [1969] 1 Lloyd's Rep 348 (CA) 9.26
Hughes v Liverpool Victoria Legal Friendly Society [1916] 2 KB 482 .... 5.12
Hussain v Brown [1996] 1 Lloyd's Rep 627 .... 2.01, 27.05
Ikarian Reefer, The [1993] 2 Lloyds Rep 68 .... 34.31
Inchmaree, The (1887) 12 App Cas 484 .... 34.30
Ingleton of Ilford Ltd v General Accident Fire and Life Assurance Corpn Ltd
  [1967] 2 Lloyd's Rep 179 .... 32.06
Insurance Company of Africa v SCOR (UK) Reinsurance Co Ltd
  [1985] 1 Lloyd's Rep 312 .... 38.21, 38.23
Insurance Corporation of Channel Islands Ltd and Royal Insurance Ltd v
  McHugh and The Royal Hotel [1997] LRLR 94 .... 27.05, 27.14
Integrated Container Service Inc v British Traders Insurance Co Ltd
  [1984] 1 Lloyd's Rep 154 .... 34.55
Interfoto Picture Library v Stiletto Visual Programmes [1989] QB 433 .... 1.14
Inversiones Manria SA v Sphere Drake Insurance Co plc, (The Dora)
  [1989] 1 Lloyd's Rep 69 .... 15.05
Investors Compensation Scheme v West Bromwich Building Society [1998]
  1WLR 896 (HL) 2.16
Ionides v Pender (1874) LR 9 QB 531 .... 6.11, 15.05
Iron Trades Mutual Insurance Co Ltd v Companhia de Seguros Imperio
  [1991] 1 Re LR 213 .... 38.16
Irving v Manning and Anderson [1847] 1 HLC 287 .... 15.05
Isaacs v Royal Insurance Co (1870) 5 LR Exch 296 .... 3.1
Islander Trucking Ltd v Hogg Robinson & Gardener Mountain (Marine) Ltd
  [1990] 1 All ER 826 .... 9.36
Italia Express (No. 2), The [1992] 2 Lloyd's Rep 281 .... 15.17
Italia Express (No. 3), The [1992] 2 Lloyd's Rep 216 .... 14.12
J Rothschild Assurance plc v Collyear [1999] Lloyds Rep IR 6 .... 37.03
J W Bollom & Co Ltd v Byas Mosley & Co Ltd [2000] Lloyd's Rep IR 136 .... 9.32
Jason v Batten (1930) Ltd [1969] 1 Lloyd's Rep 281 .... 13.09
Jester-Barnes v Licences and General Insurance Co Ltd [1934] 49 LI LR 231 .... 6.11
JJ Lloyd Instruments Ltd v Northern Star Insurance Co. Ltd (The Miss Jay
  Jay) [1987] 1 Lloyd's Rep 32 .... 34.30
Joel v Law Union & Cran Insurance Company [1908] 2 KB 863 .... 6.05
John Rigby (Haulage) Ltd v Reliance Marine Insurance Co Ltd [1956] 2 QB
  468 .... 32.03
Johnson v IGI Insurance Company Ltd [1997] 6 Re. L.R. 283 .... 1.11
Julien Praet et Cie SA v H G Poland Ltd [1960] 1 Lloyd's Rep 420 .... 10.06
K/S Merc Scandia XXXXII v Certain Lloyd's Underwriters (The Mercandian
  Continent) [2001] 2 Lloyd's Rep 563 .... 6.02, 6.19
Kacianoff v China Traders Mutual Insurance Co Ltd [1914] 3 KB 1121 .... 13.07
Kastor Navigation Co Ltd v Axa Global Risks (UK) Ltd [2004] 2 Lloyd's Rep
  277 .... 34.46
Kawasaki Kisen Kabushiki Kaisha of Kobe v Bantham Steamship Co Ltd
  [1939] 2 KB 544 .... 40.04
Kelly v Norwich Union Fire Insurance Society Limited [1989] 2 All ER 888 .... 3.5
Kelly v Solari (1841) 9 N&W 54 .... 15.26
Kennecott Utah Copper Corp v Cornhill Insurance plc (T/A Allianz Cornhill
  International) 1999 2 All ER (Comm) 801 .... 8.12
Kiel, The [1991] 2 Lloyd's Rep 546 .... 3.2
Kier Construction Ltd v Royal Insurance Co (UK) Ltd [1994] 30 Con LR 45 ...... 28.08
Kier Construction Ltd v Royal Insurance Co (UK) Ltd 30 Con LR 45 .... 24.02

PARA

King v Brandywine Reinsurance Co (UK) Ltd [2004] Lloyd's Rep IR 554 .... 2.06
King v Chambers & Newman [1963] 2 Lloyd's Rep 130 .... 9.32
King v Victoria Insurance Co [1896] AC 250 .... 16.12
Kingscroft Insurance Co Ltd v Nissan Fire & Marine Insurance Co Ltd
    [1999] Lloyd's Rep IR 371   .... 6.31
Kingscroft Insurance Co Ltd v Nissan Fire & Marine Insurance Co Ltd (No 2)
    [1999] Lloyd's Rep IR 603   .... 38.10
Kitchen Design & Advice Ltd v Lea Valley Water Co [1989] 2 Lloyd's Rep
    221   .... 15.25, 16.17
Knowles v Liverpool City Council, The Times, 15 October 1993 .... 30.08
Koonjul v Thameslink Healthcare Services (2000) 30.08
Kruger Tissue (Industrial) Ltd v Franks Gallier Ltd (1998) 57 Con LR 1 .... 16.06
Kumar v AGF Insurance Ltd [1999] 1 WLR 1747 .... 1.10
Kuwait Airways Corp v Kuwait Insurance Co SAK [1999] 1 Lloyd's Rep
    803   .... 25.13
Kyle Bay Ltd (T/A Astons Nightclub) v Underwriters [2007] EWCA Civ 57 ...... 15.26,
                                                                              15.27
Kyriaki, The [1993] 1 Lloyds Rep 137 .... 14.10, 34.46
Kyzuna Investments Ltd v Ocean Marine Insurance Association (Europe)
    [2000] Lloyd's Rep IR 513   .... 34.09
Lake v Reinsurance Corporation Limited [1967] (3) SA 124 (W) 5.03
Lamb Head Shipping Co Ltd v Jennings (The Marel) [1992] Lloyd's Rep 402;
    [1994] 1 Lloyds Rep 624   .... 14.06, 34.31
Lambert v Co-operative Insurance Society Ltd [1975] 2 Lloyd's Rep 485 .... 6.05, 38.07
Lambert v Keymood Limited [1997] 2 EG LR 70 .... 17.08
Lane v Shire Roofing Co Ltd [1995] IRLR 493 .... 30.09
Lane (W & J) v Spratt [1970] 2 QB 480 .... 32.06
Langford & Langford v Legal and General Assurance Society Ltd
    [1986] 2 Lloyd's Rep 103   .... 32.06
Larizza v Commercial Union Assurance Co [1990] 68 DLR (4th) 460 .... 3.4
Latimer v AEC [1953] AC 643 .... 30.06
Lawrence v Accidental Insurance Company (Limited) (1881) 7 QBD 216 .... 13.05
Le Banque Financiere de la Cite SA v Westgate Insurance Co Ltd
    [1990] 2 All ER 947   .... 6.38
Leathley v Tatton [1980] RTR 358 .... 35.10
Leeds v Cheetham (1827) 1 Sim 146 .... 15.30, 17.08
LeFevre v White [1990] 1 Lloyd's Rep 569 .... 14.10, 20.07
Legal and General Insurance Society Ltd v Drake Insurance Co Ltd
    [1992] 2 QB 887   .... 18.06
Lek v Mathews [1927] 29 Ll LR 141 .... 14.08
Leo Rapp Ltd v McClure [1955] 1 Lloyd's Rep 292 .... 32.05
Leppard v Excess Insurance Co Ltd [1979] 2 All ER 668 .... 15.11, 15.31
Leyland Shipping Co Ltd v Norwich Union Fire Insurance Society Ltd
    [1918] AC 350   .... 13.05
Liberian Insurance Agency Inc v Mosse [1977] 2 Lloyd's Rep 560 .... 5.02, 6.18
Lidgett v Secretan (1871) LR 6 CP 616 .... 15.23
Lister v Romford Ice and Cold Storage Co Ltd [1957] AC 555 .... 30.07
Lloyd Instruments Ltd v Northern Star Insurance Co Ltd [1987] 1 Lloyd's
    Rep 32   .... 13.06
Lloyd v Fleming (1872) LR 7 QB 299 .... 16.22
Locker & Woolf Ltd v Western Australian Insurance Co Ltd [1935] 153 LT
    334   .... 6.11
London & Provincial Leather Processes Ltd v Hudson [1939] 2 KB 724 .... 32.07
London and Lancashire Fire Insurance Co v Bolands [1924] AC 836 .... 40.09
London and Manchester Plate Glass Co v Heath [1913] 3 KB 411 .... 40.08
London and Provincial Leather Processors v Hudson [1939] 2 KB7 24 .... 15.02
London Life Association, Re (21st February 1989, unreported) 42.12

PARA

London Steamship Owners Mutual Insurance Association Ltd v Bombay
Trading Co Ltd (The Felicie) [1990] 2 Lloyd's Rep 21 .... 14.10
London Tobacco (Overseas) Ltd v DFDS Transport Ltd [1994] 1 Lloyd's Rep
94 .... 32.03
Lonsdale & Thompson Ltd v Black Arrow Group plc [1993] 3 All ER 648 .... 15.16
Lord Napier and Ettrick v Kershaw [1993] 1 All ER 385 ..... 16.01, 16.09, 16.12, 16.14,
16.17, 16.18, 16.19
Louden v British Merchants Insurance [1961] Lloyds Reports 154 .... 35.04
Lucena v Craufurd (1806) 2 B & P (NR) 269 .... 4.02, 4.06
Macaura v Northern Assurance Co Ltd [1925] AC 619 .... 4.13
Mackie v European Insurance Society (1869) 21 LT 102 .... 1.13
MacMillan v AW Knott Becher Scott Ltd [1990] 1 Lloyd's Rep 98 .... 9.38
Magee v Pennine Insurance Co [1969] 2 QB 507 .... 15.26, 35.02
Mandrake Holdings Ltd v Countrywide Assured Group plc [2005] EWCA Civ
840 .... 15.17
Manifest Shipping & Co. Ltd v Uni-Polaris Insurance Co Ltd (The Star Sea)
[1997] 1 Lloyd's Rep 360; [2001] Lloyd's Rep IR 247; [2003] 1 AC 469 ...... 6.02,
6.19, 34.08, 34.17
Mann, Macneal and Steeves v Capital and Counties Insurance Co Ltd [1921]
2 KB 300 .... 6.16
Marc Rich & Co AG v Portman [1996] 1 Lloyd's Rep 430 .... 6.08
Mardorf v The Accident Insurance Company (Limited) [1903] 1 KB 584 .... 13.05
Marel, The [1992] Lloyd's Rep 402; [1994] 1 Lloyds Rep 624 .... 14.06, 34.31
Maritime Insurance Company v Assecuranz-Union von 1865 [1935] 2 Ll
LR16 .... 38.17
Mark Rowlands Ltd v Berni Inns Ltd [1985] 3 All ER 473 .... 16.07, 17.08
Martin P, The [2004] 1 Lloyd's Rep 389 .... 6.16, 17.05, 18.05
Martin v Lancashire County Council [2000] (CA) 30.13
Maurice v Goldsbrough Mort & Co Ltd [1939] AC 452 .... 27.15
McDonnell Information Systems Limited v Swinbank [1999] 2 All ER
(Comm) 722 .... 37.04
McLean Enterprises Ltd v Ecclesiastical Insurance Office plc [1986] 2 Lloyd's
Rep 416 .... 15.16
McNealy v The Pennine Insurance Co Ltd [1978] 2 Lloyd's Rep 18 .... 9.29
McNeil v Law Union and Rock Insurance Co Ltd [1925] 23 Ll LR 314 .... 9.26
Meadows Indemnity Co Ltd v The Insurance Corporation of Ireland plc
[1989] 2 Lloyd's Rep 298 .... 38.03
Medical Defence Union v Department of Trade [1979] 2 All ER 421;
[1980] Ch 82 .... 1.03, 12.04
Mercandian Continent, The [2001] 2 Lloyd's Rep 563 .... 6.02, 6.19
Merrett v Capitol Indemnity Corporation [1991] 1 Lloyd's Rep 169 .... 9.34, 11.09
Midland Mainline v Eagle Star Insurance Co Ltd [2004] 2 Lloyd's Rep 604 .... 13.06
Mirvahedy v Henley [2003] 2 AC 491 .... 26.06
Miss Jay Jay, The [1987] 1 Lloyd's Rep 32 .... 34.30
Monk v Warbey [1935] 1 KB 75 .... 35.09
Moonacre, The [1992] 1 Lloyd's Rep. 501 .... 4.13
Moonacre, The [1992] 2 Lloyd's Rep 501 .... 6.11, 9.30
Moore v Evans [1918] AC 185 .... 15.02
Morris v Ford Motor Co Ltd [1973] QB 792 .... 30.07
Morrison v Universal Marine Insurance Company (1873) LR 8 Ex 197 .... 6.17
Motor & General Insurance Co v Cox [1991] WLR 1443 .... 35.14
Myatt v National Coal Board [2007] 1 All ER 147; [2007] 1 WLR 554 .... 33.03
Nash v Prudential Assurance Co [1989] 1 Lloyd's Rep 379 .... 27.11
Nassau Bay, The [1979] 1 Lloyd's Rep 395 .... 40.11
Natal Land Co v Pauline Syndicate [1904] AC 120 .... 17.06
National Benefit Insurance Co, Re [1933] 45 Ll LR 147 .... 24.02, 32.09

PARA

National Employers Mutual General Insurance Association v Haydon
[1980] 2 Lloyd's Rep 149 .... 18.04
National Farmers Union Mutual Insurance Society Ltd v Dawson [1941] 2 KB
424 .... 35.04
National Insurance and Guarantee Corporation v Imperio Reinsurance Co
(UK) and Russell Tudor-Price & Co Ltd [1999] Lloyd's Rep IR 249 .... 9.37
National Justice Compania Naviera SA v Prudential Assurance Co. Ltd (The
Ikarian Reefer) [1993] 2 Lloyds Rep 68 .... 34.31
National Oil Company of Zimbabwe (Private) Ltd v Sturge [1991] 2 Lloyd's
Rep 281 .... 40.07, 40.13
National Oilwell (UK) Ltd. v Davy Offshore Ltd [1993] 2 Lloyd's Rep 582 .... 4.13
National Oilwell (UK) Ltd v Davy Offshore Ltd [1993] 2 Lloyd's Rep 582 . 9.03, 16.06,
16.10, 17.05, 17.06, 17.07, 17.08, 34.55
Naumann v Ford [1985] 2 EGLR 70 .... 16.12
Nelson v Board of Trade [1901] 84 LT 565 .... 1.02
New Hampshire Insurance Co Ltd v MGN Ltd [1996] 5 Re LR 103; [1997]
LRLR 24 .... 2.08, 2.15, 17.03
Newbury v Davis [1974] RTR 367 .... 35.11
Nigel Upchurch Associates v Aldridge Estates Investment Co Ltd
[1993] 1 Lloyd's Rep 535 .... 20.08
Noble Resources Ltd v Greenwood (The Vasso) [1992] 2 Lloyd's Rep 582;
[1993] 2 Lloyd's Rep 309 .... 16.13, 34.55
Norman v Aziz [2000] Lloyds Rep IR 52 .... 35.09
Normhurst Ltd v Durnoch Ltd [2004] EWHC 567 .... 15.17
Normid Housing Association Ltd v Ralphs [1989] 1 Lloyd's Rep 265 .... 20.06
North & South Trust Co v Berkeley [1970] 2 Lloyd's Rep 467 .... 9.33
North British and Mercantile Insurance Co v London, Liverpool and Globe
Insurance Co (1877) 5 Ch D 569 .... 18.05
North British Fishing Boat Insurance Co Ltd v Starr [1922] 13 LlL Rep 206
(KB) 6.14
North Star Shipping v Sphere Insurance plc [2005] Lloyd's Rep IR 404 .... 6.11
Norwich Union Fire Insurance Society Ltd v Price Ltd [1934] AC 455 ..... 15.26, 34.46
Norwich Union Insurance Ltd v Meisels [2007] Lloyd's Rep IR 69 .... 6.11
Nukila, The [1997] 2 Lloyd's Rep 146 .... 34.34
NV Rotterdamse v Golding Steward Wrightson, unreported, 1989 .... 9.26
O'Brien v Hughes-Gibbs & Co Ltd [1995] LRLR 90 .... 26.05
O'Connor v Kirby & Co [1972] 1 QB 90 .... 9.30
O'Kane v Jones (The Martin P) [2004] 1 Lloyd's Rep 389 .... 6.16, 17.05, 18.05
OLL v Secretary of State for Transport [1997] 3 All ER 897 .... 16.16
O'Mahony v Joliffe [2000] RTR 245 .... 35.10
Orakpo v Barclays Insurance Services Co Ltd [1995] LRLR 443 .... 14.08
Orion Compania Espaniola de Seguros v Belfort Maatschappij voor Algemene
Verzekeringen [1962] 2 Lloyd's Rep 257 .... 38.17
Osman v J Ralph Moss [1970] 1 Lloyd's Rep 313 .... 9.29
P Samuel & Co Ltd v Dumas [1924] AC 431, 445 .... 17.02, 17.03, 17.07
Page v Scottish Insurance Corpn [1928] 33 LlLR 134 .... 16.11
Pan American World Airways Inc v The Aetna Casualty & Surety Co
[1975] 1 Lloyd's Rep 77 .... 40.13
Pan Atlantic Insurance Co Ltd v Pine Top Insurance Co Ltd [1994] 2 Lloyd's
Rep 427; [1994] 3 All ER 58 .... 6.01, 6.07, 6.08, 6.18, 35.02, 38.11
Pangood Ltd v Barclay Brown Co Ltd [1999] Lloyd's Rep IR 405 .... 9.35
Parker & Heard v Generali Assicurazioni SpA, unreported, 1988 .... 15.10
Pasmore v Vulcan Boiler and General Insurance Co Ltd [1936] 54 Ll LR 92 ...... 35.04
PCW Syndicates v PCW Reinsurers (1996) 1 Lloyd's Rep 241 .... 6.31
Peters v General Accident Fire & Life Assurance Corporation [1938] 2 All ER
267 .... 16.22
Petrofina (UK) Ltd v Magnaload Ltd [1983] 3 All ER 35; [1984] QB 127 . 16.06, 17.07

PARA

Phoenix General Insurance Company of Greece SA v Halvanon
  Insurance Co Ltd [1985] 2 Lloyd's Rep 599 .... 38.08, 38.16
Pine Top Insurance Co Ltd v Unione Italiana Anglo-Saxon
  Reinsurance Co Ltd [1987] 1 Lloyd's Rep 476 .... 38.15
Pioneer Concrete (UK) Ltd v National Employers' Mutual General Insurance
  Association Ltd [1985] 2 All ER 395 .... 20.05
Piper v Royal Exchange Assurance [1932] 44 Lloyd's Rep 103 .... 15.26
Pipon v Cope (1808) 1 Camp 434 .... 34.35
Pitman v Universal Marine Insurance Co (1992) 9 QBD 192 .... 34.51
Plaistow Transport Ltd v Graham [1966] 1 Lloyd's Rep 639 .... 32.06
Popi M, The [1985] 2 All ER 712 .... 14.06, 34.31
Post Office v Norwich Union Fire Insurance Society Ltd [1967] 1 All ER
  577 .... 20.03, 20.04
Pozzolanic Lytag v Bryan Hobson Associates [1998] CILL 1450 .... 28.03
Prenn v Simmonds [1971] 1 WLR 1381 (CA) 2.16
Prentis Donegan & Partners Ltd v Leeds & Leeds Co. Inc. [1998] 2 Lloyd's
  Rep 326 .... 9.35
Price & Co v Al Ships' Small Damage Insurance Association Ltd (1889) 22
  QBD 580 .... 2.10
Princette Models Ltd v Reliance Fire and Accident Insurance Corporation Ltd
  [1960] 1 Lloyd's Rep 49 .... 32.06
Printpak v AGF Insurance Ltd [1999] 1 All ER (Comm) 466 .... 2.01
Promet Engineering (Singapre) Pte Ltd v. Sturge (The Nukila)
  [1997] 2 Lloyd's Rep 146 .... 34.34
Provident Life & Pensions Ltd v Sirius International Insurance Corporation
  [2005] EWCA Civ 601 .... 2.06
Provincial Insurance Co Ltd v Morgan [1933] AC 240 .... 35.03
Prudential Insurance Co v Inland Revenue Comrs [1904] 2 KB 658 .. 1.01, 12.04, 37.04
Pryke v Gibbs Hartley Cooper Ltd [1991] 1 Lloyd's Rep 602 .... 9.38, 10.04
Punjab National Bank v de Boinville [1992] 3 All ER 104 .... 9.38
Queensland Government Railways and Electric Power Transmission Pty Ltd v
  Manufacturers Mutual Insurance Ltd [1969] 1 Lloyd's Rep 214 .... 27.08
Quorum AS v Schramm [2002] 1 Lloyd's Rep 249 .... 15.12
Quorum AS v Schramm (No 2) [2002] 2 Lloyd's Rep 72 .... 15.18
R (on the application of West) v Lloyd's of London [2004] Lloyd's Rep IR
  755 .... 11.01
R v Committee of Lloyd's, ex p Moran, The Times, 24 June 1983 .... 11.03
R v Committee of Lloyd's, ex p Posgate, The Times, 12 January 1983 .... 11.03
R v Lloyd's of London, ex parte Briggs [1993] 1 Lloyd's Rep 176 .... 11.01
R v National Insurance Commissioner, ex p Michael [1977] 1 WLR 109 .... 30.04
Rayner v Preston (1881) 18 Ch D 1 .... 16.22, 16.31
Rayner v Preston (1881) LR 18 Ch D 1 .... 4.11
Reardon Smith Line Ltd v Yngvar Hansen-Tangen [1976] 1 WLR 989 (HL) .. 2.09, 2.16
Reed v Royal Exchange Assurance Co (1795) Peake, Add Cas 70 .... 4.05
Reid v Rush & Tomkins Group plc [1989] 3 All ER 228 .... 30.10
Reischer v Borwick [1894] 2 QB 548 .... 13.03
Rendall v Combined Insurance Co of America [2005] Lloyd's Rep IR 732 .... 15.05
Republic of Bolivia v Indemnity Mutual Marine Insurance Co Ltd [1909]
  1 KB 785 .... 34.33
Revell v London General Insurance Company Ltd [1934] 50 Lloyd's Law
  Reports 114 .... 1.11
Reynolds and Anderson v Phoenix Assurance Co Ltd [1978] 2 Lloyd's Rep
  440 .... 15.11
Rhesa Shipping Co SA v Edmunds (The Popi M) [1985] 2 All ER 712 ..... 14.06, 34.31
Richard Aubrey Film Productions Ltd v Graham [1960] 2 Lloyd's Rep 101 .... 15.12
Rickards v Forestal Land, Timber & Railways Co Ltd [1942] AC 50 .... 34.26
Robert Irving & Burns v Stone [1998] Lloyds Rep IR 258 .... 37.03

Roberts v Avon Insurance [1956] 2 Lloyd's Rep 240 .... 6.22
Roberts v Plaisted [1989] 2 Lloyd's Rep 341 .... 1.11, 1.12, 6.06, 9.02
Rogers v Merthyr Tydfil County Borough Council [2006] EWCA Civ 1135 .... 33.03
Rogerson v Scottish Automobile & General Insurance Co Ltd [1931] All ER
    606; [1931] 41 L1 LR 35.06
Rohan Investments Ltd v Cunningham, [1999] Lloyd's Rep IR 190 .... 2.12
Rose v Plenty [1976] 1 WLR 141 .... 30.07
Royal & Sun Alliance Insurance plc v (1) New Hampshire Insurance
    Company (2) Willis Ltd [2003] EWHC 302   .... 9.37
Royal Boskalis Westminster NV v Mountain [1997] 2 All ER 929 .... 34.19
Royal Brunei Airlines v Phillip Tank Kock Mining [1993] AC 378 .... 2.10
Royal Exchange Assurance v Hope [1928] 1 Ch 179 .... 14.14
Royal London Mutual Insurance Society Ltd, Re (2000, unreported) 42.12
Russell v Wilson, The Independent, 2 June 1989 .... 16.17
Rylands v Fletcher (1868) LR 3 HL 330 .... 31.03
Sadler Bros Co v Meredith [1963] 2 Lloyd's Rep 293 .... 32.04
Safadi v Western Assurance [1933] 46 Ll LR 140 .... 32.08
SAIL v Farex Gie [1995] LRLR 116 .... 38.10, 38.16
Salem, The [1983] 2 AC 375 .... 34.35
Sanger and another v Beazley [1999] 1 Lloyd's Rep 424 .... 32.06
Santer v Poland [1924] 19 L1 LR 29 .... 35.02
Saunders v Ford Motor Co Ltd [1970] 1 Lloyd's Rep 379 .... 15.28
SCA (Freight) Ltd v Gibson [1974] 2 Lloyd's Rep 533 .... 32.04
Scarf v Jardine (1882) 7 App Cas 345 .... 15.32
Scindia Steamships (London) Ltd v London Assce [1937] 3 All ER 895 .... 34.34
Scott v The Copenhagen Reinsurance (UK) Ltd [2003] EWCA Civ 688 .... 15.02
Seavision Investment SA v Evennett and Clarkson Puckle Ltd (The Tiburon)
    [1992] 2 Lloyd's Rep 26   .... 9.37
Secretary of State for Trade and Industry v Great Western Assurance Co
    [1999] Lloyd's Rep IR 377   .... 10.02
Sharp v Sphere Drake Insurance Co (The Moonacre) [1992] 2 Lloyd's Rep
    501   .... 4.13, 6.11, 9.30
Shell International Petroleum Co Ltd v Gibbs (The Salem) [1983] 2 AC 375 .... 34.35
Shilling v Accidental Death Insurance Co (1857) 2 H & N 42 .... 4.05
Sillem v Thornton (1854) 3 E & B 868 .... 19.02
Simmonds v Cockell [1920] 1 KB 843 .... 2.14
Simpson v Thomson (1877) 3 App Cas 279 .... 16.06
Sinnott v Bowden [1912] 2 Ch 414 .... 15.34
Sinnott v Municipal General Insurance, [1989] CLY 2051 .... 13.08
Sirius International Insurance Co (Publ) v FAI General Insurance
    [2005] Lloyd's Rep IR 294   .... 2.16
Siu Yin Kwan v Eastern Insurance Co Ltd [1994] 1 All ER 213 .... 17.05
Smith (Plant Hire) Ltd v Mainwaring [1986] 2 Lloyd's Rep 244 .... 16.17
Smith v Colonial Mutual Fire Insurance Co Ltd [1880] 6 VLR 200 .... 15.33
Smith v Lascelles (1788) 2 Term Rep 187 .... 9.29
Smith v Stages [1989] 1 All ER 833 .... 30.04
Sofi v Prudential Assurance Company [1993] 2 Lloyd's Rep 559 (CA) 6.36, 13.08
Soya GmbH v White [1983] 1 Lloyds Rep 122 .... 34.41
Sphere Drake Insurance Ltd v Euro International Underwriting Ltd
    [2003] Lloyd's Rep 1R 525   .... 9.02, 9.37
Spinney's (1948) Ltd v Royal Insurance Co Ltd [1980] 1 Lloyd's Rep 406 .... 27.10,
                                                              40.05, 40.06, 40.07, 40.08
Sprung v Royal Insurance (UK) Ltd [1997] CLC 70 .... 15.17
St Paul Insurance v Morice [1906] 22 TLR 449 .... 38.24
Standard Chartered Bank v Pakistan National Shipping Corporation
    [2003] 1 AC 959   .... 29.04
Stanley v Western Insurance Co (1868) LR 3 Ex 71 .... 13.07

PARA

Star Sea, The [1997] 1 Lloyd's Rep 360; [2001] Lloyd's Rep IR 247;
    [2003] 1 AC 469 .... 6.02, 6.19, 34.08, 34.17
Starfire Diamond Rings v Angel [1962] 2 Lloyd's Rep 217 .... 32.06
Stark v Post Office (2000) Times, 29 March 30.08
State of the Netherlands v Youell [1997] 2 Lloyd's Rep 440, [1998] 1 Lloyd's
    Rep 236 .... 34.55
Stavers v Mountain, (1912) Times, 27 July 27.15
Stephen v Scottish Boat Owners Mutual Insurance Association (The Talisman)
    [1989] 1 Lloyd's Rep 535 .... 34.55
Stockton v Mason, Vehicle and General Insurance Company Limited and
    Arthur Edward (Insurance) Limited [1978] 2 Lloyd's Rep 430 .... 1.13, 9.02
Stockwell v RHM Outhwaite (Underwriting Agencies) Ltd, unreported, 1991 ...... 10.06
Stone Vickers Ltd v Appledore Ferguson Shipbuilders Ltd [1992] 2 Lloyd's
    Rep 578 .... 16.06
Strive Shipping Corp v Hellenic Mutual War Risks Association (Bermuda) Ltd
    (The Grecia Express) [2002] 2 Lloyd's Rep 88; [2002] Lloyd's Rep IR
    669 .... 6.11, 34.09, 34.39, 38.16
Structural Polymer Systems Limited v Brown, unreported, May 1999 .... 18.04
Stuart v Freeman [1903] 1 KB 47 .... 3.3, 5.05
Sun Fire Office v Hart (1889) 14 App Cas 98 (PC) 2.12, 3.4
Sword-Daniels v Michael Pitel & Ors [1994] 4 All ER 385 .... 11.01
Symington & Co v Union Insurance Soc of Canton Ltd [1928] 44 TLR 635 .... 13.07
T O'Donoghue Ltd v Harding [1988] 2 Lloyd's Rep 281 .... 32.06
Tai Hing Cotton Mill v Liu Chong Hing Bank Ltd [1986] AC 80 .... 9.35
Talbolt Underwriting v Nausch Hogan & Murray (The Jackson 5)
    [2006] 2 Lloyd's Rep 195 .... 17.05
Talisman, The [1989] 1 Lloyd's Rep 535 .... 34.55
Tate & Sons v Hyslop (1885) 15 QBD 368 .... 16.08
Tattersall v Drysdale [1935] 52 L1 LR 21 .... 35.06
Taylor v Allon [1966] 1 QB 304 .... 5.06
Taylor v Eagle Star Insurance Company Ltd [1940] 67 Lloyd's Law Reports
    136 .... 1.11
Tektrol Ltd v International Insurance Co of Hanover [2005] EWCA 845 .... 27.09
Thames & Mersey Marine Insurance Co v Hamilton, Fraser & Co Ltd (The
    Inchmaree) (1887) 12 App Cas 484 .... 34.30
Theobald v Railway Passengers' Assurance Co (1854) 10 Exch 45 .... 16.04
Thor Navigation v Ingosstrakh Insurance Co Inc [2005] 1 Lloyd's Rep 547 .... 34.09
Tiburon, The [1992] 2 Lloyd's Rep 26 .... 9.37
Tinsley v Milligan [1994] 1 AC 340 .... 37.04
TM Noten BV v Harding [1990] 2 Lloyds Rep 283 .... 34.41
Tomlinson (A) (Hauliers) Ltd v Hepburn [1966] AC 451 .... 32.01
Tonkin v UK Insurance Ltd [2006] 2 All ER (Comm) 550; [2007] Lloyd's
    Rep. IR 283 .... 15.16, 15.17
Total Graphics Ltd v AGF Insurance Ltd [1997] 1 Lloyds Rep 599 .... 37.04
Touche Ross & Co v Baker [1992] 2 Lloyd's Rep 207 .... 11.07
Traill v Baring (1864) 33 LJ Ch 521 .... 38.10
Transit Casualty Co v PPB [1992] 2 Lloyd's Rep 358 .... 7.03
Trickett v Queensland Insurance Co Ltd [1936] 53 LI LR 225 .... 35.04
Trinity Insurance Co Ltd v Overseas Union Insurance Ltd [1996] LRLR 156 ...... 38.16
Tyrie v Fletcher (1777) 2 Cowp 666 .... 5.10
United Shoe Machinery v Brunet [1909] AC 330, 340 .... 17.02
Universo Insurance Co of Milan v Merchants Marine Insurance Co
    [1897] 2 QB 93 .... 5.09
Vacuum Oil Co v Union Insurance Society of Canton Ltd [1926] 25 LI LR
    546 .... 34.46
Vasso, The [1992] 2 Lloyd's Rep 582; [1993] 2 Lloyd's Rep 309 .... 16.13
Ventouris v Mountain (The Italia Express (No. 2)) [1992] 2 Lloyd's Rep 281 ...... 15.17

PARA

Ventouris v Mountain (The Italia Express (No. 3)) [1992] 2 Lloyd's Rep 216 ...... 14.12

Verderame v Commercial Union Assurance Co plc [1992] BCLC 793 .... 9.38

Verelst's Administratrix v Motor Union Insurance Co Ltd [1925] 2 KB 137 .... 14.02

Victor Melik & Co Ltd v Norwich Union Fire Insurance Society Ltd
[1980] 1 Lloyd's Rep 523 .... 9.32

Vural v Security Archives Ltd [1990] 60 P & CR 258 .... 17.08

Vural v Security Archives Ltd [1990] 60 P&CR 258 .... 15.30

W & J Lane v Spratt [1970] 2 QB 480 .... 32.06

Wainwright v Bland (1835) 1 Moo & Rob 481 .... 4.05

Walker v Pennine Insurance Co [1980] 2 Lloyd's Rep 156 .... 14.11

Warren v Sutton [1976] 2 Lloyd's Rep 276 .... 9.30

Waters v Monarch Fire and Life Assurance Co (1856) 5 E & B 870 .... 4.13

Wayne Tank and Pump Co Ltd v Employers' Liability Assurance
Corporation Ltd [1974] QB 57 .... 13.06

Wealands v CLC Contractors Ltd [1999] 2 Lloyd's Rep 739 .... 21.06

Webster v General Accident Fire and Life Assurance Corporation Limited
[1953] 1 QB 520 .... 15.02

Weddell v Road Traffic and General Insurance Co Ltd [1932] 2 KB 563 .... 18.04

Welch v Royal Exchange Assurance [1939] 1 KB 294 .... 14.03

West of England Fire Insurance Co v Isaacs [1897] 1 QB 226 .... 16.09

West Wake Price & Co v Ching [1957] 1 WLR 45 .... 37.04

Wharf v Buildwell Installations Ltd [1999] 10 CL 312 .... 30.09

White v Jones [1995] 2 AC 207 .... 37.01

Williams and Thomas and Lancashire & Yorkshire Insurance Co, Re [1902]
19 TLR 82 .... 14.02

Williams v Atlantic Assurance Co Ltd [1933] 1 KB 81 .... 15.10

Williams v Natural Life Health Foods [1998] 2 All ER 577 .... 29.04

Wilson and Clyde Coal Ltd v English [1938] AC 57 .... 30.06

Wilson v Avec Audio-Visual Equipment Limited [1974] 1 Lloyd's Rep 81 .... 5.08

Wimbledon Park Golf Club Ltd v Imperial Insurance Co Ltd [1902] 18 TLR
815 .... 15.34

Winspear v The Accident Insurance Company (Limited) (1880) 6 QBD 42 .... 13.05

Woolcott v Excess Insurance Co Ltd and Miles Smith Anderson and
Game Ltd(No 2) [1979] 2 Lloyd's Rep 210 .... 9.02

Woolcott v Sun Alliance and London Insurance Ltd [1978] 1 All ER 1253;
[1978] 1 Lloyd's Rep 629 .... 6.11, 17.03

Wooldridge v Canelhas Comercio [2004] EWCA Civ 984 .... 27.11

Wright & Pole, Re (1834) 1 Ad & El 621 .... 27.15

Wright v Romford Blinds (2003) 30.08

Wulfson v Switzerland General Insurance Co Ltd (1940) 67 Ll LR 190 .... 32.05

Yangtsze Insurance Association v Indemnity Mutual Marine Insurance Co
[1908] 2 KB 504 (CA) 2.11

Yasin, The [1979] 2 Lloyd's Rep 45 .... 17.07

Yorke v Yorkshire Insurance Co Ltd [1918] 1 KB 662 .... 2.09

Yorkshire Dale Steamship Co Ltd v Minister of War Transport, The Coxwold
[1942] AC 691 .... 13.04

Yorkshire Insurance Co Ltd v Nisbet Shipping Co Ltd [1962] 2 QB 330 ... 16.01, 16.19

Youell v Bland Welch and Co Ltd [1990] 2 Lloyd's Rep 431;
[1992] 2 Lloyd's Rep 127 .... 2.16, 9.28, 11.07, 38.05, 38.14

Young v Sun Alliance and London Insurance Ltd [1976] 3 All ER 561;
[1976] 2 Lloyd's Rep 189 .... 2.12, 27.07

Zephyr, The [1984] 1 Lloyd's Rep 58; [1985] 2 Lloyd's Rep 529 ...... 1.17, 9.38, 11.06,
38.05

Zurich Insurance Co v Shield Insurance Co [1988] IR 174 .... 18.05

Canada

Shakur v Pilot Insurance Co (1991) 73 DLR (4th) 337 .... 14.06

Table of cases

PARA

European Union
Bernaldez, Re, Case C-129/94 [1996] All ER (EC) 741 .... 35.04

New Zealand
State Insurance Office v Bettany [1992] 2 NZLR 275 .... 15.12

South Africa
Steams v Village Main Reef Gold Mining Co [1905] 21 TLR 236 .... 16.02

United States
Burnand v Rodocanachi Sons & Co (1882) 7 App Cas 333 .... 16.02
Property Insurance v National Protector Insurance [1913] 108 LT 104 .... 38.12
Sumitomo Marine & Fire Insurance Company v Cologne Reinsurance
     Company, 552 NYS 2d 891 [1990] 38.12

PART 1

The Insurance Contract

Chapter 1
Contract of insurance

- General definition of insurance
- Contract formation
- Formation of a contract at Lloyd's
- The policy

General definition of insurance

1.01 It is important to define 'insurance' for a variety of reasons. Firstly, some doctrines of the common law apply only to insurance contracts – most importantly, the rules relating to insurable interest and the principle of utmost good faith. Secondly, legislation, particularly tax legislation, lays down special rules for insurance contracts. Thirdly, and perhaps most significantly, there is comprehensive statutory regulation of the insurance industry, including the carrying on of insurance business in the UK (see 10 INSURANCE COMPANIES).

A frequently quoted definition of insurance (but not necessarily an exhaustive one) is that of Channell J in *Prudential Insurance Company v Inland Revenue Comrs [1904] 2 KB 658*. In that case, three elements of insurance were identified:

(*a*) it is a contract whereby for some consideration (generally but not necessarily for periodic payments called premiums), the insured secures some benefit on the occurrence of an event;

(*b*) the event must be uncertain as to whether it will happen or not, or if the event will happen, there must be uncertainty as to when; and

(*c*) the event must be adverse to the insured, in that he possesses an insurable interest (see 17 INSURABLE INTEREST) in the subject matter insured.

Premiums

1.02 In most forms of insurance the insured pays a sum, identified as the 'premium', to the insurer. A premium is a single payment, buying cover for a specified period (generally one year). If the insurer's premium income is insufficient to cover losses, the insurer cannot seek a further payment from the insured during the policy year. This position should be contrasted with that under mutual insurance, where the member of the mutual insurer (the insured) may be required to pay additional calls to the insurer during the currency of the policy.

Premiums take the form of money payments. There is no rule of law which prevents an insurance premium from constituting part of a wider payment, for example, the membership fee of a society providing benefits other than insurance (*Nelson v Board of Trade [1901] 65 JP 487* concerned a retailer promising pensions in order to promote the sale of tea). Combined payments are less common than was once the case.

The benefit payable to the insured

1.03 The insurer's primary obligation is to provide a money indemnity to the insured. However, in policies on property, the insurer will generally reserve the right to repair damage or to replace destroyed items. Equally, there is no reason why payment cannot be in the form of services to the insured, such as the provision of transport (*Department of Trade and Industry v St Christopher Motorists Association Ltd [1974] 1 WLR 99* is a case involving mobility insurance where the insured was unable to drive his vehicle). To that extent, payment can be in a form other than money as long as it is measurable in monetary terms.

The insured must, however, be entitled to some benefit under the policy. If the insurer has a discretion, but not an obligation, to make payment upon application by the insured, the contract is not one of insurance. This is so even if the evidence demonstrates that the 'insurer' always exercises its option to make payment (*Medical Defence Union Ltd v Department of Trade [1980] Ch 82*).

Uncertain events

1.04 Insurance is against contingencies and not certainties. The insured cannot insure against events which have taken place, neither can he insure against certain events. There must always be an element of uncertainty. In the case of indemnity insurance (fire, theft, etc), the uncertainty is whether there will be a loss at all. In the case of contingency insurance (the principal example of which in modern insurance is life assurance), the uncertainty relates not to the event but rather to the date at which it might occur (*Gould v Curtis (Surveyor of Taxes) [1913] 3 KB 84*).

Contract formation

1.05 The common law permits insurance contracts to be made orally, but there are statutory inroads into this principle which effectively require various insurance contracts to be in writing. One notable example is *s 22* of the *Marine Insurance Act 1906*, which provides that a contract of marine insurance is not admissible in evidence unless embodied in a policy.

The negotiations leading up to a contract of insurance are often found in the proposal form, the cover note and the policy document itself. In relation to Lloyd's policies, the proposal form can in effect be replaced by a slip, and a binding contract is concluded as soon as the slip is initialled ('scratched') by the underwriter.

The offer

1.06 Generally speaking the offer is made by the insured to the insurer, by means of a proposal form or other application. For example, the insurer may have written to the insured direct inviting him to complete the proposal form for consideration or the invitation may have come through an advertisement ('invitation to treat'). In these circumstances, the offer emanates from the insured who either completes the proposal form himself or has it completed on his behalf by the broker. If the proposal form is filled out on the insured's behalf, the insured is nonetheless responsible for ensuring that the answers on the proposal form are true and complete to the best of his knowledge so that all material facts have been disclosed to the insurers.

Any counter-proposal made by the insurer puts the onus back on the insured to accept the counter-offer (and thus a contract is made at that stage) or to make a further counter-proposal. It is to be noted that in the case of life insurance the letter of acceptance emanating from the insurer is treated as being an offer by the insurer.

The proposal form

1.07 Once completed, the proposal form can be looked at as an offer to accept insurance by the insured. The offer made by the insured will be made open for acceptance by the insurer for a specified time, or if none is specified, for a reasonable time. It is open to the proposer to withdraw his offer to take insurance at any time before it is accepted by the insurer (see *Dickinson v Dodds (1875–76) LR 2 Ch D 463*).

'Basis of the contract' clauses

1.08 Without more, the proposal form does not form part of the contract of insurance, but if it has a 'basis of the contract' clause, that will be effective to incorporate all statements made by the insured in the proposal form as terms of the contract. The proposal form and/or policy terms normally state that any terms incorporated in this way will either be warranties or conditions precedent to insurers' liability under the policy (*Dawsons Ltd v Bonnin [1922] 2 AC 413*).

A typical basis of the contract clause provides that:

> 'The proposer warrants that the answers provided in this proposal are true and understands that these answers will form the basis of the contract of insurance.'

Some basis of the contract clauses state that the proposer declares that all the facts stated on the proposal form are true, that they are material and that they form the basis of the contract. The effect of this is to relieve insurers of the need to prove materiality in the event of any non-disclosure or misstatement.

The strict legal rules regarding the effect of basis of contract clauses are modified in the case of 'personal lines' contracts of insurance by the Insurance Conduct of Business Rules (ICOB) outlined in the FSA's handbook. ICOB 7.3.6 states that an insurer must not, except where there is evidence of fraud, refuse to meet a claim made by a retail customer on the grounds 'of misrepresentation of a fact material to the risk, unless the misrepresentation is negligent' or 'of breach of warranty or condition, unless the circumstances of the claim are connected with the breach'.

The cover note

1.09   On receipt of the completed proposal the insurer is of course allowed time to consider the proposal and a cover note can provide temporary cover in the interim, cover being fully effective from the date of issue of the cover note. Alternatively, the grant of temporary cover is frequently conditional upon the completion by the insured of the proposal form for full cover. The use of cover notes is common in personal lines insurance, for example household and motor, and it is particularly convenient for risks, which are subject to compulsory insurance, such as motor.

Cover notes may be issued by insurers themselves, or by brokers authorised by insurers under binding authorities. If the latter, the broker will be in possession of blank cover notes printed in common form which he will fill out and issue on behalf of the insurer, thereby binding the insurer (*Mackie v European Insurance Society (1869) 21 LT 102*)Alternatively, the company may send a cover note to the broker for the broker to sign and issue to the insured. In these circumstances, the broker has no general authority to grant cover. Temporary cover could also be given verbally by the broker or the insurer (*Stockton v Mason [1978] 2 Lloyd's Rep 430*).

If a policy is subsequently issued, the cover note ceases to have any effect. It is usual for the cover note to remain in force for a fixed period of time, generally a maximum of 30 days or so, but the insurer can give notice to terminate the cover note at any time during that period.

If the cover note obliges the insurers to notify the insured if his proposal is rejected, the cover note will remain in force until the insurer takes this step (*Hawke v Niagara District Mutual Fire Insurance Co (1876) 23 Gr 139*).

If the cover note provides that the insurers, as well as notifying the insured of the rejection of the proposal, must also repay any deposit paid, the insurers must ensure that they fully discharge obligations. In the case of *Grant v Reliance Insurance Company (1879) 44 UCR 229*, it was held that the insurance was not terminated unless insurers complied with the term to give ten days' notice of their intention to terminate the insurance and also with the term to repay the premium (this would be the pro rata return of the premium based upon the number of days the insurers were on risk). If the terms of the cover note provide either that the insurers must intimate their acceptance of the proposal, or that they are not bound until a policy is issued, then cover will cease at the end of the period specified in the cover note unless such a term has been complied with. Insurers should take care to ensure that the cover note clearly states the precise period they are on risk for.

The cover note is a binding contract of insurance and will bind the insurer exactly as if a full policy had been issued. If the insurer decides he is not prepared to accept the risk, he will still be liable for any claim arising prior to the cover note expiring or being cancelled.

Most cover notes provide that the cover provided is that contained in the insurer's standard form of policy. In the event that a loss occurs during the period before the policy is issued, the insured may have some difficulty in knowing precisely what formalities he has to meet in order to make a claim. In *Coleman's Depositories Ltd and Life & Health Assurance Association's Arbitration, Re [1907] 2 KB 798*, the insured employer under a employers' liability insurance cover note failed to give immediate notice to the insurers of an injury sustained during the period of the cover note, contrary to the terms of the insurer's standard policy wording. The policy had not been issued to the insured at this point. Insurers repudiated liability on the grounds (among others) that the employer had not given immediate notice in accordance with the policy conditions. The injured workman died on 15 March 1905, having been injured on 2 January 1905, the insurers only being notified the day before his death. The Court of Appeal held, by a majority, that the requirements for immediate notice did not defeat the claim as:

(*a*)   it was impossible for the employer to comply with a policy term which he had no knowledge of; and

(*b*)   because the claim arose before the employer had knowledge of the notice provision, the true inference was that the condition was never imposed on the employer.

If the cover note does not incorporate the terms of the policy, insurers will need to demonstrate that the insured was aware of the terms and conditions of the policy, or had the means of becoming aware of the terms or that the insured had actually agreed the terms and conditions of cover.

During the period of the cover note, it is open to both the insured and insurers to decline to continue with the insurance after expiry of the cover note. If cover is to continue, the note will usually be replaced by a policy.

The acceptance

1.10   No particular form of acceptance is required and the offer can be accepted by the insurer in a number of ways, for example:

(*a*)   the insurer may notify the insured of its acceptance (orally or in writing); or

(b)   acceptance may be implied from conduct including:

  (i)   the execution of the policy;

  (ii)   where the insured has tendered and the insurer accepted the premium; or

  (iii)   where the premium has been demanded or the policy issued.

Whatever means of acceptance is used, the insurer's acceptance must be unconditional for a binding contract to come into effect and, according to general contractual law principles, the insurer's silence cannot amount to acceptance (unless, of course, there has been a previous agreement that silence is to be regarded as consent). However, the law is different on this point in the United States, where the insurer can find himself on risk if he has failed to respond to the proposal within a reasonable period.

The insurer's 'acceptance' may be conditional. If the insurer's acceptance is on different terms to the offer, the acceptance is itself a counter-offer (*Canning v Farquhar (1886) 16 LR QBD 727*).

Generally speaking, acceptance must be communicated to the offeror for the contract to be concluded. However, if, for example, the insured sends his proposal to the insurer by post, he impliedly authorises the insurer to use the same means of communication and thus the insurer's acceptance is effective when the letter is posted, notwithstanding that it may never be received by the insured, and the contract is in force.

The making of the contract is not necessarily the same thing as the commencement of the risk, as the insurer will commonly refuse to allow cover to commence until the first premium has been paid or some other formality has been completed (eg the issue of a policy). The distinction between the making of the contract and the commencement of the risk is of importance mainly in relation to the insured's duty of utmost good faith, which obliges the insured to avoid misrepresentations and to disclose material facts (see 6 POLICYHOLDER DUTIES). The duty to disclose material facts relating to the underwriting of the risk (although not the duty of utmost good faith) comes to an end when the contract is made, and not at any later date at which the risk commences, so that a change of circumstances prior to the commencement of the risk need not be notified to the insurer, unless the policy states otherwise.

An applicant for insurance is deemed to have applied for a policy issued on the insurer's standard terms, whether or not the applicant knows of those terms (*General Accident Insurance Corporation v Cronk [1901] 45 Sol Jo 261, 17 TLR 233*). Consequently, once the contract is made, the insured cannot take objection to any terms which are found in the policy even though he has not received a copy of the policy. This position is modified to some extent in consumer cases falling within the jurisdiction of the Insurance Ombudsman Bureau, as the ombudsman has ruled that an insurer cannot rely upon policy terms which, although standard, are unusual and onerous unless they have been brought specifically to the insured's attention prior to the making of the contract, a principle derived from the common law (*Interfoto Picture Library v Stiletto Visual Programmes [1989] QB 433*).

If the insurer, having received a proposal, wishes to vary his standard policy terms, or charge a premium other than at the rate originally quoted, the insurer's response to the proposer is treated as a counter-offer which has to be accepted by the proposer before a contract can come into being. This was held to be the case in *Canning v Farquhar* (referred to above), in which a proposal for life insurance was replied to by the insurers with a quotation for the premium and a statement that the policy would come into effect when the premium was paid. The proposer died four days before the premium was tendered by his administrator. The Court of Appeal held that the insurers were not liable; the insurers had, by their reply, made a counter-offer which required acceptance, and acceptance was not possible after the proposer had died.

Intention to create legal relations

1.11 It is usually self-evident that the parties to the insurance contract intend to create legal relations, any problems with this aspect of the law of contract usually being confined to non-commercial contracts.

Consideration

1.12 In order for the insurance contract to be enforceable, the insured must have given something of value to the insurer for the contractual promise. This aspect is also unlikely to cause any practical problems as the premium is normally the consideration under an insurance contract. It is usually the obligation to pay the premium, rather than actually paying the premium that is required.

Formation of a contract at Lloyd's

The slip

1.13 Insurance is placed at Lloyd's by means of a slip. The slip contains a summary of the essential features of the proposed cover. The broker prepares the slip, on behalf of his client, the insured, and takes it round the Lloyd's market. Contracts can also be concluded electronically.

In *Balfour v Beaumont [1984] 1 Lloyd's Rep 272; (1984) 81 LSG 197*, Webster J described the slip as 'a document prepared by a broker, setting out a proposal to be made to an underwriter which when accepted by the underwriter becomes binding on him'. The broker drafts the slip in accordance of the instructions received from his client. As the slip is designed to be concise, it is in abbreviated form and thus commonly refers to standard market clauses by description, showing any appropriate deletions or alternatives contemplated to a standard form of wording. However, the slip must include the following essential elements:

- the identity of the insured;
- the nature of the risk;
- the duration of the insurance;
- the limits of the indemnity; and
- the premium.

If the underwriter wants to accept the business, he will initial ('scratch') the slip indicating the percentage of the risk he is prepared to write. On initialling the slip, the underwriter is contractually bound. The broker continues to present the risk to the market until it has been fully subscribed or, perhaps more usually, oversubscribed (with the amount of each subscription being later 'signed down').

It is possible that the broker will ask an underwriter for a 'pencilled line' which is understood to be a 'promised' line. The underwriter is committed to take the promised line when the broker returns with a finalised slip. In the case of *General Accident, Fire and Life Assurance Corporation v Tanter, The Zephyr [1985] 2 Lloyd's Rep 529*, the judge recognised this market practice: 'a promised line is, by practice of the market, of the same effect as if it was written on the slip itself. It gives both parties the right to have that promised line written on the slip'. The situation is different where the broker uses a 'quotation slip' to test the market to ascertain likely insurance support and current rates. Unless a promised line is requested, the fact that the underwriter has indicated on the slip the terms and the rate is seen merely as a non-binding quotation.

An account of the way business is placed at Lloyd's can also be found in the case of *General Reinsurance Corporation v Forsakringsaktiebolaget Fennia Patria [1983] QB 856, [1983] 2 Lloyd's Rep 287* (see 11 LLOYD'S).

It is possible that an underwriter, usually the leader, may want to amend one or more of the terms of the slip before putting down his line. In the *General Reinsurance* case referred to above, the Court of Appeal recognised this possibility. Kerr LJ stated:

> 'where an underwriter varies the terms of the slip with the consent of the broker before writing his line, this would accordingly constitute a counter-offer which is accepted by the broker on behalf of his client.'

LMP/MR Slip

1.14 The London insurance market has been the subject of a Market Reform Programme which consists of a number of projects sponsored by the Market Reform Group designed at increasing efficiency in placing business, processing claims and settling accounts.

The first significant reform achievement was the introduction and adoption as a standard of the London Market Principles (LMP) Slip. The LMP slip was introduced in October 2001 and was mandated by the Lloyd's Franchise Board for business incepting from 2 January 2004. This ensured a common format and content to the way that business was introduced to the market and represented a significant cultural change. This was followed by the introduction of the Market Reform Slip in June 2006, building on the LMP Slip and further increasing the efficiency of the placement process by providing an enhanced standard for introducing business to London. In June 2007 this was replaced by the Market Reform Contract (MRC) – the name change reflecting the fact that the document presented by the broker to underwriters is that that forms the contract of insurance. Today a large proportion of business introduced to the London Market is presented using the MRC.

The benefits of the MRC contract are that a standard paper form layout:

- makes it easier for carriers to assess risks offered to them;

- makes subsequent processes more efficient (eg creation of any separate insurance policy); and

- enables mapping to the ACORD Reinsurance & Large Commercial (RLC) 'Placement' XML message – so that as and when business partners start to move towards electronic trading, there is compatibility of information used within the paper placing process.

The MRC is made up of the following sections:

(a) Risk Details – details of the risk/contract involved, such as insured, type, coverage, conditions, etc.

(b) Information – free text additional information.

(c) Security Details – includes Reinsurer's Liability; Order Hereon; Basis of Written Lines; Basis of Signed Lines, Signing Provisions, insurer(s)/reinsurer(s) 'stamp' details. These indicate each insurer(s) share of the risk and their reference(s).

(d) Subscription Agreement – this establishes the rules to be followed for processing and administration of post-placement amendments and transactions.

(e) Fiscal and Regulatory – fiscal and regulatory issues specific to the insurers involved in the risk.

(f) Broker Remuneration & Deductions – information relating to brokerage, fees and deductions from premium.

It should be noted that the requirement to conform with the guidelines set down for MRC does not apply to:

- Binding Authority Agreements and line slips.

- contracts that fall within the 'Market Reform Exempt – Client Requirement' category (ie the client has expressed a preference to use a London placing document in a different format).

- slips which relate to motor, personal lines or term life insurance business which are not processed by Xchanging Ins-sure Services (providing services formerly offered by the Lloyd's Policy Signing Office).

The MRC standard has become mandatory for all other London Market placements since 1 November 2007.

The policy

1.15   Lloyd's policies and policies issued by insurance companies will vary as to their form and contents and should be drafted with care.

Insurance company policies

1.16   Insurance companies will generally use their own standard forms of policy wording which will also vary according to the type of insurance. The old-style narrative policies are generally a thing of the past and are today only of academic interest. Rather than adopting the narrative style, modern policies are 'scheduled' policies. The various parts of the policy will be in clearly defined sections which are identical within a class of business except for that part of the policy called the 'schedule' which will list all information particular to that individual risk. Scheduled policies are convenient for insurers, allowing them to keep on file a copy of the master policy and individual schedules.

Lloyd's policies

1.17   Following completion of the slip, the policy wording is drawn up. Where this happens, the wording supersedes the slip, although this does not affect the insured's duty of disclosure which ceases when the slip is initialled. *Section 21* of the *Marine Insurance Act 1906* provides:

> 'A contract of marine insurance is deemed to be concluded when the proposal of the assured is accepted by the insurer, whether the policy be then issued or not; and, for the purpose of showing when the proposal was accepted, reference may be made to the slip or covering note or other customary memorandum of the contract ...'

Where there is an apparent inconsistency between the wording of the slip and the subsequent policy, the court may refer to both documents in an attempt to reconcile the terms (*HIH Casualty & General Insurance Ltd v New Hampshire Insurance Co [2001] 2 Lloyds Rep 161*).

Sometimes policy wordings are often not drawn up and the slip remains of paramount importance embodying the terms of the contract.

Lloyd's policies will be in a standard form and will deal with the same matters as any other policy. However, points worthy of note are the premium and underwriters' liability. In relation to the premium, the policy will usually acknowledge that this has been paid which means that the insured can enforce the policy even if the premium has not in fact been paid. Underwriters' liability is several, not joint, nor joint and several. This means that underwriters' liability is restricted to the amount of their line. Properly analysed, therefore, the insured has entered into a number of separate contracts with each individual underwriter.

If Lloyd's are only writing part of a risk, and the insured also has insurance with an insurance company or companies, the Lloyd's policy will usually include a clause referring to the other policy and may provide that the Lloyd's policy is subject to the same conditions as the company's policy.

Policy conditions can be classified as two types, express conditions and implied conditions. Express conditions will vary according to the type of insurance cover. Generally, express conditions will include what constitutes notice to the insurer, cancellation, contribution, any arbitration or court jurisdiction clause, adjustment of premium and claims procedure. Implied conditions will include matters such as the existence of an insurable interest and the existence and identity of the subject matter. Express and implied conditions can be further categorised into conditions precedent to the policy, conditions subsequent to the policy and conditions precedent to liability (see 2 TERMS IN INSURANCE CONTRACTS).

Contract certainty

1.18 In December 2004, the FSA challenged the London Market to devise a solution to what it characterised as a 'deal now, detail later' culture – that is that the precise wording of an insurance contract was often not agreed at the time that parties committed themselves to that contract; and that the end client did not receive evidence of cover until after the business was on risk. In the worst cases, litigation had occurred without the terms and conditions of the contract having been agreed and without the client ever having received a copy of the contract.

The challenge related to the whole UK insurance industry. London set a series of targets for itself to demonstrate that it was seriously pursuing a market solution to this issue. Achievement of these objectives would persuade FSA that direct regulatory intervention – by introducing prescriptive rules to ensure full agreement of all terms prior to the formation of a contract – was not necessary.

The target for end 2006 was for the market to achieve contract certainty, that is, the complete and final agreement of all terms between insured and insurers before inception of the risk, in at least 85% of cases. This was achieved and surpassed and the FSA recognised this at a meeting in January 2007.

In June 2007 a consolidated Contract Certainty Code of Practice was published. This was the first publication ever to apply to the entire UK insurance industry – subscription and non-subscription; commercial and retail. Many firms are using this Code of Practice as the basis for rolling out Contract Certainty as global best practice across all their offices and branches.

Chapter 2
Terms in insurance contracts

- Classification of terms
- Construction of terms

Classification of terms

Warranties

2.01   A warranty in insurance law has a different meaning from a warranty in the general law of contract. In insurance law, a warranty is typically a promissory term where the insured promises that either a particular state of affairs exists at a particular point in time, usually at inception (a present warranty) or the insured makes a promise that a particular state of affairs will exist over a period of time, usually over the period of the insurance policy (a continuing warranty).

The essential characteristics of a warranty are:

(*a*)   It must be a term of the contract.

(*b*)   The matter warranted need not be material to the risk.

(*c*)   It must be strictly and literally complied with.

(*d*)   A breach of warranty automatically terminates the contract notwithstanding that the loss has no connection with the breach (or that the breach has been remedied before the time of loss).

Warranties must be strictly complied with and, if they are not, the effect of breach of warranty is to automatically terminate the insurance contract, without requiring insurers to make any decision or exercise any option to repudiate or avoid the contract of insurance.

Section 33 of the *Marine Insurance Act 1906* defines a promissory warranty as a term 'by which the insured undertakes that some particular thing shall or shall not be done, or that some conditions shall be fulfilled, or whereby he affirms or negatives the existence of a particular state of facts ...'. It is clear from *s 34(3)* of the *Marine Insurance Act 1906* that 'breach of warranty may be waived by the insurer'. This had been taken to suggest that an election on the part of insurers was required to avoid an insurance contract in the event of breach of warranty, notwithstanding that *s 33(3)* of the *Marine Insurance Act 1906* provides that if a warranty is not 'exactly complied with', then 'subject to any express provision in the policy the insurer is discharged from liability as from the date of breach of warranty, but without prejudice to any liability incurred by him before that date'.

In *Bank of Nova Scotia v Helenic Mutual War Risks Association [1992] 1 AC 233* the House of Lords held that the words of *s 33(3)* are clear. Discharge of the insurer from liability is automatic upon breach of warranty, and is not dependent upon any decision by the insurer to treat the contract of insurance as at an end. Although that case concerned a contract of marine insurance, the same principle applies to non-marine contracts of insurance.

The mere fact that a term is labelled a warranty will not always mean that it will be treated as such by the court. As warranties are terms with a draconian nature, often the courts will try and limit their operation. If there is any ambiguity in the wording the court will try and restrict the application of a warranty: *Printpak v AGF Insurance Ltd [1999] 1 All ER (Comm) 466*. The courts are also very reluctant to find that a warranty is a continuing warranty unless the wording is very clear indeed: *Hussain v Brown [1996] 1 Lloyd's Rep 627*.

Conditions precedent

2.02   There is some confusion in the law as to the difference between a warranty and a condition precedent. This confusion was not helped by Lord Goff's description of a warranty in *The Good Luck* (see 2.01 above), as 'a condition precedent to the liability of an insurer'.

Whereas a warranty is a term where the insured promises that a particular state of affairs exists or will exist, a condition precedent to the insurance is a condition or state of affairs that must be fulfilled before the insurance contract comes into existence. At the other end of the scale, a condition precedent to liability to meet a particular claim is a condition or state of affairs which needs to be met before insurers have a liability to deal with a particular claim made under the policy. With conditions precedent, it is for the insured to prove that the condition has been met which would entitle him to make a valid claim under the contract of insurance. If there is breach of a condition precedent to the insurance, then insurers probably never come on risk. If there is breach of a condition precedent to liability to meet a claim, then insurers are still on risk but not in respect of that particular claim. Insurers will therefore have to meet claims prior to the breach of the condition precedent to their liability to meet the claim, and any subsequent claims.

Simply labelling a term a condition precedent may not be conclusive. Where, for example, a policy attempts to make every term a condition precedent to the liability of insurers, the courts are unlikely to give this effect (see *In Re Bradley and Essex and Suffolk Accident Indemnity Society [1912] 1 KB 415*).

Reference can sometimes be found in the textbooks to conditions subsequent which are conditions that must be fulfilled at some point after the commencement of insurance cover. In an insurance contract such a condition might typically relate to an agreement by the insured to notify insurers of any increase in the risk during the life of the policy. There is little authority that adopts this classification of these terms because the courts will normally find that such terms can also be classified as warranties, conditions precedent or mere conditions.

Suspensive conditions

2.03 Warranties and conditions precedent must also be distinguished from suspensive conditions. These are terms which limit the risk covered under the policy with the effect that while the promise made by the insured is being broken, the insurer is not on risk and the cover is temporarily suspended until the breach is remedied.

Exclusion clauses

2.04 It is also necessary to distinguish between warranties and exclusion clauses. Both types of clause have the effect of limiting the cover provided by the insurer, but they operate in different ways.

If a warranty is broken, cover is automatically terminated, but if an exclusion clause operates, cover simply does not apply. For example, in an 'All Risks' policy (which insures property against 'all risks') insurers' liability under the policy may be limited by an exclusion clause which states:

> 'This policy will not cover:
>
> War risks, any consequence of war, invasion, acts of foreign enemies, hostilities (whether war be declared or not), civil war, rebellion, revolution, insurrection, military or usurped power.'

Insurers' liability under the policy does not automatically terminate in the event of war, but the insured risks are limited so that they do not include damage which occurs to the property as a result of war.

Exclusions may be express or implied. Express exclusions will be terms of the insurance contract. It is sometimes possible to argue that there is an implied exclusion in the insurance contract on the basis of limits inherent in the usual meaning of the cover written by the contract of insurance. For example, an 'All Risks' policy does not cover loss caused by inevitable deterioration.

Mere conditions

2.05 Where a term of the policy is neither a warranty, condition precedent, suspensive condition nor an exclusion clause, it will be a mere condition. Breach of a mere condition by the insured will give rise to an action in damages by the insurers against the insured. The size of damages will be proportionate to the prejudice caused to insurers as a result of the breach. Having said that, it is unusual for insurers to sue insureds for damages.

Innominate terms

2.06 An innominate term in an insurance contract is a term which is neither a warranty, a condition precedent nor a mere condition as described above. With these terms the consequences of any particular breach by the insured cannot be laid down in advance, but will depend on the nature and gravity of the particular breach. In *Alfred McAlpine plc v BAI (Run-Off) Ltd [2000] 1 Lloyd's Rep 437*, the court had to consider the nature of a condition in the insurance policy which required the insured to give notice of any occurrence which might give rise to a claim under the policy 'in writing with full details as soon as possible'. The insurers argued that the clause was a condition precedent whereas the court held that it was not. The Court of Appeal held that the notice clause was an innominate term and breach of it, however serious, would be unlikely to permit insurers to repudiate the whole contract of insurance. Following the decisions in *Friends Provident Life & Pensions Ltd v Sirius International [2005] EWCA Civ 601* and *King v Brandywine Reinsurance Co (UK) Ltd [2004] Lloyd's Rep IR 554* it has been confirmed that the breach of a claims notification clause (which is not in the nature of a condition precedent) will only result in insurers being able to claim damages.

Construction of terms

2.07 The courts have developed various rules of construction to assist in the process of interpretation of written contracts; contracts of insurance are no different from commercial contracts in this respect and are subject to the same principles of interpretation.

The intention of the parties must prevail

2.08 The most basic principle of interpretation is that the court must interpret the contract so as to give effect to the parties' intention. Nothing is relevant to the interpretation of a written contract unless it was known to or reasonably capable of being known to both parties at the time the contract was made (see *New Hampshire Insurance Co Ltd v MGN Ltd [1996] 5 Re LR 103*). This intention is to be gathered from the written language of the contract of insurance, including all documents which may be incorporated into that contract. An undisclosed intention held by one of the parties to the contract is not admissible in evidence for the purposes of interpretation. In addition, particular clauses in the policy will not be looked at in isolation; it is the policy as a whole which will be considered.

Words should be given their ordinary and natural meaning

2.09 There is a rebuttable presumption that the words of a written contract should be construed according to their ordinary and natural meaning since the parties to the contract must be taken to have intended, as reasonable men, to have used the words and phrases in their commonly understood and accepted sense (see *Yorke v Yorkshire Insurance Co Ltd [1918] 1 KB 662*, per McCardie J). If the ordinary meaning of the word has already been judicially established the courts will have regard to this earlier interpretation under the doctrine of precedent (see *Reardon Smith Line Ltd v Yngvar Hansen-Tangen [1976] 1 WLR 989*). The court will generally give effect to the ordinary and natural meaning of the language used by the parties, provided the language is clear and unambiguous, even if, with the benefit of hindsight such an interpretation is unfortunate. The court will not re-write a contract to create a better deal for the parties.

Technical or trade meaning

2.10   There are some circumstances, however, in which the court may not construe the words used by the parties according to their ordinary and natural meaning. This occurs where the words used in the contract are words which frequently have a highly technical or trade meaning. If a word has acquired a technical meaning in the usage of a particular trade or business, the court will assume that the parties intended their words to receive that customary meaning. In the case of *Price & Co v A1 Ships' Small Damage Insurance Association, Ltd (1889) LR 22 QBD 580*, the Master of the Rolls held that the word 'average' used in the context of marine insurance was clearly a technical expression whose meaning (a partial as opposed to a total loss) had been well established.

Similarly, a word or phrase which has a recognised technical meaning in law will be given that meaning. For example, the word 'dishonest' which often appears in insurance policies is construed in accordance with its definition in *s 2(1)* of the *Theft Act 1968*, although the courts have gone on to consider the standard of dishonesty to be applied in civil cases in the cases of *Royal Brunei Airlines v Phillip Tan Kok Ming [1995] AC 378* and *Abbey National plc v Solicitors Indemnity Fund [1997] PNLR 306*.

Meaning may be limited by the context

2.11   The meaning of a word is to be construed with reference to its context, and its ordinary meaning may be restricted by that context. This rule was stated by Farwell LJ in *Yangtsze Insurance Association v Indemnity Mutual Marine Assurance Co [1908] 2 KB 504*. The Master of the Rolls in *Arbuthnott v Fagan: Deeny v Gooda Walker Ltd [1996] LRLR135*, also confirmed this:

> 'the courts will never construe words in a vacuum. To a greater or lesser extent, depending on the subject matter, they would wish to be informed of what may variously be described as the context, the background, the factual matrix'.

Surrounding words

2.12   This rule of construction is a particular application of the general principle that the primary meaning of words may be affected by their context. The construction of words can be affected by their immediate environment or surrounding words within the contract.

The *eiusdem generis* rule provides that where specification of particular things are followed by general words, the general words are to be limited to matters *eiusdem generis* (ie of the same kind) with those specifically mentioned. In an insuring clause there may be a specific list of insured perils which is followed by more general words such as 'all other perils'. Here the general words would be construed to be limited to matters of the same kind as those specifically mentioned.

This rule does not, however, always apply. For example, where the preceding words do not contain a specification of particulars, but rather a description of a complete genus, later general words would not be construed as being limited by the genus of the particular thing. In *Sun Fire Office v Hart (1889) LR 14 App Cas 98*, a fire insurance policy had a condition empowering the insurers to terminate the policy if they should wish to do so for various specified reasons or 'from any other cause whatsoever'. The words 'from any other cause whatsoever' were not construed by the court as limited to the type of reasons specified earlier in the policy, but as allowing the insurers the option of terminating the policy at will.

There is a rule that words may be limited by proximity where the meaning of one word within a list of words is limited by proximity to other words. For example, in *Young v Sun Alliance and London Insurance Ltd [1976] 3 All ER 561*, the Court of Appeal held that a policy which provided cover against damage for 'storm, tempest or flood' did not apply to a claim for damage where three inches of water seeped into the insured's bathroom from an underground spring. The word 'flood' was held in this case to be treated as being limited by its proximity to 'storm' and 'tempest' and in this context a flood was 'something large, sudden and temporary, not naturally there …'. In *Rohan Investments Ltd v Cunningham [1999] Lloyd's Rep IR 190*, the Court of Appeal upheld the insured's claim under the 'storm, tempest or flood' section of his policy where, following a period of heavy rainfall, water built up on the roof and entered the insured's house over the flashings, causing an ingress of water three to four inches deep. The Court of Appeal stated that whilst the events giving rise to the flood had to be abnormal, the trial judge was entitled to find on the evidence that the accumulation of water from rainfall was sufficiently rapid to be abnormal. The abnormal accumulation of water could therefore be distinguished from the seepage which formed the substance of the claim in *Young v Sun Alliance*.

Business-like interpretation

2.13   Another accepted principle of construction is that a commercial document such as an insurance policy should be construed in accordance with sound commercial principles and good business sense, so that its provisions receive a fair and sensible application. A literal interpretation of the words will therefore not be allowed where this would produce a result which is unrealistic and unanticipated. In *Fraser v B N Furman (Productions) Ltd [1967] 1 WLR 898* the court held that in a policy, where the main purpose was to insure against damage arising from negligent acts of the insured, a condition that 'the insured shall take reasonable precautions' could not be construed so that every negligent act by the insured was in breach of that clause. The reason for this was that the insured had taken out the insurance policy specifically to cover his own acts of negligence, and the policy would be worthless to him if this construction of the words was permitted.

Resolution of ambiguity

2.14 Where there is true ambiguity in a contract of insurance or reinsurance the court is entitled to rely on a rule of interpretation known as the *contra proferentem* rule. This rule states that where contractual language is capable of two alternative interpretations, it will be construed against the party which drafted the contract of insurance or reinsurance and in favour of the party who accepts the wording. The reasoning behind this rule is that the party drafting the policy will have chosen the language used and should not therefore be able to rely on any ambiguity contained in it. This principle was established in *Simmonds v Cockell [1920] 1 KB 843*. In the direct insurance context, this rule protects insureds against some of the more onerous consequences of standard form policies imposed on them by insurers. However, in the case of reinsurance contracts, and some commercial insurance contracts and in cases where the policy has been drafted by the broker (the insured or reinsured's agent), the principle can operate in favour of the insurer or reinsurer (see *Abrahams v Mediterranean Insurance and Reinsurance Co Ltd [1991] 1 Lloyd's Rep 216*). Where the wording of the contract of insurance has been penned both by the insured and the insurer, this rule is unlikely to apply.

Where the words of a policy are capable of two constructions, the reasonable construction is to be preferred as representing the presumed intention of the parties.

Implied term

2.15 Where there is a gap in the meaning of the contract the court will imply a term to fill that lacuna, but there is no principle going wider than that (see the *New Hampshire* case at 2.08 above). The language of the policy may be unclear, not only because of it being susceptible of more than one interpretation but also due to the technical nature of the language used or its silence on a particular issue. The court may, in limited circumstances, imply certain terms into the contract to clarify the meaning of the words of the contract. The party seeking to imply a term must show that it is necessary to give efficacy to the contract, it is consistent with the express terms of the contract, and it would have been agreed by both parties, or the implied term is one that is considered to have widely established market usage which the contracting parties, if asked, would agree formed part of their contract. The courts are generally reluctant to imply terms into insurance contracts in this way. However, courts are generally more willing to imply a term that the insurance market would expect the parties to have included in the contract, or a term that a party has sanctioned the use of in a course of previous dealings.

Extrinsic evidence

2.16 Sometimes, the express language of the contract of insurance can be supplemented by the introduction of evidence other than the terms of the written contract itself relevant to the interpretation of the contract. This 'extrinsic evidence' will often not be permitted by the court because of the parol evidence rule. This rule states that when a contract has been committed to writing, oral or other extrinsic evidence may not be relied on for the purpose of adding to, varying or contradicting the written document. The purpose of this rule is to uphold the finality of the agreement intended by the parties when they put the contract in written form. As a consequence of this rule, the court may not consider either oral evidence or draft versions of the agreement as aids to the interpretation of the parties' intention. In *Youell v Bland Welch & Co Ltd [1992] 2 Lloyd's Rep 127* the judgment of the Court of Appeal gives contradictory authority as to whether or not this type of extrinsic evidence is relevant or admissible as a construction aide. The case of *Prenn v Simmonds [1971] 1 WLR 1381*, establishes that evidence of negotiations is not admissible as a construction aid. However, where a contract wording has superseded a previous version, for instance an agreed wording has followed a slip policy, the courts will look to the slip as an aid to construction (see *HIH Casualty and General Insurance Ltd v New Hampshire Insurance Co [2001] Lloyd's Rep IR 224*).

The courts have however held that contracts are not made in a vacuum and that the courts should know the commercial purpose of the contract and the background and the market in which the parties are operating (see *Reardon Smith Line* at 2.09).

In recent cases, the courts have tended to view the starting point for construction as the common sense principles of interpretation laid down by Lord Hoffmann in *Investors Compensation Scheme Ltd v West Bromwich Building Society [1998] 1 WLR 896*. These principles are as follows:

(a)   Interpretation is the ascertainment of the meaning which a document would convey to a reasonable man having all the background knowledge which would be reasonably available to the parties.

(b)   The background includes everything which would have affected the way in which the language would have been understood by a reasonable man.

(c)   The law excludes from the admissible background the previous negotiations between the parties.

(d)   The meaning of the document is different from the meaning of the word – the meaning of the document is what the parties using those words against the relevant background would reasonably have understood them to mean.

(e)   The rule that words should be given their natural and ordinary meaning reflects the common sense proposition that courts do not usually accept that parties to a contract have made linguistic mistakes.

The commercial approach taken by the courts to the interpretation of contracts was emphasised by Lord Steyn in *Sirius International Insurance Co (Publ) v FAI General Insurance Ltd [2005] Lloyd's Rep IR 294:*

'The aim of the inquiry is not to probe the real intention of the parties but to ascertain the contextual meaning of the relevant contractual language. The inquiry is objective: the question is what a reasonable person, circumstanced as the actual parties were, would have understood the parties to have meant by the use of specific language. The answer to that question is to be gathered from the text under consideration and the relevant contextual scene.'

Chapter 3
Duration of insurance contracts

- Duration of cover
- Termination of cover

Duration of cover

When does cover commence?

3.01 There is a distinction between the date of the contract and the date of the risk attaching. In principle, cover commences as soon as the contract is made.

In practice, however, policy terms may vary this possibility and may specify that cover is stated to commence:

(*a*)   on a given date and time;

(*b*)   on the occurrence of a given event (as in the case of a marine voyage policy where cover commences at the start of the voyage – see 34 MARINE INSURANCE); or

(*c*)   on the payment of premium by the insured to the insurer.

It is the first of these contract terms which provides the most difficulties. If cover runs 'from' a specified date, the legal presumption is that this date is excluded (*Isaacs v Royal Insurance Co (1869–70) LR 5 Ex 296*). Clear wording is needed to oust this presumption, for example, that the risk runs from a stated day inclusive or, as in the case of *Cornfoot v Royal Exchange Assurance Corp [1904] 1 KB 40*, that cover is for a period 'beginning with' a stated day.

Termination of cover

Expiry of cover

3.02 The duration of cover will depend upon the policy wording. If the cover is for a particular event, such as a marine voyage, the policy will come to an end when the voyage is completed, although it is the practice for policies to continue for a specified number of days following the safe arrival of the vessel in port. In the case of *Cornfoot v Royal Exchange* (see 3.01 above), in which marine cover was to run for 30 days from the arrival of the vessel in port, it was held that the additional days are to be counted in consecutive periods of 24 hours, commencing from the precise time at which the vessel arrived at port, so that in this case, the vessel completed its voyage at 11.30am and was covered for a further 30 days, such that a loss occurring at 5.30pm on the 30th day was not covered.

Some policies are stated to run from one day to another. As stated at 3.01 above, in the case of *Isaacs v Royal Insurance* it was held that the first-mentioned day was excluded. In this case it was also held that the last-mentioned date was included. Thus, if the insurer offers cover from 1 May 1993 to 1 May 1994, the effect of the *Isaacs* case is to allow the insured to recover for a loss on 1 May 1994, while at the same time, by excluding 1 May 1993, ensuring that the insurer is liable for a calendar year and not a year plus a day.

Ambiguities in the termination date of policies are generally to be construed in favour of the insured. In *Henrich Hirdes GmbH v Edmund [1991] 2 Lloyd's Rep 546*, a marine policy commenced on 16 June 1981, was stated to run for '12 months at June 16 1981', and was renewed 'for a period of one month … until 16 July 1982'. It was held that the policy was in force on 16 June 1982, even though this meant assuming that either the original policy or the subsequent renewal lasted for one day longer than the stated fixed period. As such, the principle in the *Isaacs* case still applies despite the stated duration of the total policy.

Renewal of cover

3.03   Life insurance policies are written in the form of continuing commitments on the parties and are therefore regarded as perpetual, subject to the insured tendering the premium when it falls due. Thus, even where the premium is paid annually (although it is more common these days for payment to be made by instalments), the cover does not come to an end at the end of the year, and the insured has the right to maintain the policy by making payment by the stated date and within any days of grace allowed by the policy (*Stuart v Freeman [1903] 1 KB 47*).

Indemnity policies, by contrast, are periodic, which means that at the end of the policy period a fresh contract has to be granted. The policy will come to an end at the time stated in it, or on the occurrence of a stated event. The main significance of this is that the insured is under a duty of utmost good faith when applying for renewal, and must disclose all material changes in circumstances to the insurer. The insurer may, however, waive the right of disclosure by providing in the policy that the insured is entitled to an extension either on request (which is a feature of 'held covered' clauses in marine insurance and may also be found in construction insurance where the duration of the risk is uncertain), or automatically, unless the insurer has taken the positive step of giving notice of cancellation within a specified period if there is a reservation of a right to cancel in the policy (*Commercial Union Assurance Co plc v Sun Alliance Insurance Group plc [1992] 1 Lloyd's Rep 475*).

Early termination

3.04   A policy may be terminated early, either because of a breach of duty under the policy, or alternatively the insured may in some cases be given the right to terminate the policy by notice. The date from which a notice to terminate takes effect will depend upon the wording of the policy and the words used in the notice of cancellation. There is no English authority on the effect of notice, but it has been held in Canada that a notice of termination takes effect at the end of the day on which it is received by the insurers, so that an accident on that day after the notice has arrived is still insured (*Larizza v Commercial Union Assurance Co [1990] 68 DLR (4th) 460*). Some types of policy allow a proportionate return of premium on early cancellation. In the absence of such an express right, the insured has no entitlement to a rebate, the risk having run.

The insurer may also reserve the right to give a notice of early termination. Some such conditions may require the insurer who seeks to cancel to show cause, but this is not essential. An old decision of the Privy Council holds that the insurer may rely upon a policy provision which gives him the right to cancel at any time and for any reason whatsoever (*Sun Fire Office v Hart (1889) LR 14 App Cas 98*). These clauses are however, relatively unusual in England other than in the marine context where policies are cancellable on 30 days' notice.

The effect of termination on claims

3.05   The expiry of the policy will prevent recovery for any losses arising after that date subject to two modifications:

(*a*)   In liability insurance, the policy may provide an indemnity on a 'claims made' basis or on an 'occurrence of event' basis. In the former case, the insurer is liable only for those claims made by or against the insured during the currency of the policy. In the case of 'occurrence of event' liability policy, the insurer is liable for negligent acts by the insured in the policy period, even though the award of damages against the insured does not occur until some years after the policy has run off.

(*b*)   In property insurance, the general principle is that the insurers' liability under a property policy is based on the time of the occurrence of the peril and not on the time at which damage becomes apparent. Thus, in a claim for heave, the policy covering the year in which the heave occurred is responsible for the loss, and not the policy covering the subsequent year in which damage to the property first began to appear (*Kelly v Norwich Union Fire Insurance Ltd [1989] 2 All ER 888*). This rule is logical, but may cause real practical difficulties where there has been a change of insurer and the precise date at which the heave occurred cannot easily be ascertained.

Chapter 4
Insurable interest

- Introduction

- Definition

- The requirement of an insurable interest: non-indemnity and indemnity insurance

- Non-indemnity insurance: life and non-life insurance

- Indemnity insurance: marine insurance and non-marine insurance

- The indemnity principle

Introduction

4.01 The essence of an insurance contract is that the insurer pays a sum of money to the insured upon the happening of a contingency. Payment of a sum of money on the happening of a contingency is also the essence of a wager. Prior to the passing of the Gambling Act 2005 (which came into force on 1 September 2007 and which applies to contracts created on after that date), wagers were unenforceable. What distinguished a wager from an insurance contract and so made the latter enforceable was the existence of an insurable interest. Since the Gambling Act 2005 the position has become less clear cut.

Since the legal position may be different in relation to a particular contract of insurance depending on when it is created (i.e. before or after 1 September 2007) and, indeed, what type of insurance it is there are a number of stages to the analysis. First it is necessary to consider the concept of insurable interest since this must be present in any contract of (re)insurance created before 1 September 2007. Second, it is necessary to consider the different types of insurance since the point in time when the insurable interest must exist varies and, further, as regards contracts created after 1 September 2007, the Gambling Act does not dispense with the need to show an insurable interest in respect of all contracts of insurance. Third, and in any event, it is necessary to consider the "indemnity principle" which is an overriding principle of insurance law. This principle has the effect of rendering the effect of the Gambling Act 2005 on the requirement of insurable interest largely academic, at least in relation to indemnity insurance.

Definition

4.02 Insurable interest requires that the policyholder should have an interest in the subject matter of the policy. This can either be in its preservation or if they would suffer some loss in the event of a diminution of its value. The classic legal definition of insurable interest was given by Lawrence J in *Lucena v Craufurd (1806) 2 B & P (NR) 269*, at p 302:

> 'where a man is so circumstanced with respect to matters exposed to certain risks or dangers as to have a moral certainty of advantage or benefit but for those risks or dangers, he may be said to be interested in the safety of the thing. To be interested in the preservation of a thing is to be so circumstanced with respect to it as to have benefit from its existence, prejudice from its destruction.'

The modern definition was provided by Waller LJ in *Feasey v Sun Life Assurance Co of Canada [2003] Lloyd's Rep IR 637* at para 95:

> '(5) It is not a requirement of property insurance that the insured must have a 'legal or equitable' interest in the property as those terms might normally be understood. It is sufficient for a sub-contractor to have a contract that relates to the property and a potential liability for damage to the property to have an insurable interest in the property. It is sufficient under section 5 of the Marine Insurance Act for a person interested in a marine adventure to stand in a 'legal or equitable relation to the adventure.' That is intended to be a broad concept.
>
> (6) In a policy on life or lives the court should be searching for the same broad concept. It may be that on an insurance of a specific identified life, it will be difficult to establish a 'legal or equitable' relation without a pecuniary liability recognised by law arising on the death of that particular person. There is however no authority which deals with a policy on many lives and over a substantial period and where it can be seen that a pecuniary liability will arise by reference to those lives and the intention is to cover that legal liability.'

The requirement of an insurable interest

4.03 The requirement to show an insurable interest is a rule that is governed by different statutes, depending on the type of insurance.

A crucial element in the development of the principle of insurable interest was the Gaming Act 1845. This act provided that wagers were not enforceable in English law. The led to the position that insurable interest was a necessity to escape the provision of the Gaming Act; it prevented contracts of insurance being void. However, the Gaming Act has been repealed by the Gambling Act 2005. This has, in effect, created two regimes. Any contract effected before 1 September 2007 will be subject to the Gaming Act 1845. However, any contract effected on 1 September 2007 and onwards is subject to the Gambling Act 2005 (insofar as it applies at all).

The distinction between indemnity and non indemnity insurance

4.04   The insurable interest that must be shown will depend on whether the policy is one of indemnity or one of non-indemnity. In its paper on insurable interest the Law Commission provided a definition of indemnity and non indemnity insurance (The Law Commission, Insurance Contract Law, Issues Paper 4, Insurable Interest, 2008, p3):

'Type 1 – Indemnity insurance

1.16 Indemnity contracts are governed by the indemnity principle. The indemnity principle simply means that insured's can only recover what they have lost. To make a successful claim, policyholders have to show that they incurred loss. They are compensated for the amount of that loss and no more. It follows that in order to suffer a loss, the insured must have had some kind of an interest in the subject matter. This interest is not the same as the strict insurable interest required by statute.

Type 2 – Non-indemnity insurance

1.17 Non-indemnity insurance pays a set amount on the occurrence of a specified event. Most life insurance policies are non-indemnity contracts as they pay a fixed sum on the death of the person insured. Likewise, policies that pay a specified sum on the occurrence of a defined event, such as personal accident policies or valued policies, are also non-indemnity policies.'

Non-indemnity insurance and insurable interest

4.05   As regards non indemnity insurance the rules concerning the demonstration of an insurable interest will vary, subject to whether the policy in question is a life policy or a non-life policy.

As regards life insurance, this is governed by the Life Assurances Act 1774. Section 1 prohibits the making of life insurance when there is no insurable interest. Any policy will be rendered null and void. This provision exists independently of the Gaming Act 1845. The position has not been changed by the Gambling Act 2005. Insurable interest in the life of another rests, with limited exceptions, upon financial interest. Insurance on the lives of family members is, therefore, not always permissible.

The basic rules are as follows:

(a)   A person is conclusively presumed to have an unlimited insurable interest in his own life (*Wainwright v Bland (1835) 1 Moo & Rob 481*). If a spouse and children are the nominated payees, s 11 of the Married Women's Property Act 1882 creates a statutory trust of the proceeds in their favour.

(b)   Spouses are conclusively presumed to have unlimited insurable interests in each other's lives (*Reed v Royal Exchange Assurance Co* (1795) Peake, Add Cas 70) (policy on husband); *Griffiths v Fleming [1909] 1 KB 805* (policy on wife)).

(c)   In the absence of proof of financial interest, a parent cannot insure a child (*Halford v Kymer* (1830) 10 B & C 724), although under a policy issued by a friendly society such insurance may be taken out up to a limit of £800.00 (Friendly Societies Act 1992, s 99). Equally a child cannot insure its parent without proof of financial interest (*Shilling v Accidental Death Insurance Co* (1857) 2 H & N 42).

(d)   Siblings cannot insure each other's lives without proof of financial interest (*Howard v Refuge Friendly Society (1886) 54 L T (NS) 644*), and the same obviously applies to more distant family relationships.

Business relationships involving financial interest may give rise to insurable interest. Thus an employer may insure the life of a key employee, the members of a partnership may insure each other's lives, and a creditor may insure the life of his debtor (*Hebdon v West (1863) 3 B & S 579*). The recent case of *Feasey v Sun Life Assurance Co of Canada [2003] Lloyd's Rep IR 637*, raised a new approach to insurable interest in the context of business relationships. In this case, the insurer's (or reinsured's) insurable interest was expressed to be in the lives of employees and other persons injured who might make claims against the underlying insured. The Court of Appeal held that there was no objection to the insurer's (or reinsured's) insurable interest being classified as a contingent one on the lives of the underlying insured's employees rather than as a simple liability cover. In this instance, such insurable interest was capable of a pecuniary evaluation and the policy itself was capable of being construed as covering that interest.

As regards non life insurance, the requirement for an insurable interest will depend on when the contract was effected. An insurable interest is required if the contract was created before 1 September 2007 by virtue of the Gaming Act 1845. If the contract was created after 1 September 2007 there is no need to show an insurable interest – by virtue of the change made by the Gambling Act 2005.

Indemnity insurance and insurable interest

4.06   The rules that govern indemnity insurance are more complicated. They are governed by a patchwork of statutes, with some dating from 1745. The important distinction for the purposes of the effect of the Gambling Act 2005 is between marine and non-marine insurance. This distinction is discussed separately below.

It follows from the definition of insurable interest in *Lucena v Craufurd (1806) 2 B & P (NR) 269*, that the crucial time for the existence of an insurable interest from the insured's point of view is the time at which he makes a claim on his insurer. If the insured has no insurable interest at that point, there will be no valid claim under the insurance contract, even if the insured had an insurable interest at the time that the insurance contract was entered into.

On the other hand, it is not necessary that the insured's insurable interest should have existed at the date that the insurance contract was made, provided only that the insured does not enter into the insurance contract without any *bona fide* expectation of acquiring an insurable interest at some point in the future.

Marine insurance

4.07 Marine insurance is still governed by The Marine Insurance Act 1906 and the Marine Insurance (Gambling Policies) Act 1909. The effect of these statutes is that prior to 1 September 2007 there is a legal requirement for an insurable interest for a valid contract to exist. Furthermore, the 1909 Act makes it a criminal offence to make a marine policy without any insurable interest.

The effect of the Gambling Act 2005 may be that there is no longer a need for an insurable interest in order to create a valid policy. However, the criminal prohibition on effecting such a policy remains. This means that even though the contract might be enforceable, the parties will be prevented from gaining a benefit from the enterprise.

Non-marine insurance

4.08 The law before 1 September 2007 is governed by the Gaming Act 1845. It provides that non marine indemnity policies cannot be wagers or will be void. As such there is a need to show insurable interest.

However, the Gambling Act 2005 has removed this requirement for contracts that are made from 1 September 2007 onwards. As such there is no requirement for insurable interest in contracts for non marine indemnity insurance which are made today. However, the overriding indemnity principle remains which means that the insured must suffer an actual loss in respect of the subject matter of the policy (and so have some relationship to the subject matter) in order to be able recover under the policy. This is discussed further below.

Marine insurance

The time when the insurable interest must exist

4.09 As previously mentioned, the insured must possess an actual insurable interest at the date of loss, or he can make no claim (*MIA 1906, s 6(1)*). The only exception to this principle is where the policy is made 'lost or not lost'. The type of policy caters for the possibility of a purchase of a vessel or cargo during the course of a voyage, at a time when it is assumed, but not certain, that no casualty has occurred. By insuring 'lost or not lost' the insured will be covered even though a loss has occurred prior to the completion of the sale, but only if the insured was unaware of that loss (*MIA 1906, s 6(1)*). It is not possible for a person to insure once he has become aware that a loss has occurred.

If an insured does not possess insurable interest at the outset of the policy, but genuinely expects to obtain insurable interest (eg the case of a prospective purchaser of a vessel or cargo), the policy is not void by way of gaming or wagering. His ability to recover under the policy will depend upon his obtaining an insurable interest before the casualty occurs. As previously mentioned, if he has not obtained an insurable interest by that date, he will be unable to recover under the policy (*MIA 1906, s 26(2)*) although he will have a claim for his premiums (*MIA 1906, s 84(3)(c)*).

Illustrations of insurable interest in marine insurance

4.10   A variety of interests may be insured under a marine policy:

(*a*)   the hull and machinery of the vessel;

(*b*)   the cargo carried on board the vessel – if the cargo is in the form of a undivided bulk, consisting of goods to be allocated to individual purchaser when the vessel unloads, each has an insurable interest in a proportionate part of the bulk (*MIA 1906, s 8*);

(*c*)   the freight, that is, the hire paid to the owner of the vessel either for space on the vessel for the carriage of cargo or for the use of the entire vessel under a chartering agreement;

(*d*)   liability which is faced by the owner of the vessel either to the owners of other vessels or to cargo owners.

(*e*)   the mortgagor and the mortgagee of the vessel (*MIA 1906, s 14*); and

(*f*)   the master and crew, in respect of their wages (*MIA 1906, s 11*).

Non-marine indemnity insurance: illustrations of insurable interest

Owner of property

4.11   The owner of property has an insurable interest in it for the full value of the property, even though he has entered into a binding contract for its sale (*Rayner v Preston (1881) LR 18 Ch D 1*), and despite the fact that the property would have been subject to seizure by the customs authorities for evasion of excise duty (*Geismar v Sun Alliance and London Insurance Ltd [1978] QB 383*).

Vendor and purchase of buildings

4.12   On exchange of contracts for the sale of a building or land, a binding contract of sale comes into existence. At that stage, the vendor remains the owner, but the risk will, unless the contract otherwise provides, pass to the purchaser. If this is the case, the purchaser must pay the full purchase price on completion, whether or not the building has suffered loss between exchange and completion. The result is that the vendor can insure the building, by reason of his ownership, and the purchaser can insure by reason of being on risk (*Collingridge v Royal Exchange Assurance Corpn (1877) 3 QBD 173*). If the building is damaged between exchange and completion, each party can recover the value from their respective insurers, although the vendor's insurers will be able to reclaim payment from the vendor by way of subrogation when the purchaser pays the price on completion, as the vendor would otherwise receive a double indemnity.

Possessor of property

4.13   A person in possession of goods or land, even though not the owner, may have an insurable interest in the property in question. This will be the case when his possession is coupled with a right to use or enjoy the property; a thief, or a person who is in possession of goods because they have been deposited on his land, has no insurable interest (*Macaura v Northern Assurance Co Ltd [1925] AC 619*), whereas a person who has been given a right to use and enjoy property does possess an insurable interest (Anthony John *Sharp and Roarer Investments Ltd v Sphere Drake Insurance plc Minster, Insurance Co Ltd and E C Parker & Co Ltd (The 'Moonacre')* [1992] 1 Lloyd's Rep 501*). There are two forms of insurable interest which may be claimed by a person in possession of property:

(*a*)   his personal interest; or

(*b*)   the full value of the property.

The position may be illustrated by reference to a warehouseman storing property belonging to third parties. The warehouseman's personal interest consists of any liability which he may face to the owners of the property should it be damaged (because he has not taken proper care of it), and of the amount of any charges which he may be able to levy upon the owner as payment for his storage services. Alternatively, the warehouseman has the right to insure the subject matter for its full value, and if it is lost he is able to claim the full value from the insurers (*Waters v Monarch Fire and Life Assurance Co (1856) 5 E & B 870*). The warehouseman may, however, retain only those sums representing his personal interest; the surplus insurance moneys are held for the true owner by the warehouseman as the owner's debtor. However, the warehouseman will hold the surplus on trust if the contract between the parties obliged the warehouseman to insure the property (*Re E Dibbens & Sons (In Liquidation) [1990] BCLC 577*). Whether the surplus is held as debtor or trustee will be significant if the warehouseman becomes insolvent, for in the latter case the owner has a secured claim on the surplus.

Given that insurance can be either personal or for full value, it becomes necessary to determine exactly which interest is being covered. The rule here is that the policy will be presumed to be one on the full value of the property unless there is clear wording to the contrary. This recognises those situations where the insured will insure the full value of loss even where this exceeds his personal interests as where a head contractor and subcontractor each have an insurable interest in the entire contract works, despite lack of ownership or even possession. The subcontractor may only be responsible for a small part of the works but has a sufficient connection with the entire works to justify insurable interest (*National Oilwell (UK) Ltd v Davy Offshore Ltd [1993] 2 Lloyd's Rep 582*).

The indemnity principle

4.14   Regardless of the question of insurable interest, indemnity insurance contracts (marine and non-marine) are governed by the indemnity principle. This requires the insured to suffer a loss in order to recover under the insurance contract. This will be implied into a policy if it is not expressly provided for in the contract. This means that the insured must have an interest in the subject matter of the insurance or exposure to legal liability for the loss of another in order to have a valid claim under the insurance. The law on the indemnity principle has not been affected by the Gambling Act 2005. Accordingly, the essential practical effect of the indemnity principle is to keep alive the requirement to demonstrate an insurable interest in the case of indemnity insurance contracts.

Chapter 5
Premiums

- Definition
- Amount of premium
- Payment of premium
- Renewal of premium
- Role of brokers
- Return of premium

Definition

5.01 'Premium' can be defined as the consideration paid by the insured, in return for which the insurer undertakes to insure the risks in the policy of insurance. The premium will normally take the form of a monetary payment, although it can take other forms. Once paid, the premium applies to the whole duration of the policy, and the insured cannot be required to pay a supplement should the insurer find itself faced with an undue number of claims, unless the policy contains a provision requiring payment of additional premium in these circumstances. This position can be contrasted with mutual insurance, where strictly speaking a premium is not paid. Members of the mutual insurance organisation will generally pay a sum at the beginning of the policy year. This amount may then be increased by a 'call' from the insurer during the year, or after the year in question until it is 'closed', in order to maintain the adequacy of the insurance fund for claims.

Amount of premium

5.02 In most types of insurance, the insurer will determine the amount of the premium at the outset. This, again, contrasts with the position in respect of mutual insurance which is not ascertained until the cover period has ended. In those rare cases where there is no express agreement to set the premium at the time of the contract, there is a risk that the contract may be held to be void for uncertainty. One way to avoid this is if the court construes the contract as meaning that the insured shall pay a reasonable sum to be determined by market forces. In the case of marine insurance, there is a specific statutory provision for the fixing of a reasonable market premium in the absence of agreement (*Marine Insurance Act 1906, s 31(1)*). Some policies do contemplate that the insurer may be called upon to accept additional risk during the currency of the agreement. This is particularly common in marine insurance, where the insurer is obliged under 'held covered' provisions to offer cover where the insured has deviated from the agreed route, has broken a warranty or has entered into a war zone. Here the insured will be required to pay an additional premium to be determined on market principles (*Marine Insurance Act 1906, s 31(2)*), although if a premium cannot be agreed and there is no market rate the insurers' obligation to offer additional cover is discharged (*Liberian Insurance Agency Inc v Mosse [1977] 2 Lloyd's Rep 560*).

Payment of premium

5.03 In principle, at least, premiums are payable in cash to the insurer at its principal place of business. It is for the insured to seek out the insurer and effect this payment, which should be in the form stipulated in the contract. It is more usual now for payment to be made by cheque or direct debit.

What is the effect of non-payment? Where the insured has not paid the premium on the due date the insurer may have a number of remedies. These include bringing proceedings to compel payment of the premium. Alternatively, non-payment may be regarded as a repudiatory breach giving the insurer the right to terminate the contract. In the absence of a non-forfeiture provision in a policy, and where the insurer has a contractual right to treat the policy as having been forfeited due to late payment of premium, the courts appear to be reluctant to exercise their equitable discretion to grant relief from forfeiture. In commercial cases, where premiums are handled by brokers acting for the parties, non-payment may be little more than an accounting error. It was held in *Fenton Insurance Co Ltd v Gothaer Versicherungsbank VVag [1991] 1 Lloyd's Rep 172*, a reinsurance case, that non-payment for a period of some eight years was not sufficient to amount to a repudiatory breach. A similar approach was taken in *Figre Ltd v Mander [1999] Lloyd's Rep IR 193*.

What then is the position if the policy takes effect even though the premium has not been paid? One has to look to the contract of insurance to determine whether or not the insurer is entitled to reject a claim until the premium is tendered. The position in the absence of a statement of this type was considered by the Supreme Court of South Africa in *Lake v Reinsurance Corporation Ltd [1967] (3) SA 124 (W)*. In that case the claimant was the liquidator of an insolvent insurance company. The premiums, under a reinsurance agreement, had not been paid but the reinsured suffered losses for which the liquidator commenced proceedings. The court ruled that the reinsurer was on risk despite the reinsured's non-payment. In spite of this, the reinsurer could not be obliged to meet any claim until the premiums had been tendered. Thus, when the reinsured submitted a claim, the reinsurer had the right to deduct outstanding premiums from the sum due to the reinsured under the policy. This did not, however, apply in this case, as the premium due exceeded the claims.

The payment of the premium is, in marine insurance law, a condition concurrent with the obligation of the insured to issue the policy (*Marine Insurance Act 1906, s 52*). The effect of this is, subject to a contrary provision in the contract, that the risk may commence from the agreed date of event, but that the insured will not be entitled to a policy (and therefore cannot enforce the contract – *Marine Insurance Act 1906, s 22*) until the premium has been tendered.

Renewal of premium

5.04   It is now common for insurers to accept payment by instalments, or even by monthly direct debit. Irrespective of whether premiums are paid monthly, or in a single lump sum at inception, the insured will be asked at the end of the policy period either to pay the renewal premium, or to complete a further bank mandate to ensure the continuation of the direct debiting arrangement. What is the position, then, if the insured is late in complying with the insurer's instructions? A large number of insurance contracts provide that, until the premium is paid, there shall be no insurance cover. In the absence of an express contractual provision, it is unlikely that such a term would be implied. The policy, therefore, commences at its inception date and continues until lateness of payment becomes fundamental. Once time becomes of the essence, however, non-payment constitutes default whatever the reasons for, or circumstances surrounding, the non-payment. The position may be further complicated by the insurer's grant of 'days of grace' for the payments of premium. The position also varies as between life (non-indemnity) policies and all other types of policy.

Life insurance

5.05   Given the nature of life contracts, it is unsurprising that the punctual payment of the premium is regarded as a condition precedent to the liability of the company. The insurance is regarded by the law not as periodic, but as continuing, subject to renewal by the insured. Failure to pay the premium by the due date will cause the policy to lapse, and if cover is to be reinstated, the insured will have to make a fresh application. The consequences of this can be extremely harsh. In order to avoid this, the insurer may give the insured a period of 'days of grace' for payment of the renewal premium. The effect of this is to allow the insured an extension of time for the payment of such premiums. If a loss should occur in that period, the insurer will be liable to meet the loss, for the simple reason that a life policy is to be regarded as continuing in force. This was the ruling of the Court of Appeal in *Stuart v Freeman [1903] 1 KB 47*.

Indemnity insurance

5.06   An indemnity policy, unlike a life policy, is periodic and comes to an end at the end of a stated period. Renewal by the insured creates a totally new contract. The grant of days of grace by the insurer for payment of the renewal premium does not, therefore, amount to an extension of the old policy, but is an offer to the insured of fresh cover should the premium be paid in the days of grace. It follows that the insurer is not automatically liable for a loss during the days of grace; this will depend upon whether the insurer has indicated to the insured that it is prepared to accept liability in that period, and also upon whether the insured has, by conduct or otherwise, accepted the insurer's offer of temporary cover. It was held in *Taylor v Allon [1966] 1 QB 304* that the driver of a motor vehicle was not insured during the days of grace because he had, by seeking quotes from other insurers, intended to reject the offer of temporary cover, so that merely driving his vehicle on the strength of the insurer's offer was insufficient acceptance of it.

The role of brokers

5.07   The rules applicable to the payment of premiums through brokers vary considerably as between, on the one hand, insurance placed at Lloyd's and marine policies and, on the other hand, all other policies. Lloyd's and marine insurances are governed by exceptional rules which have been long established by custom. Ordinary principles are considered first in what follows.

General principles

5.08   As a general rule, the insurance broker is the agent of the insured for most purposes (see 7 BROKERS). Payment of the premium to the broker will not, therefore, satisfy the requirement to pay premium to the insurers. Payment is not, in fact, effective until the amount has actually been received by insurers. One consequence of this is that, in practice, the risk of the broker's insolvency or misconduct is borne by the insured. There is, then, no legal relationship between the broker and the insurer. The law is illustrated by the unusual facts of *Wilson v Avec Audio-Visual Equipment Limited [1974] 1 Lloyd's Rep 81*, in which the defendant insured had placed insurances with the insurer through the claimant broker, but no premiums had been paid. The insurer became insolvent, and premiums were demanded from the brokers, who duly paid the premiums and sought reimbursement from the insured. The Court of Appeal held that the broker had no obligation to the insurer to pay the premium and, as this payment had not been authorised by the insured, the broker had no right to be reimbursed by the insured.

Lloyd's policies and contracts of marine insurance

5.09   *Section 53(1)* of the *Marine Insurance Act 1906* codifies a market usage of the marine market at Lloyd's dating back at least to the beginning of the nineteenth century, which states that the broker is directly responsible to the insurer for the premiums. It is doubtful whether this usage applies to non-marine business at Lloyd's. In the event of non-payment, the insurer must look to the broker and not to the insured for payment, although this will be of little use to the insurer where the reason for the broker's non-payment is insolvency, as the broker is a mere debtor of the insurer and does not hold any premium paid to him by the insured on trust for the insurer. The real effect of this rule is to transfer the risk of the broker's insolvency to the insurer, as the insured cannot be made to pay the insurer once he has made payment to the broker (*Universo Insurance Co of Milan v Merchants Marine Insurance Co Ltd [1897] 2 QB 93*).

The strict legal position as set out above was avoided by an agreement made in October 1997 between the Lloyd's Insurance Brokers' Committee (LIBC), Lloyd's and the Institute of London Underwriters (now called LIRMA) that insurers would not, notwithstanding *s 53(1)* of the *Marine Insurance Act 1906*, hold brokers responsible for payment of premiums in the event of a default by the insured. As far as Lloyd's is concerned, this principle applied to all business incepting after 31 August 1996, in relation to the Institute of London Underwriters, the agreement took effect in respect of all business closed on Institute policies incepting after 31 August 1997. In both cases, the agreement remained in place until 31 August 2001. The agreement has been allowed to lapse and no business going forward from 31 August 2001 is subject to it. The terms of the agreement are nonetheless summarised here as it will continue to have effect on business incepting whilst it remained in place.

The agreement not to hold brokers personally liable for premiums was conditional, since it was subject to the proviso that the broker concerned should not be in breach of any of the following three broad principles:

(*a*)   brokers and underwriters should not knowingly do business with clients likely to default;

(*b*)   brokers should inform underwriters without delay when a likely default becomes known; and

(*c*)   brokers should make every endeavour to collect monies owing and pass them to underwriters without delay, and underwriters should support such endeavours.

If a broker has been in breach of any of the above principles and the relevant policy is governed by English law, then the underwriters have the option to invoke *s 53(1)* of the *Marine Insurance Act 1906* in respect of that policy and claim the unpaid premium from the broker.

The scope of the agreement appears not to be limited to any particular categories of insurance or reinsurance.

An undertaking given by the LIBC in connection with the agreement states that the brokers 'acknowledge *s 53(1)* of the *Marine Insurance Act 1906* ... but no broker will be held liable for premium unless it is evidenced that the broker has been in breach of any of the three broad principles'. This acknowledgement presumably recognises that the legal position is clear in respect of marine

insurance and marine facultative reinsurance, subject to the opening words of
s 53, which provide for the broker to be liable for premium 'unless otherwise
agreed'. Such liability attaches, however, at the time of conclusion of the contract.
The LIBC undertaking referred to above is, therefore, presumably intended to fall
within the 'unless otherwise agreed' proviso on a conditional basis, so that the
primary liability for premium falls on the insured, subject to resumption of the
broker's liability if the broker is in breach of any of the three broad principles.

At Lloyd's, brokers and underwriters operate periodic net accounting agreements, under which the broker receives the premiums and pays losses, and settles
with the underwriter at the end of each periodic accounting period. Where this
operates, premiums will not be paid as such. The insured's position, so far as
marine business is concerned, is protected by a combination of market practice
and s 54 of the *Marine Insurance Act 1906*. The policy, when issued, will acknowledge receipt of the premium, and the section provides that such an acknowledgement is binding as between insurer and insured, so that the insurer cannot go
behind the agreement and claim the premium from the insured. The acknowledgement is not, however, binding as between the insurer and the broker.

Return of premium

Indivisibility of premium and total failure of consideration

5.10 Notwithstanding the payment of any premium, it will be recoverable if
there has been a total failure of consideration.

The common law recognises two propositions as stated by Lord Mansfield in the
case of *Tyrie v Fletcher (1777) 2 Cowp 666*.

(*a*) If the risk never attaches, the insurer has not earned any part of the
premium and the insured is entitled to recover the full premium on the
ground of total failure of consideration.

(*b*) If the risk has attached, even for a day, there is no total failure of
consideration and the insured is not entitled to a return of any part of his
premium. In such a case, the insured's right to recover any part of his
premium will rest upon the policy itself.

It is worth noting that these principles may be reflected in, or modified by, the
express terms of the contract.

Application of the law

5.11 The return of premium depends upon whether or not the risk is attached.
The following situations may arise.

Lack of an insurable interest

5.12   Where the insured has no insurable interest in the subject matter but is required to have one, the risk can never attach and the premium is returnable (*Marine Insurance Act 1906, s 84(3)(c)*). However, there is no return of premium if the insured under a life policy does not have an insurable interest, as the policy is illegal (*Life Assurance Act 1774, s 1*, as applied by *Harse v Pearl Life Assurance Co [1904] 1 KB 558*); although if the policy was induced by the fraud of the insurer's agent, the premium will be returnable (*Hughes v Liverpool Victoria Legal Friendly Society [1916] 2 KB 482*).

Loss of an insurable interest during the currency of the policy, for example, by sale of the subject matter, will not justify a return of premium, as the risk has been run, albeit temporarily (*Marine Insurance Act 1906, s 84(3)(d)*).

Risk not attaching

5.13   If the risk under the policy never attaches, for example, because the goods insured have never been transported, the premium is returnable (*Marine Insurance Act 1906, s 84(3)(b)*).

Mistake

5.14   If the contract is void for mistake, the consideration will fail and the premiums paid are returnable.

Avoidance for misrepresentation or non-disclosure

5.15   If the policy is set aside by the insurer for breach by the insured of its duty of utmost good faith, the policy is avoided *ab initio*, and the risk is deemed never to have attached. The insured will, therefore, be entitled to a full return of premium, although this right is lost if the insured's breach of duty was fraudulent or illegal (*Marine Insurance Act 1906, s 84(3)(a)*), or if the policy provides that the insurer reserves a right to retain premiums to cover administrative costs.

Divisibility of risk

5.16   If the risk attaches to some part of the policy but not to the remainder, the insured cannot recover the premium. The position differs, however, if the contract can be shown on its true construction to be severable. The insured will be entitled to a partial return of premium to reflect those risks which have not attached at the time of loss.

Breach of warranty

5.17   The position varies depending upon whether the warranty is present or continuing. If the warranty is a statement of fact made at the outset of the contract, and that fact is untrue, the insurer is never on risk and the premium is returnable (subject to the insured not having acted fraudulently). If, by contrast, the warranty is a continuing one, and is broken by misconduct by the insured during the period of the policy, the risk terminates as from the date of breach so that the premium is not returnable.

Over-insurance

5.18   If the insured has insured under a single policy for a sum greater than his insurable interest, he cannot reclaim the excess premium, although the position is different in marine insurance (see *Marine Insurance Act 1906, s 84(3)(e)*). Similarly, if the insured has over-insured by taking out two or more policies, each insurer is potentially on risk for the full amount of its liability, and the over-insured proportion of the premium is not returnable, although again the position is different in marine insurance (*Marine Insurance Act 1906, s 84(3)(f)*).

Chapter 6
Policyholder duties

- Duty of utmost good faith
- Disclosure
- Misrepresentation
- Fraud
- Minimising loss and alteration in the risk

Duty of utmost good faith

6.01 A contract of insurance is based upon the principle of utmost good faith, or *uberrima fides*. This principle can be traced back to the eighteenth century (*Carter v Boehm (1766) 3 Burr 1905*) and was adopted by the courts in recognition of the fact that it is often difficult for an insurer to ask questions about the wide range of facts which might be material to the underwriting assessment, but which are known only to the insured.

The duty of good faith was codified in *s 17* of the *Marine Insurance Act 1906 (MIA 1906)* which provides that:

> 'A contract of marine insurance is a contract based upon the utmost good faith and if the utmost good faith be not observed by either party the contract may be avoided by the other party.'

The principle of utmost good faith imposes two essential duties on the insured: the duty to disclose (*MIA 1906, ss 18, 19*) and the duty to make true representations (*MIA 1906, s 20*). The House of Lords in *Pan Atlantic Insurance Co Ltd v Pine Top Insurance Co [1994] 2 Lloyd's Rep 427* affirmed that the provisions of *MIA 1906* dealing with utmost good faith, disclosure and misrepresentation were intended to codify the common law relating to all forms of insurance, including non-marine insurance and reinsurance, and are not confined to marine insurance.

Continuing duty of utmost good faith

6.02   The duties of utmost good faith, disclosure and representation are all applicable during the negotiations and placement of the insurance contract. *Section 17 of MIA 1906* is silent on whether the duty of utmost good faith continues during the operation of the contract. In *Manifest Shipping Co Ltd v Uni-Polaris Insurance Co Ltd (The 'Star Sea') [2001] Lloyd's Rep IR 247*, the insured had failed to disclose, after litigation had commenced, a number of documents relevant to the claim. The insurers argued that this non-disclosure was fraudulent and thus in breach of *s 17 of MIA 1906*. The House of Lords appeared to treat this as a case of fraud, and so distinct in law from any ongoing duty of good faith, so that no issue arose of a breach of the duty of utmost good faith.

Nevertheless, whilst it was accepted that there was a continuing and reciprocal duty of good faith, the House of Lords was clear that the duty after a contract is concluded was different and more limited than the duty prior to the formation of the contract. The House of Lords also found that the continuing duty of good faith comes to an end once the insurer has rejected a claim and litigation in respect of that claim has commenced. At that point, the parties obligations are as set out in the Civil Procedure Rules, governing the conduct of litigation.

Another decision which limited the scope of the continuing duty of good faith was *K/s Merc-Scandia XXXXII v Certain Lloyd's Underwriters Subscribing to Lloyd's Policy No. 25t 105487 and Ocean Marine Insurance Co Ltd (The 'Mercandian Continent') [2001] 2 Lloyd's Rep 563*, in which the Court of Appeal dealt with the question of when the continuing duty of good faith applied and what the appropriate remedy was in the event of breach. The Court of Appeal held that a post-contractual duty of good faith arises where the insured has a contractual duty to provide the insurer with information, and in circumstances where a liability insurer takes control of the defence of an insured in litigation.

The Court of Appeal also held that the only remedy available for breach of the continuing duty of good faith is avoidance *ab initio*. Before it can avoid, the insurer must satisfy a two-stage test, namely:

(*a*)   there must be a breach of the continuing duty of good faith; and

(*b*)   the insurer must show that the breach of the continuing duty of good faith was of such a degree of severity that the insurer would be justified in treating the contract as repudiated and at an end.

Disclosure

6.03   In the general law of contract, a contract will be voidable if its making has been induced by a false statement or misrepresentation. In insurance law the duty to provide information during pre-contractual negotiations is more onerous. Not only does the usual principle of misrepresentation operate, but the insured is under an additional obligation to volunteer to the insurer all facts which are material to the risk, regardless of whether the insurer has asked any express questions. This obligation characterises the contract of insurance as one of utmost good faith, or *uberrima fides*.

Today the duty of disclosure is of diminished importance in the consumer insurance field. The Statement of General Insurance Practice (SGIP) (see 41 REGULATION OF SALES OF INSURANCE PRODUCTS) was replaced in a modified form by the Insurance Conduct of Business Rules with effect from 14 January 2005. The Statement of Long Term Insurance Practice survives. However, although the SGIP has been replaced, the Financial Ombudsman Service ('FOS') has issued guidance which states that the Ombudsman will continue to treat the SGIP as an example of good industry practice and will therefore still take it into account.

Under r 7.3.6 of the Insurance Conduct of Business Rules,

> 'an insurer must not unreasonably reject a claim made by a customer. Except where there is evidence of fraud, an insurer should also not refuse to meet a claim made by a retail customer on the grounds:
>
> (a)   of non-disclosure of a fact material to the risk that the retail customer could not reasonably be expected to have disclosed; and
>
> (b)   of misrepresentation of a fact material to the risk, unless the misrepresentation is negligent.'

The SGIP required the insurer to ask questions (generally in the proposal form) concerning all facts generally found to be material, and even where a consumer has been guilty of non-disclosure, the ombudsman will only allow an insurer to avoid a policy if there has been fraud. It seems likely that this will remain the position under r 7.3.6 of the ICOB rules.

The duty of disclosure remains fully operative in commercial insurance. Nevertheless, the position is currently under review by the Law Commission and changes are likely at a future stage.

The nature of the obligation to disclose

Definition of disclosure

6.04   *Section 18(1) of MIA 1906* requires the insured to disclose to the insurer 'every material circumstance' known to the insured.

Section 20 of MIA 1906 in turn requires 'every material representation' to be truthful. All facts material to the risk must therefore be disclosed.

Section 18(2) of MIA 1906 defines as material 'every circumstance which would influence the judgement of a prudent underwriter in fixing the premium or determining whether he will write the risk' (see 6.07 below).

The House of Lords in the case of *Pan Atlantic* (see 6.01 above) held that for a fact to be material, it was not necessary to show that full and accurate disclosure would have led a prudent insurer either to reject the risk, or at least to have accepted it only on more onerous terms. It was sufficient to show that the relevant fact would affect the judgement of the insurer in the sense that it would have been taken into account as part of the evaluative process. It is therefore generally enough for the insured to alert the insurer that the risk has particular character-istics, and the onus is then on the insurer to make further enquiries. If the insurer fails do so, he may be taken to have waived the right to the additional information (see 6.16 below). Equally, if the insured prepares detailed documentation for the insurer containing all material facts, and the insurer chooses not to read the documents but relies upon summary (but not misleading) statements made by the insured, the insured is likely to have complied with his duty of disclosure (see *Pan Atlantic* at 6.01 above).

The duty of disclosure is tempered by the concept of 'fair presentation' of the risk. This principle, as summarised by Kerr LJ in *Container Transport International Inc and Reliance Group Inc v Oceanus Mutual Underwriting Association Ltd [1984] 1 Lloyd's Rep 476*, recognises that there is often a limit on the amount of information that the insured can disclose. The insured must make a judgement as to what information will be material for a prudent underwriter in order to ensure that a 'fair presentation' is made. All such information must then be supplied.

Innocent non-disclosure

6.05   The insured's duty is to disclose facts of which he is aware and facts of which he ought to be aware (eg in the ordinary course of business). The insured can therefore be guilty of non-disclosure for failing to disclose a fact which he should have known, but did not. Recent cases, and in particular *Pan Atlantic* (see 6.01 above), have assumed that the insured constructively knows facts which he ought to know for the purposes of disclosure. However, In *ERC Frankona Reinsurance v American National Insurance Company [2006] Lloyd's Rep IR 157* Andrew Smith J noted that 'the courts do not readily impute to an insured information that he did not know on the basis that he ought to have known it'. It is also important that it is irrelevant that the insured did not know he was under a duty to disclose material facts. Innocence of this nature does not prevent non-disclosure from being actionable.

It is not just the insured's own knowledge which is relevant, but also that of his agents. If a broker is aware of facts material to the risk, or ought to be aware of such facts (*MIA 1906, s 19(1)*) then the broker's knowledge is deemed to be that of the insured (*Blackburn, Low & Co v Thomas Vigors (1887) LR 12 App Cas 531*) and must be disclosed. Equally, the insurer cannot avoid the policy on the basis of the facts which the insured or his brokers or agents had no way of knowing. In this sense, innocent non-disclosure has no legal consequences.

This should be contrasted with the position where the insured is aware of a particular fact, but chooses not to disclose it in the genuine belief that it is not material. The law here is clear – materiality is a matter to be assessed by the standard of the prudent insurer, not by the prudent or honest insured – and the insured's belief as to materiality, whether or not reasonably held, is irrelevant (*Joel v Law Union and Crown Insurance Co [1908] 2 KB 863* (life insurance); *Lambert v Co-Operative Insurance Society Ltd [1975] 2 Lloyd's Rep 485* (burglary insurance); *Pan Atlantic* (see 6.01 above)). This area of the law is under review by the Law Commission and there have been indications that changes may be recommended.

The use of agents

6.06 If the insured completes a proposal form or discusses matters to be disclosed in the presence of an agent who is acting for the insurer or who is authorised by that insurer to obtain the completed proposal, disclosure to the insurer's agent will generally be treated as disclosure to the insurer itself. All will depend, however, on the authority that has been given to the agent by its principal, the insurer.

A different situation arises where the negotiations with the insurer are conducted by a broker (which will always be the case at Lloyd's), as the broker is deemed to be the agent of the insured. This rule has the consequence that disclosure by the insured to the broker, or the broker's knowledge of the true position, is not sufficient to satisfy the insured's duty of disclosure to the insurer (*Kenneth Roberts v Patrick Selwyn Plaisted (1989) 2 Lloyd's Rep 341*). The insured, or his agent, must make sure that material information is communicated to the insurer. The existence of a separate obligation on the broker to disclose material facts was confirmed by the House of Lords in *HIH Casualty and General Insurance Ltd v Chase Manhattan Bank [2003] 2 Lloyd's Rep 61*. It is therefore important for the insured to keep the broker informed of any change in the insured's circumstances, so that relevant information can be passed to the insurer. However, if the insured becomes aware of a material fact too late to communicate this to the broker before the contract is concluded, the insured's non-disclosure will be excused (*MIA 1906, s 19*). However, given the speed of modern communications it is difficult to imagine circumstances where this provision would be successfully invoked.

Materiality and inducement

6.07 First, materiality. A fact is material, and has to be disclosed to the insurer, if it would 'influence the judgment of a prudent insurer in fixing the premium or in determining whether he will take the risk' (*MIA 1906, s 18(2)*). 'Every material circumstance' known to the insured must be disclosed to the insurer (*MIA 1906, s18(1)*).

The test of materiality is objective. It is normally established by way of expert underwriting evidence. In order for a fact or circumstance to be material it does not need to be shown that the the prudent underwriter would have charged a different premium or refused the risk had he known the truth; the question is whether a prudent insurer would have been influenced by the facts withheld in the sense that he would have wanted to have known about them.

Prior to *Pan Atlantic*, the test of materiality was held, in the case of *Container Transport International v Oceanus* (see 6.04 above), to be whether the fact or circumstance was one which a prudent insurer would have wished to take into account when deciding whether or not to write the risk. In the case of *Pan Atlantic* (see 6.01 above) the House of Lords conducted a complete review of the law applicable to disclosure of material facts. Their Lordships held:

(*a*)   that for a fact to be material, it was sufficient to show that the relevant fact would have affected the judgement of a prudent insurer, in the sense that he would have taken into account as part of the evaluative process that fact, even if it was not ultimately decisive; but

(*b*)   a material non-disclosure would entitle an insurer to avoid a contract only if that non-disclosure actually induced the underwriter to subscribe to the contract on the relevant terms (the actual inducement test).

Turning now to inducement. Although the first part of the test (ie materiality) is objective, the House of Lords introduced an important subjective element in that the insurer who wrote the risk cannot avoid the contract for non-disclosure if the underwriter was not in fact influenced by the non-disclosure in question, despite the fact that a hypothetical prudent insurer may have been affected. (This subjective element has been confirmed in numerous cases including by the Court of Appeal in *Assicurazioni Generali SpA v Arab Insurance Group [2003] 1 WLR 577*.)

A presumption of inducement

6.08   The test established by *Pan Atlantic* (see 6.01 above) raises the possibility that the insured or his broker may attempt to pass poor quality risks to the insurer, relying on the fact that the underwriter may not, in actuality, be influenced by full disclosure. Lord Mustill in the *Pan Atlantic* case, anticipating this problem, commented specifically that once the facts are shown to be material (in other words the first limb of the *Pan Atlantic* test has been satisfied) a presumption arises that the non-disclosure of that fact did induce the underwriter to enter into the contract on the relevant terms. This comment has subsequently been considered by the courts and in the case of *Marc Rich & Co AG v Portman [1996] 1 Lloyd's Rep 430*, the court was asked to consider whether there was evidence to rebut a presumption of inducement. The court held that a presumption would arise only where the actual underwriter was not available to give evidence and there was no reason to suppose he acted other than prudently in writing the risk. If the actual underwriter did give evidence, but that evidence was inconclusive on the question of inducement, the presumption would not operate and the burden of proving inducement would remain on the insurer.

The position has been clarified by the Court of Appeal in *Assicurazioni Generali v Arab Insurance Group* (see 6.07 above), in which Clarke LJ summarised the position as follows:

'An insurer or reinsurer must prove on the balance of probabilities that he was induced to enter into the contract by a material non-disclosure or a material misrepresentation.

There is no presumption of law that an insurer or reinsurer is induced to enter in the contract by a material non-disclosure or misrepresentation. The facts may, however, be such that it is to be inferred that the particular insurer or reinsurer was so induced in the absence of evidence from him.'

Illustrations of material facts

6.09   There are many reported cases, relating to all classes of insurance, in which the courts have been required to consider whether a particular fact was or was not material in the circumstances. General guidance only may be given here. The basic principle is that a fact may be material because it contributes either to the physical hazard or to the moral hazard of the risk underwritten.

Physical hazard

6.10   Physical hazard is constituted by those facts which increase the immediate risk to the insured subject matter. To give some obvious examples: material facts for a fire or burglary policy will include the location of the property, the uses to which the premises are put and the adequacy of security arrangements. Material facts for a life or accident policy are likely to include the insured's medical record, his occupation and his spare-time activities. Material facts for a liability policy will include the nature of the insured's activities and his knowledge of the likelihood of any claim against him arising from earlier events. Material facts for a marine, aviation or motor policy will include the qualifications of the person in control of the transport, the purposes for which the transport is required and its physical condition.

Moral hazard

6.11   Moral hazard is concerned not with the physical condition of the subject matter itself, but rather with the character of the insured and the risk that the insured in question is more likely to suffer losses or make a claim. The most important forms of moral hazard are the following.

(*a*)   Previous losses and insurance claims. What is important for this purpose is not necessarily the amount of a loss, but the mere fact that a loss has taken place (Anthony John *Sharp and Roarer Investments Ltd v Sphere Drake Insurance plc Minster, Insurance Co Ltd and E C Parker & Co Ltd (The 'Moonacre') [1992] 2 Lloyd's Rep 501*). To be safe, an insured may need to disclose previous claims even if they relate to other classes of insurance (*Becker v Marshall [1922] Ll L Rep 413*).

(*b*)   Previous refusals by other insurers to issue a policy, and previous refusals to insure without additional conditions or the charging of a higher premium, are potential material facts. This may be so even if the refusal related to a different class of insurance, as in *Locker & Woolf Ltd v Western Australian Insurance Co Ltd [1935] 153 Ll L Rep 325*, where a fire policy was held to be voidable in the light of the insured's failure to disclose a previous motor car insurance refusal.

(c) Double insurance or overinsurance of the insured subject matter may be material, but only if the degree of overinsurance suggests that a fraudulent claim is a possibility (*Ionides v Pender(1873–74) LR 9 QB 531*).

(d) Previous Criminality on the part of the insured is likely to be a material fact. Previous criminal convictions may be material if they are directly linked to the subject matter concerned (*Jester-Barnes v Licences & General Insurance Co Ltd [1934] 49 Ll L Rep 231* – drunken driving offences not disclosed for the purposes of a motor policy) or if they indicate general dishonesty of a nature likely to pose a threat to the insurer (*Woolcott v Sun Alliance and London Insurance Ltd [1978] 1 All ER 1253*). Criminal convictions are deemed to be immaterial once they are 'spent' under the *Rehabilitation of Offenders Act 1974* (an Act which wipes clean the record of a convicted person after a period of time, the relevant period being determined by a sliding scale based upon the seriousness of the offence). It is irrelevant that dishonest behaviour on the part of the insured has not come to the attention of the authorities; such dishonest behaviour is still potentially material. This includes an acquittal of a material criminal offence, which must be disclosed if the insured in fact committed the offence. An acquittal is a material fact even where the proposer maintains his innocence because it might lead the prudent underwriter to make further enquiries (*Strive Shipping Corpn v Hellenic Mutual War Risks Association (The 'Grecia Express') [2002] 2 Lloyd's Rep 88*).

Criminal charges (and similar specific allegations of dishonesty or misconduct) outstanding against the insured at the time the insurance contract is made, are material facts, even when the insured knows that he is innocent (*Brotherton v Aseguradora Colseguros SA (No 2) [2003] Lloyd's Rep IR 746*), although the insured can include within his disclosure evidence of his innocence. Colman J followed the Court of Appeal's reasoning in the *Brotherton* case in *North Star Shipping Ltd v Sphere Drake Insurance plc [2005] Lloyd's Rep IR 404*. In this case, it was held that the policy was voidable as the insured had failed to disclose, among other matters, four separate pending criminal proceedings against them in the Greek courts and a civil action in Panama, all of which alleged fraud. These proceedings were held to be material facts even though the insured may have genuinely believed that the allegations were groundless, and that three of the Greek cases had either been withdrawn or dismissed by the time of the loss. Colman J held that allegations of fraud in proceedings are material facts going to moral hazard in the sense that they would be taken into account by an underwriter in forming a view as to the acceptability of the risk. The materiality of the information is not diminished by exculpatory evidence. If exculpatory evidence is available, it should be given to the underwriter so that he has the opportunity of considering all the evidence in forming his opinion. Colman J's decision was upheld by the Court of Appeal ([2006] 2 Lloyd's Rep 183).

However, it is not always necessary for every allegation known to the insured to be disclosed. In *Norwich Union Insurance Ltd v Meisels [2007] Lloyd's Rep IR 69* the insurer asserted that the insured had failed to disclose irregularities in the filing of accounts and returns of companies of which he was a director, which has led to penalties being imposed and, in some cases, dissolution of the relevant companies.

The insured had further failed to disclose that four of his companies had been liquidated. The facts of the case did not indicate any dishonesty. The court held, in considering generally how 'moral hazard' should be dealt with, that allegations of misconduct were not always material. There was room for a test of proportionality based on the nature of the risk. The court held that exculpatory material relating to the allegations is relevant in determining whether acts are material, or whether the insurer would have accepted the insured's explanation and disregarded the allegations.

Limitations on the duty of disclosure

6.12 *Section 18(3)* of *MIA 1906* sets out four types of facts which need not be disclosed to the insurer and which are immaterial unless an express question is asked.

Facts diminishing the risk

6.13 Under *s 18(3)(a)* of *MIA 1906*, the insured need not disclose any circumstance which diminishes the risk. An illustration of this situation is *Inversiones Manria SA v Sphere Drake Insurance Co plc, Malvern Insurance Co Ltd and Niagara Fire Insurance Co Inc (The 'Dora') [1989] 1 Lloyd's Rep 69* in which the insured was held not to be in breach of the duty of disclosure for failing to disclose that the yacht to be insured was not ready to sail, and was still being worked upon some time after the inception of the risk.

Facts within the knowledge of the insurer

6.14 *Section 18(3)(b)* of *MIA 1906* stipulates that the insured need not disclose 'any circumstance which is known or presumed to be known to the insurer'. The insurer is presumed to know matters of common notoriety or knowledge and matters which an insurer in the ordinary course of business, ought to know. There are three types of facts which fall within this provision.

(a) *Facts which are actually known to the insurer.* In *Cape plc v Iron Trades Employers Association Ltd [2004] Lloyd's Rep IR 75* it was held that the assured could not, on renewal of a liability policy, be required to disclose to insurers the fact that there had been a huge rise in the incidence of claims for mesothelioma, as insurers were aware of such claims and had in fact paid them.

(b) *Facts or circumstances which the insurer ought to know in the ordinary course of his business, or facts of notoriety which the insurer ought generally to know.* Facts which have been held to fall into this category include the existence of war in a particular region and the dangerous properties of particular substances used in the insured's business.

(c) *Facts which are specific to the form of business carried on by the insurer and which ought to be known by an insurer involved in that form of business.* An insurer of fishing boats is assumed to know that boats of that class have been subject to an exceptionally large number of claims in recent years (*North British Fishing*

Boat Insurance Co Ltd v Starr [1922] 13 Ll L Rep 206). Despite this expected knowledge, an insurer will not be expected to know specific circumstances affecting limited groups within the overall market in which he works, or carry in his head information in which he has no interest.

Waiver of the duty to disclose

Express waiver

6.15   The insured need not disclose 'any circumstances as to which information is waived by the insurer' (*MIA 1906, s 18(3)(c)*). The simplest form of waiver is an express clause in the proposal form which states that the insured's duty of utmost good faith is satisfied by answering the questions put to him on the proposal. Less obvious wording may have the same effect. In *Hair v The Prudential Assurance Co Ltd [1983] 2 Lloyd's Rep 667* the proposal form concluded with a warranty by the insured that 'all the information entered above is true and complete and that nothing materially affecting the risks has been concealed.' This was held by Woolf J to mean that the insured was warranting that the answers given to express questions were true and complete, and that the disclosure of anything further had been waived.

The House of Lords in *HIH Casualty and General Insurance v Chase Manhattan Bank* (see 6.06 above) accepted that it was possible for an insured to contract out of (a) a duty of disclosure or the duty to ensure that any representation made was correct; and (b) the consequences of non-disclosure or misrepresentation by the insured (although, as a matter of public policy, the insured could not contract out of the consequences of his own fraudulent conduct).

Implied waiver

6.16   The insurer may be held by its conduct to have waived disclosure. Waiver may arise in the following circumstances.

(*a*)   The insurer has been alerted by the insured to the possible existence of special circumstances, but has failed to make further inquiry. If, for example, the insurer has been told that the insured vessel is to be carrying cargo, but the insurer neglects to seek further information as to the nature of the cargo, the insurer cannot complain if the cargo proves to be inflammable (*Mann Macneal and Steeves Ltd v Capital and Counties Insurance Co Ltd [1921] 2 KB 300*).

(b)   The insurer has chosen to ask a specific question on a particular matter, but has by the question restricted the amount of information required (*O'Kane v Jones (The 'Martin P') [2004] 1 Lloyd's Rep 389*). Proposals for life policies, for example, normally ask the insured about previous medical treatment, but limit the question to the previous five years. In *Roberts v Plaisted* (see 6.06 above), the Court of Appeal commented that the duty of disclosure has to be considered in the light of the wording of the proposal form presented to the insured.

(c)   Section 18(3)(d) of MIA 1906 states that the insured need not disclose 'any circumstance which is superfluous to disclose by reason of any express or implied warranty'. If the policy contains an express warranty, the insurer is automatically discharged from liability in the event the warranty is broken and so is not reliant upon disclosure.

(d)   The failure by an insurer to ask any questions at all on a particular matter cannot generally be regarded as waiver of disclosure of facts concerning that matter, as a finding of that sort would run counter to the very doctrine of disclosure. However, in consumer cases the insurer is obliged by the Statements of Insurance Practice (see 6.03 above and 41 REGULATION OF SALES OF INSURANCE PRODUCTS) to ask questions on matters generally found to be material, and the insurance ombudsman has taken the view that a failure to ask questions on a point makes it increasingly difficult for the insurer to argue that the information concerning the point is material. It was also held in the case of *Société Anonyme d'Intermédiaries Luxembourgeois v Farex GIE [1995] LRLR 116* that if the reinsurer makes no enquiry about the cedant's retention, he must be taken to have waived disclosure of such information.

Waiver or affirmation

6.17   The insurer can waive a breach of the duty of utmost good faith (or affirm the insurance contract notwithstanding the breach) but in order to be found to have done so, the insurer must be shown to have been fully aware of the insured's breach of duty and to have choosen to regard the contract as continuing regardless of that breach (*Liberian Insurance Agency Inc v Mosse [1977] 2 Lloyd's Rep 560*; *Container Transport International v Oceanus* (see 6.04 above); *Pan Atlantic* (see 6.01 above)).

Duration of duty of disclosure

6.18   The duty of disclosure is intended primarily to assist the insurer in his assessment of the risk. *Section 18(1) of MIA 1906* states that the insured's duty of disclosure arises 'before the contract is concluded'. After the contract has been agreed, the duty of disclosure is more limited but will revive if the insurers need further information to make a relevant underwriting decision (*Manifest Shipping Co. Ltd. v Uni-Polaris Insurance Co Ltd (The 'Star Sea'), K/s Merc-Scandia XXXXII v Certain Lloyd's Underwriters (The 'Mercandian Continent')*, both at 6.02 above). It will be noted that the relevant date is the conclusion of the contract and not the date at which the insurer comes on risk.

The duty of disclosure also revives when a fresh contract of insurance is made. This will occur in three situations.

(a)   On renewal, the renewal operating as the making of a fresh contract.

(b)   In the case of risks written on a subscription basis, separate disclosure is required to each of the subscribing underwriters. This is so because a subscription policy is in effect a composite contract between the insured and each individual underwriter.

(c)   In the case of a framework contract for insurance, such as an open cover, the insured is entitled to cover for all risks of the agreed description up to fixed or aggregate monetary limits, subject only to making appropriate declarations to the insurer. If the open cover is non-obligatory as far as the insurer is concerned, ie the insurer can reject individual declarations, the duty of disclosure applies to each declaration (*Berger and Light Diffusers Pt. Ltd v Pollock [1973] 2 Lloyd's Rep 442*). By contrast, if the cover is obligatory, no duty of disclosure arises with each declaration, but the duty of disclosure attaches to the cover itself (*Glasgow Assurance Corporation Ltd v William Symondson [1911] 2104 LT 254*).

Superfluity

6.19   The insured need not disclose 'any circumstance which it is superfluous to disclose by reason of an express or implied warranty' (*MIA 1906, s 18(3)(d)*). If the policy contains a warranty (or in the case of marine insurance an implied warranty), the insurer is automatically discharged from liability in the event that the warranty is broken. Consequently, there is little point in the insured having to disclose facts or circumstances which mean the insurer is in any event off risk as a result of a breach of warranty.

The insurer's remedies for breach of duty to disclose

6.20   If the insured has failed to disclose a material fact, the policy is rendered voidable *ab initio*, so that the insurer has the right to treat the contract as if it had never existed. The insurer has no right to maintain the contract in force and to reject the insured's claim. On avoidance of the contract, the insured is entitled to a full return of premium on the basis of total failure of consideration. The insured's premium may be forfeited if the insured is guilty of fraud or if the policy states that the insurer is entitled to keep the premium in the event that the policy is avoided (see 6.26 below). In consumer cases, the financial ombudsman is reluctant to allow insurers to rely upon an express forfeiture of premium clause, and will permit this only if the clause has been drawn to the insured's attention prior to the making of the contract.

Damages are not available for breach of the duty of disclosure. This is because the duty does not operate as an implied contractual term (breach of which would give rise to damages for breach of contract), but rather as a rule of law.

The judicial discretion contained in *s 2(2)* of the *Misrepresentation Act 1967*, under which, following misrepresentation, the court can, instead of ordering rescission, declare that the contract is subsisting and award damages to the innocent party, has no application where there has been non-disclosure in relation to a contract of insurance. The insurer cannot, as a matter of law, be prevented from avoiding the contract, although in consumer cases, as a matter of practice, the financial ombudsman may require the insurer to make a full or proportional payment of a claim despite non-disclosure, but in practice only in cases where the insured has not been fraudulent.

Misrepresentation

6.21 As stated above, contracts of insurance are contracts of utmost good faith. This means that the insured, when applying for a policy, not only has a duty to disclose all material facts to the insurer (see 6.03 above), but has a duty also to avoid making false statements to the insurer. If the insured fails in this latter duty, the insurer has the right to avoid the contract. In consumer cases, this is subject to the operation of r 7.3.6 of the Insurance Conduct of Business Rules (see 41 REGULATION OF SALES OF INSURANCE PRODUCTS) and the jurisdiction of the financial ombudsman, who will take the Statements of Insurance Practice into account. The principles applicable to misrepresentation are largely the same as those relating to non-disclosure, and therefore this section considers only those aspects of utmost good faith which are pertinent only to the law of misrepresentation.

A misrepresentation must be one of fact if it is to be actionable. Statements of opinion, intention, law or expectation are not normally capable of amounting to a misrepresentation. However, such statements may amount to an implied representation of fact as to the maker's state of mind, and so must be made honestly (see *Edgington v Fitzmaurice (1885) LR 29 Ch D 459* and *Economides v Commercial Union Assurance Co plc [1998] Lloyd's Rep IR 9*).

A misrepresentation is any false statement made to the insurer by the insured or his agent prior to the making of the contract. A statement will not be regarded as false if it is substantially true (*MIA 1906, s 20(4)*).

Misrepresentation may take one of three forms:

(*a*) a false statement made by the insured in response to a question put to him by the insurer, normally by means of a proposal form;

(*b*) a false statement made by the insured in volunteering information to the insurer – without a question having been asked by that insurer; or

(*c*) failure by the insured to answer a question put to him by the insurer – if the insured leaves a blank space in response to a question on the proposal form, his answer may be assumed to be in the negative (*Roberts v Avon Insurance Ltd [1956] 2 Lloyd's Rep 240*). Thus, in some circumstances silence may amount to misrepresentation as opposed to a breach of the duty to disclose (*HIH Casualty and General Insurance v Chase Manhattan Bank (2003)* at 6.06 above).

Materiality and inducement

6.22 A misrepresentation will give the insurer the right to avoid only if it is material and the underwriter can show that he was induced to subscribe to the contract on the relevant terms by the misrepresentation (see *Pan Atlantic* at 6.01 above). A material statement is defined as a statement which would influence the judgement of a prudent insurer in accepting the risk or in determining the amount of premium (*MIA 1906, s 20 (2)*). As with non-disclosure, the misrepresentation must be shown to have been something that would have affected the judgement of the prudent insurer in the sense that he would have taken it into account as part of the evaluative process that misrepresented fact, or circumstance, even if that was not ultimately decisive (*Pan Atlantic*). It must also be shown that the misrepresentation induced the actual underwriter as a matter of fact. It also follows that the innocence or otherwise of the insured has no bearing on the matter since a false statement represents a misrepresentation whether the insured acted fraudulently or innocently.

It is the practice in some forms of insurance for the insurer to stipulate on the proposal form that the insured's answers are deemed to be the 'basis of the contract' of insurance. Such wording converts all statements made in the proposal form into warranties, with the result that, in the event of falsity, the insurer is discharged from liability from the date of the breach. Where a statement has been converted into a warranty, the materiality or otherwise of the falsity is irrelevant to the insurer's liability (see 2 TERMS IN INSURANCE CONTRACTS). Basis clauses are not generally used in consumer cases. Nevertheless, even in the absence of a basis clause, there is a general presumption that the questions on the proposal form relate to material matters, and this is particularly so since the Statements of Insurance Practice (see 6.03 above and 41 REGULATION OF SALES OF INSURANCE PRODUCTS) applicable to consumer insurances provide that insurers are to ask express questions on matters which they have generally found to be material to their underwriting assessment.

The construction of statements made by the insured

6.23   As most misrepresentations are made in response to specific questions, the issue of whether or not there has been a misrepresentation often depends on what question the insured has been asked. A question which asks the insured to proffer his opinion or expectation should not be construed as one which demands a statement of absolute fact; in such a case, there can be a false statement only when the insured puts forward an opinion which he does not genuinely hold, or an expectation which he does not genuinely believe to be met (*MIA 1906, s 20(3)(5)*).

A question which is very broad in its ambit will be construed as being subject to a reasonableness limitation; for example, a question asking about the insured's past health record will not require him to disclose every illness, however slight, or every personal injury (*The Connecticut Mutual Life Insurance Co of Hertford v Kate Douglas Moore (1880–81) LR 6 App Cas 644*).

An ambiguous question is not falsely answered if the interpretation put upon it by the insured is reasonable in the circumstances. This principle is a specific application of the general doctrine of *contra proferentem*, whereby ambiguities are to be construed against the party drafting the wording.

A modern illustration is *Roberts v Plaisted* (see 6.06 above) where the insured completed a proposal form for insurance on his motel and, having given answers to specific questions concerning his use of the motel, left blank the general question 'Any other uses?', without stating that there was a discotheque on the premises. The Court of Appeal held that the negative answer to the general question did not amount to misrepresentation, as that question could be construed either as requiring an answer only if the specific questions which had been asked were not applicable to the risk, or as requiring disclosure of an activity which was carried on in the premises as a whole and not merely a specific part of the premises.

The insurer's remedies for misrepresentation

6.24   A policy which has been initiated following a material misrepresentation by the insured is voidable at the option of the insurer. The policy is set aside *ab initio*, and is therefore treated as if it had never existed. This means that the premium paid by the insured is recoverable by him, although the insurer may be permitted to retain the premium where the insured was guilty of fraudulent misrepresentation, or where the policy expressly provides that the premium is to be forfeited to the insurer in the event that the policy is set aside. Forfeiture terms are valid at common law, but will be enforced by the insurance ombudsman in the context of consumer insurance only if expressly drawn to the insured's attention prior to the inception of the policy.

The court also has a discretionary power, contained in *s 2(2)* of the *Misrepresentation Act 1967*, to refuse to allow a contract to be avoided, on the ground of misrepresentation, and instead to award damages to the innocent party. The purpose of this provision is to mitigate the harshness of avoidance where the party making the misstatement has not been guilty of fraud and otherwise merits generous judicial treatment. The courts have held that it is not appropriate to exercise this discretion in reinsurance cases, and in other cases of commercial insurance, on the basis that the obligation to avoid false statements, and the consequences of failing to comply with this obligation, are well known to the parties (*Highlands Insurance Co v Continental Insurance Co [1987] 1 Lloyd's Rep 109, HIH Casualty and General Insurance v Chase Manhattan Bank [2001] Lloyd's Rep IR 702* per Rix Lj in the Court of Appeal). This leaves open the possibility that the courts might, in consumer cases, refuse to allow an insurer to avoid a contract for innocent misrepresentation. This is in fact the position reached by the financial ombudsman in his decisions on misrepresentation, a view justified by the Statements of Insurance Practice (see 6.03 above and 41 REGULATION OF SALES OF INSURANCE PRODUCTS).

Although there is no possibility of damages at common law for breach of the duty of utmost good faith, the effect of *s 2(1)* of the *Misrepresentation Act 1967* is that, if a false statement is made by one contracting party which induces the other to enter into the contract, then the other is entitled to recover damages, measured on the basis of the tort of deceit, unless the person making the statement can demonstrate that he was not negligent in making the statement. Although the question of whether *s 2(1)* applies to insurance contracts has not been discussed in detail by the courts, this was assumed without argument by the House of Lords in *HIH Casualty and General Insurance Ltd v Chase Manhattan Bank* (see 6.06 above).

Fraud

6.25   Questions of fraud may arise in relation to all contracts, including contracts of insurance. Fraud arises in insurance contracts most obviously in the case of fraudulent misrepresentation. However, it should also be remembered that it is not only during the negotiations before the insurer chooses to accept the risk that fraud is an issue. Fraud often arises in the presentation of claims, particularly in commercial insurance.

The definition of fraud

6.26   In order to establish a fraudulent misrepresentation, an insurer must show that a statement made by the insured was:

(*a*)   false;

(*b*)   made dishonestly, or without belief in the truth of it or being reckless as to whether it is true;

(*c*)   induced the underwriter into making the insurance contract in question.

It was the case of *William Derry, J C Wakefield, M M Moore, J Pethick, and S J Wilde v Sir Henry William Peek, Baronet (1889) LR 14 App Cas 337* which put dishonesty, as defined above, at the heart of the definition of fraud, and it remains of central importance today. There is clearly a line which must be carefully trodden between fraud and carelessness, even where that carelessness seems unacceptably extreme. Fraud must be interpreted strictly along the lines set out in *Derry v Peek*. It is, therefore, fraud if an insured makes a statement knowing that he is entirely ignorant as to its truth, but it is not a fraud if a false statement is made simply as a result of failing to investigate the relevant facts.

The effect of fraudulent statements

6.27   An insured's fraudulent statement gives the insurer the option of avoiding the contract. He may, as in the general law of contract, rescind the insurance contract and recover back any monies paid out under that contract.

Where the insurer has decided to rescind the policy on the ground of fraud, there is authority that he may cancel that policy without offering to return the premiums as would be the case if the contract was if avoided for any other form of misrepresentation or non-disclosure. Under *s 84(1)* of *MIA 1906*, in marine insurance there can be no return of premium where the insurer has avoided the policy because of fraud by the insured. The reason for this rule is public policy, *viz* to discourage fraud. There is no clear statement that this section applies in cases of non-marine insurance. However, it is likely the courts will apply the *MIA 1906* principle as a non-marine insurance contract is clearly still a contract of utmost good faith. There is support for this view from earlier 18th and 19th century case law (*Chapman v Fraser [1793] Marshall on Marine Insurances (4th edn) 525*; *British Equitable Insurance Co v Musgrave (1887) 3 TLR 630*) which decided that in cases where fraud was perpetrated by the insured, or his agent, he cannot recover premium previously paid.

Materiality and inducement

6.28 A fraudulent statement, unlike a non-disclosure or misrepresentation, does not need to be a material fact (ie satisfy the first 'objective' part of the usual test) in order to be actionable. This law was well established in the 19th century and was reaffirmed in the *Pan Atlantic* case (see 6.01 above). However, it must still be shown that the fraudulent statement induced the insurer to underwrite the contract if it is to be actionable. Nevertheless, if the fraudulently statement was not material (in the objective sense), it will probably be difficult in practice to prove that it induced the insurer to write the contract of insurance.

Fraudulent claims

6.29 The other area where fraud can arise is in the making of claims by the insured. If the insured makes a fraudulent claim (ie a claim which he knows is inflated or does not care), the insurer can treat the policy as terminated for breach, or refuse to pay the particular claims tainted by fraud. However, if there is innocent or negligent conduct by the insured in connection with the making of a claim, this will not give rise to any remedy. It is, however, open to insurers to include provisions in the policy for the forfeiture of benefits in such circumstances.

In *Axa General Insurance Ltd v Gottlieb [2005] Lloyd's Rep IR 369*, the court made it clear that the remedy available to insurers in relation to a fraudulent claim is forfeiture of the relevant claim, rather than avoidance of the entire contract. It was held that Axa could not recover the sums paid by it in respect of the separate valid claims prior to the fraud as pre-existing genuine claims would be unaffected by the fraud.

Agents of the insured

6.30 It is a general principle of contract, and insurance contract law, that the principal whose agent has made a misrepresentation must take responsibility for the representations of that agent. The basis for this rule is the agency principle of imputation of the knowledge of an agent to its principal and the doctrine of vicarious liability.

Section 18(1) of *MIA 1906* provides that the insured is deemed to know every circumstance which in the ordinary course of business ought to be known by him. This includes the knowledge of agents conducting the insured's business, which is imputed to the insured. However, the knowledge of an agent is not imputed to the insured in circumstances where the agents have committed a fraud upon, or other breach of duty towards, the insured, and therefore the dishonesty of an agent is not one of the matters which an insured, in the ordinary course of business, ought to know for the purpose of *s 18(1)* of *MIA 1906 (PCW Syndicates v PCW Reinsurers [1996] 1 Lloyd's Rep 241; Kingscroft Insurance Co Ltd v The Nissan Fire & Marine Insurance Co Ltd [1999] Lloyd's Rep IR 371)*.

Criminal liability for fraudulent statements

6.31   *Section 397* of the *Financial Services and Markets Act 2000* makes it a criminal offence for any person to make a statement, promise or forecast which he knows to be misleading, false or deceptive in a material particular, or which is made recklessly (dishonestly or otherwise), if its effect is to induce the making of an insurance contract.

Under *s 2 of the Fraud Act 2006,* which came into force on 15 January 2007, a person will be guilty of fraud if they dishonestly make a false representation and intend, by making that representation, either to make a gain for themselves or another or to cause a loss to another or to expose another to a risk or loss.

Under *s 3 of the Fraud Act 2006*, which also came into force on 15 January 2007, a person will be guilty of fraud if they dishonestly fail to disclose to another person information which they are under a legal duty to disclose and they intend, by that failure to disclose information, either to make a gain for themselves or another or to cause a loss to another or expose another to a risk of loss.

Minimising loss and alteration in the risk

6.32   There is no common law duty in the law of insurance requiring the insured to minimise the risk of the loss insured. The courts assume that the insurer has taken account of the possibility that the level of risk may increase throughout the duration of the contract *(Baxendale v Harvey (1859) 4 H&N 445)*. In what circumstances, then, may an increase in risk give an insurer the right to refuse to pay claims or avoid the contract? The courts at common law have stipulated that an increase in risk will only allow the insurer to be protected where the nature of the risk itself is changed. In other words, an increase in risk is generally not actionable if not disclosed, as long as the subject matter of the contract and the nature of the contract has not changed.

Clearly where the insured intended before the making of the contract to increase the risk during the duration of the policy, there is a straightforward non-disclosure (as discussed in 6.05 above), which is therefore actionable. Linked to this, where the insured is a perpetrator of a fraud, as discussed in 6.26 above, and as a result of that fraud there is an increase in risk and/or the increase in risk is not disclosed to the insurer, then equally this will be actionable.

However, there is no clear rule as to when an increase in risk amounts to a change in subject matter. It is a matter of degree. Insurers have generally been dissatisfied with the lack of protection at common law and have therefore instituted specific policy provisions in an attempt to protect themselves. They have done this via a number of standard clauses as follows.

Increase in hazard clauses

6.33 These clauses vary in their wording, but the courts have shown themselves to be extremely wary, of clauses which instead of relating to a specific concern of the insurer, attempt to cover a possible increase in all possible dangers. In dealing with these clauses, the courts do not alter the common law position; see the case of *Exchange Theatre Ltd v Iron Trades Mutual Insurance Co Ltd [1984] 1 Lloyd's Rep 149* in which a bingo hall was destroyed by fire following the introduction to the premises of petrol and a petrol generator. The condition provided:

> 'This policy shall be avoided with respect to any item thereof in regard to which there be any alteration after the commencement of this insurance whereby the risk of destruction is increased.'

The court held in this case that there had been an alteration to the contents, but no alteration to the building. Had the building itself been turned into a petrol store, the case would probably have been decided differently (see also *Farnham v Royal Insurance Co Ltd [1976] 2 Lloyd's Rep 437*).

Continuing warranties

6.34 These are otherwise known as 'basis of contract' provisions. They have the purpose of turning each declaration on the proposal form into a warranty, irrespective of the materiality of that declaration (see 6.07 above).

Reasonable care clauses

6.35 A typical clause of this nature will state that

> 'although I take the risk of insuring against certain unexpected events, I expect you to take reasonable care of the insured property during the currency of the policy.'

The courts have, unsurprisingly, been reluctant to enforce these clauses if they conflict with the very underlying purpose of the insurance, which is to protect the insured from loss resulting from his own negligence (see *Fraser v B N Furman (Productions) Ltd [1967] 2 Lloyd's Rep 1*). Although the insurer may be able to rely on a clause of this nature where the insured has recognised the risk, but failed to act upon it, it is more difficult where the insured has failed to recognise the risk at all, even though a reasonable person would have done so. In those cases, the court will allow the insurer to rely upon the clause only when the insured can be shown to have acted recklessly. Leaving jewellery in the glove compartment of a car, whilst taking travellers cheques and money with you and locking the car has been held not to be reckless (*Sofi v Prudential Assurance Co Ltd [1993] 2 Lloyd's Rep 559*). A householder failing to lock his backdoor or activate his alarm system upon noticing that he was being followed home, was, on the other hand, found to be reckless (*Gunns v Par Insurance Brokers [1997] 1 Lloyd's Rep 173*).

It is worth noting that in property insurance, there is a simple option for insurers, which is to include a clause in the policy which requires the insured to maintain his or her property in a sound condition. This can be measured more objectively.

Fire protection clauses

6.36   Property insurers will often give a discount on the premium if the insured promises to keep fire extinguishing protection at the premises and to keep that in good working order. Usually the insured is also required to warrant that the maintenance of the fire protection system will be carried out by an approved specialist contractor. In this way insurers have successfully contracted to reduce the risk throughout the period of the contract.

Duty on the insurer

6.37   It should be noted that the insurer also has a duty to observe utmost good faith in its dealing with policyholders and prospective policyholders (*La Banque Financière de la Cité SA (Formerly Banque Keyser Ullmann en Suisse SA) v Skandia Insurance Co Ltd Westgate Insurance Co Ltd (Formerly Hodge General & Merchantile Insurance Co Ltd)[1990] 2 All ER 947*).

It has been recognised by the Court of Appeal in the cast of *Drake Insurance plc v Provident Insurance plc [2004] 1 Lloyd's Rep 268* that if an insurer avoids a contract in bad faith, that avoidance may be nullified.

Chapter 7
Policyholder protection

- Introduction

- Liability of insolvent insurers to policyholders

- The Financial Services Compensation Scheme

- Amounts payable under the Financial Services Compensation Scheme

- Summary

Introduction

7.01   Provisions relating to the establishment of the Financial Services Compensation Scheme (FSCS) are to be found in *ss 212–224* of the *Financial Services and Markets Act 2000* (*FSMA 2000*). The FSCS came into being on 1 December 2001. Many of the rules and procedures applicable to the *FSCS* replicate similar provisions contained in the *Policyholders Protection Act 1975* and/or *Policyholders Protection Act 1997* which were repealed when the FSCS came into being. This chapter does not deal with different rules applicable to contracts of insurance issued prior to 1 December 2001 nor with the *FSCS*'s responsibility to compensate depositors or the holders of certain investment products which are not applicable to insurance companies. The Compensation sourcebook of the FSA's Handbook (COMP) sets out the rules under which the FSCS operates.

Liability of insolvent insurers to policyholders

7.02   In order to understand the extent of the liability of the FSCS in the event of the insolvency of an insurer, it is necessary to understand the nature of the rights which insolvency law gives to policyholders against an insolvent insurer, as the word 'claim' is defined for the purposes of COMP as a valid claim made in respect of a civil liability owed by a person against whom the compensation scheme provides cover.

Valuing claims

7.03   The *Insurers (Winding Up) Rules 2001 (SI 2001/3635)*, which replaced the *Insurance Companies (Winding Up) Rules 1985 (SI 1985/95)*, establish how insurance policies are to be valued upon the winding-up of an insurance company. Where a claim has fallen due for payment before the date of the winding-up order, the position is simple – the policyholder is admitted as an unsecured creditor for the amount of the claim (but, unless the policyholder is a reinsured, subject to the priority over other unsecured creditors referred to below). Where the claim has not fallen due for payment before the date of the winding-up order, there are complicated provisions in *SI 2001/3635* which apply to the valuation of long-term policies.

In the case of general business policies, the relevant valuation principle is derived from *r* 6 of and *Sch 1* to *SI 2001/3635*. *SI 1985/95* contained similar provisions which were interpreted by the High Court in *Transit Casualty Co (In Receivership) v Policyholders Protection Board [1992] 2 Lloyd's Rep 358,* and approved by the Court of Appeal subsequently in *Scher v Policyholders Protection Board [1994] 2 WLR 593 (Note),* as meaning that, if the event giving rise to the claim has occurred before the date of the winding-up order or resolution to wind up the company (liquidation date), and even if the policyholder was not notified of the claim, or was not otherwise aware of the claim at that time, then the amount of the claim will be admissible as an unsecured claim in the liquidation. If the claim is still unliquidated when proofs are called the liquidator will place a value on the claim for distribution purposes. The policyholder under a general policy will also have a claim, if the premium has been paid in advance, to a refund of that proportion of the premium paid as relates to the period the policy still had to run from the liquidation date. It is important, when a policyholder is on notice of the insolvency of an insurer, that alternative cover should be arranged to take effect no later than the liquidation date, as the FSCS will have no power in relation to general business to make payments to insureds in respect of insured events occurring on or after the liquidation date. The position in relation to long-term policies is rather more complicated, but again a policyholder should consider whether alternative cover should be obtained.

Historically in the UK, policyholders have had equal priority to other unsecured creditors on a winding-up of an insolvent insurer. However, the EU *Directive on the Reorganisation and Winding-up of Insurance Undertakings*, which was implemented in the UK in April 2003, changes this by providing that *insurance claims* (amounts owed by the insurance company to its policyholders under insurance contracts, not including reinsurance contracts) have priority over other unsecured creditors in a winding-up of an insurer.

The Financial Services Compensation Scheme

Powers

7.04   The FSCS may, where it is not reasonably practicable or appropriate for the FSCS to take steps to secure continuity of insurance for the eligible claimant, pay compensation to an eligible claimant (subject to the provisions of COMP 11 which deals with circumstances where the compensation may go to other people) if the FSCS is satisfied that the claim is in respect of a protected claim against a relevant person who is in default. In the case of long-term insurance contracts, if it is reasonably practical to do so, there is an obligation on the FSCS to make arrangements to secure continuity of insurance for eligible claimants under protected contracts of insurance.

The FSCS may determine an insurer to be in default if it is subject to one or more of the following proceedings in the UK (or equivalent or similar proceedings in another jurisdiction):

(*a*)   passing of a resolution for a creditors' voluntary winding-up;

(*b*)   determination by its regulator that it appears unable to meet claims and has no early prospect of doing so;

(*c*)   appointment of liquidator or administrator or provisional liquidator or interim manager;

(*d*)   the making of an order for its winding-up or administration; and/or

(*e*)   the approval of a company voluntary arrangement.

There are analogous trigger provisions for insurers who are not companies.

In the case of long-term insurance contracts where arrangements are not made to secure continuity of insurance cover the FSCS must calculate the liability of the relevant insurer in accordance with the terms of the contract as valued in a liquidation, or (in the absence of such relevant terms) in accordance with such reasonable valuation techniques as the FSCS considers appropriate. Any bonus provided under a long-term insurance contract must be declared before the beginning of the liquidation to be eligible to be considered in any compensation calculation. If the FSCS considers that the benefits or future benefits provided for under a protected long-term insurance contract are or may be excessive in any respect, having regard to the premiums paid or payable and to any other terms of the contract, the FSCS must refer the contract to an actuary who is independent of the claimant and of the insurer and if, following the actuary's written recommendation, the FSCS is satisfied that any of the benefits provided for under the contract are or may be excessive, it may treat the liability of the relevant insurer under the contract as reduced.

Funding of the Financial Services Compensation Scheme's obligations

7.05   The FSCS imposes levies on authorised persons in order to meet its expenses. These expenses include in particular expenses incurred, or expected to be incurred, in paying compensation, borrowing or insuring risks.

The FSCS may impose two types of levy: a management expenses levy, and a compensation costs levy. The FSCS has discretion as to the timing of the levies imposed.

In calculating a compensation costs levy, the FSCS may include anticipated compensation costs for defaults expected to be determined in the 12-month period following the date of the levy.

In making rules to enable the FSCS to impose levies (which for insurers are generally a levy on a percentage of premium income over a relevant period), the FSA must take account of the desirability of ensuring that the amount of the levies imposed on a particular class of authorised person reflects, so far as practicable, the amount of claims made, or likely to be made, in respect of that class of person. Thus insurers of long term business only are not generally levied in respect of the failure of companies underwriting general business.

Amounts payable under the Financial Services Compensation Scheme

7.06   A protected contract of insurance for the purposes of the FSCS is one relating to a protected risk or commitment issued by the insolvent insurer through an establishment in the UK, another European Economic Area (EEA) state or the Channel Islands or the Isle of Man. Generally speaking the insolvent insurer must have been authorised by the FSA. Special provisions apply to the circumstances where firms who are regulated in another EEA state conduct regulated activities in the UK.

To be a protected risk or commitment the risk must generally be situated in the UK (there are special rules relating to the Channel Islands and the Isle of Man). The situation of a risk or commitment is determined as follows:

(*a*)   for a contract of insurance relating to a building or a building and its contents (insofar as the contents are covered by the same contract), the risk or commitment is situated where the building is situated;

(*b*)   for a contract of insurance relating to vehicles of any type the risk or commitment is situated where the vehicle is registered;

(*c*)   for a contract of insurance lasting four months or less covering travel or holiday risks (whatever the class concerned) the risk or commitment is situated where the policyholder took out the contract; and

(*d*)   in cases not covered by any of the above, where the policyholder is an individual the risk or commitment is situated where he has his habitual residence at the date when the contract commenced and where the policyholder is not an individual the risk or commitment is situated where the establishment to which the risk or commitment relates is situated at the date when the contract commenced.

The following classes of general insurance contracts are excluded from compensation in any circumstances:

(i)   aircraft;

(ii)   ships;

(iii) goods in transit;

(iv) aircraft liability;

 (v) liability of ships; and

(vi) credit.

COMP 4.2 defines who is an eligible claimant. Broadly speaking (except in relation to compulsory insurances) only individuals and certain small businesses are entitled to claim but there are exceptions.

Compulsory insurances

7.07 The FSCS will pay in full the liability of the insolvent company (calculated as referred to at 7.2–7.3 above) in respect of compulsory insurance under the following legislation:

- s 1(4A)(d) of the *Riding Establishments Act 1964*;

- s 1 of the *Employers' Liability (Compulsory Insurance) Act 1969*;

- *Part VI* of the *Road Traffic Act 1988* (third party liability); and

- a contract of insurance effected for the purposes of s 19 of the *Nuclear Installations Act 1965*

  to the extent the policy covers a liability required under any of those enactments to be covered by insurance. This compensation is payable in relation to all policies regardless of the identity of the policyholder (ie large businesses are covered too).

General insurance other than compulsory insurance policies

7.08 The FSCS, if it is unable to secure continuity of insurance cover or determines that the cost of so doing would be unreasonable, will pay cash compensation of 100% of the first £2,000 and 90% of the remainder of the liability of the insolvent company where the policies are held by eligible claimants and are not within the excluded classes referred to in 7.6 above.

The FSCS's liability in relation to long-term policies

7.09 If the FSCS secures continuity of insurance for eligible claimants, they will not necessarily receive any cash, but will continue to be insured (though possibly with lower benefits than before).

The FSCS's liability to pay compensation, in respect of a long term insurance contract, is limited to ensuring that the claimant will receive at least 100% of the first £2,000 and then 90% of any further benefit under his contract of insurance due to him from the insolvent insurer in excess of £2,000, subject to and in accordance with terms corresponding (so far as it appears to the FSCS to be reasonable in the circumstances) to those which have applied under the contract of insurance.

Insolvent insurance intermediaries

7.10   With effect from 14 January 2005, the COMP sourcebook was amended to provide for compensation for those persons who have a claim against an insolvent insurance intermediary in relation to a protected non-life investment insurance mediation. The contract must be a general insurance contract and the insurance mediation must have been conducted from an establishment of the insurance intermediary in the UK, or a branch of a UK intermediary (who has its head office in the UK) established in another EEA state as a result of the 'passporting rights' as afforded by the EU Insurance Mediation Directive.

7.11   However the FSCS will not cover any claims made against an intermediary, where the claimant was introduced to the intermediary via another intermediary who does not come within the eligibility criteria above. Furthermore the FSCS will not cover any claims made in respect of intermediaries who are not 'relevant persons', for example a retailer who sells extended warranties. There are special provisions governing the extent to which insurance mediation business conducted in the UK by branches of intermediaries whose home regulator is in another EEA state may be subject to FSCS compensation and levies.

7.12   Similarly to the provisions governing general insurance policies, the FSCS are liable to compensate claimants in full for the first £2,000, and then 90% of the remainder of the insolvent intermediary's liability (save for those claims in respect of a liability under compulsory insurances).

7.14   In the case of the intermediation of long-term insurance contracts there may be a claim against the FSCS if the intermediary becomes insolvent, particularly if there is an investment element to the policy. The compensation in such cases is limited to a maximum payment of 100% of the first £30,000 of the loss and then 90% of the next £20,000.

Summary

7.15   The effect of the legislation contained in *FSMA 2000* and the associated rules in COMP, is to enable those policyholders who qualify for protection generally to recover over 90% of their claim (or 100% in the case of compulsory insurances) relatively quickly. The FSCS then claims against the insurer in respect of the amount paid to the policyholder, and will take an assignment of the policyholder's claim against the insurer for this purpose.

Chapter 8
Global insurance programmes

- Introduction
- Retaining risk
- Vertical contractual chains
- 'Difference in conditions' cover
- Problems with global programmes
- Summary

Introduction

8.01   In most industry sectors, the last 20 years have seen the development of the multinational group. Not unnaturally, it has been common for such multi-billion dollar conglomerates to seek consistent insurance coverage throughout their organisation. Such consistency is best obtained by central purchasing, which also has the advantage of enabling the corporation to use its size to keep down premium rates.

Obstacles to a single global policy

8.02   Thus, brokers and insurers have been challenged to develop global insurance programmes. However, there exist three, perhaps more, obstacles to insurers providing a single global policy.

(*a*)   *Regulation.* There are still many nations throughout the world which maintain considerable regulatory control over the local insurance and, in some cases, reinsurance industry. This has resulted in it being impractical for some foreign insurers to become admitted. It is certainly the case that there has been a recent trend towards deregulation but, on occasions, regulation still provides a formidable barrier.

(*b*)   *Lack of global reach of insurance companies.* Until recently other sectors of industry have developed internationally ahead of the insurance sector.

71

Insurers have therefore found it difficult to provide either the capacity or the global reach to provide one policy worldwide.

(c)   *Underlying liabilities.* It is also difficult to produce a wording which will cover the different types of liability that may occur throughout the world. Recently, the harmonisation of insurance regulation within Europe has allowed the creation of Europolicies, but the drafting of such policies has not been without its difficulties.

Retaining risk

8.03   Another trend which has been developed over the last 20 years has been the desire on the part of multinationals to retain a greater part of the risk and, in effect, insure on a catastrophe basis. Rather than each subsidiary simply retaining a larger amount per occurrence, it has been common for large industrial groups to set up their own wholly-owned subsidiary, which acts as an insurer for the group, and is commonly described as a captive insurer. Many of these captives have diversified so as to provide a wide range of services to the group, and even to corporate entities outside of the group. Generally, however, their primary purpose is to retain the risk. To maximise tax advantages, captives are frequently located offshore.

The use of a captive insurer also has the added advantage of enabling the group to have direct access to the reinsurance market. Therefore, barriers between the insurance and reinsurance markets are broken down, with both direct insurers and reinsurers frequently being found as security on such programmes. A disadvantage is that the captive must comply with regulations which exist in each territory. Imagine for example a US multinational in Switzerland and Austria. Non-admitted insurance (from an insurer not licensed in the territory) is not allowed in Switzerland, while in Austria it may be subject to punitive premium tax.

Vertical contractual chains

8.04   For these reasons, and others, it is not unusual for there to be a need for local-fronting insurance companies, thus a vertical chain of risk transfer may occur, with the insured transferring the risk to a fronting insurer. This fronting insurer then retains only a very small percentage of the risk, passing the balance of the risk through to the captive insurer. The captive insurer, in turn, may have several insurance/reinsurance programmes. It may purchase a multi-layer excess of loss protection whilst still retaining a substantial part of the risk. Frequently, the lead insurer/reinsurer on the main programme will provide the fronting facility to the captive. Also, it frequently occurs that the captive purchases a separate stop-loss reinsurance for its retention.

'Difference in conditions' cover

8.05   If the above factual scenario occurs, then the fronting company in various regulatory locations may find it difficult to provide consistent coverage. Therefore, the insurance policy issued at a local level may only provide the basic cover needed to comply with the local regulations. The insurers or reinsurers on the main programme may issue what is commonly known as a master policy, providing 'difference in conditions' (DIC) cover which will be issued to the multinational's head office.

Therefore, in circumstances where the cover provided by the master policy is greater than that provided by the local policy, a gap payment will be paid to the group head office.

Problems with global programmes

8.06   The one key problem characteristic of most global programmes is the poor quality of the draftsmanship. By their very nature they are complex, on occasion transferring billions of dollars of risk and requiring tailor-made solutions. Frequently, however, insufficient thought is given to the wording. Particular problems which can arise are set out below.

Jurisdiction and choice of law

8.07   It is not uncommon to see different parts of the programme incorporating different choice of law and jurisdiction clauses. More frequently, however, it is common to find them omitted altogether, thus relying upon local conflict of law rules.

The effect is to create inconsistency within the programme, both in respect of underlying liabilities and contractual enforcement. A relatively simple solution is to incorporate a comprehensive arbitration clause throughout the programme, but this rarely occurs.

Inconsistency between the local and master policy

8.08   Frequently, local policies are issued without reference to the master policy. Unless the master policy is properly drafted so as to control the programme, inconsistencies, for example between limits in the local policies and the master policies, can occur.

A problem which often occurs in respect of business interruption claims is whether or not a temporary supply of goods provided by another part of the group attracts a profit element, and is thus claimable as part of the business interruption loss for the local subsidiary. Such problems can be overcome by payback provisions in the master policy.

Controlling claims

8.09 One of the central difficulties in global programmes is that the real risk taker, namely the insurance or reinsurance market above the captive, may be several contractual steps away from the insured which will be paying the claims. Thus, for example, a claims control clause between the insurance market and the captive may provide the market with little control over claims paid by the insured. Sometimes quite complex contractual arrangements and side agreements are necessary, to ensure that the market retains a degree of control over claims exceeding specific levels.

Contractual inconsistency

8.10 On occasions, inconsistencies also arise in the coverage provided by the various vertical layers of risk transfer. A programme which is not carefully drafted may result, for example, in a claim being paid by the captive but excluded by the insurance/reinsurance market. Great care is needed to ensure consistency.

Captive insolvency

8.11 It is unusual for captives to be rated for solvency in the same way that one might expect from other insurers. Thus the fronting insurer may be taking a risk as to the ongoing solvency of the captive. Again, the parties may decide to use various side agreements and on occasions may utilise guarantees from the parent company. Considerable care has to be taken in drafting this type of agreement to ensure that each contracting party retains an insurable interest, that the separate contracts of insurance and reinsurance are not regarded as sham transactions and that any guarantee arrangements will not simply be overturned by the laws governing insolvency in the relevant jurisdictions.

Summary

8.12 Surprisingly, few of these global programmes have as yet found their way to the courts. This is probably due to the fact that most disputes are settled because of the bargaining power of each party, rather than as a result of the quality of the contractual documentation. Recently, however, the RTZ Group, and its captive Three Crowns, sued its brokers and the reinsurance market, following the explosion of its smelter and acid plant at Kennecott in Ohio (*Kenecott Utah Copper Corp v Cornhill Insurance plc [1999] 2 All ER (Comm) 801*). This particular case involved many issues, including the attachment to the risk at reinsurance level, whether the claim was excluded as a result of the property being untested and uncommissioned, and other issues involving the application of various exclusions in the underlying policy. The amount of this claim totalled in excess of US$250 million, and it is the potential size of the claims arising out of global programmes which, in the future, will lead to disputes.

PART 2

The Parties

Chapter 9
Brokers

- Brokers and agency law
- The regulation of brokers
- The rights of brokers
- The duties of brokers
- The liabilities of brokers

Brokers and agency law

The broker as the insured's agent

9.01   A broker is an independent insurance intermediary, appointed by the insured to perform various duties for him relating to the setting up and operation of insurance contracts, and to assist the insured in the event of a claim. The broker is, therefore, the agent of the insured and not the agent of the insurer. He cannot act for the insurer, or in any manner inconsistent with his duties to the insured, without the express consent of the insured. The most important consequences of the broker being regarded as the insured's agent are that:

(*a*)   any information which is communicated to the broker by the insured is generally not deemed to have been received by the insurer – this may be relevant in relation to pre-contract disclosure by the insured and the giving by the insured of notice of loss; and

(*b*)   payment of the premium by the insured to his broker is not generally treated as payment to the insurer (see 9.31 below), and payment of losses by the insurer to the broker is treated as receipt by the insured – the insured, therefore, bears the risk of fraud or insolvency on the part of his broker.

Practical difficulties

9.02   The simple legal concept that the broker is the insured's agent is blurred in practice, as brokers do not operate quite in this way. A number of areas of difficulty may be found.

(*a*)   Brokers receive their commission not from the insured but from the insurer (see 9.26 below).

(*b*)   Under *s 19* of the *Marine Insurance Act 1906* (*MIA 1906*), where an insurance is effected for the insured by a broker, the broker must disclose to the insurer every material circumstance which is known to himself and to the insured. In *HIH Casualty and General Insurance Ltd v Chase Manhattan Bank [2003] UKHL 6*, the House of Lords held that the effect of *s 19* is to impose a duty of utmost good faith on the broker independent of that imposed on the insured by *s 18* of the *MIA 1906*.

(*c*)   In the London market there is a long tradition, which has been criticised by the courts, of brokers acting for both the insured and the underwriters in the event of a loss. The nature of the London market means that there is necessarily a close relationship between brokers and underwriters, yet the position in law is that the broker is the agent for the person who has instructed him (and whom the broker may never before have met) rather than the agent of underwriters with whom the broker is in daily contact.

(*d*)   A broker may be given a binding authority by an insurer, which authorises the broker to accept risks on behalf of the insurer. The fact that the broker is a coverholder acting on behalf of an insurer may not always be obvious to an insured who seeks independent advice on insurance.

(*e*)   The large international broking firms play an active role in promoting various forms of new insurance where a market gap is perceived. This may involve a broker preparing wordings for use by insurers for insurances which are obtained by the broker for their insured clients.

(*f*)   A broker instructed to obtain insurance may, particularly in the London market, first seek reinsurance, which enables the broker to offer to insurers a risk which is substantially covered by reinsurance, and thus makes the task of finding insurance somewhat easier (see 38 REINSURANCE).

In the light of these practical considerations, it is by no means clear that the broker should always be the insured's agent as a matter of law. In *Roberts v Plaisted [1989] 2 Lloyd's Rep 341*, a Lloyd's broker failed to inform underwriters that the insured's motel included a discotheque, and the underwriters sought to avoid the policy for material non-disclosure and misrepresentation. The Court of Appeal was able to find on the facts that there had been no breach of duty, but went on to suggest that the law on the agency of brokers should be reconsidered, if necessary, by the Law Commission. However, in *Sphere Drake Insurance Ltd v Euro International Underwriting Ltd [2003] EWHC 2376*, it was held that a broker is free to present whatever business he thinks fit to the insurer, even if it is loss-making: the broker does not owe any duty of care to the underwriter as to the quality of business presented. The obligation of the broker is to make a fair presentation, and as long as this is done the insurer cannot expect the broker to make underwriting decisions on his behalf.

There are also cases in which it has been held that information received by a broker from the insured is deemed to be received by the insurer without further communication (*Stockton v Mason [1978] 2 Lloyd's Rep 430*, where a broker authorised by insurer to issue cover notes); *Woolcott v Excess Insurance Co Ltd and Miles Smith Anderson and Game Ltd (No 2) [1979] 2 Lloyd's Rep 210*), although the actual status of the intermediary in these cases is unclear.

Authority

9.03   The extent to which a broker can bind an insured depends upon his authority, which may be express, usual or apparent. The insured may also, by ratification, adopt the unauthorised acts of his broker. If, therefore, a broker has entered into a contract of insurance on the insured's behalf without the insured's authority, the insured may simply adopt the contract for his own benefit. Ratification is possible even after a loss has occurred (*National Oilwell (UK) Ltd v Davy Offshore Ltd [1993] 2 Lloyd's Rep 582*) but the insurer must have been aware that the broker was not acting on his own account and was a mere agent.

The regulation of brokers

9.04   Up until 14 January 2005 insurance brokers were subject to an industry-developed system of self-regulation called the General Insurance Standards Council (GISC). Since that date, brokers have been regulated by the Financial Services Authority (FSA).

A major factor in the decision of the Treasury to transfer responsibility for the regulation of the activities of insurance brokers to the FSA was the need for the United Kingdom to comply with Directive 2002/92/EC of the European Parliament and of the Council of 9 December 2002 on insurance mediation (IMD).

Insurance broker wishing to carry out any activities regulated by the FSA now need to apply for authorisation by the FSA or become appointed representatives of an FSA authorised firm.

The FSA has set out, by way of rules and guidance in the FSA Handbook, the standards that they consider insurance brokers should meet in order to comply with the requirements of the IMD. On 20 January 2004, the FSA published a Policy Statement (PS04/1: Insurance Selling and Administration & Other Miscellaneous Amendments: Feedback on CP187 and made text) setting out their final rules for the regulation of the sale and administration of general insurance (eg motor and household insurance) and pure protection contracts (eg critical illness and income protection) ('non-investment insurance contracts') but not long-term care insurance contracts (eg life assurance), which are subject to the Conduct of Business Rules of the FSA which apply to all firms conducting designated investment business and are outlined in a separate sourcebook within the FSA's handbook.

The rules and guidance applicable to non-investment insurance contracts are outlined in a separate sourcebook within the FSA's handbook. This is called the

Insurance: Conduct of Business sourcebook (ICOB). The eight chapters in the ICOB are referred to as ICOB 1, ICOB 2 etc and we will comment on each in turn.

Application of ICOB (ICOB 1)

9.05 ICOB 1 sets out the scope of ICOB, including to whom they apply, to what activities the rules apply and where the rules apply.

In each chapter, different rules apply depending on whether the insurance broker is dealing with an individual buying insurance for himself and his family (retail customer) or a business buying insurance (commercial customer). Where it is not clear whether a customer is a retail or commercial customer, insurance brokers must comply with the rules that apply to retail customers.

The following points should also be noted about the application of ICOB rules:

(*a*) Although we comment on its application to insurance brokers only, ICOB applies to all insurance intermediaries (including insurers when selling directly and in their role as product providers).

(*b*) ICOB only applies to the insurance broker in contact with the customer – not to insurance brokers who are in the middle of the distribution chain.

(*c*) ICOB does not apply to reinsurance contracts or to transactions involving large risks where the risk is located outside the EEA.

(*d*) ICOB applies in a limited way only to transactions involving commercial customers and large risks where the risk is located inside the EEA.

General rules (ICOB 2)

9.06 ICOB 2 outlines the general requirements of ICOB which relate to communication, reliance on others, unfair inducements and record keeping. In particular, ICOB 2 states that:

(*a*) Any communication with customers must be clear, fair and not misleading.

(*b*) An insurance broker should not offer or accept an inducement if it is likely to conflict with the duty it or the recipient firm owes to its customers.

(*c*) For distance contracts with retail customers, insurance brokers must provide a paper copy of the contract terms and conditions if requested.

Financial promotion (ICOB 3)

9.07 ICOB 3 contains rules on financial promotion (eg product brochures, advertising, and websites). Those insurance brokers subject to the financial promotion rules need to show they have taken reasonable steps to ensure that the promotion is clear, fair and not misleading.

The rules require insurance brokers to check that the promotion they intend to use is compliant with the rules. When communicating a promotion provided by another insurance broker, the communicating insurance broker can rely on the providing insurance broker to check that it complies with the rules.

Advising and selling standards (ICOB 4)

STATUS DISCLOSURE

9.08 Status disclosure refers to the information that insurance brokers must provide about themselves and any fees that they charge. In summary, the information insurance brokers need to give to customers before the contract is concluded includes:

(*a*)   name and address of the insurance broker;

(*b*)   statutory status of the insurance broker;

(*c*)   a statement that the name, address and statutory status of the insurance broker can be checked on the FSA register (along with details of how to check);

(*d*)   details of any holding of 10% or more of voting rights or capital that the insurance broker has in an insurance undertaking;

(*e*)   details of any holding of 10% or more of voting rights or capital that an insurance undertaking (or a parent of an insurance undertaking) has in the insurance broker;

(*f*)   the basis on which the insurance broker provides advice or information;

(*g*)   how to complain to the insurance broker (including notification that complaints may be referred to the Financial Ombudsman Service where relevant);

(*h*)   that compensation may be available; and

(*j*)   details of any fees.

The disclosure requirements for insurance brokers making introductions are significantly reduced so that they need only disclose their name, address, statutory status, whether they are part of the group they are making an introduction to, and details of any fees the customer will have to pay for their services.

In order to meet the status disclosure requirements, insurance brokers can use either the initial disclosure document (IDD), or if the sale includes a mortgage or packaged investment product, the combined initial disclosure document (CIDD). The IDD and CIDD are set out in the annexes to ICOB 4.

SUITABILITY

9.09 The rules differ depending on whether advice is given in the form of a personal recommendation or not. When an insurance broker makes a personal recommendation, the rules require that the recommended non-investment insurance contract is suitable for the customer's demands and needs. This means an insurance broker must:

(*a*)   assess the customer's demands and needs by:

    (i)   asking for all relevant information;

    (ii)   having regard to any details the insurance broker already holds about the customer that are available and accessible to it; and

    (iii)   explaining to the customer his duty to disclose all circumstances material to the insurance, and taking this into account; and

(*b*)   assess the suitability of the contract recommended against the customer's demands and needs by:

    (i)   checking that cover is sufficient for the risks the customer wants to insure;

    (ii)   taking account of any relevant exclusions or conditions in the contract; and

    (iii)   considering the cost of the contract where this is relevant to the customer's demands and needs.

STATEMENT OF DEMANDS AND NEEDS

9.10   The rules require that customers be provided with a statement of their demands and needs which must reflect the complexity of the contract. In addition, the statement must confirm whether or not the contract has been personally recommended. If a recommendation has been made, the reasons for that recommendation must be given in the statement.

COMMISSION DISCLOSURE AND EXCESSIVE CHARGES

9.11   With respect to commission disclosure, ICOB 4 requires that when dealing with a commercial customer, the insurance broker must, if asked, disclose the commission that he and any associate of his would receive in connection with the contract being sold.

With respect to excessive charges, ICOB 4 requires an insurance broker to ensure its charges to retail customers are not excessive. The rule on excessive charges does not cover premiums but does include any fees that an insurance broker charges (including fees they charge where they receive no commission from the insurer).

UNSOLICITED SERVICES

9.12   In order to meet the requirements of Directive 2002/65/EC of the European Parliament and of the Council of 23 September 2002 concerning the distance marketing of consumer financial services, ICOB 4 states that insurance brokers cannot supply a distance contract to a retail customer without the customer's prior consent. However, this rule does not apply where the insurance broker has a right to renew a policy without consent, for example in accordance with the contract terms and conditions.

Product disclosure (ICOB 5)

RESPONSIBILITIES ON INSURERS AND INSURANCE BROKERS

9.13 Insurers are generally responsible for producing information and for its content, while insurance brokers are responsible for providing the information to customers. In cases where the FSA does not regulate the insurer, the insurance broker is responsible for producing the information, and for its content.

RETAIL CUSTOMERS

9.14 ICOB 5 covers information about the product that must be given to customers. In summary, the following information must be provided to retail customers:

(*a*) Policy Summary including:

    (i) The name of the insurance undertaking;

    (ii) The type of insurance and cover;

    (iii) Significant features and benefits;

    (iv) Significant and unusual exclusions;

    (v) Cross-references to exclusions in the policy document;

    (vi) Contact details for notification of claims; and

    (vii) The key facts logo.

(*b*) Statement of Price including:

    (i) The total amount of premium (where the policy is sold with other goods and services, the premium must be shown separately from all other prices);

    (ii) Additional fees, charges, and taxes payable, including any interest; and

    (iii) The total price to be paid for the insurance contract.

(*c*) Directive-required information.

(*d*) Information about cancellation including:

    (i) The existence or absence of a right to cancel;

    (ii) Duration of the cancellation period;

    (iii) How to exercise the right to cancel including what the customer may have to pay; and

    (iv) The consequences of non-cancellation.

(*e*) Information about the claims handling process including:

   (i) The point of contact for notifying a claim; and

   (ii) What information must be provided to the insurer when a claim is notified.

(*f*) Policy document including all the terms and conditions of the contract.

(*g*) Renewal information. The following information must be given at least 21 days before the expiry of a non-investment insurance contract with a retail customer:

   (i) Renewal terms or a statement that renewal will not be invited;

   (ii) Details of any changes to policy terms and the premium; and

   (iii) That the customer has a right to request a new policy document.

The timing and medium in which this information must be provided varies according to the channel through which the non-investment insurance contract is sold.

The FSA requires that the customer be told orally of the importance of reading the policy summary, especially the section on significant and unusual exclusions. If advice is given, insurance brokers will also need to ensure their staff understand the implications of any significant and unusual exclusions for any personal recommendations they make.

The FSA has made clear that the policy summary is a generic document, but insurance brokers can personalise it if they wish. The FSA restricts the information that can be included in the policy summary, so that the important information stands out. However, the FSA has allowed insurance brokers to include the policy summary as part of another document providing it is a prominent and distinct section.

The rules allow insurance brokers to provide a key features document which follows the content requirements of the investment conduct of business rules if they wish, instead of the policy summary.

COMMERCIAL CUSTOMERS

9.15 For commercial customers, the FSA require insurance brokers to provide:

(*a*) Certain directive-required information, information on premium and fees and other information sufficient to enable the customer to make an informed decision about the contract pre-sale;

(*b*) The policy document promptly after conclusion of the contract; and

(*c*) Renewal terms, or notification that the insurer does not intend to invite renewal in good time before the policy expires.

GROUP POLICIES

9.16   For group policies , the FSA requires that the commercial customer who is the legal holder of the policy be provided with a policy summary and policy document. The insurance broker must also advise the commercial customer to provide a copy of the policy summary to each policyholder and inform them that a copy of the policy document is available on request.

WHITE LABELLING

9.17   The rules do not contain any restrictions on 'white labelling' (ie where an insurance broker labels and sells a product under its own name, when in fact that product is created by another firm). However, the FSA has included guidance to state that insurance brokers should make clear to the customer the identities of both the insurer and the insurance broker and should ensure that their communication with customers is clear, fair and not misleading.

Cancellation (ICOB 6)

9.18   The requirements apply to all insurance contracts bought by retail customers, irrespective of whether they are bought face-to-face or at a distance, with some limited exceptions. For example, the cancellation rules do not apply to contracts where the activity or event being insured is of less than one month's duration. For general insurance contracts, the cancellation period is 14 days and for pure protection contracts it is 30 days.

When a contract is cancelled, insurers can charge for services they have provided in connection with a general insurance contract as long as the charge cannot be considered a penalty. However, insurers cannot charge when a customer cancels a pure protection contract. The FSA has made it clear that where insurance brokers charge customers for the service provided in the cancellation period, they will not be allowed to recover any property or money provided to settle a claim during the cancellation period.

Claims handling (ICOB 7)

9.19   Insurers are responsible for the prompt and fair handling of claims on policies they write. If they outsource claims handling to another company, the insurer retains responsibility for compliance with the rules. The rules set out a series of standards for handling retail customer claims from when a claim is first notified through to when the settlement terms are agreed.

Insurance brokers are required to act with due care and skill when acting on behalf of a customer in relation to a claim. They are also required to avoid conflicts of interest when they are acting for the customer at the claims stage. In addition, the FSA now requires that if an insurance broker acts for an insurer in respect of a claim on a policy it sold to the customer, the insurance broker must inform the customer that he is acting on behalf of the insurer, not the customer, at the point of claim.

THIRD PARTY CLAIMANTS

9.20   The FSA does not require insurers to treat third party claimants as if they were customers, as this would not align well with the current legal position and could give rise to conflicts of interest. The FSA has, however, added guidance reminding insurers of their obligations under the Principles for Businesses when dealing with third party claimants.

Distance non-investment mediation contracts (ICOB 8)

9.21   ICOB 8 sets out the information that must be provided by insurance brokers to retail customers when there is a distance non-investment mediation contract (being a distance contract to provide advice or information on non-investment insurance products, other than simply as part of the marketing stage in the sale of a contract). This information includes a description of the main characteristics of the contract, the total price to be paid for the contract and the customer's cancellation rights. This information must be provided in addition to that required by ICOB 4. The FSA thinks these contracts will rarely exist in the retail market.

Other amendments to the FSA Handbook

9.22   As well as ICOB, insurance brokers must comply with the relevant rules in the other FSA sourcebooks. PS04/1 makes a number of changes to these sourcebooks, and two of the most significant changes are explained below.

Complaints handling

9.23   The rules for complaints handling for eligible complainants (being private individuals, commercial customers with a group annual turnover of less than £1 million, charities with an annual income of less than £1 million and trustees of a trust with a net asset value of less than £1 million) are contained in the Dispute Resolution: Complaints Sourcebook (DISP). The main provisions relate to insurance brokers acknowledging and settling complaints within set time limits and informing the complainant that they may refer the matter to the Financial Ombudsman Service (FOS). For persons who are not eligible complainants, insurance brokers must have appropriate and effective procedures for registering complaints.

Insurance brokers are subject to the compulsory jurisdiction of the FOS. All businesses covered by the FOS pay a general levy to contribute to its costs. For businesses regulated by the FSA, to help simplify administration, the FSA collects the levy at the same time that it collects both its own regulatory fees and the levy for the Financial Services Compensation Scheme (FSCS).

Training and competence

9.24 The rules on training and competence are contained in the Training and Competence Sourcebook (TC). For all staff carrying out insurance mediation activities, insurance brokers will need to comply with the training and competence 'Commitments'. Although the FSA does not impose any examination requirements, insurance brokers will need to ensure their employees are and remain competent for the work they do, are appropriately supervised, and that their competence is regularly reviewed.

For staff giving advice (not just personal recommendations) to retail customers, the more detailed rules in the TC sourcebook will apply.

Enforcement

9.25 The FSA has an extensive range of disciplinary, criminal and civil powers to take action against regulated and non-regulated firms and individuals who are failing or have failed to meet the standards required and protect the interests of consumers. These are outlined in the Enforcement Sourcebook within the FSA's handbook. Examples of the FSA's powers include the ability to:

(*a*) withdraw a firm's authorisation;

(*b*) prohibit an individual from operating in financial services;

(*c*) prevent an individual from undertaking specific financial activities;

(*d*) censure firms and individuals through public statements;

(*e*) impose financial penalties;

(*f*) seek injunctions;

(*g*) apply to court to freeze assets;

(*h*) secure the return of money to customers; and

(*j*) prosecute firms and individuals who undertake regulated activities without authorisation.

The FSA works closely with other law enforcement agencies.

The rights of brokers

Commission

9.26 As noted above, the broker's commission is paid by the insurer rather than by the insured, even though the broker is the insured's agent. This rule is anomalous, in that it contravenes the basic agency rule that an agent may not profit from his office other than with the express consent of his principal. However, the exception in favour of insurance brokers is well established, and is subject only to the condition that the payment by the insurer conforms to usual market practice in terms of amount (*Hugh Allen & Co Ltd v A Holmes [1969] 1 Lloyd's Rep 348 (CA)*) and circumstances of payment (*NV Rotterdamse v Golding Steward Wrightson, unreported, 1989*). A broker is entitled to commission from the insurer only if the broker can demonstrate that his actions were the effective cause of the contract between the insured and insurer (*McNeil v Law Union and Rock Insurance Co Ltd [1925] 23 Ll LR 314*).

It should be noted that ICOB 4 requires an insurance broker to disclose the commission that he receives if he is asked to do so by a commercial customer (see 9.11 above).

Lien

9.27   A lien is a common law possessory security, entitling a creditor in lawful possession of the debtor's property to retain that property as security for the debt. In certain forms of insurance (for example marine insurance) the premium is paid by the broker. If the policy is then issued to the broker by the underwriters, the broker may retain the policy as security for the payment of the premium by the insured to the broker (*Marine Insurance Act 1906, s 53*). The lien does not extend to a composite policy (*Eide UK Ltd v Lowndes Lambert Group Ltd [1998] 1 Lloyd's Rep 389*).

The duties of brokers

Nature of the duties

9.28   Brokers, as agents, owe two classes of duty to the insured. Firstly, brokers owe to the insured the duty to obey instructions by the use of reasonable care and skill. The fact that the broker has failed to achieve what has been requested by the insured does not automatically mean that the broker is in breach of duty; it is sufficient if the broker exercises reasonable care. If the broker cannot obtain what is required, he must report in what respects he has failed and seek his client's alternative instructions (*Youell v Bland Welch and Co Ltd – the Superhulls Cover Case (No 2) [1990] 2 Lloyd's Rep 431*). Secondly, the broker owes fiduciary duties to the insured, which require the broker not to act in a manner which creates a conflict between his duty to the insured and his personal interest or duty to a third party. The practical limitations of this duty have been noted at 9.2 above.

Finding insurance

9.29   The primary obligation of the broker is to use all reasonable care and skill to obey the instructions given to him as to the insurance required. A number of aspects of this duty have emerged from the cases.

(*a*)   The broker must consider the market as a whole and seek to obtain the widest cover at the lowest premium. If the risk is uninsurable, the broker must inform the insured promptly (*Smith v Lascelles (1788) 2 Term Rep 187*).

(b)   The broker must ensure the security offered by the insurer or reinsurer is appropriate for the type of business being insured or reinsured (*Berriman v Rose Thomson Young (Underwriting) Ltd [1996] LRLR 426*).

(c)   A broker who knows an insurer to be in financial difficulties, but nevertheless continues to place insurance with the insurer will be liable in negligence (*Osman v J Ralph Moss [1970] 1 Lloyd's Rep 313*).

(d)   The policy must suit the insured's needs. If the broker has failed to procure insurance within the required time, or of the required scope, he will be in breach of duty. There are many illustrations of this in the insurance cases. Firstly, in *Youell v Bland Welch* (see 9.28 above) the broker had procured reinsurance for 48 months only, to cover a marine construction insurance risk of unlimited duration. Secondly, in *Forsikringsaktieselskapet Vesta v Butcher (No 1) [1989] 1 All ER 402*, the broker obtained reinsurance governed by English law, which gave less protection to the reinsured than the liability which it faced to its own insured under a policy governed by Norwegian law; however, the judges of the Queen's Bench Division, Court of Appeal and House of Lords all allowed recovery on the policy of reinsurance by a variety of different arguments so no question of liability on the part of the brokers arose. However the House of Lords added that the brokers would have faced liability if the reinsured's claim under the policy failed. Lastly, in *McNealy v The Pennine Insurance Co Ltd [1978] 2 Lloyd's Rep 18*, the broker procured a motor policy which excluded part-time musicians, into which category the insured fell. It was held that the brokers ought to have asked the insured whether the exclusion applied to him.

Completing the proposal form

9.30   In *O'Connor v BDB Kirby & Co [1972] 1 QB 90*, a proposal form completed by the broker and subsequently signed by the insured was found to contain material false statements, and the insurer avoided the policy. The Court of Appeal accepted that the broker owed a duty of care to the insured to transcribe the insured's answer in an accurate fashion, but found the broker not to be liable because firstly, the insured had not shown that the error was due to the broker's negligence, and secondly, the insured, by failing to check the form before signing it, had been the cause of his own loss.

The *O'Connor* case does not remove all possibility of action against the broker. In *Warren v Henry Sutton & Co [1976] 2 Lloyd's Rep 276*, the broker made false statements to the insurer about the driving record of a person to be a named driver under a motor policy. The broker was held to be in breach of duty for having failed to make the necessary inquiries of the insured himself. Moreover, if the completion of the proposal is entrusted to the broker due to the insured's absence, the broker is under a personal duty to check the answers. An extreme example is *Sharp v Sphere Drake Insurance Co (The Moonacre) [1992] 2 Lloyd's Rep 501*, where the broker had not only failed to inform the insured of the significance of an exclusion clause, but had also forged the insured's signature on the proposal, and had thereby submitted a proposal form to the insurers containing the material false statement that the insured had personally checked the form. The broker was held to have acted negligently in these circumstances.

The common law duty outlined above is replicated in the terms of ICOB 4 (see 9.8-9.12 above).

Payment of the premium

9.31   In marine insurance, the broker undertakes personal responsibility to the insurer to pay the premium (*Marine Insurance Act 1906, s 53(1)*), so that the insured is immune from an action by the insurer for the premium. The most important effect of this is that if the broker becomes insolvent having received the premium from the insured, the insured cannot be called upon to pay the premium again. This rule does not apply to other forms of insurance, and the general principle remains that the broker is the insured's agent, so that payment of the premium to the broker is not deemed to be payment to the insurer (see 5 PREMIUMS).

Post-formation duties

9.32   Once the insurance has been arranged, the broker is under a range of further duties.

(*a*)   If the policy is delivered to the broker, the broker must read the policy to check that it complies with the cover requested from the insurer (*King (Or Fiehl) v Chambers & Newman (Insurance Brokers) [1963] 2 Lloyd's Rep 130*).

(*b*)   The broker must, if asked by the insured whether particular conduct is or is not permitted under the policy, act reasonably in providing advice. In the event of lack of clarity, it will not be enough for the broker to form a view of what the policy wording means (*Melik & Co v Norwich Union Fire Insurance Society and Kemp [1980] 1 Lloyd's Rep 523*), and it may be necessary for the broker to seek clarification from the insurer.

(*c*)   When a policy is about to expire, the broker's duty may, depending upon the instructions given by the insured, be either to renew automatically, or to inform the insured as to the imminent lapse of cover. If the broker's duty is to effect renewal he must

   (i)   ensure that all material facts are communicated to the insurer (*Coolee Ltd v Wing Heath & Co (1930) 38 Ll L Rep 157* Cf *Dunbar v A&B Painters Ltd and Economic Insurance Co Ltd and Whitehouse & Co [1986] 2 Lloyd's Rep 38*); and

   (ii)   inform the insured of any changes in cover imposed on renewal and obtain an acknowledgement from the insured of his willingness to accept such changes on renewal (*Great North Eastern Railway Ltd v Avon Insurance plc [2001] 2 Lloyd's Rep 649*).

(*d*)   If the insured wishes to alter his insurance arrangements and requests that the broker make the necessary adjustments, the broker must act with reasonable care. In *Cherry Ltd v Allied Insurance Brokers Ltd [1978] 1 Lloyd's Rep*

274, the broker was instructed to cancel a policy, but informed the insured that this could not be done. The insured, acting on this advice, cancelled a substitute policy, and was subsequently left uninsured when the broker did manage to cancel the original policy without informing the insured. The broker was held liable for a loss later suffered by the insured which was not covered by any policy.

(e)   A broker will, depending on the type of policy, be under a duty to take reasonable steps to ensure that the client is aware of the nature and terms of the insurance, and, in particular, to draw attention to and explain (if necessary) any terms, the breach of which might result in his being uninsured (*JW Bollom & Co Ltd v Byas Mosley & Co Ltd [2000] Lloyd's Rep IR 136*).

(f)   A broker must exercise all reasonable care and skill in order to be in a position to collect claims when called upon to do so. This obligation means that the broker must retain the necessary documents to enable him to collect the insured's claims. The information need only be retained so long as a reasonable broker would regard a claim as possible (*Grace v Leslie & Godwin Financial Services Ltd [1995] LRLR 472*).

Claims

Making the claim

9.33   The broker is required under his duty to the insured to seek payment of the claim from the insurer following loss. In *North & South Trust Co v Berkeley [1970] 2 Lloyd's Rep 467*, the broker acted simultaneously for the insured and underwriters. The broker, on behalf of underwriters, commissioned a report on the insured's loss. The insured sought possession of the report, on the basis that the broker was his agent, and held the report in that capacity, rather than as agent for the underwriters. Donaldson J (at 479) rejected the insured's claim, but issued a firm warning that a broker could not act for both parties in this fashion, and that in future cases less leniency would be shown. It is common market practice, despite this ruling, for brokers – particularly at Lloyd's – to obtain surveys and other reports for underwriters, and on request to appoint solicitors for underwriters. Such conduct is almost certainly a breach of duty towards an insured who has not been made aware of the practice.

ICOB 7 (see 9.19-9.20 above) states that an insurance broker must not put itself in a position where its own interest, or its duty to any person for whom it acts, conflicts with its duty to any customer, unless it made proper disclosure to its customer of all information needed to enable its customer to give informed consent to the arrangement; and it has obtained the prior informed consent of the customer.

Payment of the loss

9.34   In many cases, particularly at Lloyd's, the broker has an accounting arrangement with underwriters whereby the broker pays losses and subsequently is indemnified by the underwriters. If the broker pays the insured in anticipation that the underwriters will accept liability, and they refuse, the sum paid by the broker to the insured may be treated as a gift. If the payment is so treated, this means that:

(*a*)   if the underwriters are not liable, the insured retains the sums paid by the broker;

(*b*)   if the underwriters are liable, the insured can probably recover the full amount of his loss from the underwriters, irrespective of the fact that he has been paid by the broker, and can retain both sums. In *Merrett v Capitol Indemnity Corporation [1991] 1 Lloyd's Rep 169*, the brokers paid the reinsured's claim against the reinsurers gratuitously for commercial reasons (see 11 LLOYD'S).

In the absence of any accounting arrangement, the insurer may pay the loss directly to the broker. As the broker is the insured's agent, payment to the broker is deemed to be payment to the insured, so that if the broker becomes insolvent, the insured cannot require the insurer to pay again. If the insurer, having paid the broker, discovers that the payment was made in error, the insurer can only recover the payment from the broker before the broker paid over or accounted for the money to the insured (*Holland v Russell (1863) 4 B&S 14*). The insurer must thereafter reclaim the payment from the insured himself.

The liabilities of brokers

Contract and tort

9.35   There has been a move in the general law since 1986 against the co-existence of duties of care in contract and tort, the principle being that if the parties have a contract, the contract should provide an exhaustive statement of their rights and liabilities (*Tai Hing Cotton Mill v Liu Chong Hing Bank Ltd (No 2) [1986] AC 519*). This principle does not, however, apply to insurance brokers (and possibly not to other providers of professional services). The position is that a broker owes a duty to the insured to exercise reasonable care and skill in carrying out his instructions, both in contract (by means of an implied term) and in tort (by means of a duty of care). Consequently, in the event of a negligent breach, the insured may choose whether to sue in contract or in tort.

A sub-broker, who is usually the agent of the producing broker, will normally have no contractual relationship with the insured (*Pangood Ltd v Barclay Brown Co Ltd [1999] Lloyd's Rep IR 405*). A sub-broker does not owe any general duty of care to the insured, but such a duty may exist depending on the circumstances of the case. See, for example, *Prentis Donegan & Partners Ltd v Leeds & Leeds Co Inc [1998] 2 Lloyd's Rep 326* where it was held that a sub-broker owes a duty of care to the insured but there was no contract between them.

Limitation of actions

9.36   Under *s 5* of the *Limitation Act 1980*, an action for breach of contract must be brought within six years of the date of breach. In the case of an action in tort, the action may be brought either within six years of the date of the loss, or three years from the date on which a reasonable person would have the knowledge required to bring the action, whichever date is later (*Limitation Act 1980, ss 2* and *14A,* the latter inserted by the *Latent Damage Act 1986*). It is a feature of breach of duty by a broker that it may not come to light for some years after it has occurred, for example when a policy is procured by means of false information given by the broker in year one, and a loss occurs in year ten, at which date the insurer denies liability. In both contract and tort, time begins to run in year one, which is the date of the breach of contract for the purposes of *s 5* of the *Limitation Act 1980* and the date of damage for the purposes of *s 2* of the *Limitation Act 1980* (*Islander Trucking Ltd (In Liquidation) v Hogg Robinson & Gardener Mountain (Marine) Ltd [1990] 1 All ER 826*). In such a case, it is possible to sue only in tort, by relying on the three-year 'discoverability' period under *s 14A* of the *Limitation Act 1980.* There is a long-stop period of 15 years from the date of breach of duty after which no action may be brought.

Measures of damages

9.37   It makes little difference whether the insured sues his broker in contract or tort, as the cases have established that the same measure of damages applies and the same deductions in favour of the broker are available. The basic measure of damages against a broker whose breach of duty has rendered a loss irrecoverable from the insurer is the amount of the loss itself, not the amount insured (*Charles v Altin (1854) 15 CB 46*). This is coupled with any costs incurred by the insured in unsuccessfully pursuing the insurer (*Seavision Investment SA v Evennett (The Tiburon) [1992] 2 Lloyd's Rep 26*). Damages recoverable by reinsureds from their brokers, for breach of duty in obtaining cover, which underwriters are entitled to later avoid for non-disclosure of material facts, were in general limited to the value of the cover which they were instructed to obtain and reported that they had obtained. However, if the scope of the duty was wider and involved undertaking to advise on the course of action which the reinsured should pursue, the damages recoverable would be greater (*Aneco Reinsurance Underwriting Ltd (In Liquidation) v Johnson & Higgins Ltd [2002] Lloyd's Rep IR 91*).

The amount recoverable will be reduced in two situations. First, if the broker can demonstrate that the insurer would, irrespective of the broker's breach of duty, not have paid the full amount of the loss, the broker's liability is limited to the amount which the insurer would have been likely to pay. This situation arises most commonly where the insurer has a defence against the insured which has nothing to do with the broker's breach of duty. In *Everett v Hogg, Robinson and Gardner Mountain (Insurance) Ltd [1973] 2 Lloyd's Rep 217*, both the insured and the broker had given false information to the insurer. The insurer relied upon the broker's error to deny liability. The court held that the insurer, faced with the insured's breach only, would have settled for two-thirds of the claim, and that was, therefore, the amount which the broker's duty had cost the insured and was the appropriate measure of damages.

The second situation is that in which the insured has in some way contributed to his own loss. In *Forsikringsaktieselskapet Vesta* (see 9.29 above), the Court of Appeal held that the *Law Reform (Contributory Negligence) Act 1945*, which allows the apportionment of damages where it is shown that the insured is guilty of contributory negligence and where the broker's liability in contract is the same as in tort. The level of deductions has been fairly low, as the courts have taken the view that the insured, having appointed a broker, is not under a duty to monitor the manner in which the broker performs his duty. In *Youell v Bland Welch* (see 9.28 above), reinsurance brokers had sent details of cover to the reinsureds, but had failed to clarify in the document the fact that reinsurance cover was to be limited to 48 months. The reinsureds either did not read the document or, having read it, did not appreciate the restriction. The court felt that a deduction of 20% from the damages against the broker following a loss outside the period of cover was appropriate in the circumstance. In *National Insurance and Guarantee Corporation v Imperio Reinsurance Co (UK) and Russell Tudor-Price & Co Ltd [1999] Lloyd's Rep IR 249* damages payable by a broker to a reinsured, in circumstances where the broker had produced a policy amendment which plainly did not have its intended effect, but which were, nevertheless, approved by the reinsured were reduced by 30%. By contrast, in *The Moonacre* (see 9.30 above), another case in which the insured had failed to read or appreciate policy wording, the court refused to make any deduction from the insured's damages against the broker. *The Moonacre* is likely to represent the position where the insured is not an expert in insurance matters. The courts are more likely to find a reinsured guilty of contributory negligence compared with an insured (but see *(1) GE Reinsurance Corporation (2) Great Lakes Reinsurance (UK) plc (3) Sphere Drake Insurance Ltd (4) Royal & Sun Alliance Insurance plc v (1) New Hampshire Insurance Company (2) Willis Ltd [2003] EWHC 302*).

Persons to whom duties are owed

9.38 The fact that the broker has a contract with the insured does not necessarily mean that the broker does not owe a tortious duty of care to third parties. The cases have established the following principles:

(a) A broker appointed to arrange insurance, who seeks reinsurance first on behalf of insurers yet to be identified, and who gives a signing indication to the reinsurers, must use its best endeavours to obtain the promised level of subscription (*General Accident Fire and Life Assurance Corporation v Tanter, The Zephyr [1985] 2 Lloyd's Rep 529*; see 38 REINSURANCE).

(b) A broker who is asked by the purchaser of a car to transfer the insured's motor policy to the third party purchaser to accompany the sale of the car, owes a duty of care to the third party to effect the insurance as required, and is in breach of that duty if it fails to inform him that the transfer has not been accepted (*Bromley LBC v A Ellis (Luff & Sons, Third Party) [1971] 1 Lloyd's Rep 97*). Similarly, if the broker is aware that the policy is to be assigned to a third party, the broker owes a duty of care to the third party to ensure that the policy is valid from its inception (*Punjab National Bank v de Boinville [1992] 3 All ER 104*). This is so because the third party in these cases has been identified, and there is no danger of the broker facing liability to a large unidentifiable class of persons.

(c)   A broker does not owe a duty of care to the public at large. In *MacMillan v AW Knott Becker Scott Ltd [1990] 1 Lloyd's Rep 98,* the broker made false statements to the insurer on the insured's behalf when the insured's liability policy was obtained. This rendered the policy voidable. The insured subsequently became insolvent, and various third parties who had claims against the insured commenced proceedings against the insured's liability insurers in accordance with the *Third Parties (Rights Against Insurers) Act 1930* (see 20 THIRD PARTIES (RIGHTS AGAINST INSURERS) ACT 1930). The claimants thus sought to sue the brokers, alleging a duty of care owed to them. The court felt that it would not be appropriate to impose a duty of care upon brokers placing a liability policy, towards any person who might be injured by the insured.

(d)   If a broker is appointed by a company to procure insurance, his duty is – under the corporate veil principle – owed only to the company, and not to the individual shareholders. This rule may prove to be harsh in the case of a small private company where the use of corporate form was a matter of pure convenience. In *Verderame v Commercial Union Assurance Co plc [1992] BCL.C. 793*, the Court of Appeal held that the brokers did not owe a duty of care to the two shareholders of a company to procure a valid policy for the company, and that the duty was owed to the company itself. This was significant on the facts, as the company had become insolvent so that any successful claim by the company would lead to recovery by it for the benefit of its creditors, so that the shareholders themselves received very little by way of compensation.

(e)   A broker does not normally owe any duties in contract to an insurer. A broker can, however, assume specific obligations to an insurer or reinsurer (see *The Zephyr* at (a) above and *Pryke v Gibbs Hartley Cooper Ltd [1991] 1 Lloyd's Rep 602*).

If the policy wording has been prepared by the broker, as agent of the insured, the doctrine of *contra proferentem* will operate against the insured in the event of ambiguity (*Bartlett & Partners Ltd v Meller [1961] 1 Lloyd's Rep 487*). In such circumstances the broker must exercise particular care to ensure that the wording which he has prepared meets the needs of each insured (see *Forsikringsaktieselskapet Vesta* at 9.29 above).

Chapter 10
Underwriting agencies

- Nature of underwriting agencies
- Underwriting agencies and Lloyd's
- Underwriting agencies and reinsurance pools

Nature of underwriting agencies

Definition

10.01   An underwriting agent is a person given authority by an insurer or reinsurer to write insurance or reinsurance business on the insurer or reinsurer's behalf. Underwriting agencies are primarily used in order to establish some form of presence in a territory where the insurer is itself not otherwise represented; to this extent, selling insurance through an underwriting agent is an alternative to the insurer establishing a full branch in the territory in question. In practice, underwriting agencies are most widely used by Lloyd's underwriters and in the placing of reinsurance risks.

The scope of an underwriting agent's authority depends upon the terms of his appointment. Some underwriting agents are given the right to accept business on behalf of the insurer, while others merely obtain proposals for transmission to and decision by the insurer.

Authorisation

10.02   Under the *Financial Services and Markets Act 2000 (FSMA 2000)*, no firm or person may carry on a regulated activity in the UK unless authorised or exempt (the 'General Prohibition'). In relation to insurance generally, the regulated activities, which are regarded as separate activities, are:

(*a*)   effecting contracts of insurance; or

(*b*)   the carrying out of contracts of insurance.

In relation to Lloyd's, the regulated activities are:

(i) advising a person to become or continue or cease to be a member of a particular Lloyd's syndicate;

(ii) managing the underwriting capacity of a Lloyd's syndicate; or

(iii) making arrangements for another person to buy, sell, subscribe for or underwrite syndicate capacity or a person's membership.

Additionally, under the FSA's Insurance Conduct of Business ('ICOB') rules (as amended), with effect from 14 January 2005 (when the *Insurance Mediation Directive (2002/92/EC)* was implemented in the UK), intermediaries involved in the sale and administration of general insurance will also be carrying on regulated activities where they are:

- arranging the purchase of insurance policies;

- advising on insurance policies;

- dealing as an insurance agent; or

- assisting in the administration and performance of insurance policies.

Underwriting agents will normally carry on one or more of the regulated activities set out above in the ordinary course of their business. Where they do so, they must either be exempt from requiring authorisation, or be authorised, either by applying to the Financial Services Authority for a Part IV permission, or by qualifying for automatic authorisation through the exercise of passport rights under EU law. In this regard, where a European Economic Area firm seeks to establish a branch in the UK they will be automatically authorised to carry on regulated activities if certain 'establishment' conditions (generally relating to confirmation from the firm's home state regulator that it has given the firm consent to establish a branch in the UK) are met. Note that under *s 316(1)* of the *FSMA 2000*, members of Lloyd's do not require authorisation from the FSA in order to carry on insurance business at Lloyd's.

Where an underwriting agent requires authorisation, it will also be required to abide by certain of the FSA's high-level principles, which largely involve acting with due care, skill, diligence and integrity and observing proper standards of market conduct. It will also be required to abide, where applicable, by the FSA Rules and Handbook generally, of which the high level principles and ICOB rules form a part.

FSMA 2000 also introduces a regime relating to authorised persons, under which key personnel working within authorised firms have to be approved directly by the FSA. Once approved, they are directly subject to FSA rules and FSA disciplinary action for failure to comply. Under this regime, where a firm allocates significant responsibility to a senior manager of a significant business unit, that manager will be required to be approved by the FSA. Where an underwriting agency is actually underwriting insurance policies, any senior manager of the underwriting agency who has responsibility for a significant underwriting unit is likely to require approval. Approved persons must also comply with the FSA's high level principles.

The application of the *FSMA 2000* authorisation requirements to an overseas insurer in the UK who is selling insurance through an underwriting agent operating in the UK may give rise to difficulty. If the underwriting agent has no power to grant cover, but merely transmits proposals to the insurer for decision, it is clear that – prior to 14 January 2005 – the underwriting agent itself is not carrying on regulated activities in the UK. However, after 14 January 2005, such activities will become regulated activities. Furthermore, it is also arguable, following *Secretary of State for Trade and Industry v Great Western Assurance Co SA [1999] Lloyd's Rep IR 377,* that in such circumstances the insurer is also carrying on regulated activities in the UK. If, instead, the underwriting agent is making underwriting decisions in the UK on behalf of the insurers, it may be that all of the parties are carrying on business in the UK and require authorisation. This was the ruling in *DR Insurance Co. v Seguros American Banamex [1993] 1 Lloyd's Rep 120,* in which the underwriting agent, located in London and acting on behalf of a number of reinsurers, received proposals and provisionally accepted risks and submitted them to the reinsurers for acceptance. The court found that the details submitted by the underwriting agent were insufficient for any judgement to be made by the reinsurers, and that the reality was that the underwriting agent was itself taking underwriting decisions on behalf of the reinsurers. As a result, the underwriting agent and the reinsurers were carrying on insurance business in the UK, and had to be authorised.

Where insurance contracts are made by an entity that does not have proper authorisation, or which is not otherwise exempt from authorisation, *ss 26–28* of the *FSMA 2000* provide that such contracts remain enforceable against the insurer by the original insured if he so elects, but are not enforceable by the insurer (for example the insurer would be unable to enforce the provisions enabling it to receive premiums). However, this is subject to the discretion of the court to decide that the contract is enforceable on the ground that it is just and equitable to enforce it. This decision will largely revolve around whether the entities concerned reasonably believed they were not contravening the General Prohibition. *Sections 26–28* of the *FSMA 2000* also provide that the insured is entitled to recover any money or property paid by him under the contract if it is not enforced, and compensation for any loss sustained by him as a result of having parted with that money or property.

Special note should be taken of *ss 23–24* of the *FSMA 2000*, which provide that a person who contravenes the General Prohibition or who describes himself as authorised or exempt, or who behaves or otherwise acts in a manner which indicates that he is an authorised or exempt person when he is not, is guilty of a criminal offence and is liable to imprisonment.

Underwriting agencies and Lloyd's

10.03 Insurance business carried on by Lloyd's is sometimes arranged through underwriting agents acting on behalf of Lloyd's syndicates. The agreement by which the underwriting agent is authorised to accept risks on behalf of the participating syndicates is known as a binding authority or binder. Under the

Lloyd's regulatory structure, the holders of binding authorities must be approved by Lloyd's, and agreements with approved holders are then registered at Lloyd's. The relationship between the syndicates and the underwriting agent must be conducted through a Lloyd's broker. Note that the FSA now requires that binding authorities must expressly provide that the underwriting agent is to act as agent of the insurer for the purpose of receiving and holding premiums (if the agent has the authority to commit the insurer to risk), claims monies (if the agent has the authority to settle claims on behalf of the insurer) and premium refunds (if the agent has the authority to make refunds of premiums on behalf of the insurer).

The current regulatory framework is contained in:

(a)   the Delegated Underwriting Byelaw (No 1 of 2004);

(b)   the Overseas Underwriting Byelaw (No 2 of 2004);

(c)   the Definitions Byelaw (No 7 of 2005);

(d)   Chapter 2 of the Lloyd's Underwriting Requirements;

(e)   an internet based registration scheme; and

(f)   a Code of Practice for Delegated Underwriting established under the byelaws.

The Code of Practice, which highlights the main risks associated with delegating authority and provides practical guidance to help manage such risks, covers the assessment of new coverholders, the production and provision of contracts for delegating authority, the monitoring of contracts of delegation and the cancellation or non-renewal of such contracts. In addition, Lloyd's have produced a Coverholder Handbook which explains to coverholders their part in the Lloyd's franchise, and a Coverholder Undertaking which sets out Lloyd's expectations of coverholders when dealing with the Lloyd's market.

Underwriting agencies and reinsurance pools

10.04   Much reinsurance business is conducted through reinsurance pools, the business being negotiated on behalf of the pool participants by an underwriting agent. The role of the underwriting agent acting for the pool will vary from case to case. Sometimes the agent will only be the conduit for the passing of reinsurance business to the pool participants. In the majority of cases, however, the agent is given authority by the pool participant to accept risks on their behalf or on behalf of one or more pool participants nominated to accept risks as a 'front' for the pool.

Since the underwriting agent is, in effect, exercising its own discretion on behalf of the pool, the contract for the appointment by the pool of the underwriting agent gives rise to a duty of disclosure by the underwriting agent (*John W Pryke v Gibbs Hartley Cooper Ltd [1991] 1 Lloyd's Rep 602*). An underwriting agent entering into agreements on behalf of the pool may sue and be sued on those agreements in its own name, unless it is made clear that the underwriting agent is acting purely as an agent for the principal (*Ernest Scragg & Sons Ltd v Perseverance Banking and Trust Co Ltd [1973] 2 Lloyd's Rep 101*).

Underwriting agent's authority

10.05   The relationship between the underwriting agent and its principal is governed by the agency agreement.

The extent of the agent's actual authority will be defined by any express agreement between the parties, and will be a matter of the construction of the agreement. In addition to any express authority, the underwriting agent will have implied authority to do whatever is necessary in order to comply with his duties. The scope of the agent's authority will also be judged according to any trade practice or usage of the particular market in which the agent is operating. Any implied term must not, however, conflict with the express terms of the agency agreement.

The underwriting agent may also bind its principal to the extent of any apparent or ostensible authority. Third parties are, therefore, entitled to rely on any act of an underwriting agent if it is within the scope of the agent's usual authority.

If the underwriting agent exceeds his authority, his principal can ratify the actions of the agent. If the principal does not wish to ratify any act of the agent, it should make this clear to the third party as soon as possible.

An underwriting agent cannot, in the absence of express or implied authority from its principal, delegate its authority to a third party or appoint a sub-agent to perform any act within the scope of its authority. The agent must perform its fiduciary duties to its principal.

In the event of an underwriting agent both acting as an agent for a buyer of insurance by broking an insurance policy to that customer and acting as an agent for the insurer in relation to any claim made under that policy, the ICOB rules as amended provide that in a situation of this type, the agent must inform the customer that it is acting on behalf of the insurer in relation to that claim. The underwriting agent is also obliged by the ICOB rules to avoid conflicts of interest of this type unless it can manage them by disclosure to, and the obtaining of informed consent from its customer.

Underwriting agent's duties

10.06   The agency agreement will usually deal with the duties of the agent. Clear underwriting guidelines should be given to the agent, whether orally or in writing.

An underwriting agent is likely to be negligent if he does not act in accordance with the basic principles of insurance; for example, he must ensure that he has spread any risk to his principal. He must also act with the reasonable skill and care expected of an underwriting agent.

An underwriting agent also has an implied duty (if the agreement does not so provide) to prepare and maintain records of the business written, the premium income received, and the claims history. It is also common practice to find a clause in the agency agreement whereby the principal has the right to inspect the books and records maintained by the agent.

The agent also has an obligation not to act in furtherance of its own interests over those of its principal. In the case of *Julien Praet et Cie, S/A v H G Poland Ltd [1960] 1 Lloyd's Rep 420*, which involved a motor insurance binder given by a Lloyd's syndicate to a Belgian insurance broker, the broker terminated the binder and offered to the insureds new policies with another Lloyd's syndicate on the expiration of their current policies. The court held that the broker was not entitled to terminate the existing policies as this interfered with the contractual rights of the parties to the policies and was contrary to the interests of the underwriters.

Where an underwriting agent is authorised by the FSA to carry on regulated activities relating to insurance, the underwriting agent is under a duty to comply with the FSA Rules and Handbook.

Chapter 11
Lloyd's

- History and structure
- Regulation of Lloyd's
- The course of business at Lloyd's
- Payment obligations at Lloyd's

History and structure

11.01   Lloyd's of London began life as a coffee house owned by Edward Lloyd in the 17th century. The premises were a popular meeting place for merchants, and rapidly became the focus for the underwriting of marine policies. Lloyd's developed rapidly, and by 1696 had begun to publish *Lloyd's News,* which gave details of marine casualties, and which may be regarded as the forerunner of *Lloyd's List.* Lloyd's is now located in Lime Street in the City of London. More recently, fundamental changes in the structure of Lloyd's have occurred, as a result of the many challenges faced by the market in the last decade.

Underwriting takes place at Lloyd's through syndicates. A syndicate is an unincorporated association of various capital providers known as 'Names', grouped together for one year at a time for the purpose of underwriting. Up to the end of 1993, Lloyd's Names were solely comprised of individuals who had unlimited liability in respect of their Lloyd's underwriting liabilities. As a response to the substantial losses suffered by Names in the 1980s and early 1990s, Lloyd's introduced, in January 1994, limited liability membership of Lloyd's syndicates through corporate membership. Individual members have not been permitted to join Lloyd's on an unlimited liability basis since 2003. Instead, they now become corporate members and are generally assisted through the process of forming or joining a corporate member by a members' agent.

Another of the responses of Lloyd's to the serious losses of the 1980s was the creation of a reinsurance company called Equitas. The purpose of this company is to ring fence the 1992 and prior years' liabilities of Names through a reinsurance of these liabilities. This has enabled Lloyd's to trade forward without the burden of dealing with these earlier years.

Insurance decisions for each Syndicate are taken by the active underwriter (or his or her deputy or class underwriter), the remaining members of the Syndicate being passive investors. The interests of Names are protected by members' agents, whose function is to ensure that the investment in Lloyd's made by a Name is spread appropriately amongst suitable syndicates, and also to ensure that the funds provided by Names are to be used for genuine underwriting purposes (*Boobyer v David Holman & Co Ltd (No 2) [1993] 1 Lloyd's Rep 96*; *Brown v KMR Services Ltd, Sword-Daniels v Michael Pitel [1995] 2 Lloyd's Rep 513*). Each syndicate is run by managing agents. A managing agent may run more than one syndicate. Each Name has an agency agreement with a members' agent, and some Names contract directly with managing agents, while others deal with managing agents through their members' agent. It was held by the House of Lords in *Arbuthnott v Feltrim [1995] CLC 437*, that a managing agent (whether or not he has a direct contract with the Name) owes a duty of care to each Name on the Syndicate which it manages in respect of the underwriting activities of those syndicates.

The Society of Lloyd's itself is, however, immune from suit by Names unless bad faith can be established (*s 14* of the *Lloyd's Act 1982* as applied in *Ashmore v Corp of Lloyd's (No 2) [1992] 2 Lloyd's Rep 620*). The Society of Lloyd's (interchangeably referred to as the Corporation) is a body of individual underwriters incorporated by statute and authorised by its constitution to exercise supervisory, regulatory and disciplinary powers over its members. It has also been held that the Society of Lloyd's does not exercise public functions and thus is not susceptible to judicial review proceedings brought by members (*R v Lloyd's of London, ex p Briggs [1993] 1 Lloyd's Rep 176*) which was approved in *R (on the application of West) v Lloyd's of London [2004] Lloyd's Rep IR 755* (but see 11.05 below for the contrasting position of the Disciplinary Committee).

Lloyd's underwriters do not deal directly with the general public, and all negotiations for insurance are conducted only with Lloyd's brokers. A non-Lloyd's broker who wishes to seek cover from Lloyd's must instruct a Lloyd's broker to act as sub-broker for this purpose.

The duties owed by (re)insurance brokers are dictated by the law of agency and London market practice. They are also regulated by the FSA.

The Lloyd's Franchise Board controls the registration of and withdrawal of registration from Lloyd's brokers. An applicant will only be registered if it is either (a) registered with a competent authority, if it is established in a member state, or (b) if it is not established in a member state, it has demonstrated to the satisfaction of the Franchise Board that it meets strict professional requirements in relation to its competence, good repute and financial capacity.

Regulation of Lloyd's

11.02   The regulation of Lloyd's was reviewed during the consultation process behind the *Financial Services and Markets Act (FSMA 2000)*. Although under FSMA 2000, much of the previous self-regulatory regime remains, the FSA now has disciplinary powers in respect of breaches of FSA principles. Lloyd's retains its own investigation and disciplinary powers however, for suspected breaches of its own byelaws and rules, and the FSA will liaise with Lloyd's and will use its discretion in determining whether or not to intervene.

The Lloyd's regulatory framework is governed partly by the *Lloyd's Act 1982* and the *FSMA 2000*. The *Lloyd's Act 1982* established the Council of Lloyd's. The Council consists of elected working members of Lloyd's and elected or nominated external members. It is the senior body of Lloyd's, performing its statutory role in relation to the legal and disciplinary functions of Lloyd's. The Council delegates many of its functions (except for those that cannot be delegated under the Lloyd's Act) to the Franchise Board. There are a large number of byelaws and regulations governing the entire conduct of business at Lloyd's.

Part XIX ss 314–324 of the *FSMA 2000* governs the regulation by the FSA of the Lloyd's markets. *Part XIX* makes the Society of Lloyd's an 'authorised person', and gives the FSA certain powers to direct the affairs of the Society, its members and Lloyd's managing and members' agents. In general terms, the FSMA allows Lloyd's to self-regulate although the FSA retains powers to ensure that Lloyd's regulatory approach is consistent with that of the FSA. The FSA's general duty is to keep itself informed about the way in which the Council of Lloyd's self-regulates the market, and to keep under review the desirability of exercising its powers in relation to Lloyd's.

The FSA will intervene, having regard to the interests of existing and potential policy holders, and where the Society of Lloyd's may have failed to satisfy any obligations under the byelaws and regulations governing its business.

Before the FSA intervenes with the regulation of Lloyd's, it must issue an insurance market direction to the Council, the Society or both. After the publication of a draft direction, the Act provides for a period of consultation, and thereafter for publication of the FSA's response to the consultative process and the final direction.

Persons who ceased to be an underwriting member of the Society on or after 24 December 1996 are regulated under a modified regime. A former underwriting member may carry out each contract of insurance that he has underwritten at Lloyd's, without applying for authorisation to do so from the FSA. The FSA may however impose such requirements as appear to it to be appropriate for the purpose of protecting policy holders against the risk that the underwriting member in question may not be able to meet his liabilities. There is provision in the Act for a period of consultation before any such requirements are imposed.

On 30 June 2003 the Council passed the Underwriting Byelaw (No 2 of 2003) and related Underwriting Requirements, the Definitions Byelaw (No 3 of 2003, now replaced by the Definitions Byelaw No 7 of 2005) and Runoff Guidelines. The Underwriting Byelaw implements new business planning and performance arrangements and provides a framework under which the Franchise Board can make and modify rules which are tailored to market risks and underwriting conditions.

Challenging the imposition of fines or suspension

11.03 Any member of Lloyd's who is accused of infringing rules of conduct is subject to disciplinary proceedings before the Disciplinary Committee , which have the power to impose fines and, ultimately, to suspend membership. There is an appeal from these proceedings to the Appeal Tribunal, except where the Disciplinary Committee has imposed a fixed penalty. Lloyd's disciplinary proceedings are subject to challenge by way of judicial review (*R v Committee of Lloyd's, ex p Moran, The Times, 24 June 1983*; *R v Committee of Lloyd's, ex p Posgate, The Times, 12 January 1983*).

The course of business at Lloyd's

The Lloyd's slip

11.04 Insurance at Lloyd's is often initiated by the preparation of a 'slip' by the broker. Some business, however, such as personal lines, is commenced by proposal terms. The slip sets out the basic details of the risk, and proposes the terms upon which the risk is to be accepted. The slip is then presented by the broker to an underwriter who is known to specialise in insurance of the class sought. If the leading underwriter is prepared to accept the risk, he will 'initial' (sign) the slip on behalf of his syndicate for a given amount, and thereby bind his syndicate to accept the stated part of the risk. The broker will then present the slip to underwriters acting on behalf of other syndicates, and by this process will seek to obtain full coverage of the risk. The number of syndicates involved in a particular risk will vary. To expedite this procedure, syndicates may authorise one particular syndicate to bind them up to given financial limits in respect of risks of a particular type. This type of authority, known as a 'line slip', means that a broker can obtain a substantial proportion of the required cover by obtaining the subscription of an underwriter administering a line slip.

Once the slip has been fully subscribed, unless it is in the form of a slip policy, it will be replaced by a detailed policy issued by Lloyd's Policy Signing Office.

Binding nature of a slip

11.05 As soon as an underwriter initials a slip, he creates a binding contract between himself and the insured for the sum specified by the underwriter. As the slip progresses, and more underwriters subscribe to it, further contracts are made. By the time the slip is fully subscribed, therefore, it will amount to a composite document evidencing a series of individual contracts with the insured. This method of contract formation gives rise to a number of issues.

(*a*)   If a slip is not fully subscribed, and the broker is unable to obtain any further subscriptions, neither the insured nor the subscribing underwriters can withdraw from the contract unless there is some mutual agreement to this effect (*General Reinsurance Corp v Forsakringsaktiebolaget Fennia Patria [1983] 2 Lloyd's Rep 287*).

(*b*)   If the leading underwriter has initialled the slip on its original terms, and following underwriters insist upon new terms, the leading underwriter cannot claim the benefit of the new terms.

(*c*)   If a loss occurs prior to full subscription, and the subscribing underwriters are on risk those underwriters who have subscribed are liable.

(*d*)   The insured owes a duty of utmost good faith to each subscribing underwriter separately (*Bank Leumi Le Israel BM v British National Insurance Co Ltd [1988] 1 Lloyd's Rep 71*). A misrepresentation or non-disclosure by the insured to a leading underwriter may only be relied upon by a following underwriter where it is established that the following underwriters, in initialling the slip, would have relied on the leader's acceptance as having been procured through a proper presentation when they agreed to subscribe to the contract themselves (*Aneco Reinsurance Underwriting Ltd (In Liquidation) v Johnson & Higgins Ltd [2001] UKHL 51*).

Oversubscription

11.06   The only situation in which the initialling of a slip may be varied unilaterally is where the broker has obtained over 100% subscription to the slip. Oversubscription is of little use to the insured, as he can never recover more than an indemnity. A custom has arisen at Lloyd's, which was given judicial approval in *General Accident Fire and Life Assurance Corp v Tanter, 'The Zephyr' [1985] 2 Lloyd's Rep 529*, whereby the subscriptions of the underwriters can be signed down proportionately, giving no more than 100% cover. This case further decides that a broker who indicates to the leading underwriter that he intends to seek oversubscription from the market, and thereby induces the leading underwriter to accept a greater liability than he would otherwise have done, is under a duty to use his best endeavours to obtain the level of oversubscription specified so that the leading underwriter is not left overexposed. A signing down indication given to the leading underwriter alone is not, however, deemed to have been made to the following market, so that subsequent underwriters who rely on the conduct of the leading underwriter in accepting a greater initial exposure will have no remedy against the broker.

Effect of the issue of the policy

11.07   *Relationship with the slip.* As the slip constitutes a binding contract between the insured and the underwriters, the policy should not contradict what is in the slip. If there is inconsistency between the two documents, the insured is entitled to seek rectification of the policy so that it accords with the original agreement. It is unclear whether the underwriters can seek rectification, for it was held in *Eagle Star Insurance Co v Spratt [1971] 2 Lloyd's Rep 116* that the Lloyd's Policy Signing Office is the authorised agent of the underwriters. If, therefore, the policy gives the insured a concession which was not contained in the slip, the underwriters are probably bound by the more generous terms of the policy.

While a slip may be used to rectify the policy, it cannot generally be used as evidence in any dispute as to the meaning of policy wording although the terms of the slip may well be relevant to the factual matrix against which the policy will be construed. If the policy is unclear, generally courts seek to ascertain its meaning without reference to the slip (*Youell v Bland Welch and Co Ltd [1992] 2 Lloyd's Rep 127*). However, in certain circumstances, for example where the slip contains a fundamental term of the insurance whereas the policy wording is silent, it may be held that the slip has not in fact superseded the policy wording, as so may be used as evidence of the contract terms (*HIH Casualty and General Insurance Ltd v New Hampshire Insurance Co Ltd [2001] 2 Lloyd's Rep 161*).

Composite nature. A Lloyd's policy, when issued, is, like a slip, a composite contract between the insured and the several syndicates subscribing to the policy. In *Touche Ross & Co v Baker (Colin) [1992] 2 Lloyd's Rep 207*, a Lloyd's liability policy issued to leading firms of accountants provided that if it was not renewed, cover would nevertheless be provided in respect of events which had occurred during the currency of the policy (the 'discovery extension' clause). One underwriter of those subscribing decided not to renew, and argued that he was not bound by the discovery extension clause as that clause could operate only if there had been a collective decision not to renew. The House of Lords held that the discovery extension clause bound each underwriter individually, so that any one under-writer who refused to renew could not evade his obligations under the clause.

Payment obligations at Lloyd's

Premiums

11.08   Marine premiums at Lloyd's are, by custom, payable by the broker rather than by the insured. This is codified in *s 53(1)* of the *Marine Insurance Act 1906*. It is doubtful whether this custom applies to non-marine premiums. The legal basis for this principle is the fiction that the premium has been paid by the insured to the broker, passed on by the broker to the underwriter and then loaned back to the broker by the underwriter. The most significant legal consequence of the rule is that if the insured has actually paid the broker, but the broker has not paid the underwriter (generally because of insolvency), the underwriter must look to the broker and cannot make the insured pay again. If payment has been made by the broker before the insured has himself paid, the broker is entitled to retain possession of the policy by way of lien until the insured has indemnified the broker (*Marine Insurance Act 1906, s 53(2)*).

The strict legal position, as set out above, regarding the Lloyd's broker's personal liability for marine premiums is now only of academic interest. This is because of an agreement reached in October 1997 between the Lloyd's Insurance Brokers' Committee (LIBC), Lloyd's and the Institute of London Underwriters (now called IUA) that insurers would, notwithstanding *s 53(1)* of the *Marine Insurance Act*, not hold brokers responsible for the payment of premiums in the event of a default by the insured (see 5 PREMIUMS).

Losses

11.09   The Lloyd's market operates a net accounting system, under which premiums and losses are paid centrally for each accounting period. An insured is not bound by the practice of crediting losses in an account between Lloyd's underwriters and a Lloyd's broker, unless the insured has express knowledge of the practice or has adopted the transaction. It follows that if the broker becomes insolvent before he has paid the claim, the insured has a right to recover and claim direct from the Lloyd's underwriters. The net accounting system to some extent breaks down when the broker funds to the insured a loss, but subsequently finds that the underwriter relies on a defence to the claim. The broker is under no legal obligation to the insured to make payment, so the payment is usually classified as a gift, which in turn means that there is no basis upon which the broker can recover the payment. It appears that there may be nothing to stop the insured bringing an action against the underwriter despite having received payment from the broker (*Merrett v Capitol Indemnity Corp [1991] 1 Lloyd's Rep 169*). The double recovery in this case was avoided by an undertaking given by the reinsured to pay any recovery to the broker.

Chapter 12
Insurance companies

- The authorisation requirement
- Regulated activities
- Defining what constitutes a contract of insurance
- Consequences of conducting unauthorised insurance business
- Legal and procedural requirements for authorisation by the FSA
- Ongoing supervision

The authorisation requirement

12.01 *Section 19* of the *Financial Services and Markets Act 2000 (FSMA 2000)* provides that no person may carry on (or purport to carry on) a regulated activity in the United Kingdom unless he is an authorised person or an exempt person (what is defined in *FSMA 2000* as the 'general prohibition').

Contravention of the general prohibition is a criminal offence, which can carry an unlimited fine and/or imprisonment for up to two years. It is also an offence under *s 24* of *FSMA 2000* for a person to describe himself (in whatever terms) as an authorised or exempt person or behave, or otherwise hold himself out, in a manner indicating or which is reasonably likely to be understood to indicate, he is authorised or exempt when he is not.

Section 31 of *FSMA 2000* provides that the following categories of people are authorised persons:

(*a*) a person who has permission from the Financial Services Authority (FSA) to carry on one or more regulated activities (a *Part IV permission*);

(*b*) an EEA firm or a Treaty firm qualifying for authorisation under *Schs 3 or 4* to *FSMA 2000*, respectively (Sch 3 relates to so-called EEA Passport Rights under which (amongst other types of financial services business) insurance companies which are headquartered in another EEA State and regulated by the relevant regulator in that EEA State may obtain permission from their regulator to provide services into, or establish a branch in, another EEA State); and

(c)   a person who is otherwise authorised by a provision of, or made under, *FSMA 2000*.

Exempt persons include appointed representatives of authorised persons, to the extent the authorised person has agreed in writing to accept responsibility for the activities of that representative. Also exempt are those specified in an exemption order pursuant to *s 38* of *FSMA 2000*. The *Financial Services and Markets Act 2000 (Exemption) Order 2001 (SI 2001/1201)* (as amended) provides for various exemptions (eg trade unions providing provident benefits or strike benefits are exempt from the general prohibition against effecting or carrying out contracts of insurance).

Section 418 of *FSMA 2000* (as amended), contains five scenarios where a person is 'deemed' to carry on an activity in the UK even if, on the ordinary meaning of the words, he is not. For example, one such scenario is where a company has a head office outside the UK but a regulated activity is carried on from an establishment maintained by it in the UK.

Regulated activities

12.02   *Section 22(1)* of *FSMA 2000* provides that a 'regulated activity' is an 'activity of a specified kind' which is 'carried on by way of business' and relates to an investment of a specified kind.

The *Financial Services and Markets Act 2000 (Regulated Activities) Order 2001 (SI 2001/544)* (as amended) sets out the 'regulated activities' and the 'investments' in relation to which authorisation is required. For an activity to be a regulated activity, it must be carried on in relation to one of the specified investments. 'Rights under a contract of insurance' is a specified investment.

Effecting contracts of insurance as principal and carrying out contracts of insurance as principal are two of the regulated activities prescribed by *SI 2001/544*.

Defining what constitutes a contract of insurance

12.03   There is no exhaustive statutory definition of what constitutes a 'contract of insurance' for the purposes of *SI 2001/544*. The SI, somewhat unhelpfully, defines a 'contract of insurance' as meaning any contract of insurance which is a contract of long-term insurance or a contract of general insurance, and then goes on specifically to include some types of contract which common law has not regarded as contracts of insurance, such as fidelity bonds, performance bonds, administration bonds, bail bonds, customs bonds or similar contracts of guarantee.

Part 1 of Sch 1 of *SI 2001/544* sets out the description of 18 classes of contracts of general insurance for regulatory purposes and *Part II* of that Schedule sets out brief descriptions of nine classes of contracts of long-term insurance for regulatory purposes.

The headings are:

(*a*)   General insurance:

- Accident.
- Sickness.
- Land vehicles.
- Railway rolling stock.
- Aircraft.
- Ships.
- Goods in transit.
- Fire and natural forces.
- Damage to property.
- Motor vehicle liability.
- Aircraft liability.
- Liability of ships.
- General liability.
- Credit.
- Suretyship.
- Miscellaneous financial.
- Legal expenses.
- Assistance.

(*b*)   Long-term insurance:

- Life and annuity.
- Marriage and birth.
- Linked long term.
- Permanent health.
- Tontines.
- Capital redemption.
- Pension fund management.
- Collective insurance etc.
- Social insurance.

Some of the descriptions under the headings are broad, whilst others are very narrow.

It is therefore necessary to consider case law to assist in trying to define a contract of insurance (see 12.04 below).

As a consequence of the lack of a clear statutory definition, the FSA has considerable discretion as to whether a particular business is to be challenged on the ground that it is conducting an unlawful insurance business. The FSA has issued some guidance (in PERG 6) on how it approaches the issue of whether a particular contract is or is not a contract of insurance, although ultimately this is subject to the decision of the courts.

Characteristics of an insurance contract

12.04   Whilst there have been some reported decisions of UK courts addressing the issue of what does or does not constitute a contract of insurance, they are based on the particular facts before them; the courts have been careful not to define conclusively what is and what is not a contract of insurance.

The most widely quoted definition of an insurance contract is that of Channell J in *Prudential Insurance Company v Commissioners of Inland Revenue [1904] 2 KB 658*. In that case, three elements were identified which, if present in a contract, were likely to cause it to be construed as an insurance contract:

(*a*)   it is a contract under which, in return for the making of a payment or payments (generally called premiums) the insured secures some benefit on the occurrence of an event;

(*b*)   that event must be uncertain as to whether it will happen or not, or if the event is inevitable, there must be uncertainty as to when; and

(*c*)   the event must be adverse to the insured (though it is to be noted that cases since have drawn a distinction between indemnity and contingency insurance, for example the event triggering endowment and annuity policies and certain other forms of contingency insurance may not be adverse).

In many cases, if a claim can properly be made under the policy, the benefit receivable by the insured will be a money payment. However, 'payment' can take the form of services to the insured, or the repair or replacement of damaged items.

For instance, in *Department of Trade and Industry v St Christopher Motorists' Association Ltd [1974] 1 All ER 395*, the High Court held that payment in the form of services to the insured (in this case the provision of transport if a driver was disqualified from driving) should be characterised as an insurance contract.

Whilst household insurance policies might offer repair or replacement services, not all repair or replacement contracts are insurance contracts. Contracts under which the provider undertakes to provide periodic maintenance of goods or facilities, whether or not any uncertain or adverse event (in the form of, for example a breakdown or failure) has occurred, are unlikely to be contracts of insurance. Warranties given by manufacturers or retailers in connection with the sale of goods are not generally regarded as insurance contracts; if they were, then most manufacturers and retailers would need to be authorised as insurance companies. The FSA draw a distinction between such manufacturing and retailers warranties (which it recognises will not usually be defined as contracts of insurance) and warranties given by other parties (which it argues will generally be contracts of insurance). The FSA, in PERG 6.7, argue that a warranty given by a seller which is of the same nature as a seller's usual obligations as regards the quality of goods or services of that kind is not a contract of insurance, but that if, for instance, an extended warranty has to be paid for or is provided by third parties, then that is likely to be insurance. That analysis is not accepted by everyone and does not at the time of writing have English case authority to support it.

There are exemptions for certain organisations which confer only benefits in kind which may otherwise be regarded as insurance, for example, art *12* of *SI 2001/ 544* exempts contracts when the primary benefit is the provision of motor vehicle breakdown services generally by employees of the provider.

Sometimes public policy considerations appear to colour the determination of a court in deciding whether or not a particular contract is an insurance contract or not. An example, perhaps, is the case of The *Medical Defence Union Ltd v The Department of Trade [1979] 2 All ER 421*. This case considered whether or not the Medical Defence Union (MDU), which indemnifies doctors against claims alleging professional negligence, was carrying on an insurance business. If the MDU was carrying on insurance business, its members would have had to contribute a substantial capital sum to enable it to meet the capitalisation requirements of the legislation governing insurance companies. It was held that the contracts issued by the MDU were not insurance contracts because the MDU had a discretion, but not an obligation, to provide benefits to a member (although in practice the discretion was always exercised).

Consequences of conducting unauthorised insurance business

12.05　An agreement made by a person in the course of carrying on a regulated activity in breach of the general prohibition will generally be unenforceable against the other party (*s 26* of *FSMA 2000*). The other party is entitled to recover any money paid or transferred by him under the agreement, with compensation for any loss sustained by him as a result.

A person who is authorised with a *Part IV permission* who carries on a regulated activity outside the scope of his permission is not guilty of an offence and the transaction is not void or voidable (*s 20(2)* of *FSMA 2000*).

Legal and procedural requirements for authorisation by the FSA

12.06 The FSA publishes a Handbook of Rules and Guidance. This is divided into over 50 separate manuals or sourcebooks (each of which is divided into chapters) commonly referred to by an acronym – for instance, the Supervision Manual is 'SUP', so 'SUP 3' means chapter 3 of the Supervision Manual and the Perimeter Guidance Manual is PERG. Not all of these manuals are relevant to insurance companies because the FSA also regulates other financial services providers, but most are relevant to insurance companies.

Under *s 41(2)* of *FSMA 2000*, the FSA must, in granting a *Part IV permission*, ensure that the applicant will satisfy, and continue to satisfy, the 'threshold conditions' in relation to all of the regulated activities for which it has, or will have a *Part IV permission*. The threshold conditions are set out in *Sch 6* of *FSMA 2000* and guidance is given on them in COND 2.

Perhaps the most important threshold conditions are: the need for the FSA to be satisfied that if any person has close links to the applicant and that person is subject to any foreign law or enforcement requirement, the FSA's effective supervision of the applicant will not be prevented (as a consequence the FSA generally requires information about all persons owning 10% or more of the equity of the applicant or of any of its parent companies (20% in the case of insurance intermediaries which are not also insurance companies); the need for the applicant to have adequate resources in relation to the activities it is to conduct and the need for the applicant and its senior managers to be fit and proper people who are capable of conducting the business soundly and prudently.

The FSA has six months to make its determination as to whether to authorise an applicant following submission of a completed Application Pack, although this may vary depending on the complexity of the application. The FSA prefers to discuss applications to authorise new insurance companies in draft, prior to their formal submission as applications.

FSMA 2000 confers broad powers on the FSA to determine the procedure for applications and details relating to the granting of permissions. The FSA, on granting the permission, specifies the permitted regulated activity or activities, but may describe them in such manner as it thinks appropriate (*s 42(6)* of *FSMA 2000*). The permission granted will consist of three elements:

(1)   a description of the activities including any limitations;

(2)   the specified investments involved; and

(3)   any requirement to be imposed pursuant to *s 43(1)* of *FSMA 2000*.

Before providing services into another EEA State or establishing a branch of its business in another EEA State application must be made to the FSA for an extension to the *Part IV permission*. This can take up to a month to process in the case of providing services, three months in the case of establishing a branch.

Ongoing supervision

12.07 *FSMA 2000* requires the FSA to 'maintain arrangements designed to enable it to determine whether persons on whom requirements are imposed by or under this Act are complying with them' (*para 6(1)* of *Sch 1* to *FSMA 2000*).

The Supervision Manual (SUP) and the Decision Procedure and Penalties Manual (DEPP) form the regulatory processes part of the Handbook. The FSA relies on a mixture of receiving regular returns from the insurer in prescribed forms, meetings with management and disclosure of other material information from management in a timely manner to maintain its supervision, with an armoury of disciplinary weapons to encourage compliance.

The FSA publishes high level standards, breach of which is likely to lead to disciplinary action against the regulated entity and/or its directors/senior managers. The basic principles are set out in the PRIN section of the FSA Handbook. These state that the authorised entity must:

(*a*)   conduct its business with integrity;

(*b*)   conduct its business with due skill, care and diligence;

(*c*)   take reasonable care to organise and control its affairs responsibly and effectively with adequate risk management systems (the SYSC section of the FSA Handbook sets out more guidance in relation to this);

(*d*)   maintain adequate financial resources;

(*e*)   show proper standards of market conduct;

(*f*)   pay due regard to the interests of its customers and treat them fairly;

(*g*)   pay due regard to the information needs of its customers and communicate in a way which is clear, fair and not misleading;

(*h*)   manage conflicts of interest fairly;

(*j*)   take reasonable care to ensure the suitability of its advice and discretionary decisions for any customer who is entitled to rely upon its judgement;

(*k*)   arrange adequate protection for clients' assets when it is responsible for them;

(*l*)   deal with its regulators in an open and cooperative way; and

(*m*)   disclose to the FSA appropriately anything relating to the organisation of which the FSA would reasonably expect notice.

SUP 10.4.5 specifies numerous management functions (not all of which are relevant to insurance companies) which are 'controlled functions' for the purposes of the FSA's regulation of an authorised person. Every person who holds a controlled function with an authorised person must be individually approved by the FSA as a fit and proper person.

The FSA has wide powers to discipline individuals approved by them who fall short of the standards required by the principles or the rules, including the power to fine them and to issue orders prohibiting them from holding any management function in any FSA regulated entity. A director or senior manager who delays in reporting material breaches of regulatory requirements to the FSA is likely to increase the severity of the sanctions applied against them compared to what would have prevailed if the delay had not occurred.

The prudential business standards with which authorised insurers must comply are to be found in several of sourcebooks within the FSA Handbook, including INSPRU and COBS which relates to conduct of business. Prevention of money laundering is a matter the regulators take very seriously. Failure to maintain and enforce effective anti-money laundering systems and controls can lead to substantial fines and other disciplinary action.

PART 3

The Claim

Chapter 13
Causation

- Proximate cause

- Sequential causes of loss

- Concurrent causes of loss

- Mitigation

- Insured's negligence

- Alternative policy formations

Proximate cause

13.01 The insurer is liable only for those losses proximately caused by an insured peril (*Marine Insurance Act 1906, s 55(2)(a)*), and it is for the insured to prove that his loss was so caused. If the policy is All Risks, meaning that the insured's burden is simply to demonstrate that he has suffered a loss, the insurer can escape liability by demonstrating that the loss was proximately caused by an uninsured peril.

Sequential causes of loss

13.02 Causation is a crucial matter, but it is not possible to lay down any single test for ascertaining the proximate cause of a loss where there has been a series of contributing factors. Each case must turn on its own facts. The most difficulty is occasioned by cases in which there are two operative and interacting events occurring sequentially. The law does not accept that the last event is necessarily the proximate cause of the loss, and a court might take the view that the earlier event was the start of an unbroken chain of events leading to the loss. The cases fall into three general classes: unbroken chain of events, broken chain of events and linked events.

Unbroken chain of events

13.03   In this type of case, the first peril to occur is bound ultimately to lead to a loss, and the occurrence of the second peril is simply the inevitable or other means by which that loss occurs. The position may be illustrated by *Reischer v Borwick [1894] 2 QB 548*, in which a vessel was holed following a collision, and was lost due to the ingress of water. The court held that the proximate cause of the loss was collision, and that the ingress of water was an inevitable consequence of the collision.

Broken chain of events

13.04   Perhaps the best illustrations of this situation are provided by a series of wartime marine cases in which a vessel, seeking to avoid enemy submarines, has deviated from its course and has been lost in bad weather, for example *Yorkshire Dale Steamship Co Ltd Appellants v Minister of War Transport Respondent [1942] AC 691*. In those cases, the proximate cause of loss is clearly perils of the sea, and not war risks.

Linked events

13.05   The most complex cases are those in which the first and second perils are equally efficient in their operation, in the sense that the loss would not have taken place had just one of the perils occurred. The decided cases are all borderline. In *Leyland Shipping Co Ltd, Appellants v Norwich Union Fire Insurance Society, Ltd Respondents [1918] AC 350*, the insured's vessel was holed by a torpedo, and put into the port of Le Havre for repairs. The port authorities refused to allow the vessel to berth, as storms were expected and the authorities feared that the vessel would sink in the port's vicinities. The vessel left port, and was subsequently lost outside the vicinity of the port in a storm. The House of Lords held that the proximate cause of the loss was war risks and not perils of the sea, as the storm had not broken the chain of causation. Similar results were reached in a serious of accident policy cases, of which *Mardorf v Accident Insurance Co [1903] 1 KB 584* is typical. In this case, the insured under an accident policy was accidentally scratched, a wound which became infected and resulted in blood poisoning from which the insured died. The cause of death was held to be the accidental scratch, and not natural causes.

These cases may be contrasted with two other accident policy claims. In *Winspear v The Accident Insurance Company, Limited (1880–81) LR 6 QBD 42*, the insured suffered a fit, which caused him to fall into a river and to drown. It was held that his death was proximately caused by accidental drowning rather than by the natural cause of the fit. A similar decision was reached soon afterwards in *Lawrence v The Accidental Insurance Co (Ltd) (1880–81) LR 7 QBD 216*, where the insured's fit lead to him falling onto a railway line in front of a train.

Concurrent causes of loss

13.06 A loss may be attributable to two events working chronologically along-side each other. Here, the issue is not whether the chain of causation from one event has been broken by the second event, but rather which of the two events is the greater contributor to the loss. This is again a question of fact in every case. It may not always be possible for the court to disentangle the causes, in which case it must conclude that the loss has been proximately caused by two concurrent causes.

Such a finding is of little significance for the insured where the concurrent causes consist of an insured peril and a peril which is not specifically excluded under the policy, as the rule here is that the uninsured peril is disregarded. In *JJ Lloyd Instruments Ltd v Northern Star Insurance Co Ltd [1987] 1 Lloyd's Rep 32*, the insured's vessel, which was unseaworthy, was lost in bad weather. As the vessel was insured under a time policy there was no warranty of seaworthiness under *s 39(1)* of the *Marine Insurance Act 1906*, and the insurers were unable to rely upon *s 39(5)* of the *Marine Insurance Act 1906* (which provides a defence under a time policy where a loss is attributable to seaworthiness) because the insured had not been aware of the unseaworthy state of his vessel (see 34 MARINE INSURANCE). The Court of Appeal was thus faced with a situation in which there were concurrent perils operating: perils of the sea (an insured peril); and unseaworthiness (an uninsured, but not excluded, peril). The insured was held to be able to recover, as he had proved that his loss had been proximately caused by an insured peril.

A finding that a loss has concurrent causes is, however, fatal to the insured's claim if the loss caused by one of those two perils is specifically excluded under the policy. In *Wayne Tank and Pump Co Ltd v Employers Liability Assurance Corporation Ltd [1974] QB 57*, the insured installed into premises, belonging to a third party, equipment for storing and cooling wax. The equipment malfunctioned, causing a disastrous fire for which the insured was held to be liable to the third party on two grounds: (*a*) unsuitable material had been used in the manufacture of the equipment; and (*b*) the insured had failed to carry out proper monitoring tests. The insured's liability policy covered the second of these risks, but specifically excluded 'damage caused by the nature or condition of any goods', the first of the risks. The Court of Appeal held that the proximate cause of the loss was the condition of the equipment, so that the insured was unable to recover. However, the Court of Appeal went on to suggest that, even had it not been possible to distinguish the two causes of loss, thereby rendering them concurrent causes, the insured would also have failed to recover. The reason was that if a loss is caused proximately by the interaction of an insured risk and an excluded risk, the exclusion takes priority.

This principle was applied by the Court of Appeal in *Midland Mainline Ltd v Eagle Star Insurance Co Ltd [2004] 2 Lloyd's Rep 604*. Following a rail disaster which had been caused by a rail fracturing, restrictions were imposed by the rail network operator on other parts of the railway network where it was known the rails were also suffering from stress fatigue. The claimant, a train operating company, had an insurance policy covering business interruption losses, but excluding liability for losses arising from wear and tear. The Court of Appeal held that there were two concurrent causes of the loss, wear and tear and the imposition of emergency speed restrictions, and applied the rule that in cases of concurrent causes any specific exclusion prevailed over the cover. Therefore the insurers could rely upon the exception.

Mitigation

13.07 As a general principle, the insured has a duty to take steps to avoid or mitigate a loss, and within the policy of insurance this obligation generally takes the form of a reasonable care clause. As noted below, such clauses do not have the effect of preventing recovery when mere negligence by the insured has been involved.

Whether or not the insured is under a duty to take steps to avoid a loss, the fact that he has done so may give rise to causation issues. The general principle is that, as long as the insured has acted reasonably, steps taken by him to avert loss by a peril insured against will not prevent recovery, even if the steps taken by the insured result in loss from an uninsured peril. This point was made by Kelly CB in *Stanley v The Western Insurance Co (1867-68) LR 3 Ex 71*:

> 'I agree that any loss resulting from an apparently necessary and *bona fide* effort to put out a fire, whether it be by spoiling the goods by water or throwing the article of furniture out of a window, or even the destroying of a neighbouring house by an explosion for the purpose of checking the progress of flames, in a word, every loss that clearly and proximately results, whether directly or indirectly, from the fire, is within the policy.'

This principle was applied by the Court of Appeal in *Symington & Co v Union Insurance Society of Canton, Ltd (1928) 32 Ll L Rep 287*. In this case a fire broke out at a quay. A quantity of cork was stored on the quay, some of which was doused with water and some of which was thrown into the sea in order to prevent loss by fire. The Court of Appeal held that the water damage to the cork had been proximately caused by fire.

All depends, however, upon the insured having acted reasonably. If the insured, anticipating the occurrence of an insured peril, takes avoidance measures which result in loss by an uninsured peril, the insurer will not be liable if it can be demonstrated that the likelihood of loss from an insured peril was remote in the extreme (see *Kacianoff v China Traders Insurance Co Ltd [1914] 3 KB 1121*).

Insured's negligence

13.08 Negligence by the insured has a neutral effect on his ability to recover. This is stated specifically by *s 55(2)(a)* of the *Marine Insurance Act 1906*:

'[the insurer] is liable for any loss proximately caused by a peril insured against, even though the loss would not have happened but for the misconduct or negligence of the master or crew.'

The effect of this provision is that negligence is not regarded as a peril in its own right, but merely as the method by which a peril can be brought into existence. The only question, therefore, is whether the peril occasioned by the insured's negligence is an insured or excluded peril. The point is illustrated by *Harris v Poland [1941] 1 KB 462*, in which the insured, for safety reasons, hid her jewellery in a fire grate. She subsequently forgot what she had done, and lit a fire as a result of which the jewellery was lost. The judge, allowing recovery under her householder's policy, held that the loss had been caused by the insured peril of fire, and the fact that the loss by fire had resulted from the insured's negligence did not defeat the claim. The position is not affected by a clause requiring the insured to take reasonable care of property, as such a clause has been held to mean no more than that there can be no recovery where the insured has deliberately or recklessly caused the loss.

As a review of recent cases demonstrates, there is an implied duty on every insured at common law to take reasonable care for his property, and to act as though he was uninsured. Whether an insured has deliberately or recklessly caused the loss will depend upon the factual circumstances of each case. The following cases demonstrate the different factual circumstances that the court will need to consider.

Sinnott v Municipal General Insurance [1989] CLY 2051: The claimant was moving property with a total value of £3,000 from her flat to a house some miles away. She stopped in a city area she knew to have a high incidence of car theft and left her car unattended for 30 minutes while she visited a library. The car was stolen (with the contents) and never recovered. The insurers argued that the claimant had failed to take 'reasonable precautions'. It was held that the claimant was entitled to recover her insured loss. It would have been otherwise if she had left the goods on view in the car (they were in the boot) or if there had been an express clause that such goods were not to be left an unattended motor car.

Devco Holder Ltd and Burrows & Paine Ltd v Legal & General Assurance Society Ltd [1993] 2 Lloyd's Rep 567: The claimant company purchased a Ferrari and insured it with the defendant against theft. One of the claimant's employees left the car temporarily unattended in a station car park, with the keys in the ignition, while he went to his office on the first floor of the building opposite the station. The car was stolen and damaged. It was a term of the policy that the claimant take all reasonable steps to protect the car against loss or damage. The question was whether reasonable steps had been taken. The judge found that the employee had not taken reasonable steps by leaving the car unlocked in a public place with the key in the ignition deliberately, rather than inadvertently. The defendant appealed.

It was held, in dismissing the appeal, that (i) by deliberately leaving the key in the ignition of a car attractive to thieves, the employee deliberately courted a danger in the breach of the condition; (ii) there was a breach even though the employee underestimated or did not contemplate the risk of theft or thought the absence from the car park would be short; and (iii) (*obiter*) the position might have been different if the keys had been left inadvertently.

Sofi v Prudential Assurance Co Ltd [1993] 2 Lloyd's Rep 559: The insured had a household policy covering theft and a travel policy. Both obliged him to take 'all reasonable steps to safeguard … property'. The claimant decided to take jewellery valued at £42,000 away on holiday as he had been burgled at home. After a discussion with members of his party, the claimant decided to leave the jewellery locked in the glove compartment of a car for 15 minutes while visiting Dover Castle, the car being in view for most of that time. The car was ransacked and the jewellery and all of the claimant's suitcases were stolen. The insurer argued that the claimant failed to take reasonable steps and should have taken the jewellery with him or left someone in the car. The judge found in favour of the claimant and the insurer appealed.

It was held, in dismissing the appeal, that (i) the burden was on the insurer to prove a breach of the condition; (ii) the correct test was to consider the recklessness on the part of the claimant and there was no distinction between property and liability insurance; and (iii) in applying the test, it was relevant to take into account the value of the goods at risk, but the claimant was not reckless as he had considered the security position and was not away from the car for a long period.

Alternative policy formations

13.09   The principle of causation is a default rule, and can be ousted by contrary wording. The policy may, for example, state that the insurer is liable for loss by a particular peril only if that peril is the 'direct and sole' or an 'independent' cause of the loss. This means that the operation of any other peril, even in a minor role, will deprive the insured of an indemnity. The same will follow if the insurer is stated to be discharged from liability where an excluded peril has indirectly caused the loss. Both possibilities are illustrated by *Jason v Batten (1930) Ltd [1969] 1 Lloyd's Rep 281*, in which the insured, who suffered from heart disease, was involved in a motor accident. Six days later, he suffered a heart attack, which disabled him for a year. The insured claimed under his accident policy, which stated that he could recover for disablement sustained in any accident, and independently from all other causes, but that the insurers were not liable for disablement directly or indirectly caused by pre-existing physical defect. Fisher J held for the insurers: while it was the case that the insured's heart attack would not have occurred without the accident, the insured's disablement was not caused independently by the accident, and in any event, the insured's latent medical problem had been an indirect cause of his disablement within the meaning of the exclusion. The advantages to the insurer of a widely-phased exclusion are also demonstrated by *Coxe v Employers' Liability Assurance Corporation, Ltd [1916] 2 KB 629*, where the insured's death resulted from being hit by a train during a blackout enforced under wartime regulations. The insurers were held not to be liable under the policy, which excluded death caused directly or indirectly by war risks.

Chapter 14
Claims

- Notification of claims
- Proof of loss
- Fraudulent claims
- Limitation

Notification of claims

14.01   The simple existence of a policy of insurance to cover a particular type of loss does not mean that payment under the policy automatically follows upon the event of the loss occurring. Having issued the policy, the insurer is likely to be oblivious to the subject matter of the policy, and remain so unless and until the insured notifies the insurer that he suffered a loss in respect of which he believes he has cover under the policy.

If the insured fails to give proper notice of loss to the insurer, then the insurer may be prejudiced by being unable to respond under the policy to the loss. Can the insurer confirm that the policy covered the loss? Is the insurer able to investigate the circumstances in which the loss is alleged to have occurred? Can the loss be properly quantified? Can the insurer be satisfied that the insured is complying with his duty to act in good faith? Is it a fraudulent claim?

Most policies stipulate the manner and time within which a loss is to be notified to the insurer. If the notice clause is a condition precedent to the insurers' liability, breach of its terms will entitle the insurer to refuse to pay the claim, even if there is no actual prejudice to the insurer. If the clause is a bare condition, then, depending on the wording of the clause itself, the insurer may still be liable to pay the claim even though there has been a breach by the insured.

Unless expressly stated in the policy as a requirement, notification of a claim to the insurer may be given verbally and by someone other than the insured. While notice may be given to an agent of the insurer duly authorised to receive it, notice to the insured's broker does not amount to notice to the insurer, as the broker is the agent of the insured.

Time for giving notice

14.02   Notice of loss provisions tend to fall into three categories.

(*a*)   Provisions under which the insured is required to give immediate notice of loss. If the provision is a condition precedent to liability, an insured who delays in any way in giving notice under this type of claim will lose his right to claim. The cases are clear that the insured's obligation is absolute, and is not excused by events beyond his control. In *Re Williams and Thomas and Lancashire & Yorkshire Insurance Co [1902] 19 TLR 82*, the insured's obligation was to give notice of any accident causing injury to a third party. An accident occurred, but the injury to the third party did not become manifest for some seven weeks, at which point notice of loss was given. It was held that the insured had failed to comply with his notice obligation. However, conditions precedent such as this are extremely rare today.

(*b*)   Provisions under which the insured is required to give notice of loss or of an event likely to lead to a loss within a specified period, generally seven or fourteen days of the loss occurring. Once again, if the provision is a condition precedent, the insured cannot successfully plead any excuse for failing to notify. In *Cassel v Lancashire & Yorkshire Insurance Co (1885) 1 TLR 495*, the insured under a policy against accidents was required to give notice to the insurer within 14 days of the occurrence of an event giving rise to a claim against the insured. An accident to the third party occurred, but it did not become clear for some nine months that the third party had suffered injury. The insured was held to be too late to seek an indemnity despite the surrounding circumstances.

(*c*)   Provisions under which the insured is required to give notice of loss as soon as is reasonably practicable. This type of clause is much more generous, and even if it is a condition precedent to liability, permits the insured some leeway if for good reason the claim could not be presented immediately. Such a case was *Verelst's Administratrix v Motor Union Insurance Co Ltd [1925] 2 KB 137*, in which a claim on an accident policy was allowed even though it was not made for a year after the insured's death, as the existence of the policy had not been known to the insured's representatives until that time.

In consumer cases, the Statements of Insurance Practice prevent the insurer from relying on an immediate or fixed-term notification clause, and provides that the insured must be given a reasonable time in which to make a claim (see 41 REGULATION OF SALES OF INSURANCE PRODUCTS regarding the Statements of Insurance Practice).

Proof of loss

14.03   In the same way that the insurer needs to know of a loss occurring, the insurer also needs to know the nature and extent of the loss that has to be met. Accordingly, the policy will normally stipulate in what manner and what particulars of loss are to be notified to the insurer, usually requiring the completion of a claim form. The policy will require the insured to provide particulars of the loss with such detail as is reasonably practicable, and he must do so within the time specified in the policy.

While the insurer is entitled to seek more detailed information about the circumstances of the loss or the quantification of the claim, in order to decide whether or not he is obliged to indemnify under the policy, the insurer cannot make unreasonable demands. The insurer must limit the enquiry to information that appears to be relevant to the claim, in which event the insured must comply with the request, even though the information supplied subsequently is found to have been irrelevant. This is demonstrated by *Welch v Royal Exchange Assurance [1939] 1 KB 294*, in which the insured refused to provide information concerning certain bank accounts in his mother's name. These ultimately proved to have no connection with the loss, but the insured was nevertheless held to have failed to comply with a condition precedent in the policy.

In certain situations, for example where the insured has lost documentary evidence that would substantiate his claim, the insurer may require the insured to complete a Statutory Declaration detailing his loss and entitlement to claim. However, such a Statutory Declaration does not override the insured's duty to prove his loss in any subsequent trial should the insurer continue to refuse to meet the claim. In the alternative, the insurer can request an indemnity from the insured or claimant.

In relation to life insurance, the rules in respect of proof of title are the same as for other forms of policy. However, in situations where there is uncertainty as to survivorship, all the evidence of the circumstances that is available should be submitted to either a registrar or district registrar at the earliest opportunity. The registrar or district registrar can then decide whether a grant of representation may be issued on that evidence or whether further enquiries should be made (see *Practice Direction (PDAD: Commorientes Grants) [1964] 1 WLR 1027*). Therefore, for example, the insurer may, within a reasonable time, require a post-mortem examination of the deceased (*Ballantine v Employers Insurance Co of Great Britain [1893] 21 R 305*).

Waiver of breach of condition precedent

14.04   An insurer may lose the right to rely upon a breach of condition precedent if his conduct has been such as to lead the insured to believe that the claim will be paid, and the insured has in some way relied upon the insurer's conduct. In all cases there can be only be waiver if the insurer is aware of the insured's breach. An insurer who proceeds with arrangements to deal with the insured's claim may potentially be treated as having waived the breach, whereas an insurer who does nothing while considering his position will not be taken to have waived the breach (*Allen v Robles [1969] 3 All ER 154*).

Burden of proof

14.05   When a claim is made by an insured against an insurer, a number of issues may be in dispute between them. They may relate to the circumstances of the loss, the amount of the loss or the possibility that the insured has broken a term of the contract. The law has developed a series of rules for determining which party bears the burden of proving these respective issues. The general principle is that he who alleges must prove, so that the insured must prove his loss and the insurer must prove any exception or fraud by the insured, but there are various special cases where the burden is reversed.

The standard of proof required is the usual civil standard of the balance of probabilities. However, if the insurer is alleging fraud on the insured's part, this will have, in practice, to be demonstrated to a higher standard approaching the criminal 'beyond reasonable doubt' standard.

Proof of loss by an insured peril

General rule

14.06 The insured bears the burden of proving that he has suffered a loss and that the loss was attributable to a peril insured against under the policy. Unless this can be done, there is no possible claim. If, therefore, the insured has suffered a loss but cannot demonstrate how it has occurred, his claim will fail. This possibility is most likely in the context of marine insurance, where a vessel is lost without explanation. This situation faced the House of Lords in *Rhesa Shipping Co SA v Edmunds (The Popi M) [1985] 2 All ER 712*, and their Lordships ruled that the insured could not recover without proving that an insured peril had occurred. The House further determined that, in such cases, the court is not required to adjudicate between possible explanations in order to determine which of them is the least implausible and for this to be taken as the likely cause of the loss. In *The Popi M*, the insured relied upon evidence that submarines had been seen in the area, and that the most likely explanation for the loss was caused by accidental collision. The insurers asserted by way of defence that the vessel was probably unseaworthy. As there was no evidence for either argument, the claim was dismissed. The position is that unless the insured can produce an explanation which on the balance of probabilities is correct, he must lose. The House of Lords did concede that it is possible that the insured might be able to demonstrate that an insured peril has caused the loss by showing that all other possible causes could not have operated, but the prospects of success by elimination are not great, simply because no evidence is available (*Lamb Head Shipping Co Ltd v Jennings (The Marel) [1994] 1 Lloyd's Rep 624*).

At this stage in the process, the insured does not have to prove that the loss was accidental and unforeseen, as it is enough for the insured to show that a loss has taken place. If the insurer wishes to allege that the insured was in some way implicated in the loss, by fraud, and the insurer's response to the claim is that the entire loss was a figment of the insured's imagination, then the insured is required to prove that the loss actually occurred. To this extent the insured bears the burden of disproving fraud at the outset. An illustration is the Canadian decision in *Shakur v Pilot Insurance Co (1991) 73 DLR (4th) 337*, where the insured asserted that she had been mugged and that jewellery which she had been carrying had been stolen. The court ruled that the onus was on the insured to prove that a mugging had taken place and, as she was unable to do so, her claim failed.

All Risks insurance

14.07 Under an All Risks policy, the insured need only prove that he has suffered a loss, without having to point to the precise event which has caused that loss (see 24 ALL RISKS INSURANCE).

Fraudulent claims

14.08 If the insured submits a fraudulent claim to the insurer, the insurer has the right at common law to reject the claim while maintaining the policy in force, or he may simply treat the contract as terminated for breach of contract by the insured. Most policies contain provisions governing fraudulent claims, conferring one or both of these rights upon the insurer independently of the insurer's common law rights.

Fraudulent claims can take many forms, of which the following are the most common.

(*a*)   *Deliberate destruction of the subject matter by the insured.*

(*b*)   *An exaggerated claim by the insured.* This is the most frequent problem faced by insurers but one where the courts have singularly failed to give clear guidance. Overvaluation of a loss is not evidence of fraudulent conduct on the part of the insured, whereas if the overvaluation is particularly gross or excessive, having regard to all the circumstances of the case, then that may constitute fraud. Fraud relating to just part of a claim will vitiate the entire claim. In *Lek v Mathews [1927-28] 29 Ll L Rep 141*, the insured claimed for the loss of his stamp collection, including for the loss of some stamps which he did not own. The court held that the entire claim was fraudulent, even thought the insured's apparent purpose was to ensure that he did not suffer a financial loss on the stamps which were actually lost.

The difficulty for the insurer in establishing that a claim is fraudulent rather than merely inadvertently exaggerated by the insured was recognised by the Court of Appeal in *Orakpo v Barclays Insurance Services Co Ltd [1995] LRLR 443*. The court recognised that where an insured places an inflated value on the claim, and provided that nothing is misrepresented or concealed, his actions may be regarded as no more than an legitimate starting point for negotiations with the insurer or the insurers appointed loss adjuster.

(*c*)   *Fraudulent description of the circumstances of the loss.* This will prevent proper investigation by the insurer. In *Cox v Orion Insurance Co Ltd [1982] RTR 1*, the insured claimed that his vehicle had been stolen and damaged, when in fact the damage had been caused by the insured himself while intoxicated. The insured's claim was held to be fraudulent even though, had the truth as to the circumstances of the loss been disclosed to the insurers, they would have been liable.

A claim which is not fraudulent, but which involves false statements, cannot be rejected. A merely innocent misrepresentation does not give the insurer the right to reject the claim or to terminate the contract (*Bucks Printing Press Ltd v Prudential Assurance Co [2000] CLY 880*).

Proof of fraud

14.09 Any defence of fraud must, other than in the exceptional case of perils of the sea, be made out on the basis of evidence produced by the insurer. As an allegation of fraud is also an allegation of potential criminal offence by the insured (seeking to obtain money by deception or, possibly, criminal damage) the insurer must demonstrate fraud according to the criminal burden of proof (*Broughton Park Textiles (Salford) Ltd v Commercial Union Assurance Co Ltd [1987] 1 Lloyd's Rep 194*). There may nevertheless be a number of indications that the loss was brought about by the insured's connivance. These will include:

(*a*)   over-insurance;

(*b*)   inability of the insured to produce proof of loss (in the case of a business, this will often mean evidence of stock in trade);

(*c*)   the insured's insolvency or urgent need for funds;

(*d*)   loss occurring in unexplained circumstances;

(*e*)   failure by the insured to make any inquiries into the circumstances of the loss; and

(*f*)   refusal by the insured of assistance (eg in the case of a stranded vessel, failing to take advantage of the offer of salvage).

Limitation

The Limitation Act 1980

14.10 The *Limitation Act 1980* provides that an action for breach of contract is to be brought, by the issue of a writ, within six years of the date of breach. An action on an insurance contract is treated by the law as one for breach of contract, and the breach of contract is deemed to be the loss itself.

Consequently, in the case of a life, marine or property policy, the insured has six years from the date of his loss to bring an action against the insurer. It is important to stress that time begins to run at this early date, and not at any later dated at which the insurer refuses to pay (*Bank Of America National Trust & Savings Association v Christmas (The Kyriaki) [1993] 1 Lloyd's Rep 137*). The insured must, therefore, disregard events taking place after the loss should it be necessary for proceedings to be commenced.

As far as liability is concerned, the insured's loss occurs when he has been found to be liable to a third party. The six-year limitation period will thus commence when there is a judgment or award against the insured, or when a settlement is reached with the third party (*London Steamship Owners Mutual Insurance Association Ltd v Bombay Trading Co Ltd (The Felicie) [1990] 2 Lloyd's Rep 21*). There may have been prior negotiations between the insurer and the insured in the course of which the insurer has indicated that it does not intend to indemnify the insured in the event that the insured is found to be liable to the third party. The position here is that the insurer's mere denial of liability does not start the limitation period running, although if the insured informed the insurer that he regards the insurer as in breach of contract the limitation period will begin to run there and then. If, therefore, the insured under a liability policy wishes to preserve his six-year limitation period running from the date at which he is found liable, he must refrain from acknowledging any earlier breach of contract by the insurer (*Lefevre v White [1990] 1 Lloyd's Rep 569*).

Contractual limitation periods

14.11 Some types of policy substitute a lesser contractual limitation period for the statutory six years. In *Walker v Pennine Insurance Co [1980] 2 Lloyd's Rep 156*, a motor policy provided that the insured had to commence an action against the insurer within twelve months from the date on which the insurer denied the insured's claim. The clause was enforced against the insured, and it was held to be irrelevant that at the date of the insurer's denial of liability, the injured third party had not obtained judgment against the insured. The insured was, therefore, in the unfortunate position of having time running against him, and potentially expiring, before he could know whether or not there was a successful claim against him.

The insurer's obligation to pay

14.12 The insurer's obligation to make payment arises as soon as the insured's loss occurs as that is the date on which the insurer is deemed to be in breach of contract. Any delay by the insurer in making payment is not, therefore, a further breach of contract in respect of which additional damage can arise (*Ventouris v Mountain (The Italia Express) (No 3) [1992] 2 Lloyd's Rep 281*). Instead, the insured will be entitled to interest for late payment, and this will generally be calculated to run from the date at which the insurer, acting reasonably, would have made payment. In exceptional cases, the insured may also be entitled to damages to compensate him for the distress caused to him in consequence of the insurer's delay.

Payments in respect of assigned policies

14.13 As a result of the *Policies of Assurance Act 1867* and *s 136* of the *Law of Property Act 1925*, it is possible for the benefit of a life insurance policy to be assigned at law. If an assignment fails as a legal assignment, it may still operate as a valid equitable assignment. A legal assignment gives the assignee the right to sue for the debt at law, and therefore the ability to give the company good legal discharge, without having to join the assignor. Furthermore, the whole or part of any proceeds of an insurance policy are also assignable in equity. An equitable assignment gives the equitable assignee, either with the consent of the insured, the right to sue the insurer in the name of the insured or, without such consent, the right to join the insured as a joint defendant in an action against the insurer.

Payments in respect of policies under trust

14.14 If an express trust has been created, either of a policy or alternatively of the payments under a policy, the beneficiary should invite the trustee who contracted under the policy to carry out the trust in his favour. If the trustee refuses to hand over insurance money to the beneficiary, the beneficiary may sue the trustee for the money. If a trustee refuses to sue the insurer to recover the money due, the beneficiary is 'entitled to sue in his own name in presence of the trustee, whom he may make a defendant' (*Royal Exchange Assurance v Hope [1928] 1 Ch 179*).

Chapter 15
Valuation of Loss

- Loss
- Indemnity
- Valued policies
- Unvalued policies
- Insurance on a 'reinstatement' basis
- Late payment by the insurer
- Restrictions on recovery
- The insurer's right of salvage
- Reinstatement

Loss

General meaning of 'loss'

15.01 Most contracts of insurance are contracts of indemnity, which means that the insured must prove that he has suffered a loss in order to substantiate a claim (for the burden of proving loss, see 14 CLAIMS, and for assessing the value of a loss see 15.05 et seq below). A loss may be either total or partial, and in the case of property may take the form either of damage to or deprivation of possession of the property. Marine insurance law, by way of contrast to all other forms of property insurance, recognises an intermediate form of loss, known as constructive total loss (see 34 MARINE INSURANCE). A constructive total loss is something less than a total loss of the property, but which permits the insured to recover the full insurable value of the subject matter on a total loss basis where the property is either damaged beyond economic repair or where the property has been seized by a third party and is unlikely to be returned within a reasonable time.

Loss of possession of property

15.02 In marine insurance, an insured who has been deprived of use or possession of his property by the act of a third party – often in the form of seizure of property or arrest of a vessel – can frequently claim for constructive total loss of the property. In non-marine insurance this possibility does not exist, and the insured must demonstrate a total loss. A number of different situations might arise.

(a)   The insured's property has disappeared without explanation and cannot be found on reasonable search. Here there is clearly a loss. For example, in *Holmes v Payne [1930] 2 KB 301*, the insured's necklace went missing and she was paid by the insurers for its loss. Interestingly, the necklace was subsequently found in the lining to her cloak, but it was held by the court that the insurers were entitled only to claim the necklace and not to reclaim their payment. This was because if the insured item is missing and a reasonable time had elapsed to allow for a diligent search and that search has failed to recover the item, then it may properly be said to be lost as recovery of the item appears uncertain.

(b)   The insured's property has been stolen by persons unknown. Even though there is the theoretical prospect of recovery, because a thief cannot obtain or pass on good title to the property, the attitude taken by the insurance industry, and endorsed by the insurance ombudsman, is that goods which have been stolen are lost if their whereabouts cannot be ascertained after reasonable efforts, subject to the insurer's right of salvage if the goods are ultimately returned. Also see *Webster v General Accident Fire and Life Assurance Corporation Limited [1953] 1 QB 520*, in which it was held that a car passed to an auctioneer for sale on the purchaser's behalf, but which the auctioneer purported to sell on his own behalf, had been 'lost' because the insured had taken all reasonable steps to recover it and, having taken all reasonable steps, recovery had not been achieved and was uncertain.

(c)   The insured's property has been seized by a third party who has refused to return it. In *London and Provincial Leather Processors v Hudson [1939] 2 KB 724*, the insured sent skins to a firm in Germany to be processed. The German firm entrusted some of these skins to a subcontractor. The German firm became insolvent and the skins were retained by the subcontractor as security for sums owed to it by the German firm. This was held to be a loss of the skins, even though their whereabouts was known.

(d)   The insured's property is in safe hands but the insured cannot obtain possession of it. This was the situation in *Moore v Evans [1918] AC 185*, where pearls sent from England to potential customers in Europe were insured under a goods in transit policy, but on the outbreak of war were deposited for safekeeping with a bank in Brussels to protect them from seizure by the German authorities. The House of Lords held that the pearls were not lost, even though the insured was deprived of the use of them for four years. Equivalent facts in marine insurance would plainly have amounted to a constructive total loss.

(e)   In certain cases it may not be immediately apparent that the possibility of recovery of an insured item is subject to a 'mere chance'. Whether or not there is an uncertainty as to recovery may require a 'wait and see' period which is discussed in *Scott v The Copenhagen Reinsurance (UK) Ltd [2003] EWCA Civ 688*, where a British Airways aircraft was stranded in Iraq when war broke out in 1991 and subsequently destroyed by bombing. The court said that the 'wait and see' cases in their real sense refer to the situation where property cannot immediately be said to have been lost, but the insured has been deprived of it in circumstances which are subject to a process of development and change. The process of development and change may indicate that the prospects of recovery are uncertain. As in that case where the aircraft was subsequently blown up the development of circumstances determined what was originally not immediately apparent as a loss. The 'wait and see' test might also refer to the emergence of evidence which impacts upon the assessment of the probabilities of recovery. Thus, where a car is taken without the owner's consent, if it is discovered that the car was taken by a joy rider instead of a thief the probability may be that it will soon be found and recovered.

The defrauded insured

15.03   An insured may be tricked by fraud into giving possession of his property to a third party, who absconds with the property. The insured is *prima facie* entitled to recover even if he was negligent in his conduct, but a further question may arise as to whether there has been a 'loss' in such circumstances.

The situation must be considered where the insured has been induced to sell his property to a third party in return for what proves to be a stolen or otherwise worthless cheque. In *Eisinger v General Accident Fire and Life Corporation Ltd [1955] 2 All ER 897*, the court ruled that an insured who had exchanged his car for a cheque which was subsequently dishonoured had lost not the car, but rather the proceeds of the sale, the latter not being insured under the policy. This decision is inconsistent with a later decision of the Court of Appeal, *Dobson v General Accident Fire and Life Corporation plc [1989] 3 All ER 927*, where the insured sold jewellery to a third party who paid by means of a stolen cheque. The policy covered 'loss by theft' and the Court of Appeal ruled that, as what had occurred had amounted to 'theft' (see 27 BUILDINGS AND PROPERTY INSURANCE), the insured was entitled to recover. It was not suggested to the Court of Appeal that there had been no 'loss'. If, in the case of fraud, the insured's policy covers theft, the *Eisinger* decision would appear to have been superseded by that of *Dobson*.

Indemnity

15.04   Contracts of insurance confer upon the insured the right to receive a sum of money on the happening of an uncertain event. This is subject to the common law principle of indemnity, under which the insured is entitled to recover at most a sum equivalent to the amount which he has lost by reason of the happening of the uncertain event. Not all insurance contracts are indemnity contracts. Life and accident policies fall into this excluded category, on the basis that it is not possible to calculate the value of a life or a limb. The amount recoverable under a life or accident policy is, therefore, the amount agreed between the parties.

Property and other indemnity policies may be written on a valued or unvalued basis. If the policy is valued, the parties agree the insurable value of the subject matter, so that in the event of loss the insurer is liable for the agreed value or the relevant part of the agreed value. If the policy is unvalued, it will be necessary for a calculation of the amount actually lost to be made. The use of valued policies for the most part eliminates post-loss disputes as to the measure of indemnity, and such policies are common on items which have no readily ascertainable market value. Policies on unique items such as works of art and jewellery are often valued, as are the vast majority of marine policies.

Valued policies

Valuation

15.05   The value of the subject matter agreed between the parties for the purposes of the policy is deemed to be conclusive (*Marine Insurance Act 1906, s 27(3)* and, *inter alia*, *Irving v Manning and Anderson [1847] 1 HLC 287*). It is rarely appropriate for the insurer to contest the agreed valuation once a loss has occurred, as the premium has been paid on the basis of that valuation. There are nevertheless exceptional situations in which an excessive valuation may be relevant.

It has been said that if the insured has warranted that the subject matter is of a certain value, and this proves to be false, the insurer may apparently rely upon the breach of warranty as discharging him from liability irrespective of the small amount of any discrepancy. However, note the Court of Appeal's decision in *Economides v Commercial Assurance Co plc [1998] 1 QB 587*, in which it was held that a representation of belief or opinion as to the value of property to be insured need only be made honestly – there is no requirement of reasonable grounds for the belief or opinion. That said, however, there must be some basis for the representation before it can be said to have been made honestly. This decision has subsequently been applied in a commercial context in *Eagle Star Insurance Co Ltd v Games Video Co (GVC) SA, the 'Game Boy' [2004] 1 Lloyd's Rep 238* and *Rendall v Combined Insurance Co of America [2005] Lloyd's Rep IR 732*.

If the agreed valuation proves to be wildly excessive, to the extent that there is good reason to presume fraud, the insurer may be able to plead that there has been a misrepresentation of a material fact from the outset, entitling him to set the policy aside. The leading authority is *Ionides v Pender [1874] LR 9 QB 531*, where a cargo which had cost £8,000 was insured for £16,500. The insured's stated purpose was to insure against loss of profits on resale. There was evidence, though, that whilst profits as high as 30% were conceivable, anything higher than that would render the risk speculative and this should have been disclosed. The excessive estimation of profits had not been disclosed and the policy was therefore voidable for non-disclosure.

See also *Eagle Star Insurance Co Ltd v Games Video Co (GVC) SA, the 'Game Boy' [2004] 1 Lloyd's Rep 238* in which the vessel was insured for $1.8m but which, due to it's condition, only had a value of $100,000. This overvaluation was found to be material. The underwriting expert for the insured gave evidence that an overvaluation was only material if it was extreme. However, Simon J accepted that an overvaluation 'in multiples' was also material and Insurers were entitled to avoid for misrepresentation as to the value of the vessel.

An insured who insures property for the price paid for it by him cannot be guilty of misrepresentation if he insures for that amount, even though the price was excessive (*Inversiones Manria SA v Sphere Drake Insurance Co plc, The Dora [1989] 1 Lloyd's Rep 69*).

Total loss under a valued policy

15.06   Total loss under a valued policy is determined strictly in accordance with the agreed valuation. If the property has been insured for its full value, the insured is entitled to the full value. If the property has been insured for a sum less than the full value, the insurer is liable only for the agreed amount.

Partial loss under a valued policy

15.07   Where there has been a partial loss, the amount recoverable is again calculated in accordance with the agreed value. This will depend, however, upon whether the insured has insured for the full agreed value or a lesser sum and whether the policy is or is not subject to average (see 15.08 – 15.09 below).

Valued policy not subject to average

15.08   Under a valued policy not subject to average, the insured recovers that proportion of the agreed value of the subject matter which the amount lost bears to the true value. In *Elcock v Thomson [1949] 2 KB 755*, a building with an agreed value of £106,850, and insured for that amount, was damaged to the extent of 30%. The insured was held to be entitled to recover 30% of the agreed value and so recovered £32,055. This was so despite the court's conclusion that the true value of the building had been only £18,000 before the fire, so that the insured's actual loss was a mere £5,400.

If the insured is insured for the full agreed value, the position is governed by the *Elcock v Thomson* principle. By contrast, the insured may have deliberately insured the property for a sum less than the agreed value. If the policy is not subject to average, the fact of its underinsurance makes no difference to the *Elcock v Thomson* principle except that the insured value operates as a ceiling on recovery. Thus:

(a)   if property with an agreed value of £200,000 is insured for £100,000 and suffers a 50% loss, the insured is entitled, in accordance with *Elcock v Thomson*, to recover £100,000 whatever the actual cost of reinstatement or repairs might be; and

(b)   if property with an agreed value of £200,000 is insured for £100,000 and suffers a 75% loss, the insured can recover only £100,000 as that is the maximum sum insured under the policy.

Valued policy subject to average

15.09   If a valued policy is subject to average, the insured is deemed to be his own insurer for the uninsured proportion of the loss. The parties are deemed to have jointly insured the subject matter. For example, suppose that property with an agreed value of £100,000 is insured for £100,000 and suffers 25% damage. In these circumstances, the insured recovers £25,000, as the insurer has accepted 100% of the risk. Average does not apply.

By contrast, suppose that property with an agreed value of £100,000 is insured for £80,000 and suffers 25% damage. The loss is £25,000 but this must be divided between the insurer and the insured in accordance with their respective proportions as joint insurers, so that the insurer pays £20,000 (80%) and the insured bears a loss of £5,000 (20%).

Unvalued policies

Valuation

15.10   The insured under an unvalued policy may be required to state a valuation of the property to the insurer even though the valuation is irrelevant to the sum recoverable, as this is determined by the value at the date of the loss. The value will, however, normally be relevant in fixing the insurer's maximum liability under the policy and forms the basis for the calculation of the premium. It will rarely be a material fact, for utmost good faith purposes, for the insured to overstate the value of the subject matter, as the insured will not be able to recover any more than his actual loss and the main consequence is that the insured has paid a superfluous premium. An overvaluation which is material for the purposes of a valued policy may, therefore, not be material for the purposes of an unvalued policy. However, if the sum stated is grossly excessive and points towards potential fraud on the insured's part, the policy may be regarded as voidable. In *Parker & Heard v Generali Assicurazioni SpA, unreported, 1988*, goods worth £38,000 were insured for £200,000 (5.5 times the real value) but this was held not to be excessive. The case of *Williams v Atlantic Assurance Co Ltd [1933] 1 KB 81* is an exceptional case: a valuation of £8,000 in respect of goods worth £250 (32 times the real value) was held to be sufficient to allow the insurer to avoid the contract.

Total loss under an unvalued policy

Valuing the insured's loss: buildings

15.11   Under an unvalued policy, the sum insured under the policy is normally the maximum amount which may be recovered in respect of a loss. The sum which is recoverable will, subject to that ceiling, depend upon the actual amount of the insured's loss. This is determined by the value of the insured property immediately prior to the loss. The method of determining the value may vary according to the intentions of the insured and so the basis of the calculation may vary from case to case. A good example would be a restaurant being operated in ornate Victorian premises in a busy city centre. If the building is totally destroyed, the insured's loss may be calculated on one of three assumptions.

(a) The value of the building to the insured was its uniquely ornate construction and décor. Here, the insured will be entitled to recover the cost of reinstating the building in more or less its original form (*reinstatement cost*).

(b) The value of the building to the insured was its city centre location and its actual appearance was of marginal significance. In such a case, the insured's indemnity is to be calculated on the provision of a *modern equivalent cost* building.

(c) The insured had, prior to the loss, evidenced an intention to sell the building. Here, the value of the building to the insured is its investment worth and not its physical appearance or location. The insured's loss will, therefore, be determined in accordance with *market value*. This is likely to be a sum less than both reinstatement cost and modern equivalent cost.

Reinstatement cost is the appropriate measure where a building's particular features are the reason for the insured's occupation of the building. In the case of a domestic dwelling of unique characteristics, this is almost certain to be the case. In the case of commercial premises all will depend upon the evidence. In *Reynolds and Anderson v Phoenix Assurance Co Ltd [1978] 2 Lloyd's Rep 440*, the insured purchased for £18,000 an old maltings, which he used for the storage of grain. The building was insured for £628,000 and was destroyed by fire. The cost of reinstating the maltings in their original condition was £250,000, while the cost of erecting a modern equivalent building was £50,000. The trial judge was persuaded that the insured used the maltings in the light of their aesthetic features and awarded £250,000. An insured who is paid on a reinstatement basis is not generally obliged as far as the insurer is concerned to use the money to reinstate the premises, although the insured may be under a contractual duty to a third party to reinstate (as in the case of a landlord insuring a building for the benefit of tenants – see 15.30 *et seq* below). A person interested in the property may, however, under *s 83* of the *Fires Prevention (Metropolis) Act 1774* require the insurer to use the insurance monies to reinstate the property rather than pay the proceeds of the policy over to the insured (see 15.34 below).

Modern equivalent cost is appropriate for business premises which are used without regard to their particular aesthetic qualities. In *Exchange Theatre Ltd v Iron Trades Mutual Insurance Co Ltd [1983] 1 Lloyd's Rep 674*, the building in question was a Victorian public hall, which was used by the insured to operate a bingo hall and discotheque. The Court of Appeal ruled that the insured was entitled to a modern equivalent reinstatement, although a retrial was subsequently ordered on the basis of an allegation of fraud.

Market value is appropriate where the insured's intention, at the time of the loss, had been to dispose of the property. This was the position in *Leppard v Excess*

Insurance Co Ltd [1979] 2 All ER 668, in which the insured's house was destroyed by fire. Before the fire, the market value of the property had been £4,500. After the fire, its market value was £1,500. The reinstatement cost would have been £8,694 and the sum insured covered the cost of reinstatement, but the insured was held to be entitled only to the lower figure of £3,000 (ie the difference between the market value before the fire (£4,500) and the market value after the fire (£1,500)), in the light of his intention at the time of the loss to sell the property.

Valuing the insured's loss: goods

15.12   In the event of a total loss the general principle remains that the insured can recover the value of the goods immediately prior to the loss. In the case of mass-produced goods, this figure will nearly always be the cost of replacing the goods in their actual condition immediately prior to the loss. However, if the policy is written on a 'new for old' basis, the insured will be entitled to a sum sufficient to enable the insured to purchase new goods without any reduction for wear and tear.

Where the market value test is applicable, the fact that the insured originally acquired the goods cheaply is immaterial, as this does not bear upon the market value of the goods at the date of their loss (*Dominion Mosaics and Tile Co Ltd v Trafalgar Trucking Co Ltd [1990] 2 All ER 246*). In *Quorum v Schramm [2002] 1 Lloyd's Rep 249* where there were two markets (the auction market and the private dealers' market) for determining the value of a damaged pastel by Degas, the court in determining the value decided that it should have regard to the market where it was likely that the higher price would be obtained. In any event, on the facts this was the market where the picture was likely to be sold. Therefore, it more accurately reflected the loss. The market value of goods is to be assessed on an objective basis and disregards the vagaries of particular potential buyers. In *State Insurance Office v Bettany [1992] 2 NZLR 275*, the insured's car was written off in an accident and the insured claimed for the market price of the car immediately prior to the loss (US\$5,750). On inspection of the car by the insurers, it was found to have a serious fault which would not have been discoverable on ordinary inspection, but which reduced the market value of the car to US\$2,500. The insured was held to be entitled to the higher figure, as that was the sum which he would have obtained had he attempted to sell the car. This principle was adopted by the insurance ombudsman in the following year.

It should also be noted that when dealing with complaints about motor valuations the Financial Ombudsman defines 'market value' as the 'likely cost to the customer of buying a car as near as possibly identical to the one which has been stolen or damaged beyond economic repair' and not the value which could have been obtained upon sale.

In determining the value of goods, other forms of loss are to be disregarded. The loss of a treasured heirloom or article of sentimental value does not entitle the insured to any sum in excess of market value (*Re Earl of Egmont's Trusts, Lefroy v Earl of Egmont [1908] 1 Ch 821*) and for this reason items of that sort are commonly insured under valued policies. Equally, the loss of an article used in a process of manufacture does not, unless the policy expressly provides, justify a claim by the insured for loss of profits pending the replacement of the item. The exclusion of less tangible forms of loss is illustrated by *Richard Aubrey Film Productions Ltd v Graham [1960] 2 Lloyd's Rep 101*, in which a film nearing completion was lost. The court allowed the difference between the market value of the completed film and the costs of completion and excluded any claim based upon emotional and aesthetic loss.

Partial loss under an unvalued policy

The general measure of loss

15.13   If a building or goods are damaged but not totally destroyed, the insured will normally be entitled to the reasonable cost of effecting repairs. This may be subject to the principle of average: if the insured is under-insured and the policy is subject to average, the insured and the insurer are treated as co-insurers for their respective proportions of the market value of the loss, so that an insured who is 30% under-insured will have to bear 30% of the cost of repairs (see 15.09 for the application of average to partial loss under a valued policy, where precisely the same principles apply).

The fact that the cost of reinstating a building or repairing goods is greater than their pre-loss market value does not give the insurer any common law right to pay only the market value. Many policies do nevertheless provide that in such a case the insurer may treat the property as totally destroyed and pay only the property's market value to the insured.

Damage to a distinct part of a property

15.14   A perennial problem for insurers is the situation in which the insured suffers loss of or damage to property which forms part of a wider article, the loss diminishing the value of the wider article despite lack of physical harm to it. For example, damage to the fabric covering an armchair forming part of a three-piece suite, where the fabric is no longer available. The insured can clearly claim the cost of re-covering the armchair, but he is left with a non-matching three-piece suite. The question here, which has yet to reach the English courts, is whether the insured can claim the cost of re-covering the entire three-piece suite. In the absence of a clear legal principle, the insurance ombudsman has adopted as a rule of thumb the practice of awarding to the insured one-half of the cost of re-covering the remaining items.

Consequential loss

15.15   As with total losses, consequential losses – loss of profits, compensation for sentimental value – are not recoverable where goods have been partially damaged. One exception to this principle would appear to be depreciation. If an item (eg a car) is damaged and repaired, it will probably be less saleable whatever the quality of the repair, and the insurance ombudsman has stated that the insured should be entitled to recover the amount of depreciation suffered by his goods due to repair as a part of his ordinary loss under the policy.

Insurance on a 'reinstatement' basis

15.16 Policies on buildings are commonly written on a 'reinstatement' basis. This does not mean that the insured is entitled to have his building reinstated, but merely that the cost of reinstatement is recoverable under the policy (always assuming that the insured intends to reinstate). In most cases, the reinstatement value will represent the actual value of the premises to the insured. In particular, where the insured is under a contractual duty to reinstate the premises, the amount recoverable is based upon the reinstatement cost (*Lonsdale & Thompson Ltd v Black Arrow Group plc [1993] 3 All ER 648*). Such costs are to be assessed as at the date of loss: *Tonkin v UK Insurance Ltd [2006] 2 All ER (Comm) 550*.

An issue may arise where the insured wishes to undertake some improvements to the building as part of the reinstatement. *Tonkin* provides useful guidance on what information an insured should provide to insurers in order to calculate the value of a claim. Where minor improvements are to be undertaken the insured needs to make it plain to the insurer at the outset that the scheme will include some elements of improvement and identify those improvements. In the case of major changes to improve what was there before it may be better to draw up a notional reinstatement scheme that is accurately priced and this can be used to calculate the insurers' contribution towards reinstatement. HHJ Peter Coulson QC made it clear that an insured should never try to put forward a reinstatements scheme without identifying any improvements. 'It is never acceptable to be less than direct and open with insurers. At the worst end of the scale, such conduct can easily amount to fraud ... [at the very least it] will inevitably cause delay suspicion and antagonism. It is a clear failure on the part of the insured to comply with these obligations under the policy.'

Conversely, if the evidence demonstrates that the value of the property to the insured immediately prior to the loss was some lesser amount, the insured is entitled to recover only that amount. In *McLean Enterprises Ltd v Ecclesiastical Insurance Office plc [1986] 2 Lloyd's Rep 416*, premises with a market value of £250,000 were insured on a reinstatement basis for £375,000, the latter sum being the estimated cost of reinstatement. Prior to the loss, the insured had been involved in negotiations to sell the premises, although there was no binding contract. The premises were the subject of a partial loss and the court ruled that the insured was entitled to recover only the difference between £250,000 and the post-loss market value of the premises.

Late payment by the insurer

Damages for breach of contract

15.17 Insurance contracts are treated as contracts to hold the insured harmless against the liability or loss insured against. Therefore, a claim under a contract of insurance is properly viewed as a claim for breach of contract. In the case of a life or property policy, the date of the insurer's breach of contract will be the date of the event causing loss and in the case of a liability policy, the date of the insurer's breach of contract is the date on which the insured's liability to a third party is established. The insurer has no implied right to postpone payment for a reasonable time while investigating the claim, for example. The fact that the insurer is liable in damages from the outset necessarily means that, if payment of such damages is not made or delayed, the insurer cannot be liable for any further breach of contract.

In *Ventouris v Mountain, The Italia Express (No 2) [1992] 2 Lloyd's Rep 281*, the underwriters under a marine policy delayed in making payment and were sued for additional damages, representing distress. The judge ruled that the underwriters could not be liable for damages for distress, as to award damages would be tantamount to regarding the underwriters as being in further breach of their original breach of contract. In addition, the judge held that the *Marine Insurance Act 1906* did not contemplate any claim against the insurer other than for an indemnity calculated in accordance with that Act and, on the facts, there had been no distress as the insured was a company. This decision was approved and applied in *Sprung v Royal Insurance (UK) Ltd [1997] CLC 70*. In that case, the insured argued that he had been unable to continue to run his business and as a consequence had lost the opportunity to sell it as a result of insurers delaying payment of a material damage claim for three and a half years. The Court of Appeal approved and applied *The Italia Express* and held that there could be no recovery of damage in respect of a failure to pay or a delay in payment of the original damages and that the insured would only be compensated by payment of interest. See also *Normhurst Ltd v Durnoch Ltd [2004] EWHC 567*; *Mandrake Holdings Ltd v Countrywide Assured Group plc [2005] EWCA Civ 840*; and *Tonkin v UK Insurance Ltd [2007] Lloyd's Rep IR 283*. It is perfectly possible, however, that in appropriate circumstances in the future, a court might rule that an insured can recover damages for delay if the insurance policy contains a term (express or implied) that payment of a claim will be made without delay. This possibility was hinted at by the Court of Appeal in *AGH Sprung v Royal Insurance (UK) Ltd [1997] CLC 70*. However, to date, such arguments have not succeeded. In *Tonkin* the insured sought to claim damages for breach of contract relying on a provision that insurers would ' always try to be fair and reasonable whenever you have need of the protection of this Policy. We would also act quickly to provide that protection'. The court concluded that there was no separate breach of contract arising out of the general obligations set out in the care clause on the basis of this obligation was too general. It would appear therefore that to have any chance of succeeding in such a claim the separate provision would need to be more specific.

Interest

15.18   The proper remedy against a dilatory insurer is therefore an award of interest. The High Court has a general discretion under *s 35A* of the *Supreme Court Act 1981* to award interest on a claim for damages. As a matter of logic, it would follow from the nature of a claim under an insurance contract (see the 15.17 above) that interest should be awarded from the date of the event insured against.

The court's usual practice, however, has been to award interest from the date when the claim ought to have been paid in the ordinary course of events. Therefore, insurers will be allowed some time to consider the claim. The time will vary according to the nature of the loss, the way the claim is presented and the circumstances which require investigation. That interest may be reduced in circumstances in which the court feels that there has been unreasonable delay on the part of the insured in bringing proceedings: see *Quorum AS v Schramm (No 2)* *[2002] 2 Lloyd's Rep 72*. The power to award interest is not confined to sums unpaid by the date of the judgment; the court can order interest on sums paid at an earlier date, such as payments into court or payments on account (*Edmunds v Lloyd Italico e L'Ancora Cia di Assicurazioni e Riassicurazioni SpA [1986] 2 All ER 249*).

Restrictions on recovery

Betterment

15.19   An insured whose property is destroyed or damaged and is subsequently reinstated or repaired at the expense of the insurer may be obtaining something better than was actually lost. Where the insured does stand to make a profit, the insurer is generally accepted to be entitled to deduct from the amount payable a sum representing the notional profit to be gained by the insured as a result of receiving something better. The concept of a deduction for betterment has been objected to, however, as 'the equivalent of forcing the [insured] to invest money in the modernising of their plant which might be highly inconvenient for them' (per Widgery LJ in *Harbutt's 'Plasticine' Ltd v Wayne Tank & Pump Co Ltd [1970] 1 QB 447*). On the other hand, it is always open to an insured specifically to insure his property on a 'new for old' basis, if he is prepared to pay the additional premium.

The calculation of betterment is a somewhat arbitrary exercise and it is in practice frequently excluded in the case of household goods under 'new for old' policies.

Contractual limitations

Excess clauses

15.20   The insured is often required, and sometimes has the option, to carry an excess (or similarly a retention or deductible) in respect of every claim. Unless the claim reaches the excess figure, the insurer is not liable at all, and if the claim is greater than the excess figure the insurer is entitled to deduct the amount of the excess from its payment. The use of excesses recognises that most claims are relatively small. If the insurer was liable for small claims, the administrative and liability costs to the insurer would be greatly increased and for this reason the premium for a policy without an excess is disproportionately high. In addition, the presence of an excess means that the insured shares in the risk of loss and, therefore, is intended to encourage the insured to guard against losses.

It is particularly important to define the risk insured against, as this will determine whether the insured bears one single excess as a result of a particular incident or a number of excesses in respect of each individual claim flowing from the incident. This raises the distinction between 'events', 'occurrences', 'accidents' and 'claims'.

Franchise clauses

15.21   A franchise clause, like an excess, lays down a sum which must be exceeded before the insured can make a claim. The difference between the two types of clause is that, where the loss exceeds the amount stated in a franchise clause, the insurer bears the entire loss and not merely the amount by which the loss is greater than the franchise figure.

A series of losses

Unconnected loss

15.22   The insured may suffer a series of losses, such as burglaries, within the period covered by the policy. There will generally be a maximum sum insured under the policy. The application of the maximum liability figure will depend upon the proper construction of the policy's wording. The policy might provide that the maximum sum insured relates to single losses so that the insurer is liable for more than one loss even though their aggregate cost is greatly in excess of the maximum sum insured. Conversely, the policy may lay down a maximum figure, not just per claim, but per year. If the policy is silent, the former construction appears to be the correct one, a principle which has been codified by *s* 77 of the *Marine Insurance Act 1906*.

Successive claims for the same subject matter

15.23   If the insured's property is damaged by fire, repaired and then damaged again, the insured can, in accordance with the principles set out in 15.22 above, recover for the successive losses. The position is different, however, if the original damage has not been repaired. Three different situations might arise.

(*a*)   The insured's car is damaged in a road accident and is left in his garage pending repair. The garage catches fire and renders the vehicle a total loss. Here, the obvious solution is that the partial loss is merged into the total loss, so that the insured can recover only for the total loss (*British and Foreign Marine Insurance Co Ltd v Wilson Shipping Co Ltd [1921] 1 AC 188*).

(*b*)   The insured's car is damaged in a road accident and is deposited with a repairer (the car being uninsured while in the possession of a person other than the insured) where it is destroyed by fire. Here, the merger principle again operates, depriving the insured of the right to recover anything at all, not even for the insured partial loss. In practice, this is an unlikely event today.

(*c*)   The insured's car is damaged in a road accident and is left in his garage pending repair. The policy then expires and the insured does not renew. The car is subsequently destroyed by a fire in the insured's garage. The rule, laid down in the marine case of *Lidgett v Secretan (1871) LR 6 CP 616* is that the insured's position has to be viewed at the date of the expiry of the policy. As at that date the insured had an outstanding partial loss, he is entitled to recover for that loss.

Losses with a common cause

15.24   Rather different considerations arise where the insured suffers a series of different losses flowing from the same event. This is particularly significant in liability insurance, where one negligent act by the insured can give rise to a range of liabilities. Assuming that the policy contains a maximum liability figure faced by the insurer, it will be necessary to determine whether that figure relates to individual claims by (or in the case of liability insurance, against) the insured, or whether it relates to an aggregation of claims flowing from some single unifying factor – an event, for example. The result may vary, depending upon whether the maximum liability figure relates to 'accidents', 'occurrences', 'events' or 'claims'.

Settlements between insurer and insured

Binding nature

15.25   The payment of a loss by the insurer is frequently made conditional upon the insured entering into a contract with the insurer under which the insurer's payment is to be accepted in full and final settlement of the loss. Should additional loss subsequently come to light, the insured will have no right to claim against the insurer for that loss. In the absence of a full and final settlement agreement, the insured can look to the insurer for an indemnity for loss which comes to light at a later date. These principles are illustrated by *Kitchen Design & Advice Ltd v Lea Valley Water Co [1989] 2 Lloyd's Rep 221*, in which the claimant insured's premises were damaged by flooding caused by the defendant. The insurers paid the insured for the flood damage and recovered their payment from the defendant on a 'full and final settlement' basis. Subsequently, the insured put in a claim against its insurers for consequential loss, which the insurers had to pay as they had not settled the original claim as a full and final settlement. The insurers were, however, precluded from reopening the agreement with the defendant and were thus unable to seek indemnification from them.

Settlements made under a mistake

15.26   In English law, where the parties involved in negotiating a contract are under a common misapprehension as to a fundamental matter which affects the very basis of their negotiations, their subsequent contract is void. If the mistake is of lesser significance, the contract is not to be treated as void, but voidable, and either party may ask the court to exercise its discretion to set the contract aside. A settlement contract based on an error is, therefore, potentially void or voidable, and the insurer can either reclaim its payment or, if it has not paid, refuse to make payment.

The decided cases provide specific illustrations of these rules:

(*a*)   where the insurer makes payment under a lapsed policy, the payment may be recovered (*Kelly v Solari (1841) 9 N&W 54*);

(*b*)   where the insurer makes payment in the erroneous belief that the insured had an insurable interest, the payment may be recovered (*Piper v Royal Exchange Assurance [1932] 44 Lloyd's Rep 103*);

(*c*)   where the insurer makes payment in ignorance of the fact that the loss has not been caused by an insured peril, the payment may be recovered (*Norwich Union Fire Insurance Society v Price [1934] AC 455*); and

(*d*)   where the insurer makes payment unaware of the existence of grounds which would have entitled him to set aside the insurance contract for breach of duty by the insured, the payment may be recovered (*Magee v Pennine Insurance Co [1969] 2 QB 507* – misrepresentation by the insured when applying for the policy). Presumably the same principle would apply if the insurer was unaware of a breach of condition or warranty by the insured. The mere fact that the insurer has paid does not amount to waiver of the defence, as there can be waiver only where the insurer was aware of the facts giving rise to a defence and nevertheless made payment.

In *Kyle Bay Ltd (T/A Astons Nightclub) v Underwriters [2007] EWCA Civ 57* both the insured and insurers agreed settlement on the basis that the policy was written on a 'gross profits basis' subject to the application of average whereas it was in law a declaration linked policy to which average did not apply. As a consequence, the Insured recovered £108,319.46 less than it ought to have. The Court of Appeal upheld the first instance decision that the settlement contract was not void for mistake. The claim settled on a mistaken legal basis will not be void for mistake unless the mistake renders the agreement to settle either impossible to perform or renders the subject matter of the agreement radically different from the subject matter that the parties believed to exist. The fact that the settlement agreement is to one party's disadvantage does not render it void.

Settlements induced by misrepresentation

15.27   If the insured's claim is fraudulent, the insurer may refuse to pay it and generally has the additional right under the contract to terminate the policy (see 13 CLAIMS). If the insured's claim is not fraudulent or reckless but contains innocent misstatements, there is no breach by the insured of his continuing duty of utmost good faith and (subject to any other relevant policy conditions) the claim must be paid.

The insured can set aside a settlement contract if it has been induced by a false statement made on behalf of the insurer. In *Saunders v Ford Motor Co Ltd [1970] 1 Lloyd's Rep 379*, the plaintiff signed a document presented to him by his employers in respect of an injury at work, for a full and final settlement at £100. The plaintiff had been led to believe that this was an interim payment only and the court held that the document signed by the plaintiff could not stand.

However, in *Kyle Bay Ltd v Underwriters* the insured sought to argue that it was entitled to rescind the settlement agreement for misrepresentation on the basis that insurers had represented that the policy was not declaration linked and average applied. Jonathan Hirst QC concluded that the insurers' letter was not to be read as a representation as to the contents of the policy but rather as a statement of underwriters' opinion of the overall effect of the policy. It was, therefore, a representation as to belief or opinion and was an accurate representation of the insurers' opinion and therefore made in good faith. There had been no misrepresentation.

Unfair settlements

15.28 In general, the courts will not overturn a contract on the basis that its terms are unfair to one of the parties, as it is not regarded as the function of law to rewrite bargains. This principle is modified where a contracting party can be shown to have been pressurised into making the contract. Pressure may be physical or economic (duress) or psychological (undue influence). A possible example of economic pressure might arise where an insured trader, whose business premises are destroyed by fire in what appear to be suspicious circumstances, feels obliged to accept a low settlement offer in order to minimise disruption to the business and loss of goodwill. An example of undue influence is provided by *Horry v Tate & Lyle Refineries Ltd [1982] 2 Lloyd's Rep 416*, in which a claimant injured at work was pressurised into accepting a settlement of £1,000 by statements to the effect that he was, due to his own lack of care, probably not entitled to any payment at all. The judge held that the settlement signed by the claimant should be set aside.

The insurer's right of salvage

15.29 Once the insured and insurer have agreed upon a settlement, the insured is entitled to the policy monies. If there has been a total loss of the subject matter insured, the insurer has a common law right of salvage, that is, to take possession of whatever is left of the insured subject matter and deal with it as the insurer thinks fit. Thus, an insured whose car is treated as a total loss by the insurer must hand the wreckage to the insurer and the insurer is entitled to sell the wreckage (for scrap or repair) for its own benefit.

The principle of salvage also operates where insured subject matter, which has been lost and paid for as a total loss, once again comes into the insured's possession. This was the situation in *Holmes v Payne* (see 15.02 above) where the insured rediscovered her lost jewellery in her cape after the insurer had indemnified her for the loss. The insurers claimed repayment of the policy monies, but the trial judge held that, following settlement, the insurer was entitled only to the insured subject matter by way of salvage and could not overturn the settlement for mistake. The position is presumably the same when the insured wishes to retain the property and repay the policy monies (as will be the case where the property has a sentimental value or is underinsured); the insurer again has the right to demand the property by way of salvage.

The insurer's right of salvage is different in many ways from its rights of subrogation. One example is as follows. If an insurer takes possession of property by way of salvage and then sells it (or what remains of it) at a profit, the insurer is entitled to retain the profit. If, on the other hand, an insurer exercising its rights of subrogation, recovers from a third party a sum in excess of its outlay under the policy, the insurer holds the balance on trust for the insured. For a fuller discussion of subrogation, see 16 SUBROGATION.

Reinstatement

Definition

15.30 Reinstatement in this context is not the cost of reinstatement, as described at 15.11 above, but rather the actual repair or rebuilding of damaged property by or on behalf of the insurer. Reinstatement is only available if there is an express provision in the contract of insurance or under statute as between the insurer and a third party who, while not a party to the insurance, has some interest in the property.

The insured may himself be under an obligation to a third party to use the policy monies to reinstate the damaged property. Examples of this situation are:

(*a*) a policy procured by a landlord on a block of flats, with each lease requiring the landlord to use the policy monies to effect reinstatement;

(*b*) a hire purchase agreement on a motor vehicle under which the hirer is required to insure the vehicle and to use the insurance monies to repair it in the event of damage; and

(*c*) express provisions in a mortgage deed requiring the lender to reinstate.

Whether or not the insured is under an obligation depends upon the nature of his relationship with the third party. The general rule is that, unless there is an express obligation on the insured to reinstate, the third party has no right to require the insured to use the policy monies to do so (*Leeds v Cheetham [1827] 1 Sim 146*). However, where the insured is under a contractual duty to reinstate, he is under a corresponding implied duty to pursue the claim against the insurer and to reinstate the premises in the same condition as they were previously. In *Vural v Security Archives [1990] 60 P&CR 258* it was held that the landlord of premises was required to reinstate the building using a floor covering which was suitable for the tenant's business. Furthermore, a person interested in the property may, under *s 83* of the *Fires Prevention (Metropolis) Act 1774*, require the insurer to use the insurance monies to reinstate the property rather than pay the proceeds of the policy over to the insured. In addition, the *Contracts (Rights of Third Parties) Act 1999* provides that third parties other than the insured, who are identified in the policy by name, class or other description (and upon whom the policy purports to confer a benefit) may enforce the policy direct against the insurer. Thus, for example, a tenant or a lender whose interest is noted in the policy may be able to make a claim direct against the insurer even if he is not the insured under the policy (so long as the policy does not provide that the third party is not entitled to enforce his rights direct).

Reinstatement under the policy

The availability of reinstatement

15.31   Most policies on property confer upon the insurer the alternative rights, following damage to the property, either to indemnify the insured by means of the payment of money or to have the insured's property reinstated. The option is there for two reasons: reinstatement may be cheaper than a cash indemnity; and the insurer may suspect some form of malpractice on the part of the insured and may wish to ensure that the insured cannot gain in any way as a result of the loss. The option to reinstate is normally for the benefit of the insurer only; the insured has no right at common law to insist upon reinstatement as opposed to payment (*Leppard v Excess Insurance Co Ltd [1979] 2 All ER 668*) and policies rarely confer that right.

The obligation to reinstate

15.32   Once a loss has occurred, an insurer who has a contractual right either to pay or to reinstate must exercise the option within the time limits set down by the policy or, if no limits are specified, within a reasonable time. As soon as the insurer has unequivocally stated his intention to reinstate or to pay, that decision is binding on the insurer: *Scarf v Jardine (1882) 7 App Cas 345.*

If the insurer has chosen to reinstate, a fresh contract for repair or rebuilding between the insurer and the insured comes into being. As is the case with all contracts for the supply of work and materials, the insurer is under an implied obligation to reinstate the property to an appropriate standard and must perform this obligation within a reasonable time. An illustration of the point is a Scottish decision, *Davidson v Guardian Royal Exchange Assurance [1979] 1 Lloyd's Rep 406*, where the insured was entitled to claim damages against the insurer for the failure of its agent (a garage) to repair the insured's car within a reasonable time.

Even if the insured nominates a repairer or builder to reinstate, the contractual position would appear to remain unchanged, in that the insurer remains liable to the insured for failure to reinstate or for defective reinstatement and there is no contract between the insured and the repairer. If, therefore, the repairer is negligent, the insured's claim remains one against the insurer. Conversely, the repairer has no claim against the insured for the cost of effecting the repairs and the repairer's rights can be enforced only against the insurer (*Godfrey Davis v Culling and Hecht [1962] 2 Lloyd's Rep 349*).

Unforeseen complications

15.33   An insurer who has elected to reinstate is under a contractual obligation to do so. If it proves to be the case that the cost of reinstatement is greater than originally anticipated (and even if the cost exceeds the monetary amount which would have been payable under the policy) the insurer is not excused from the obligation to reinstate in full. An extreme illustration of the scope of insurer's liability is the Australian decision in *Smith v Colonial Mutual Fire Insurance Co Ltd [1880] 6 VLR 200*, in which the insurer was held to be liable to reinstate a building in full even though much of the original reinstatement work carried out by the insurer had been destroyed by fire.

A greater problem, however, arises in the situation in which the insurer, having opted to reinstate, finds that reinstatement is not merely more expensive than was originally contemplated, but impossible as a matter of law (for example by reason of the intervention of planning authorities). The position here is as follows.

If the insurer has not commenced reinstatement when impossibility intervenes, the insurer's exercise of the option to reinstate is frustrated and the insurer's obligation reverts to the provision of a financial indemnity under the policy (*Anderson v Commercial Union Assurance Co [1885] 55 LJQB 146*).

If the insurer has commenced reinstatement when impossibility intervenes, the same position would appear to apply. The difficulty is that the insurer will have incurred expense, but it would seem that there is no legal basis upon which the insurer can seek to deduct any expenditure already incurred from the full sum owing to the insured.

In either case, if the insured has agreed with a third party that the policy monies are to be used to reinstate the property, and reinstatement is impossible, the general principle is that the policy monies must be divided between the insured and the third party in accordance with their respective interests in the property (*Beacon Carpets Ltd v Kirby [1984] 2 All ER 726*).

Statutory reinstatement

15.34   In the 18th century a particular form of insurance fraud gave rise to great difficulty. A tenant would procure a short term (possibly weekly) lease on a building and would then start a fire having insured the building for its full value. Insurers are not, of course, liable to the insured in such circumstances (see 14 CLAIMS) but deterrence rested upon the chances of detection. Parliament ultimately rendered the practice unprofitable in an ingenious fashion, by passing *s 83* of the *Fires Prevention (Metropolis) Act 1774*, a provision which has been copied throughout the common law world. *Section 83*, which is lengthy and complex, provides that an insurer of a house or building damaged or destroyed by fire is required, on the request of any person interested in the property, to cause the insurance monies to be laid out for the purpose of reinstatement. This ensures that any person setting fire to a building for the insurance money will not actually receive the money as long as a third party interested in the property intervenes and requests reinstatement.

The operation of *s 83* is subject to a number of conditions, which are as follows.

(*a*)   The section extends to England and Wales but not Scotland, and operates only in respect of buildings rather than their contents (*Re Barker, ex parte Gorely [1864] 4 De G J & Sm 477*). Moreover, the damage must be caused by fire.

(*b*)   The section applies to insurance companies, but not to Lloyd's underwriters.

(*c*)   Application by a person interested must be made to the insurer before the insurance money has been paid to the insured. Once the insured has received the insurance monies, notice to the insurer is ineffective.

(*d*)   Persons interested in property in addition to the insured have been held to include the parties to a lease (*Wimbledon Park Golf Club Ltd v Imperial Insurance Co Ltd [1902] 18 TLR 815*), the parties to a mortgage (*Sinnott v Bowden [1912] 2 Ch 414*) and the parties to a contract of sale (see *Lonsdale & Thomson Ltd* at 15.16 above). A party to the policy cannot, however, give notice. In *Reynolds and Anderson* (see 15.11 above) a mortgagor was held not to be able to require the insurer to reinstate his house under a policy procured by the mortgagee to which the mortgagor was a named party.

(*e*)   The insurer is liable to reinstate the premises, but only to the extent of the sum payable under the policy. This should be compared and contrasted with reinstatement under contract with the insured, where the insurer is liable to reinstate whatever the cost.

(*f*)   The insurer's liability under *s 83* arises only where the insurer would otherwise be liable to the insured under the policy. If, therefore, the insurer has a defence against the insured, *s 83* cannot be relied upon. This point is particularly important where the property is damaged by fire after the insured has entered into a binding contract to sell the property. While the purchaser is an interested person, he will be unable to give notice to the insurer once he has made payment to the insured as at that stage the insured has suffered no loss. If, however, the insured vendor has agreed with a third party, such as a tenant, that he will reinstate the property in the event of loss, the insured is not indemnified by the payment by the purchaser and retains the right to claim under the policy: this will permit the purchaser to give notice to the insurer despite having made payment to the insured (see *Lonsdale & Thomson* at (*d*) above).

(*g*)   The insurer, having received a valid notice, must either apply the insurance monies to reinstate the building or may pay them directly to the insured on receipt of some security for the insured's promise to reinstate.

(*h*)   An insurer who refuses to reinstate may be restrained by an injunction in favour of the third party from making payment to the insured (see *Wimbledon Park Golf Club* at (*d*) above).

Chapter 16
Subrogation and Assignment

- Nature of subrogation

- Scope of the right of subrogation

- Indemnification of the insured

- Actions against the emergency services

- Procedural aspects of subrogation actions

- Sums recovered by way of subrogation

- Assignment

- Assignment of the policy

- Assignment of the proceeds of the policy

Nature of subrogation

Role of subrogation

16.01 The insurer's right of subrogation has been recognised in England since at least the middle of the eighteenth century. The principle is that an insurer, having indemnified the insured for his loss, is entitled to 'step into the shoes' of the insured, and may commence proceedings in the insured's name against the third party who has caused the insured's loss. The sum recovered may then be retained by the insurer. The insurer's right of subrogation is codified in *s* 79 of the *Marine Insurance Act 1906*, which states that an insurer who has indemnified the insured for a total or partial loss is entitled to exercise all the rights and remedies of the insured arising as from the date of the loss, in relation to the insured subject matter. Subrogation does not give the insurer the right to take the insured subject matter itself, although in the case of a total loss, the parallel doctrine of abandonment confers upon the insurer the right to take possession of what is left of the insured subject matter.

Subrogation has two functions. Firstly, it ensures that the person who is actually responsible for the loss will pay for it, despite the fact that the victim of the loss has private insurance. In practice, however, the wrongdoer is himself likely to be insured, so that many subrogation actions are in effect attempts to seek to move the loss from one insurer to another. Secondly, the doctrine of subrogation furthers the indemnity function of insurance, by ensuring that the insured does not recover both from his insurers and from the wrongdoer to compensate him for a single loss.

Although the conceptual origins of an insurer's right of subrogation are not entirely clear, it is suggested that, following the House of Lords decision in *The Right Honourable Francis Nigel Baron Napier and Ettrick and Richards Butler v R F Kershaw Ltd [1993] 1 Lloyd's Rep 197* subrogation is in fact fundamentally a legal doctrine which arises from the very nature of the contract of indemnity albeit that it is customarily enforced by equitable remedies. The authorities are unclear as to whether the right to subrogate arises by virtue on an implied term of the contract (*Yorkshire Insurance Co Ltd v Nisbet Shipping Co Ltd [1962] QB 330*) or arises automatically on payment of the indemnity but independently of, or at best parasitically on, the express or implied terms of the insurance contract. (Note that the concept of a common law right distinct from the express or implied terms of the insurance contract is now the favoured analytical basis for the insurer's right to decline a fraudulent insurance claim and recover payments already made to the insured in respect of that claim (*Agapitos v Agnew [2002] 3 WLR 616*).) Irrespective of how it arises, however, the operation of subrogation in insurance cases can be modified by express contractual provisions and also by various terms implied into insurance policies by the courts. Subrogation is, therefore, a combination of equitable principles and express and implied policy terms.

An excellent summary of the historical genesis of subrogation is set out in *England v Guardian Insurance Ltd [1999] 2 All ER (Comm) 481*.

Practical operation of subrogation

16.02   In *Castellain v Preston (1882–83) LR 11 QBD 380*, Brett LJ stated the principles applicable to subrogation rights in the following words:

> '... as between the underwriter and the insured, the underwriter is entitled to the advantage of every right of the insured, whether such right consists in contract, fulfilled or unfulfilled, or in remedy for tort capable of being insisted on, or in any other right, whether by condition or otherwise, legal or equitable, which can be or has accrued, and whether such right could or could not be enforced by the insurer in the name of the insured by the exercise or acquiring of which right or condition the loss against which the insured is insured, can be, or has been diminished.'

In the actual case, the insured building was destroyed by fire between contract and completion, and the vendor had received both the insurance moneys and the purchase price at the time of the action; the insurers were held to be entitled to recover the sum paid by the purchaser to the vendor by way of subrogation. The insurer is entitled to make a claim of this type only in respect of sums which have been paid to the insured by the third party to diminish his loss. This may give rise to fine distinctions. For example, in *Arthur Charles Burnand v Rodocanachi Sons & Co. (1881–82) LR 7 App Cas 333*, compensation paid to the insured by the US Government in the aftermath of the American Civil War was held, on the proper construction of the authorising legislation, to be by way of personal compensation and not in diminution of loss. Consequently, the insurer had no claim to the sum. By contrast, in *Steams v Village Main Reef Gold Mining Co [1905] 21 TLR 236*, compensation paid to the insured by the South African Government following requisition of the insured's property was held to be intended to diminish loss, and was thus subject to a subrogation recovery.

Subrogation is not in any event confined to insurers, but extends to any person giving an indemnity. An insurance-related question was discussed by the House of Lords in *Giles v Thompson [1994] 1 AC 142*. This case considered the validity of an agreement between a driver whose car had been damaged in a motor accident, and a car-hire firm. The firm agreed to provide a hire car free to the insured pending the repair of his own vehicle (such loss being generally outside the cover provided by a motor policy) in return for the transfer to the firm of the insured's right to sue the wrongdoer for damages representing these costs. The House of Lords held that the agreement was valid, and in particular did not amount to champerty (interference with a cause of action). The decision is of some disquiet to motor liability insurers, as the practical ability of the victim of a motor accident to sue the wrongdoer has been enhanced significantly.

Assignment as an alternative to subrogation

16.03   The insurer's right of subrogation arises automatically on the indemnification of the insured by the insurer, so that, in principle, an insurer can rely upon subrogation to recover from the third party a sum equivalent to that paid to the insured without having to take any further steps in relation to the insured. However, in some situations, insurers prefer to take an assignment of the insured's cause of action against the third party. Assignment has two main advantages:

(*a*)   the insurer need not pay the insured before exercising assigned rights against the third party; and

(*b*)   under an assignment, the insurer is able to retain the entire sum recovered from the third party, whereas under subrogation the insurer retains only the nominal amount actually paid to the insured.

Assignment has two potential drawbacks. Firstly, the insurer has to call upon the insured to assign his rights after the loss. However, there is no objection to a policy term which states that the insured's rights are deemed to vest in the insurer, so that the need for a formal assignment is obviated. Secondly, if the insurer has taken a legal assignment of rights the action must be brought in its own name; many insurers prefer anonymity in the process of pursuing third parties.

Scope of the right of subrogation

Indemnity contract

16.04   The doctrine of subrogation applies only to insurance contracts which are contracts of indemnity, given that one of the primary purposes of subrogation is to prevent the insured from recovering more than an indemnity. All forms of property insurances are indemnity contracts, whereas the same is not true of all forms of life policies so the holder of a life policy may be able to recover both the policy moneys and damages from the person causing the insured's death. Personal accident policies are, for subrogation purposes, classified as non-indemnity contracts, so that an insured who suffers personal injuries can claim both from the insurer and from the wrongdoer in each case without discount for the other's payment (*Theobald v Railway Passengers Assn (1854) 10 Ex 45*). As new insurance products develop, the courts may be called upon to decide whether these new policies are indemnity policies for subrogation purposes.

Insured must have a cause of action

16.05   An insurer exercising subrogation rights can obtain no better rights against the wrongdoer than the insured himself possessed at the date of the loss. If, for some reason, the insured has no cause of action against the third party, the insurer himself cannot sue the third party, although in some circumstances the insurer may have a right to proceed against the insured for failing to protect the insurer's subrogation rights. The insurer's rights will depend upon why the insured has no cause of action against the third party. A variety of situations might be found.

Wrongdoer is a party to the policy

16.06   Subrogation rights cannot be exercised against a person who is party to the contract of insurance. In *Simpson and Co. v Thomson, Burrell (1877–78) LR 3 App Cas 279* the insured's two vessels were involved in a collision. The House of Lords held that the insurers could not deny liability for the damage to one of the vessels by arguing that the damage was caused by the negligence of the insured's own agents, and that the liability was cancelled out by the right to claim the loss from the insured by way of subrogation.

The same principle applies where the wrongdoer is a co-insured (ie where the parties are co-owners or where the parties have different interests under the policy (see 17 CO-INSURANCE)). The difficulty here is in determining whether there is co-insurance. In *Petrofina (UK) Ltd v Magnaload Ltd [1983] 3 All ER 35*, a policy taken out by a head contractor for himself and all subcontractors was held to be intended to make subcontractors co-insureds. Thus, when a subcontractor negligently damaged property on the site, the insurer, having paid for the loss, was unable to exercise subrogation rights against the subcontractor. If, by contrast, the policy does not specifically state that subcontractors are to be co-insureds, and the arrangements between the contractor and the subcontractor do not contemplate that the contractor will insure on the subcontractors behalf, the subcontractor cannot claim to be party to the insurance and will face a subrogation claim (*Stone Vickers Ltd v Appledore Ferguson Shipbuilders Ltd [1992] 2 Lloyd's Rep 578*). A policy which does cover subcontractors will extend to a subcontractor who has not authorised the contractor to procure a policy, provided that he ratifies the contractor's act of insuring for him, ratification being possible even after the loss has occurred (*National Oilwell (UK) Ltd v Davy Offshore Ltd [1993] 2 Lloyd's Rep 582*). Consideration must also be given to the type of losses covered by the co-insurance: in *Kruger Tissue (Industrial) Ltd v Franks Gallier Ltd 57 Con LR 1* the policy provided co-insurance in respect of existing structures and their contents but not in respect of loss of profits or increased costs of working resulting from damage to the existing structures and their contents. Thus the insurer was able to subrogate against the contractor in respect of consequential losses although not in respect of the loss to the existing structures and contents themselves.

Wrongdoer contemplated as a beneficiary of the policy

16.07   In some situations, two parties holding different interests in the same subject matter may agree that only one of them is to be a named insured under the policy, although the intention is that the policy should cover their respective interests. This arrangement is commonly found between a landlord and a tenant: the landlord (although it may be the tenant) insures, but the premium is paid by the tenant and it is intended that the policy moneys are to be used in reinstating the premises in the event of a loss. Insurers generally require the interest of the tenant to be 'noted' on the policy, although noting does not have the effect of creating a co-insurance.

An arrangement of this type is intended to obtain insurance for the benefit of both landlord and tenant even though only the landlord is a party to the insurance. In *Mark Rowlands Ltd v Berni Inns Ltd [1985] 3 All ER 473*, the policy was taken out by the landlord with the premiums paid by the tenant, and the building was damaged by fire due to the apparent negligence of the tenant. The insurer paid the landlord, and sought to exercise subrogation rights against the tenant. The Court of Appeal held that a term was to be implied into the lease to the effect that, in the event of any loss to the premises caused by the tenant, the landlord has no right to proceed against the tenant but must instead recover from the insurers. Given that the landlord has no right to sue the tenant, the insurer has no subrogation rights against the tenant and must bear the loss.

Wrongdoer exempted from liability by contract with insured

16.08   If the insured has agreed to exempt the third party from liability, the insurer is bound by the insured's agreement. In *Tate & Sons v Hyslop (1884–85) LR 15 QBD 368*, a cargo owner entered into an agreement with carriers under which the carriers were to be liable only for negligence. The cargo owner subsequently insured the cargo, but did not disclose to the insurers the restriction on his rights. Following loss caused by the carriers without negligence on their part, it became clear that no subrogation rights could exist against the carriers. However, the insurer was held to be able to avoid the policy for the insured's failure to disclose to the insurer that subrogation rights had been prejudiced in this way.

The opposite can arise where a contractual indemnity gives rise to rights of the insured which it might otherwise not have. These indemnities are common in complex construction projects. One issue for the courts is whether the right of an insurer where such indemnities exist is one of contribution, as if the contractual indemnity were itself an insurance policy (see 18 DOUBLE INSURANCE AND CONTRIBUTION), or one of subrogation. A Scottish case arising out of the Piper Alpha oil rig disaster, *Caledonian North Sea v London Bridge Engineering [2002] 1 Lloyd's Rep 553*, decided that such contractual indemnities allocated primary responsibilities and that the insurance was in case of non-recovery under the indemnity. As such subrogation rights against the giver of the indemnity could arise.

Loss of cause of action by the insured

16.09   There is an implied term in every contract of insurance that the insured will not, after the loss, throw away his cause of action against the wrongdoer and thereby prejudice the insurer's subrogation rights (see *Lord Napier and Ettrick* at 16.01 above). If the insured does enter into arrangements with the wrongdoer under which the wrongdoer is excused liability, the insurer is bound by those arrangements, although the insurer will have an action against the insured for the loss caused by his conduct. The question whether the insured faces liability to the insurer for a post-loss settlement of rights depends upon whether the settlement was or was not *bona fide*. If the settlement is based upon the fact that the insured has received, or is to receive, an equivalent sum from the insurers, the settlement is plainly prejudicial to the insurer's rights and the insured must make up the amount lost (*West of England Fire Insurance Co v Isaacs [1897] 1 QB 226*). By contrast, if the settlement is based upon genuine negotiations, the insurer is bound by it and has no cause of action against the insured.

Waiver of subrogation rights by the insurer

16.10   An insurer may stipulate in the policy that subrogation rights are not to be exercised against named persons or classes of persons. This form of provision is common in construction contracts where co-insurance arrangements are not used, the object being to eliminate the cost of allocating any losses on site between the contractor and the various subcontractors by requiring the contractor's insurer to bear the loss. The subrogation waiver clause is not, however, effective in law. In *National Oilwell* (see 16.06 above) the High Court ruled that a subcontractor who was not party to the contract of insurance could not rely upon a subrogation waiver purported to be in his favour. If he was a party to the policy, he was a co-insured protected from subrogation, and if he was not a party to the policy, then the doctrine of privity of contract prevented reliance on the subrogation waiver clause.

Indemnification of the insured

Actual payment by the insurer

16.11   Before the insurer can be subrogated to the rights of the insured against the wrongdoer, the insurer must have provided an indemnity to the insured. If the insurer has failed to pay the entire sum due under the policy, subrogation rights cannot arise. This is illustrated by *Page v Scottish Insurance Corporation Ltd (1929) 33 Ll L Rep 134*, where insurers refused to admit liability to the insured in respect of his possible liability following a motor vehicle accident. The insurers were held not to be able to claim from a third party the costs of repairing the insured's car.

The insurer's liability to indemnify the insured

16.12   As long as the insurer has paid the insured, the insurer will obtain subrogation rights, This is so even if the payment is made by way of settlement, without the insurer's liability having been fully established as a matter of law. This was held to be the case in *King v Victoria Insurance Co Ltd [1896] AC 250*, and in *Lord Napier and Ettrick* (see 16.01 above) the Court of Appeal and House of Lords simply assumed that an insurer who settles is permitted to claim from the third party.

An insurer who pays in the clear knowledge that he is not liable under the policy will not, however, obtain subrogation rights, as subrogation is not available with respect to pure *ex gratia* payments. This rule can be sidestepped by means of express agreement between the insurer and the insured. In *Naumann v Ford [1985] 2 EGLR 70*, the insured tenant agreed with the insurer that the insurer would pay the loss *ex gratia* (the policy having lapsed), and that the insured would bring an action against the wrongdoer and would hold the proceeds on trust for the insurer. The High Court ruled that the insured's action against the wrongdoer was permissible, and was not defeated by the fact that the insured had been indemnified by the insurer.

Rights of the insurer prior to payment

16.13   The insurer has no subrogation rights against the third party prior to making payment to the insured. At this stage, the action against the third party belongs entirely to the insured, although if the insured prejudices the insurer's rights by entering into a settlement with the wrongdoer which cannot be justified on objective grounds, the insurer will have an action against the insured for breach of contract (*Faircharm Investments Ltd v Citibank International plc [1998] Lloyd's Rep Bank 127*). Most of the authorities, however, consider positive acts by the insured not acts of omission.

A further question is whether the insured is, in this pre-indemnification period, under a positive duty to preserve the insurer's rights. This creates a potential difficulty where the insurer anticipates that, unless speedy action is taken against the third party, any right of recovery against him may prove to be unenforceable. This might arise, for example, where the third party has taken steps to transfer his assets outside the UK, or where the insured is faced with a limitation period (the latter being particularly important in marine cargo claims, where the contractual limitation period may be no more than one year). In such cases, the insured is perfectly free to seek a Mareva injunction against the third party freezing his assets, or to issue a 'protective' writ preserving the cause of action against the operation of a limitation period, but an insured who is fully covered by insurance has no particular incentive to incur the expense of doing so. It is undecided whether the insurer can require the insured to take a pre-emptive step of this type.

Some policies may impose the necessary obligation upon the insured, but in the absence of an express obligation it is far from clear that the insurer could insist upon this. In *AB Svensk Exportkredit v New Hampshire Insurance Co unreported, 1998*, the Court of Appeal held that a reasonable care clause in an insurance policy (obliging the insured to take reasonable care to avoid incurring a loss) did not have the effect of allowing the insurer to control the insured's conduct prior to having been paid by the insurer. In *Noble Resources Ltd and Unirise Development Ltd v George Albert Greenwood ('The Vasso') [1993] 2 Lloyd's Rep 309*, it was held that a sue and labour clause in a marine policy did not operate to require the insured to seek a Mareva injunction, and it was not suggested by the insurers that subrogation might have had any different effect. Thus, insurers generally include a wide-ranging clause allowing them to exercise the rights of the insured and commence proceedings prior to payment of the indemnity.

Loss exceeding the sum insured

The insured's right to proceed

16.14   It is commonly the case that the amount lost by the insured exceeds the sum payable by the insurer under the policy. This may arise either because the insured bears an excess (also known as a retention or deductible) which requires him to meet the first part of his own loss, or because the insured is underinsured. The two forms have very different consequences.

Turning first to the case in which the insured bears an excess under the policy, it was held by the House of Lords in *Lord Napier and Ettrick* (see 16.01 above) that the amount of the excess is deemed not to be a loss within the terms of the policy as the insured has agreed to bear the amount of the excess. Consequently, full payment by the insurer after deducting the excess means that, as far as the insurer is concerned, the insured has received a full indemnity. In such a case, the control of the action passes to the insurer under the doctrine of subrogation, which means that the insured will recoup his excess only if the insurer is able to recover the full amount of the claim from the third party, as in such a case, the insurer can retain only the amount of its own payment and must hand over the surplus to the insured.

By contrast, if the insured is underinsured because the policy limits do not extend to the full amount of the loss, the insurer obtains subrogation rights by virtue of its payment, but the insured retains the right to control the action against the third party (*Commercial Union Assurance Co v Lister (1873–74) LR 9 Ch App 483*). The insurer is, therefore, bound by any settlement reached between the third party and the insured (although the insurer will have an action against the insured for breach of an implied term in the insurance policy prohibiting the insured from prejudicing the insurer's subrogation rights – see above). Equally, the insurer is bound by the insured's conduct of the action. In *Terence Trevor Hayler v D G Chapman [1989] 1 Lloyd's Rep 490*, a motor case, the insured obtained judgment against the wrongdoer only for the uninsured sum, as the rest of the insured's loss had been recovered from his own insurers. The insured's insurers sought to have the judgment set aside on the ground that the insured had sought an inadequate amount. The Court of Appeal ruled that a judgment could not be set aside unless fraud on the part of the defendant (or the defendant's insurers) could be shown (for example, by not contesting the insured's claim in the knowledge that an inadequate sum had been claimed). As there was no fraud, the judgment had to stand: the insured's insurers in such a case would, therefore, be required to proceed against the insured for prejudicing their subrogation rights. In *Buckland v Palmer [1984] 3 All ER 554*, another motor case, the insured commenced an action against the third party for the uninsured sum. The insurer here stepped in at an earlier stage, and before the case had been heard, the insurers issued their own proceedings against the defendant for the sum which had been paid to the insured under the policy. The Court of Appeal held that two sets of proceedings could not be commenced in relation to the same cause of action, and held that the proper approach was for the insurers to apply for the insured's action to be set aside and fresh proceedings for the entire loss to be commenced.

Stopping an action by the insured

16.15   An insurer who has subrogation rights is likely to wish to use them. However, there may be cases in which the insurer does not want proceedings against the third party to be pursued. The most likely explanation for this is the existence of a 'knock-for-knock' or equivalent agreement between the insured's motor insurer and the wrongdoer's liability insurer, under which each insurer has agreed to bear first party losses and not to pursue liability claims. This situation arose in *Hobbs v Marlowe [1978] AC 16*, however the House of Lords did not go as far as ruling that an insurer has a right under the doctrine of subrogation to halt an action by the insured, in this case such a right was to be found in the express subrogation clause in the policy. If an insured has initiated proceedings on its own initiative, then generally he cannot be restrained by the insurer.

An insured who did successfully proceed against the third party contrary to his own insurer's wishes would not, of course, be able to retain both the insurance moneys and the damages recoverable from the third party; a sum equivalent to the insurer's payment to the insured would have to be returned to the insurer.

Actions against the emergency services

16.16   The courts have been reluctant to impose a positive duty of care upon emergency services to protect property owners. They have distinguished between the statutory duty which might be owed by the emergency service, making them liable under any particular legislation, and the establishment of a common law duty of care which, if proven, may lead to the payment of substantial damages. The only authority which has led to substantial damages against an emergency service is the case of *Digital Equipment Co Ltd v Hampshire County Council and Capital &*

Counties plc v Same [1997] 2 Lloyd's Rep 161. The case established that a fire brigade did not owe a duty of care to individual owners of premises other than in special circumstances. Those circumstances would normally involve the emergency service intervening and aggravating the damage by way of a positive act of negligence. Thus, for example, if the fire brigade failed to respond in time or respond with sufficient engines, the property owner would be unable to establish the requisite duty of care. On the other hand, in this particular case, the fire brigade intervened and turned off the sprinkler protection system, thus substantially aggravating the problem. In those circumstances, the brigade had created a fresh danger or substantially increased the risk of damage. The ongoing reluctance of the courts, however, to impose such duties is demonstrated by the decision of *OLL v Secretary of State for Transport [1997] 3 All ER 897*, in which the court purported to follow the above case, but decided that the failures of the coastguard when positively misdirecting the rescue attempts of others did not create a duty and breach so as to establish a claim for damages. It is difficult to distinguish between the two cases.

Procedural aspects of subrogation actions

16.17 Subrogation proceedings must be brought by the insurer in the name of the insured. If the insured's name, for some reason, cannot be used, for example, because the insured is a company which has been dissolved and has thus ceased to exist (*M H Smith (Plant Hire) Ltd v D L Mainwaring (T/A Inshore) [1986] 2 Lloyd's Rep 244*), subrogation rights will be lost. In other cases, the insurer can compel an unwilling insured to lend his name to the action, and can also compel the insured to permit the insurer to control the conduct of the action. It was indeed suggested by the House of Lords in *Lord Napier and Ettrick* (see 16.01 above) that the insurer possesses an equitable charge over the insured's action, although their Lordships were not prepared to go any further than ruling that there is an implied term in the contract of insurance under which the insured is under a duty to allow the use of his name.

The fact that the insurer is not suing in its own name should not be overlooked. In *Russell v Wilson, Independent, 2 June 1989*, the plaintiff's insurer brought a subrogation action against the defendant motorist, represented by his liability insurer. Since the claim was for a small amount, the matter was heard under the small claims procedure in the county court, under which procedure each party bears its own costs. The insurers had lost sight of this, and had used expensive lawyers. The court ruled that the successful insurer had to bear its own costs, despite the fact that these greatly exceeded the sum in dispute.

In *Kitchen Design and Advice Ltd v Lea Valley Water Co [1989] 2 Lloyd's Rep 221*, the plaintiff was insured against property damage and consequential loss. The defendants' conduct resulted in water damage to the plaintiff's property, for which payment was made by the plaintiff's insurers. The insurers, exercising subrogation rights, then reached a full and final settlement with the defendants' insurers for a slightly smaller sum. Subsequently, the plaintiff made a further claim against its insurers for consequential loss. This claim was met, but the insurers found themselves unable, by reason of their settlement with the defendants' insurers, to seek indemnification from them. The plaintiff's insurers commenced proceedings against the defendants in the insured's name, arguing the settlement which had been reached bound only the two insurers, and that it did not affect the plaintiff and defendants themselves. This argument had become possible only because the insurers, in settling, had done so in their own names and not in the names of the parties. The High Court nevertheless dismissed the action, by holding that the plaintiff's policy was to be construed as authorising the insurer to enter into settlements on the plaintiff's behalf, so that the insurer had settled the plaintiff's rights by its agreement with the defendants' insurers.

Sums recovered by way of subrogation

Ownership

16.18   Sums in respect of which the insurer may have a subrogation claim may be received in one of two ways.

(a)   By virtue of the fact that the third party has made payment to the insured. In such a case, the insured must account to the insurer for some or all of that payment. The capacity in which the sum is held by the insured is of importance in the event that the insured becomes insolvent before payment has been made to the insurer; if the insured is merely a debtor of the insurer, the insurer is purely an unsecured creditor and will have no prioritised claim in the event of insolvency. If, by contrast, the insured holds the money in a fiduciary capacity, the insurer has a priority in any bankruptcy or liquidation proceedings. The question was resolved in the insurer's favour by the House of Lords in *Lord Napier and Ettrick* (see 16.01 above). Their Lordships ruled that the insurer has an equitable charge or lien over the money, so that it is impressed with a security interest in favour of the insurer. This conclusion was the direct result of the equitable nature of subrogation.

(b)   By means of an action against the third party brought by the insurer in the insured's name. Here, the money will go directly to the insurer. If the insurer has recovered a sum greater than its own payment to the insured, that must be paid to the insured, and pending payment is, it might be assumed in the light of *Lord Napier and Ettrick*, to be held subject to an equitable charge or lien in the insured's favour.

Allocation

16.19   When a sum of money has been obtained from the third party by either the insurer or the insured the question arises of how it is to be allocated between them. There are two general principles here.

The first is that the insurer can never recover by way of subrogation a nominal sum greater than had been paid to the insured. In *Yorkshire Insurance Co Ltd v Nisbet*

Shipping Co Ltd [1962] 2 QB 330, the insured suffered a loss of £72,000, which was paid by the insurers. The insured then recovered £126,000 from the wrongdoer (the Canadian Government). The discrepancy arose because of alterations in the exchange rate, and the reality of the situation was that the amount recovered, although nominally greater than the loss, was in practical terms equal to it. The court, nevertheless, held that subrogation operated on nominal payments, and held that the insurers could claim only £72,000 of the recovery, leaving the insured with a windfall of £54,000. In this type of situation, the insurer is better advised to seek an assignment of the insured's rights, as assignment allows the insurer to retain the full amount of any recovery.

The second general principle is that the insured is entitled to receive an indemnity, so that any moneys recovered from the third party must first be allocated to the insured to make up any shortfall between his loss and the sum recovered from the insurer. In determining the total amount of the insured's loss for this purpose, any excess borne by the insured is to be disregarded. The principle is well illustrated by *Lord Napier and Ettrick* (see 16.01 above). Here, the insureds (Lloyd's Names) were insured against underwriting losses, and also had causes of action against those responsible for the losses. The House of Lords worked on assumed figures of:

recovery from wrongdoer	£150,000
total loss	£160,000
sum insured	£100,000
uninsured excess	£25,000

The insured was paid the sum insured of £100,000, but this still left the insured with a loss of £60,000, consisting of £25,000 excess and £35,000 above the policy limits. The House of Lords held that the uninsured excess was to be disregarded in determining the insured's loss, as that sum had been agreed to be borne by the insured. This left a 'recover down' principle, under which the £150,000 recovered was to be applied in the following order:

(*a*)   the first £35,000 went to the insured, to provide him with an indemnity;

(*b*)   the next £100,000 went to the insurer, by way of subrogation; and

(*c*)   the balance of £15,000 went to the insured, on the principle that the insurer can never retain more than the nominal amount which it had paid.

The 'recover down' principle is equally applicable to a commercial insurance which is arranged in layers: any subrogation recovery goes to the top layer insurer first, on the basis that the layering arrangement is intended to ensure that he is the last insurer to bear any loss.

Assignment

16.20   English law provides different mechanisms for the assignment, or transfer, of 'choses in action', such as contractual and other rights. Insurance policies and rights of payment under insurance policies are choses in action, and are therefore, in principle, transferable from the insured to a third party. The assignment of insurance rights concerns two very different matters.

- the assignment of the policy itself; and

- the assignment of the right to recover the debt owed by the insurer under the policy.

The differences flow from the fact that where the policy itself is assigned, there is a change of insured, whereas where there is an assignment of the right to recover, the insured stays the same. It is important to note that an assignee of the policy of insurance can only recover losses sustained by him to his interest, whereas an assignee of a right of recovery can only recover for losses sustained by the insured (who stays the same).

Assignment, for the purposes of this book, is concerned only with voluntary assignment of policies and their proceeds. Transfer may also occur by operation of law, on the death or insolvency of the insured.

Assignment of the policy

General prohibition

16.21   The general rule is that a contract of insurance is a personal contract between the insurer and the insured, in that the insurer only undertakes the risk having considered with care the character of the insured and the potential for loss under the policy. The law does not, therefore, permit the insured to transfer his policy to a third party and thereby to change the nature of the risk originally accepted by the insurer.

The general rule disallowing assignment is nevertheless subject to three exceptions. A policy may be assignable if:

(*a*)   the insurer consents to the transfer;

(*b*)   the policy is a marine policy; or

(*c*)   the policy is a life policy.

Consent of the insurer

16.22   The insurer may consent to the transfer of the policy either by including a right to transfer in the policy itself, or by consenting to an express request for a transfer. An illustration of the former possibility is the clause sometimes found in policies on buildings, which states that the purchaser of the property is to be entitled to the benefit of the seller's insurance for the period between exchange of contracts and conveyance to the purchaser.

The effect of failure to obtain the insurer's consent to assignment is demonstrated by *Peters v General Accident Fire & Life Assurance Corporation (1938) 60 Ll L Rep 311*

167

which held that where the insured sold his motor vehicle and assigned his motor policy covering the motor vehicle contemporaneously to a third party, the assignment of the policy without consent had the effect of terminating the policy automatically.

Where the insurer has consented to the assignment of the policy, it is important for reasons of insurable interest that there is a simultaneous assignment to the third party of the subject matter insured by the policy and the policy itself.

If the insured purports to assign the property before he assigns the policy, his insurable interest in the policy will lapse and the policy becomes ineffective. This was so held in *Rogerson v Scottish Automobile & General Insurance Co Ltd [1931] (1931) 41 Ll L Rep 1*, in which the insured's motor policy was held to have lapsed on his selling the car which was insured under it. The policy can survive in this situation only if the insured has retained some insurable interest, for example, in the case of a motor policy where the policy covers the insured while driving other vehicles (*Dodson v Peter H Dodson Insurance Services [2001] 1 WLR 1012*, disapproving of *Boss v Kingston [1962] 2 Lloyd's Rep 431*), or in the case of a property policy where the insured retains legal ownership until the purchase price on the sale of a property has been paid (*Rayner v Preston (1881) 18 Ch D 1*).

If, by contrast, the insured purports to assign the policy before he assigns the property, the assignee of the policy does not at that stage have any insurable interest in the property. It was held in *Lloyd v Fleming (1872) LR 7 QB 299* that a third party assignee cannot recover as at the date of the assignment of the policy, as he did not possess an insurable interest, and the insured cannot recover as he has assigned the policy. This disregards the insurable interest rule that a policy on property is lawful as long as the insured has a reasonable expectation of obtaining an insurable interest (see 4 INSURABLE INTEREST). The correct rule seems to be that the insured assignee cannot recover if a loss occurs before the property is transferred to him, but he can recover if the loss occurs after the policy and the property have both fallen into his ownership.

Formalities

16.23   A contract of insurance, as a chose in action, can be assigned either at law or in equity. There is need for an express assignment in all cases, as the mere fact that the subject matter of a contract of insurance is transferred to a purchaser does not have the effect of carrying with it any policy on that subject matter (*Marine Insurance Act 1906, s 15*). A legal assignment must comply with s 136 of the *Law of Property Act 1925*, the requirements of which are that:

(*a*)   the assignment must be in writing and signed by the assignor;

(*b*)   the assignment is intended to transfer the entirety of the assignor's interest (and not merely a part of the interest, eg where the policy is mortgaged); and

(*c*)   written notice of the assignment is given to the insurer.

An assignment which fails to meet one or more of these requirements will nevertheless take effect as an equitable assignment, as long as an intention to assign can be demonstrated.

A legal assignment is preferable from the assignee's point of view, for two reasons.

(*a*)   A legal assignment allows the assignee to bring proceedings against the insurer in his own name. As the law does not recognise an equitable assignment, an action on the policy must be brought by the assignee and the assignor jointly. This is only a technical problem, as the court can force the assignor to lend his name to the proceedings.

(*b*)   Taking a legal assignment protects the assignee against fraud. Priorities of competing assignments, whether legal or equitable, are determined by the dates of notice of the assignment being given to the insurer. Thus, if the insured assigns his policy to A without giving notice to the insurer, and then fraudulently assigns his policy to B, B (assuming that he was not, at the time of assignment to him, aware of what has gone before) may obtain priority over A by being first to notify the insurer of his interest.

Marine policies

16.24   It is a long established principle in the common law, as codified in *s 50(1)* of the *Marine Insurance Act 1906*, that marine policies can be assigned. This recognises the basis upon which shipping business is transacted, and in particular the 'cost insurance freight' form of export contract, under which the seller of goods is obliged to arrange for the transport, as well as arranging the insurance policy, to be assigned to the buyer on payment for the goods.

The procedure for, and effect of, assigning marine policies is set out in *s 50(3)* and *50(2)* respectively of the *Marine Insurance Act 1906*, which provides that:

(*a*)   a policy may be assigned by endorsement or in any other customary manner;

(*b*)   assignment has the effect of allowing the assignee to proceed against the insurer in the assignee's own name; and

(*c*)   there is no requirement for the assignee to give notice of assignment to the insurer in order to create a legal assignment.

A marine policy is only assignable if it does not contain terms expressly prohibiting assignment.

Life policies

16.25   A life policy requires the insurer to make payment to the policyholder on the death of the life insured. As long as the policyholder has an insurable interest in the insured life at the date the contract is made, the policy will be freely assignable unless (which is today rare) the policy provides otherwise. Life policies may be sold or mortgaged, and there is a thriving auction market for life policies.

A life policy may be assigned in any of the following ways:

(*a*)   under the provisions of the *Policies of Assurance Act 1867*;

(*b*)   in compliance with *s 136* of the *Law of Property Act 1925*; and

(*c*)   in equity.

Policies of Assurance Act 1867

16.26   Prior to the *Policies of Assurance Act 1867*, a life policy was not assignable at law. However, under the 1867 Act, an assignment is valid if it is of the assignor's whole interest in the policy or of merely a part of it, for example by way of mortgage.

A policy may be assigned under the 1867 Act, either by endorsement on the policy, or by a separate document in the form set out in the schedule to the 1867 Act. Notice of the assignment must be given to the insurer.

Section 136 of the Law of Property Act 1925

16.27   A life policy is a chose in action, and as such can be assigned under the provisions of the *Law of Property Act 1925*. An assignment of a life policy under this provision requires that the assignment of the life policy is absolute, so that the assignor must transfer the entirety of his interest.

The formalities are as follows:

- The assignment must be in writing and signed by the assignor.

- Written notice of the assignment must be given to the insurer.

Equity

16.28   An assignment of a life policy may also be assigned in equity without formality and without notice to the insurer. Various forms of assignment will commonly overlap. Where a number of successive assignments by a fraudulent policyholder have been made, the first assignee to give notice to the insurer will take priority, as long as he was not aware of any previous assignments when he took his own assignment.

Consequences of assignment of a policy

16.29   An assignment, whether legal or equitable, of a policy has the effect of bringing into existence a new contract between the insurer and the assignee. This does not mean, however, that previous matters affecting the policy are disregarded, for the rule is that assignment is always 'subject to equities'. This means that any defence to a claim, or any right to avoid the policy, which the insurer had obtained before the assignment remains in place and can be relied upon against the assignee after the assignment. The position is spelt out by *s 50(2)* of the *Marine Insurance Act 1906* which provides that the insurer 'is entitled to make any defence arising out of the contract which he would have been entitled to make if the action had been brought in the name of the (original insured)'. A similar wording is found in *s 136* of the *Law of Property Act 1925* and *s 2* of the *Policies of Assurance Act 1867*. Matters which can be pleaded against the assignee include failure by the insured to disclose a material fact when the policy was taken out and breach of warranty by the insured.

Assignment of the proceeds of the policy

Principles governing assignment

16.30   The proceeds of the policies constitute a debt payable by the insurer to the insured. Debts are freely assignable as choses in action. The proceeds of a policy may be assigned either:

- under the terms of *s 136* of the *Law of Property Act 1925*; or

- in equity.

The differences between an assignment of the policy and an assignment of the proceeds are as follows.

(*a*)   An assignment of the proceeds does not give rise to a new contract between the insurer and the assignee, which means that the insured is still the assignor, and for that reason the consent of the insurer to assignment is not needed unless the policy expressly so provides.

(*b*)   The assignee does not need to have an insurable interest in the subject matter of the policy and as such, the subject matter does not also have to be assigned.

An assignment of the proceeds of the policy can be effected at law, by compliance with *s 136* of the *Law of Property Act 1925* or in equity (see 3.04 above). If the assignment is legal, the assignee can sue the insurer in his own name; if not, the assignor must be joined to the action. An assignee of the proceeds, nevertheless, is in a somewhat weaker position as regards the insurer than is an assignee of the policy itself. This is the case because there is no change of insured, so that the rights of the assignee are purely dependent upon the conduct of the insured. Not only is the assignee's right to recover limited by any wrongful conduct by the insured prior to the assignment (for example, breach of the duty of utmost good faith, breach of warranty, etc) (see 2 TERMS IN INSURANCE CONTRACTS) but the assignee is affected by post-assignment misconduct. The point is that the assignee can claim the proceeds only if the proceeds would have been payable to the insured.

If, therefore, the insured fails to make a claim under the policy within the time allowed by the policy, the insurer has a defence to the claim and the assignee has no rights. Similarly, if the insured, having assigned the right to recover, breaks a warranty in the policy, there are no proceeds payable, and there is no available fund against which the assignee can press his claim (*Bank of Nova Scotia v Hellenic Mutual War Risks Association (Bermuda) Ltd (The Good Luck) [1991] 3 All ER 1* – breach of warranty by the insured vessel's entering into a war zone). It is for this reason that an assignee is well advised to procure his own fall back policy which will provide an indemnity to him in the event that the insured's own policy for some reason does not provide an indemnity. An example of this would be a mortgagee's interest policy providing for indemnity in the event that the primary insurer repudiates liability.

Sale of land

16.31   The problem here is the two-stage process applicable to a contract for the sale of land. At the initial contract stage, the purchaser bears the risk while the seller remains the owner, and ownership is transferred to the purchaser only at the second stage of completion. The effect of the purchaser bearing the risk in the period between contract and completion is that the purchaser must pay the full price on completion, irrespective of any damage which may have taken place regarding the property (see *Rayner v Preston* at 3.03 above). To reverse this rule, which in effect requires both parties to maintain insurance for that period, s 47 of the *Law of Property Act 1925* provides that any sum payable to the seller under his own policy shall be held by him for the purchaser on completion. The purchaser is therefore only liable to pay the purchase price, net of the insurance recovery, by virtue of a statutory assignment of the policy proceeds. This provision is subject to various conditions including, *inter alia*, obtaining the consent of the insurer.

The section is, however, fundamentally flawed as it disregards the fact that the seller's insurer, having paid the insured, is entitled to exercise subrogation rights against the purchaser and to claim payment under the contract of sale from the purchaser (see 16 SUBROGATION). Fire policies often contain a condition giving the buyer the benefit of the insurance, thereby disallowing the insurer from exercising subrogation rights in the seller's name against the buyer. The practice has thus remained for both parties to maintain insurance. The problem was attacked in a rather different manner in 1990, when the Law Society's revised Conditions of Sale imposed an obligation on the seller to transfer the property in the same physical state as it was at the date of contract. This means that the seller retains the risk until completion.

Chapter 17
Co-insurance

- Introduction
- Joint insurance
- Composite insurance
- Co-insured subrogation immunity
- Insurance for the benefit of another

Introduction

17.01 Co-insurance is a collective term for any form of arrangement under which the interests of two or more persons are insured under a single policy. There are two forms of co-insurance: joint insurance and composite insurance. The distinction is important, for reasons that follow.

This chapter will also consider a third possibility, namely, that a policy has been taken out by a single insured, under contractual arrangements with another, whereby that other is the intended beneficiary.

Joint insurance

17.02 Joint insurance is where there is more than one insured under a policy and each has a common and indivisible interest in the insured subject matter (*General Accident Fire and Life Assurance Corp Ltd v Midland Bank Ltd [1940] 2 KB 388*). The clearest example of a common and indivisible interest sufficient to give rise to joint insurance is that of joint ownership of the insured property.

The general principle with joint insurance is that the rights of the joint insureds stand and fall together. This has the following consequences:

(a)   Any application for the policy is made by both parties, as each will have completed the application. A false statement, or a failure to disclose material facts, by one party will, therefore, permit the insurer to avoid liability against both parties (*United Shoe Machinery v Brunet [1909] AC 330, 340*).

(b)   The conditions in the policy must be complied with by both parties. If, for example, a burglary policy provides that the insured must take reasonable care to avoid a loss, and one of the joint insureds neglects to secure the premises from which the insured property is stolen, the other (innocent) party has no claim against the insurers. The same principle applies to other breaches of duty by one of the parties, such as a breach of warranty or deliberate destruction of the property (*P Samuel & Co Ltd v Dumas [1924] AC 431, 445*).

(c)   In the event of a loss, the insurer may pay the insurance moneys to any one of the joint insureds.

Composite insurance

Definition and significance

17.03   Composite insurance is where there is more than one insured and each has a diverse interest in the insured subject matter. Where the policy is composite each insured in effect has a separate contract with the insurer, albeit embodied in a single policy document. Typical examples of composite insurance are policies taken out by a mortgagor and a mortgagee, a landlord and a tenant, an owner and a hirer of goods, and a contractor and subcontractor of building works.

The implications of composite insurance are as follows:

(a)   Because the contracts are separate, if one insured has made a non-disclosure or misrepresentation at inception and the other has not, the insurer may only avoid the contract as against the 'guilty' insured (*New Hampshire Insurance Co Ltd v MGN Ltd [1997] LRLR 24, 57–58*). An illustration may be found in the context of mortgagor and mortgagee. A building society will typically procure a block insurance policy covering its interests as mortgagee in all properties. Each mortgagor choosing to insure with the mortgagee's insurers will then be added to the block policy. If the mortgagor infringes his duty of utmost good faith in applying for cover, he will be unable to recover under the policy, but the mortgagee's cover under the block policy is unaffected (*Woolcott v Sun Alliance and London Insurance Ltd [1978] 1 Lloyd's Rep 629*). A point to note, however, is that where one proposal form is completed by all the insureds or by one as agent for the others, if this contains a non-disclosure or misrepresentation then (assuming actual inducement) the insurer will be able to avoid as against all the insureds. This is because, under the present law, it is no defence to an insurers' case on avoidance that the non-disclosure/misrepresentation was made innocently.

(b)   Breach of duty by one party will preclude recovery by him but will not affect the other's right to recover. To give some examples: in the case of a life policy under which A and B insure each other's lives, and A murders B, A cannot claim under the policy but the policy moneys will be payable to B's estate (*Davitt v Titcumb [1989] 3 All ER 417*); under a policy taken out by the mortgagor of property covering the interests of himself and the mortgagee, deliberate destruction of the property by the mortgagor will not preclude recovery by the mortgagee (*P Samuel & Co Ltd v Dumas [1924] AC 431*).

(c) Losses under the policy must be paid to each composite insured in respect of his own interest (*General Accident Fire and Life Assurance Corp Ltd and Drysdale v Midland Bank Ltd [1940] 2 KB 388*). A co-insured with an insurable interest in the entire subject matter may, however, recover the full sum insured although he must account to his co-insureds for any sums which are in excess of his own interest in the subject matter.

Creation of composite insurance

17.04   A composite policy may be formed by the co-insureds making simultaneous applications to the insurer. More commonly, however, an insured will insure on behalf of himself and other persons, either specifically identified or forming part of a definable class. A good example of the position is found in the context of the insurance of a construction project, the head contractor insuring himself and all subcontractors. Whether a person is co-insured under a policy depends upon whether or not the primary insured was or was not authorised to procure insurance for that person.

Where the primary insured is authorised

17.05   Where X is authorised by Y or required by a contract with Y to take out a composite policy with Y (ie a policy under which both their respective, divisible interests in the subject matter of the insurance are covered), the policy will cover the interests of both where:

(a)   *X's authority / contractual obligation extends to procuring the policy in question*. In *National Oilwell (UK) Ltd v Davy Offshore Ltd [1993] 2 Lloyd's Rep 582*, for example, the main contractor was obliged by the terms of the subcontract to procure an all risks property insurance policy for the subcontractor, covering the equipment due to be supplied under the subcontract, up to the point of delivery of the equipment. In fact, the main contractor procured a policy which covered both itself and the subcontractor against liability incurred due to defects in the subcontract equipment occurring before or after delivery. Defects arose in the equipment post-delivery, with the result that construction was delayed , causing the main contractor to incur substantial losses. These were paid by the insurer, which sought in turn to recover its payment from the subcontractor by way of subrogation. The subcontractor resisted this claim by asserting that he was a party to the contract of insurance and, therefore, immune from subrogation proceedings in accordance with the general rule that subrogation rights cannot be exercised against an insured party (see 17.07 below). The court held that the subcontractor was not a co-insured vis-à-vis post-delivery risks, since to be a co-insured the main contractor must have been authorised to insure on the subcontractor's behalf. This had not been the case, as the subcontract obliged the main contractor to insure for the subcontractor only in respect of pre-delivery losses. The main contractor's authorisation to insure could not be any wider than his obligation. The subcontractor was, therefore, co-insured under the policy only in respect of pre-delivery risks.

(b)   *X intended to cover Y's interests, when taking out the policy*. It has been held that the question here is subjective (was it X's subjective intention for the insurance to cover Y's interest? (*O'Kane v Jones (The Martin P) [2004] 1 Lloyd's Rep 389*), but it seems that the position is not entirely clear (*Hopewell Project Management Ltd v Ewbank Preece Ltd [1998] 1 Lloyd's Rep 448, 456–457*).

(c)   *The policy does not preclude the extension of coverage to Y*. Usually, the policy will identify the insured persons, either by name or description. But the description must be apt to cover the purported co-insured in question. In *Talbolt Underwriting v Nausch Hogan & Murray Inc (The Jackson 5) [2006] 2 Lloyd's Rep 195*, for example, the question was whether the ship owner's repairers where a co-insured by virtue of policy phrase: 'and/or Subsidiary, Affiliates, Associated and Interrelated Companies and/or Joint Ventures'. The court held that they were not, since the repairer was not in the same group of companies, and something more than a repairing contract was required to give rise to a joint venture.

If the purported co-insured (Y) is not named or otherwise described as being an insured by the policy, then the question is whether the actual proposer (X) was acting as his agent, ie whether Y was X's undisclosed principal. In *Siu Yin Kwan v Eastern Insurance Co Ltd [1994] 1 All ER 213*, for example, a shipping agent was requested by a shipowner to obtain a policy covering the shipowner's potential liability to his employees. A policy was issued, but with the shipping agent named as the insured. An accident occurred for which the shipowner was held to be liable, and the Privy Council ruled that the shipowner was the proper insured under the policy by reason of the doctrine of the undisclosed principal, given that the requirements of authorisation and intention had been met.

A potential problem which may arise when a person not identified in the policy claims to be the insured on the basis that the actual proposer acted with his authorisation and intended to do so, is the duty on the proposer to disclose all material facts to the insurer. Is the existence of the undisclosed principle a material fact? In *Talbot Underwriting*, Cooke J stated *obiter* that in his view, in the connection of the marine policy there under consideration, this would certainly be the case.

If the purported co-insured is not named or otherwise described as being an insured by the policy and is unable to successfully argue that he was the actual proposer's undisclosed principal, he may still be able to enforce the policy, by virtue of the *Contracts (Rights of Third Parties) Act 1999*.

Where the primary insured is unauthorised

17.06   Where the primary insured under an insurance contract is not authorised to obtain cover for another person, that other may in some circumstances be able to ratify the unauthorised act, and thereby claim to be a party to the contract. Ratification was discussed by the court in *National Oilwell* (see 17.05 above), where the following conditions for ratification by the subcontractor were laid down:

(*a*)   The contractor had to be a person identified in the policy as a co-insured, either by name or by description. This is based on the common law rule that an undisclosed principal cannot ratify.

(*b*)   The subcontractor must have intended to insure on behalf of the subcontractor. As above, this requirement was held by the court in *National Oilwell* not to have been met, as the contractor's intention to insure could not be regarded as any wider than his obligation to do so. In the result, even though the subcontractor was stated to be a co-insured, the fact that the contractor was not obliged to insure for post-delivery losses meant that he could not have intended to do so.

Where ratification is possible, it can be effected at any time, even after the person seeking to ratify has become aware that a loss has occurred. But a company which was not formed at the date that the policy incepted cannot ratify the contract, since it did not exist at the material time (*Natal Land & Colonization Co v Pauline Colliery and Development Syndicate [1904] AC 120*).

Co-insured subrogation immunity

17.07   An insurer has no right of subrogation in the name of one co-insured against another under the same policy (*Petrofina (UK) Ltd v Magnaload [1984] QB 127*). There is debate as to the basis for this rule. On one view it is to avoid the circuity that would arise if an insurer could recover from one of its insured what it had paid out to another, under a policy insuring both (see eg *The Yasin [1979] 2 Lloyd's Rep 45*). However, in *Co-operative Retail Services Ltd v Taylor Young Partnership Ltd [2002] 1 WLR 1419*, Lord Hope stated that the better view on the facts there under consideration was that such a recovery was prevented by virtue of an implied term in the contract between the co-insureds, pursuant to which the composite policy had been taken out.

The prohibition on subrogation against a co-insured only applies to those risks in respect of which the co-insured has cover under the policy. In the *National Oilwell* case (see 17.05 above), the co-insured subcontractor was insured only against losses occurring prior to his delivery of products to the contractor. The products were allegedly defective, and caused the contractor loss due to delay in completing the project. The court held that the subcontractor was not immune from a subrogation action regarding post-delivery losses, as he was not a co-insured in respect of such losses. Also, if the co-insured is guilty of wilful misconduct and either deliberately or recklessly causes the loss, the insurer, having paid other co-insureds, is not precluded from proceeding against the guilty co-insured by way of subrogation (*P Samuel & Co Ltd v Dumas [1924] AC 431, 445*).

Insurance for the benefit of another

17.08   Where a number of interests are to be insured, an alternative to composite insurance is a policy taken out in the name of one insured but for the benefit of himself and other persons who are unidentified. The premium will often be paid, directly or indirectly (in the form of, for example, rent or other charges to the named insured) by the other persons. The interests of those other persons are frequently 'noted' on the policy, although noting probably has no legal significance. This form of insurance has the following effects:

(*a*)   *The right to sue.* There is no privity of contract between the insurer and the unnamed insureds, whether or not their interests have been noted on the policy. In the event of a loss, only the named insured can bring an action on the policy.

(*b*)   *Payment of proceeds.* All insurance proceeds are payable to the named insured, and the unnamed insureds have no general right to require the insurer to apply the insurance moneys in any other way. There is one statutory exception to this principle, contained in *s 83* of the *Fires Prevention (Metropolis) Act 1774*, under which a person with an interest in a building insured under a fire policy can require the insurer to apply the insurance funds on reinstatement of the building.

(*c*)   *Unnamed insured subrogation immunity.* While the unnamed insureds can derive no direct benefit from the policy, an indirect benefit may accrue, in the form of immunity from a subrogation action (see 16 SUBROGATION).

In *Mark Rowlands v Berni Inns Ltd [1985] 3 All ER 473* the plaintiff was the landlord of the building, the basement of which was leased to the defendant. The tenant covenanted to repair the basement, when necessary, and to pay to the landlord an insurance rent related to the premium paid by the landlord for insurance of the whole building. The lease contained a provision that, in the event of fire, the tenant was to be relieved of the duty to repair the building and the landlord was to use the insurance money to repair it. Subsequently, the whole building was destroyed by a fire. The insurer indemnified the landlord and sought to recover from the tenant, whose negligence it was alleged had caused the fire. The Court of Appeal held that, although the tenant was not a party to the insurance contract, under the lease the insurance was taken for the joint benefit of landlord and tenant; and that this arrangement revealed that the parties' intentions were that the tenant was exempt from any liability to the landlord for the loss covered under the insurance policy.

Thus, unnamed co-insured's immunity from subrogation rests upon the implication of a term in the contract with the named insured, whereby the named insured agrees to look to the proceeds of the insurance policy rather than to the co-insured for indemnification for loss. Arguably, in the absence of an obligation to insure and reinstate, and some contribution to the premium by the unnamed co-insured, it will rarely be possible for a term of the *Mark Rowlands* case type to be implied. In *National Oilwell* (see 17.05 above) the subcontractor claimed to be an unnamed co-insured for losses occurring after his delivery of products to the named insured contractor. Colman J ruled that it was not possible to imply into the subcontract any term giving the subcontractor the benefit of the contractor's insurance, not the least because the subcontractor had not contributed any part of the premium for post-delivery losses.

The essential question which the court must look at is whether it was the parties' common intention that the insurance should inure to both parties' benefit, even in the absence of one of the parties being a named insured. Indeed, in looking for that intention, the courts have now decided that they can look outside of the precise contractual arrangements between the parties, as in the case of *Lambert v Keymood Ltd [1997] 2 EG 131*, where the court determined that it was entitled to take that intention outside of the terms of the lease by examining ancillary correspondence between the tenant and the landlord.

(*d*) *Rights of the unnamed insureds against the insured.* Any rights which the unnamed insureds possess against the insured derive from the contractual relationship between them. Two particular issues arise:

   (i) Can the unnamed insureds force the named insured to make a claim under the policy? This may be a particularly important issue in the context of policies taken out by a landlord intended to benefit tenants, for if the premises are destroyed, the tenants will be under a continuing obligation to pay rent and the landlord has no incentive to make a claim against the insurers. In some cases the courts will be willing to imply a term into the contract between the named and unnamed insureds that the named insured will make a claim (*Vural Ltd v Security Archives Ltd [1990] 60 P & CR 258*), and in residential tenancies governed by the *Landlord and Tenant Act 1987* there is a statutory procedure under which the tenant can prevent the insurer from denying liability for want of a claim pending proceedings to require the landlord to make a claim (*Landlord and Tenant Act 1985, s 42(2), Sch 3, para 7*).

   (ii) Can the unnamed insureds claim any interest in the policy moneys? The general rule is that, unless the contract gives any specific right to the unnamed insureds, the named insured can deal with the insurance moneys exactly as he thinks fit (*Leeds v Cheetham (1827) 1 Sim 146*). However, if the amount recovered exceeds the insured's own loss, he will in certain circumstances have to account to third parties for the excess.

Chapter 18
Double insurance and contribution

●   Introduction

●   Double insurance

●   Double insurance and contribution

Introduction

18.01 Where the insured takes out insurance for a sum greater than his potential loss, he is said to be overinsured. Overinsurance, which occurs because there are two or more policies on a single risk, is known as double insurance. In the event of double insurance, the insured may seek indemnity from any one of the insurers involved and, in that case, the paying insurer has the right to recoup a proportion of its payment from the other insurers. This right is referred to as the insurer's right of contribution, and is only applicable to indemnity contracts.

Double insurance

The insured's rights

18.02 It is a cardinal rule of insurance law that the insured can recover only an indemnity, irrespective of whether he is insured for a greater sum. In the event of double insurance, the insured can still recover only an indemnity, but he is free to make up that indemnity from the insurers in such proportions as he thinks fit (a rule confirmed by *s 32(2)* of the *Marine Insurance Act 1906*). The surplus premium paid by the insured is recoverable from the insurers. This is clearly the case in marine insurance (under *s 84(3)(f)* of the *Marine Insurance Act 1906*) and is probably the case in other forms of insurance.

Variation by contract

18.03   Double insurance is restricted through contractual devices. Insurers are wary of overinsurance, and particularly of double insurance, as this may be an indication of potential fraud by the insured. Insurers may also be unwilling to face the entire burden of a claim when other insurances are in place. For these reasons, a number of contractual devices may be used by insurers to overcome the common law principle that the insured can claim from the insurers in such order as he thinks fit. The following are typical clauses:

- an unconditional prohibition on the taking out of further insurance;

- a prohibition on the taking out of any further insurance without the consent of the insurer;

- a postponement of the insurer's liability in the event that any other insurance covering the risk is in existence; and

- a policy provision that the contract is not to come into force if any other insurance covering the risk exists at the date of inception.

It will frequently be the case, where there is double insurance, that both policies involved contain clauses of the above types. Which of the two policies bears the risk will depend upon a number of factors, including:

(*a*)   the wording of the clauses;

(*b*)   which of the policies was incepted first;

(*c*)   whether the insurer has an independent defence to any claim under either of the policies; and

(*d*)   whether the clause is to be construed as excluding only identical double insurance, or whether it extends to accidental overlaps in cover.

Double insurance and contribution

18.04   In *Equitable Fire and Accident Office, Ltd v The Ching Wo Hong [1907] AC 96*, policy A required the insured to obtain the insurer's consent for the taking out of further cover on the same risk. The insured, without seeking the consent of the insurer, entered into an agreement for the issue of policy B, but this never came into force as the premium for it was not paid. It was held that the condition in policy A had not been broken. In *Home Insurance Co of New York v Gavel [1928] 30 Ll L Rep 139*, policy A provided that the insurer would not be liable in the event that the insured took out further insurance of which the insurer had not been notified. The insured procured policy B, which stated that it was not to come into force if an earlier policy covering the risk was in place. It was here held that the wording of policy B prevented it from coming into operation, and that the entire risk was borne by policy A.

The courts have refused to adopt a construction of contractual restrictions which leads to neither insurer being liable. If the circular position is reached whereby each policy casts the risk onto the other and that a different result is reached depending upon which policy is looked at first, the courts will disregard the contractual restrictions and hold each insurer to be liable for the full loss (*Weddell v Road Transport and General Insurance Co Ltd [1932] 2 KB 563; National Employers Mutual General Insurance Association Ltd v Haydon [1980] 2 Lloyd's Rep 149*).

Rateable proportion clauses. A rateable proportion clause is intended to restrict the insurer's liability to a proportion of the ultimate claim. If the policy issued by insurer A contains a rateable proportion clause, and the insured procures a policy from insurer B, insurer A is liable only for the proportion of the cover which its policy represents, in this case 50%. Where a policy contains both a rateable proportion clause and a clause which provides that the insurer is not liable if some other policy exists, the rateable proportion clause will be construed as the overriding clause, and the insurer will be liable for its proportion of the cover in the usual way.

The effect of a rateable proportion clause is that the insured is unable to claim against only one insurer. If he wishes to obtain his whole indemnity he must claim against all of the relevant insurers (see *Structural Polymer Systems Ltd v Brown [2000] Lloyd's Rep IR 64*).

The main disadvantage of a rateable proportion clause for the insured is that, in the event of the insolvency of any one of the co-insurers, the insured will not be able to make a full recovery, even with multiple policies.

Definition of contribution

18.05   Contribution is an equitable doctrine, and operates where there has been double insurance and the insured has claimed from one insurer rather than another. Let it be supposed that the insured has procured a policy from insurer A, and a policy from insurer B, and the claim has been made against insurer A alone. Contribution is insurer A's right to claim from insurer B a proportion of A's payment to the insured.

Contribution can operate between insurers only where, leaving aside the respective financial limits of the policies, the policies involved are more or less the same in terms of coverage. The following features must be present.

(*a*)   The policies must cover the same subject matter. It will be a matter of construction whether this is the case. Moreover, the overlap between the policies must be substantial rather than merely coincidental. If, therefore, a motor policy and a household policy both cover theft of property from a car, whichever insurer is called upon to pay by the insured has no right of contribution from the other insurer (see *Zurich Insurance Co v Shield Insurance Co [1988] IR 174*, which concerned a motor policy and an employers' liability policy).

(*b*)   The policies must cover the same insured interests in that subject matter. Different interests may exist in the same property. A quantity of goods in store may, for example, be insured by their owner for their value, and by the warehouseman in respect of his own liability for them. If the goods are destroyed, and the warehouseman's insurers make payment, those insurers have no right to seek contribution from the owner's insurers (*North British and Mercantile Insurance Co v London, Liverpool and Globe Insurance Co (1877) LR 5 Ch D 569*). Note however there will be, on the facts of some cases, the same insured interests even where there may appear to be different insureds. This was the case in *O'Kane v Jones (The 'Martin P') [2004] 1 Lloyd's Rep 389* where the manager of a ship was held to be acting as the undisclosed principal of the owner of the ship when effecting insurance on the ship (see 17 CO-INSURANCE).

The conditions for contribution

18.06   For there to be contribution, both insurers must face legal liability to the insured. The implications of this are explained in the following paragraphs, in which it is assumed that insurer A has been called upon by the insured to make payment, and then makes a claim against insurer B for contribution.

Insurer A's legal liability. If insurer A is not obliged to make payment to the insured, but does so on an *ex gratia* basis, insurer A, in effect, makes a gift to the insured. English law does not, however, allow restitutionary claims in respect of gifts. In *Legal and General Insurance Society Ltd v Drake Insurance Co Ltd [1992] QB 887*, the insured had procured two motor policies covering the same losses. The insured incurred liability to a third party, and a claim was made against insurer A, whose policy contained a rateable proportion clause. Insurer A settled the entire claim and sought contribution from insurer B. The Court of Appeal held that A's claim had to fail. A was, by the terms of its own policy, liable only for one-half of the loss, but had chosen voluntarily to pay the entire loss. There was, therefore, no legal basis upon which A could recover the excess payment from B.

Insurer B's legal liability. If insurer B has a defence against the insured, there is no concurrent liability under the two policies and insurer B has an equivalent defence against a contribution claim brought by insurer A. The time at which the right of contribution of insurer B to insurer A arises is at the date of loss not at the time of the contribution claim. This is the decision of *O'Kane* (above) which rejected the view of the Privy Council in *Eagle Star Insurance Co Ltd v Provincial Insurance plc [1993] 3 All ER 1,* and followed the view of the *Legal & General* case (above). *O'Kane* concerned two insurances taken out on a ship; one which the insurer had threatened to cancel but did not and one which was taken out in anticipation of this cancellation but which, subsequent to the loss, had itself been cancelled. If the time for assessing contribution had been at the time the claim was made then the cancellation of the second policy would mean only one policy was in force at the time. The court's decision that the relevant time was when the loss occurred meant there was double insurance and the paying insurer could claim a contribution from the other insurer.

However, a rateable proportion clause will not necessarily preclude contribution. In *Drake Insurance plc v Provident Insurance plc [2003] EWCA Civ 1834,* the Court of Appeal held that insurer A, who had the benefit of a rateable proportion clause in its policy but who was in dispute with insurer B over the validity of a concurrent policy (and therefore B's need to contribute to the settlement of the claim), was not in the position of a volunteer when it paid 100% of the claim 'under reserves'. Insurer A had made it clear to insurer B that it would pay the claim and later litigate the issue of its entitlement to a contribution if it had to. The court held that insurer B should bear the risk of the facts not supporting its avoidance of the second policy.

The amount of contribution

18.07   There are two ways of calculating the amount from which the paying insurer, insurer A, can recover from the contributing insurer, insurer B. The first is the independent liability calculation, which is applicable in liability insurance. The second is the maximum liability calculation, which applies in property policies.

Independent liability

18.08   Using this measure, the court looks at the amount of the insured's loss for which each insurer is liable, and the loss is apportioned accordingly. This means that if the loss falls within the policy limits of each insurer, each is liable for the full amount of the loss and therefore a 50% contribution is called for. In *Commercial Union Assurance Co Ltd v Hayden [1977] Q.B. 804*, policy A covered the insured's liability up to £100,000, whereas policy B covered the insured's liability up to £10,000. The insured suffered a loss of £4,425.25. The Court of Appeal held that, as each insurer would have been liable for that sum, insurer A – who had paid the loss – was entitled to recover 50% from insurer B.

The maximum amount of the liability of each insurer becomes important only when the loss exceeds the financial limits of one or both of them. If, in the *Commercial Union* case, the insured's loss had been £30,000, then the respective independent liabilities of insurers A and B for that loss would have been £30,000 and £10,000. The correct apportionment on those figures would have been insurer A bearing ¾ of the loss of £30,000 and insurer B bearing ¼ of the loss of £30,000.

Maximum liability

18.09   This measure, used in property insurance, gives paramount importance to the financial limit of each insurer's liability. By way of example, suppose that insurer A's maximum liability is £80,000 and insurer B's maximum liability is £40,000. Any loss is to be borne by the insurers, up to the financial limits of their policies, in the proportions 2:1.

Chapter 19
Average

- Average defined
- Policies subject to average

Average defined

19.01   The concept of average is intertwined with that of contribution between policies. The general term *average* may be used to describe both 'conditions' (or clauses) of average (ie the *first condition of average* and the *second condition of average*). This section only deals with the principle in the context of the first condition (for the interest of the reader, the second condition of average is concerned with the contribution between more specific and less specific insurance).

The first condition of average concerns the situation where the insured is under-insured and a partial loss has occurred. Where a policy is subject to average (for which see 19.02, below), the insured is deemed to be his own insurer for the proportion of the value of the subject matter by which he is uninsured (in the case of marine policies this is codified in *Marine Insurance Act 1906, s 81,*).

The formula for calculating how the first condition of average is applied is as follows:

$$\frac{\text{Sum insured} \times \text{loss}}{\text{True value}} = \text{Amount payable under policy}$$

Set out below are some practical examples of average.

(a)   If subject matter worth or valued at £100,000 is insured for £80,000, and is totally destroyed, the insured recovers the full amount under the policy, £80,000. This is so whether or not the policy is subject to average.

(b)   If the subject matter worth or valued at £100,000 is insured for £80,000 under a policy not subject to average, and suffers 50% damage, the insured will recover his full £50,000 loss.

(c)   If subject matter worth or valued at £100,000 is insured for £80,000 under a policy subject to average, and suffers 50% damage, the insured and the insurer are deemed to be co-insurers in the respective proportions ²⁄₁₀: ⁸⁄₁₀. The insured will, therefore recover only ⁸⁄₁₀ of his loss, namely £40,000.

Policies subject to average

19.02   All marine policies, valued and unvalued, are deemed to be the subject of average (*Marine Insurance Act 1906, ss 67(2), 81*). Fire policies on commercial property have frequently been written on an average basis by inclusion of an express clause. However, as yet, there is no clear authority as to whether, in the absence of such an express clause, average is to be implied as a matter of law. In *Carreras Ltd v Cunard Steamship Co Ltd [1918] 1 KB 118*, a case involving the insurance of goods stored in a warehouse, the court read an average clause into the contract in question without an express condition to that effect. Bailhache J's reasoning being that fire policies on goods were so often written on that basis that an average clause was to be implied. It does not appear clear, however, whether the court had heard any expert evidence to that effect, and it is at least arguable that the very existence of express clauses in the majority of fire policies is evidence that there was an intention to omit such a clause if one is not included. It is probably the better view that commercial property policies are not subject to average unless an express clause is included. In the absence of an express clause and in the case of a gross undervaluation, the only remedy available to the insurer is to allege a non-disclosure or misrepresentation (see chapter ??). However, such allegations are made difficult by the fact that the valuation representation will probably be characterised as an opinion. Therefore, to succeed, the insurer must establish that in all the circumstances the opinion could not have been honestly held.

Purely domestic property risks are not normally written subject to average (Lloyd's policies being an exception), and clear wording would be required to produce that effect (*Sillem v Thornton (1854) 3 E & B 868*). Equally, commercial policies other than those on property (eg fidelity policies) are not presumed to be subject to average (*Fifth Liverpool Starr-Bowkett Building Society v Travellers Accident Insurance Co Ltd [1893] 9 TLR 221*).

Chapter 20
Third Parties (Rights Against Insurers) Act 1930

- Background

- Conditions for the operation of the 1930 Act

- Compliance with policy terms

- Agreements between the insurer and the insured

- Limitation periods

- The third party's right to information

- Problems with the operation of the 1930 Act

- Proposals for reform

Background

20.01 In *Re Harrington Motor Insurance Co Ltd, ex p Chaplin [1928] Ch 105*, it was held that where an insured incurs a liability to a third party but then becomes insolvent, the insurance policy proceeds must be paid into the insolvent insured's estate for distribution to the insured's creditors generally, and cannot be redirected to meet the third party's claim.

The *Third Parties (Rights Against Insurers) Act 1930 (TP(RAI)A 1930)* was passed specifically to resolve the problem which had emerged in *Re Harrington*. The broad effect of the 1930 Act is to transfer to the third party the rights of the insolvent insured against his liability insurers. This means that the policy monies go directly to the third party, and do not pass into the general insolvency.

TP(RAI)A 1930 applies to all forms of liability insurance, compulsory or non-compulsory, but it does not apply to motor insurance, where the principle of the 1930 Act is embodied in the *Road Traffic Act 1988*, or to reinsurance.

Conditions for the operation of the 1930 Act

The insured's insolvency

20.02   *TP(RAI)A 1930* becomes available only once the insured has become insolvent. The triggering events are listed in *s 1* of *TP(RAI)A 1930* and include bankruptcy, voluntary or compulsory winding-up, administration and receivership.

Proof of the insured's liability

20.03   A third party cannot use *TP(RAI)A 1930* to sue the insurer directly unless and until he has first established the insured's liability to him by admission or judgment. In *Post Office v Norwich Union Fire Insurance Society Ltd [1967] 1 All ER 577*, property belonging to the claimant was damaged by the insured. Before the legal responsibility of the insured to the claimant had been determined, the insured became insolvent and the claimant commenced proceedings under the 1930 Act. The Court of Appeal held that the action against the insurers was premature and was not permitted by the 1930 Act.

Dissolved companies

20.04   The requirement to prove the insured's liability can be particularly difficult where the insured is a company and, as a result of its insolvency, it has been dissolved and removed from the Register of Companies. Once it has been removed from the Register, the company has, as a matter of law, ceased to exist and proof of its liability becomes legally impossible. This situation arose in *Bradley v Eagle Star Insurance Co Ltd Respondents [1989] 2 WLR 568*, and the House of Lords confirmed in that case that, as the insured had ceased to exist as a matter of law and its liability could not be established, *TP(RAI)A 1930* could not be used against its insurers. This problem was swiftly remedied by legislation. *Section 651* of the *Companies Act 1985*, as amended by the *Companies Act 1989*, now permits a company to be restored to the Register of Companies purely for the purposes of proceedings against it to establish its liability. Once this has been done, the third party can then proceed against the company and, in due course, against the insurer in accordance with the *Post Office* case principle (see 20.03 above).

The situations in which *s 651* of the *Companies Act 1985* permits the resurrection of a dissolved company are as follows:

(*a*)   in the case of an action for damages for death or personal injury, the action may be brought at any time after the dissolution of the company subject to there being no limitation period affecting the action; and

(*b*)   in all other cases, the action must be brought within two years of the company's dissolution.

Section 651 of the *Companies Act 1985* is due to be repealed by the *Companies Act 2006* although, at the time of publication, the date for repeal was still to be announced. However, the subject matter of *s 651* will be contained within *Part 31*, *Chapter 3* (Restoration to the Register) of the *Companies Act 2006* and, in particular, *s 1030* (When application to the court may be made).

Compliance with policy terms

20.05   On the insolvency of the insured, the rights of the insured against the insurer are 'transferred to and vest in' the third party (*TP(RAI)A 1930, s 1*). However, the third party cannot be in any better position against the insurer than the insured would have been. Thus, if the insurer has any defence against the insured, that defence can be used against the third party equally. Furthermore, if the policy imposes conditions upon the insured which have to be met before the insurer is liable, such as premium payment or claims notification, such conditions must be met before the third party can use *TP(RAI)A 1930* against the insurer. One type of policy term which causes great difficulty in this regard is one which requires the insured to give notice of the loss either immediately or within a period of time. If the insured has been dilatory (and this is certainly possible in the context of an insolvency) this policy term is likely to have been breached, and this may give rise to a defence for the insurer which will defeat the third party's action under the 1930 Act (*Pioneer Concrete (UK) Ltd v National Employers' Mutual General Insurance Association Ltd [1985] 2 All ER 395*).

All that is transferred to the third party under the 1930 Act is the insured's contractual rights against the insurer. If those contractual rights have ceased to exist or can be defeated, the third party's claim against the insurer under the 1930 Act will not succeed.

Agreements between the insurer and the insured

20.06   *Section 3* of *TP(RAI)A 1930* states that any agreement between the insurer and the insured to settle, limit or relinquish the insured's claim under the policy is void and of no effect against the third party. However, this provision deals only with agreements made after the insured has become insolvent. The 1930 Act does not deal with agreements between the insurer and the insured made before the insured's insolvency has been confirmed, and in *Normid Housing Association Ltd v R. John Ralphs, John S Mansell, Ralphs and Mansell and Assicurazioni Generali SPA [1989] 1 Lloyd's Rep 265*, the Court of Appeal held that a pre-insolvency contractual agreement to limit the insurer's liability to a fraction of the potential total fell outside the prohibition of the 1930 Act and was valid, provided that it was made in good faith.

Limitation periods

20.07   Under a liability policy, the insured has a six-year limitation period, running from the date on which his cause of action against the insurer arose, in which to issue a claim form commencing his action against the insurer. It was held in *LeFevre v White [1990] 1 Lloyd's Rep 569* that the third party inherits the insured's limitation period, with the result that, if the insured has not commenced proceedings against the insurer within six years and then becomes insolvent, the third party is himself time-barred.

A particular difficulty arises where the insured has issued a claim form against the insurer within the limitation period, but becomes insolvent during the course of his action against the insurer at a time six years after his cause of action against the insurer arose. In *LeFevre v White* it was held that the action is not transferred to the third party under the 1930 Act as the action is not a right under the policy. The third party must, therefore, commence fresh proceedings against the insurer, but if six years have elapsed he will be time-barred. The same problem arises in arbitration proceedings. In *The London Steamship Owners Mutual Insurance Association Ltd v Bombay Trading Co Ltd (The 'Felicie') [1990] 2 Lloyd's Rep 21*, it was held that if the insured becomes insolvent during the course of arbitration proceedings, the third party cannot simply take over those proceedings but must commence fresh proceedings, in which case he may be met by a limitation defence.

The third party's right to information

20.08   *Section 2 of TP(RAI)A 1930* confers upon the third party the right to obtain information from the insured as to his insurance position following the bankruptcy or insolvency event. This will include details of the policy, including premium receipts. Once this information has been obtained, the third party can obtain equivalent information from the insurer to enable the action under the 1930 Act to be brought. A serious restriction was placed upon the operation of this section by the decision in *Nigel Upchurch Associates v The Aldridge Estates Investment Co Ltd [1993] 1 Lloyd's Rep 535*, in which it was held that *s 2* can be relied upon only after the third party has established the insured's liability. This meant that the third party must successfully prosecute an action against an insolvent defendant without first knowing whether or not the defendant has an insurance policy at all, or at least one which covers that particular liability. The risk of wasting extensive legal costs for a claim which might not ultimately be met by an insurer is one which many third parties would, understandably, not be willing to take. The decision in *Upchurch Associates v Aldridge Estates* was, however, overruled by the Court of Appeal *In Re OT Computers Ltd (In Administration) Nagra v OT Computers Ltd [2004] EWCA Civ 653*, which held that the transfer to and vesting in the third party of the rights of the insured (such as they were) occurred on insolvency and were not delayed until the establishment of the substantive content of such rights. The fact that the third party might not, in the event, be able to establish either the proposed defendant's liability or his right to any insurance indemnity had nothing to do with the requirement of information concerning the defendant's insurance arrangements. *Section 2* would usually entitle the third party to obtain disclosure of such information before the establishment of the insured's liability to that third party.

Problems with the operation of the 1930 Act

20.09   Over the years a number of deficiencies in *TP(RAI)A 1930* and problems with its operation have been exposed, some of which have already been outlined above. These include the following:

(a)   the fact that third parties may go to the expense of establishing the liability of the insured only then to discover that the insurer is not liable under the insurance contract;

(b)   the requirement that third parties restore dissolved companies to the register in order to establish the company's liability and then acquire rights under *TP(RAI)A 1930*;

(c)   the ability of insurers to rely against third party claimants under *TP(RAI)A 1930* on all the defences and policy terms on which they could have relied against the insured, including those which could have been performed only by the insured personally;

(d)   the fact that the a possibly limited insurance fund, inadequate to meet the claims of all third parties, is distributed on a 'first past the post' basis rather than *pro rata* to all claimants;

(e)   the added delay and expense arising from the fact that the third party, in general, has to bring two sets of proceedings, one against the insolvent insured and then another against the insurance company; and

(f)   the fact that there is no fresh limitation period for third parties claiming under *TP(RAI)A 1930*.

Proposals for reform

20.10   In July 2001, following an initial joint Consultation Paper which appeared in 1998, the Law Commission and the Scottish Law Commission published a report entitled *Third Parties – Rights Against Insurers* (Cm 5217) in which a series of proposals for reforming the *TP(RAI)A 1930* were detailed and to which a draft *Third Parties (Rights Against Insurers) Bill* was appended. The principal recommendations of the report were as follows.

(a)   It should not be necessary for the third party first to establish the insured's legal liability.

(b)   Instead, two facts should trigger the third party's rights – firstly, that the incident giving rise to the liability has occurred, and secondly, that an insolvency event has happened. Once these two events have occurred, the third party should be entitled to establish the liability of the insured and the liability of the insurer in one set of proceedings.

(c)   Where the insured is a dissolved company that has been struck off the Register of Companies, the third party should not have to take proceedings to restore the company to the Register in order to be able to establish the company's liability.

(d)   An insurer should not be permitted to insist that policy conditions be met by the insured if the third party could meet those conditions.

(e)   The obligation to disclose policy information should not be dependent on the establishment of the liability of the insured, but should arise after the incident giving rise to the liability of the insured and after the insolvency event.

(*f*)   The duty of the insured and of the insurer to disclose policy information should arise simultaneously.

(*g*)   The distribution of a limited insurance fund to multiple claimants should be determined by a statutory scheme involving an application to the court by a third party or by the insurer, which the court will decide depending on the circumstances of the case.

(*h*)   A third party's right of action under *TP(RAI)A 1930* should be treated as a new cause of action under English law and governed by a fresh limitation period.

(*i*)   A third party should be able to substitute himself in court and arbitration proceedings already commenced by the insured against the insurer, prior to the insolvency of the insured.

(*j*)   The law should be clarified to make it clear that the provisions would apply to cases with a foreign element.

The Government signalled its acceptance of these recommendations in answer to a Parliamentary Question on 2 July 2002. In September 2002 the Law Commission and the Scottish Law Commission issued a further joint Consultation Paper (CP 08/02) on the implementation of the report by way of a Regulatory Reform Order rather than by way of primary legislation (which the draft Bill suggests is what the Law Commissions had envisaged). It was proposed in this Consultation Paper that, subject to the outcome of the consultation, the changes be implemented during 2003/2004.

However, the Department for Constitutional Affairs (formerly the Lord Chancellor's Department) stated in its February 2004 analysis of the responses to the consultation paper that the law officers had advised that the following aspects of the Law Commissions' recommendations could be carried out by way of a regulatory reform order (the others requiring primary legislation):

(*a*)   the remedy in a single set of proceedings;

(*b*)   the third party's improved rights to information about the insurance position; and

(*c*)   clarification that the law applied to proceedings with a foreign element.

Further, the Department for Constitutional Affairs said that it considered that these were the Law Commissions' core recommendations and that, rather than waiting until parliamentary time became available for primary legislation on all of the proposals, the Government intended to press on with the implementation of these elements of the Law Commissions' recommendations by way of a regulatory reform order.

At the time of publication, there is still no sign of the promised regulatory reform order and the advantage of proceeding swiftly with at least some of the recommendations has been lost.

PART 4

Dispute Resolution

Chapter 21
Arbitration

- The arbitration agreement and arbitration clause
- The scope of arbitration
- Procedure governing arbitrations
- Confidentiality
- Honourable engagement clause
- Right to appeal

21.01 Arbitration is an alternative method of dispute resolution to court proceedings. In practice, the use of arbitration in insurance disputes is largely limited to commercial insurance, and in particular to shipping and reinsurance disputes. English law on arbitration is governed by the *Arbitration Act 1996*. Arbitration is consensual and private. Parties to a contract of insurance can agree to resolve any dispute relating to that contract by reference to arbitration. The parties will agree to be bound by the decision of the arbitrators. An arbitration clause can be included in the contract of insurance or a separate agreement can be created; in whatever manner it is formulated, the arbitrators derive their powers from the agreement to arbitrate.

The arbitration agreement and arbitration clause

21.02 *Section 7* of the *Arbitration Act 1996* gives explicit statutory recognition to what has become known as the doctrine of severability. This doctrine means that the arbitration agreement contained in the insurance contract concerned is treated as separate to the main contract, unless otherwise agreed by the parties. This prevents potential legal difficulties at a later date if one party alleges that the contract in dispute has been rescinded or avoided. Logically this would result in the arbitration clause which forms part of that contract also being treated as avoided. However, by treating the arbitration agreement as a separate contract, this problem is circumvented. Arbitrators, therefore, can be appointed to adjudicate whether a party's avoidance of the contract is valid.

The scope of arbitration

21.03   The matters which can be referred to arbitration will depend upon the scope of the wording of the clause or agreement in question. An arbitration clause should be drafted in the widest possible terms to try to ensure that all disputes which could arise concerning the contract in question can be referred to arbitration for resolution. However, since arbitration is a consensual and private method of resolving disputes, it is impossible to compel third parties to join the proceedings. In the context of insurance, this may be a major drawback if a party to, for example, a dispute between an insurer and an insured, or a reinsurer and a reinsured, wishes to join the broker as a party to proceedings for misrepresentation and/or negligence.

Arbitration clauses can also state the type of person to be appointed as arbitrator and how such appointments are to be made. Such clauses in reinsurance contracts will often stipulate that the arbitrators must have requisite amounts of experience in the London insurance and reinsurance market. The advantage of this is that the panel of arbitrators will have relevant expertise to determine any dispute which arises between the parties to the contract.

There are other organisations who have drafted or recommended arbitration clauses such as ARIAS, the AIDA Reinsurance and Insurance Arbitration Society. (AIDA is the International Association for Insurance Law, known by the initials of its French title, *Association Internationale de Droit des Assurances*.)

Procedure governing arbitrations

21.04   ARIAS has produced a comprehensive set of arbitration rules to deal with the conduct of arbitration proceedings from commencement until termination. Such rules can be incorporated into the arbitration agreement.

In the absence of specific procedural rules set out in the arbitration agreement, the parties can decide between themselves how the arbitration should be conducted. In the absence of agreement between the parties, even with regard to how the arbitrators should be appointed, the *Arbitration Act 1996* sets out rules for the commencement of arbitration proceedings and the appointment of arbitrators, as well as providing those arbitrators with powers to determine the manner in which the dispute between the parties should be resolved.

Confidentiality

21.05   Arbitration decisions are confidential, although in certain circumstances the arbitrators' award will need to be disclosed if it becomes necessary, by way of example, to enforce the award.

The award of the arbitrators is only binding upon the parties to the arbitration. Thus, unlike the court system, there is no operation of precedent. This does not mean that arbitrators are not bound by the published decisions of the English courts, assuming, of course, the governing law of the contract in dispute is the law of England and Wales. The contract could be governed by the laws of other countries; therefore the arbitrators would be bound by the laws of that jurisdiction.

For this reason, the parties to arbitration proceedings will usually wish to have at least one lawyer (usually a senior QC with relevant experience) as part of the arbitration tribunal. He or she will usually chair the tribunal and prepare the reasons for the arbitrators' decision, as well as advising the other members of the tribunal (who will often be practising or recently retired market practitioners) of the details of law and procedure relevant to the particular hearing.

Honourable engagement clause

21.06   Arbitration agreements, particularly in reinsurance contracts, often include a clause known as an honourable engagement clause. In essence, an honourable engagement clause allows the arbitrators flexibility when making their decision; they can take notice of market practice based upon their own knowledge and resolve the dispute based upon what is fair and reasonable, as opposed to a strict legal approach. The courts have deemed such a clause to be valid as long as it does not attempt to alter or oust the substantive law. An example of an honourable engagement clause is as follows:

> 'The arbitrators and the umpire shall interpret this reinsurance as an honourable engagement and they shall make their award with a view to effecting the general purpose of this reinsurance in a reasonable manner, rather than in accordance with a literal interpretation of the language.'

That particular clause was the subject of a court decision in the case of *Home & Overseas Insurance Co Ltd v Mentor Insurance Co (UK) Ltd [1989] 1 Lloyd's Rep 473.* The court gave full effect to the requirement that the arbitrators in that case, in reliance upon the honourable engagement clause, should make a decision based upon equitable grounds rather than by a strict legal interpretation of the issues in dispute.

Honourable engagement clauses appear to have been given statutory effect in the *Arbitration Act 1996,* potentially rendering the necessity to include such a clause in an arbitration agreement superfluous. *Section 46(1)(b)* of the *Arbitration Act 1996* provides:

> 'The arbitral tribunal shall decide the dispute … if the parties so agree, in accordance with such other considerations as are agreed by them or determined by the tribunal.'

In a decision under *s 46(1)*, the Court of Appeal held that an arbitrator could determine any issue which the parties to a dispute chose to put before him, and that it was irrelevant that the arbitration clause was silent as to the issue in dispute (*Wealands v CLC Contractors Ltd [1999] 2 Lloyd's Rep 739*). One key question which remains is whether *s 46* will have the effect of reducing the grounds upon which parties can appeal arbitrators' awards on the grounds of an error of law to the courts of England and Wales.

Right to appeal

21.07   The right to appeal to the courts of England and Wales from the decision of an arbitration panel is restricted to questions of English law. The court has first to give leave before an appeal can take place. The *Arbitration Act 1996* (in particular *s 69*) clarifies the previous statute law and court practice. In summary, leave to appeal will only be given where the decision of the tribunal on the question of law is (a) obviously wrong or (b) of general public importance and at least open to serious doubt. It is vital that an arbitral award is in writing and fully reasoned if there is to be any possibility of an appeal by either party from the tribunal's decision.

Chapter 22
Court proceedings

- Civil Procedure Rules
- The overriding objective
- The court's case management powers
- Pre-action protocols
- The three 'tracks' to litigation
- Part 36 offers
- Disclosure
- Expert evidence
- Summary

Civil Procedure Rules

22.01 In 1999 the civil justice system in England and Wales underwent its most fundamental changes in many years. The *Rules of the Supreme Court (SI 1965/1776)* which governed procedure in the High Court, and the *County Court Rules (SI 1981/1687)* which governed procedure in the county court, were replaced by a single set of rules, known collectively as the *Civil Procedure Rules 1998 (CPR) (SI 1998/3132)*, on 26 April 1999. These rules followed Lord Woolf's proposals for reform set out in his 1996 report, 'Access to Justice'. The primary goals of the new rules were to improve access to justice, to reduce the cost of litigation and the complexity of the rules, and to remove unnecessary distinctions of practice and procedure. References to '*parts*' and '*rules*' which follow refer to Rules and Parts of the *CPR (SI 1998/3132)*.

The overriding objective

22.02 The key principle which runs through the entirety of the *CPR* is the court's overriding objective which is set out in *Part 1*. This overriding objective is for the courts to deal with cases justly. *Rule 1.1(2)* sets out the following matters, which as far as practicable must be considered by the court when dealing with a case 'justly':

'(a)   ensuring that the parties are on an equal footing;

(b)   saving expense;

(c)   dealing with the case in ways which are proportionate:

    (i)   to the amount of money involved;

    (ii)   to the importance of the case;

    (iii)   to the complexity of the issues; and

    (iv)   to the financial position of each party;

(d)   ensuring that it is dealt with expeditiously and fairly; and

(e)   allotting to it an appropriate share of the court's resources, while taking into account the need to allot resources to other cases.'

The concept of proportionality as set out above is a vital element of the new rules. The courts no longer give the parties the free hand they once had to deal with their disputes in any way that they choose, without regard to the issues and the amounts involved. The court's duty is to manage cases. That duty is set out in *rule 1.4* which states

'the court must further the overriding objective by actively managing cases'.

Rule 1.4 goes on to describe what active case management includes, for example, 'encouraging the parties to co-operate with each other in the conduct of the proceedings', 'identifying the issues at an early stage', 'encouraging the parties to use an alternative dispute resolution procedure' and 'helping the parties to settle the whole or part of the case'.

The court's case management powers

22.03   The courts have significant powers of case management to assist them with implementing the overriding objective and fulfilling their duty to manage cases. One of Lord Woolf's key concerns was that parties had previously been allowed to let the litigation process drag on unnecessarily which was wasteful, not only in terms of time, but also in terms of costs. Judges have, therefore, changed from being reactive to proactive and wide ranging case management powers have been bestowed upon the courts.

Part 3 sets out the judge's case management powers. The courts have powers to fix strict direction timetables, to adjourn or bring hearings forward, to require not only a party's legal representatives, but also the party itself, to attend before the court, and to stay the whole or any part of the proceedings to encourage the parties, for example, to explore alternative dispute resolution. The courts even have powers to decide which issues are to be tried and to exclude an issue from consideration.

In order to assist the court with its greater powers of intervention, *rule 3.3* gives the court the power to make an order of its own initiative. The court has also been given wide powers to impose sanctions on parties who fail to comply with its orders. The sanctions available to the courts include costs penalties (*r 44.3*), and even the power to strike out a party's statement of case (*r 3.3*).

In addition, the courts also have the power, for example, to strike out a party's case where 'it discloses no reasonable grounds for bringing or defending the claim' (*r 3.4(2)(a)*), or to grant summary judgment against either a claimant or a defendant in relation to the whole or part of a claim if they consider that the claim has no real prospect of being successfully made or defended, unless there is another compelling reason why a trial should take place (*Part 24*).

Pre-action protocols

22.04   The *CPR* introduced the concept of 'pre-action protocols'. These were revolutionary, because for the first time the courts are able to interfere with parties' pre-action behaviour, in order to encourage them to address the issues in dispute as they arise, with a view to reaching an early settlement if possible. This is achieved by, for example, requiring parties to disclose the nature of their case, as well as key documents, even before proceedings have commenced.

There are currently approved pre-action protocols in respect of eight types of action; construction and engineering disputes, defamation, personal injury claims, clinical dispute, professional negligence, judicial review, disease and illness claims, and housing disrepair cases. Further pre-action protocols may follow. Nevertheless, whatever the nature of the dispute, courts will expect the parties, in the light of the overriding objective in *Part 1*, to act reasonably and to exchange information relevant to the issues in dispute before proceedings commence. Pre-action conduct will be taken into account when the court considers the issues of costs at the end of the case.

In addition, pursuant to *r 31.16*, parties are entitled to make an application for pre-action disclosure of documents relevant to the claim if there has not been voluntary disclosure. The court will grant pre-action disclosure if it is satisfied it will aid the fair disposal of any proceedings brought subsequently, or in addition will assist the resolution of the dispute without the need for bringing proceedings, or to save costs generally.

The three 'tracks' to litigation

22.05   Disputes are allocated to three different tracks:

(a) *Small claims track.* This is an informal procedure with limited rights to recover costs, together with no disclosure or experts other than with leave of the court.

(b) *Fast track.* This was introduced by the *CPR* and is designed to deal with reasonably straightforward cases. Cases allocated to the fast track will be subject to a fixed timetable of 30 weeks from the date of allocation to trial. Once set, the timetable must be complied with and sanctions will be imposed in the event of default. The trial itself will normally be restricted to one day.

(c) *Multi-track.* This covers all other types of cases. On allocation to multi-track, there will usually be a case management conference to decide upon how the case is to be conducted. One important aspect is that a trial window will be fixed which will be a period of time when the trial will take place. The actual date of the trial will be fixed later.

Rules 26.6–26.9 set out the rules governing allocation of a dispute to one of the three tracks. The allocation occurs once a defence has been filed. The parties at that stage complete an allocation questionnaire. It asks the parties to consider to which track the case should be allotted. In summary, allocation depends largely on the financial value of the claim; the small claims track deals with personal injury claims under £5,000 and landlord and tenant claims under £1,000; the fast track deals with claims between these limits and £15,000; and the multi-track deals with cases over £15,000. If the court considers it so appropriate, it has the discretion to allocate a case to a different track, even if the financial value falls outside these limits.

The allocation questionnaire also asks the parties a variety of other questions relevant to case management concerns. It asks the parties to set out whether they have complied with pre-action protocols, whether there are any specific applications they wish the court to consider, details of who their witnesses of fact will be, and what expert evidence the parties require. The parties are also asked if they wish to have a one-month stay of the proceedings in order to attempt to settle. If either side indicates positively to that question the court has the power to stay the proceedings.

A failure to provide proper information concerning allocation will result in sanctions being imposed by the court on the defaulting party. Such sanctions can be punitive.

Part 36 offers

22.06   One of the most important parts of the *CPR* is *Part 36*. This aims to encourage the parties to settle cases before trial. Both claimants and defendants are able to make *Part 36* offers, either to accept or pay a certain sum, or the equivalent where a claim does not have a monetary value. Such offers are made 'without prejudice save as to costs'. This means that no admission as to liability is made, and the court will not be made aware of the existence of a *Part 36* offer until the issue of costs is dealt with after a trial (if the case proceeds that far). The making, and acceptance, of *Part 36* offers by both claimants and defendants is encouraged by a variety of provisions dealing with those costs arising after a *Part 36* offer is made. These costs consequences make *Part 36* an important tactical consideration in any litigation.

Disclosure

22.07   Disclosure is the process whereby the parties to the proceedings disclose the documents which are relevant to the issues in dispute. Disclosure is governed by *Part 31*.

The normal order will be for standard disclosure. This requires a party to disclose those documents on which it relies, those which adversely affect its case or another party's case, or those which support the other party's case. A party is only obliged to undertake a reasonable search for documents relating to the issues in dispute, and such factors as the number of documents involved will be taken into account when deciding if such a search has been reasonable.

Parties can seek disclosure of documents which fall outside the scope of the standard disclosure rules by making an application to court, if the other party will not voluntarily disclose the documents sought. The court when making its decision will consider the principles set out in the overriding objective at *Part 1*.

Expert evidence

22.08   Expert evidence is likely to have an important role in most disputes relating to insurance law. In particular, expert underwriting evidence will tend to need to be adduced to assist the court to determine what a prudent underwriter would have wanted to know by way of material circumstances in the context of a non-disclosure dispute. Expert evidence is governed by *Part 35* which, in furtherance of the overriding objective, aims to ensure that such evidence is given as objectively and efficiently as possible.

The court has case management powers to limit what expert evidence the parties can adduce, including encouraging the parties to appoint a single joint expert. If two experts are appointed, they will be expected to co-operate, and the parties will be required to disclose the substance of the instructions given to their appointed expert.

Summary

22.09   The key theme of the *CPR* is to achieve a resolution of the dispute as swiftly and economically as possible. The principles of the overriding objective will be applied to all elements of court procedure leading to trial. In order to achieve this objective, the courts have been given far reaching powers and the parties are under a duty to assist the court in achieving the overriding objective, and in many cases, litigation is now a swifter way to resolve a dispute than arbitration, where the strict rules, time limits and sanctions of the *CPR* do not apply.

Chapter 23
Alternative dispute resolution

- Mediation
- Executive tribunal (or 'mini trial')
- Expert determination
- Early neutral evaluation

23.01 Alternative dispute resolution (ADR) has taken on a new importance since the introduction of the *CPR* in April 1999, and of various practice directions which govern court procedure in England and Wales, for the simple reason that the courts are now under a duty to consider and encourage the parties in dispute to use ADR if it is considered appropriate. The court specifically asks the parties in the allocation questionnaire, which they complete after the defence has been filed, whether they have considered ADR and if they think it is appropriate.

ADR is a concept which originates from the USA. It is a generic name given to a variety of procedures which are designed to assist parties in dispute to resolve their differences. In basic terms, it is the private resolution of disputes with the use of a neutral third party. The procedures are usually without prejudice to the parties' rights to proceed to litigation or arbitration, which are mutually exclusive forums for resolving disputes. The aim of ADR is to seek a swifter resolution to the dispute than more 'traditional' processes, to save costs and hopefully, by adopting a commercial approach to resolving the dispute, the parties at the end of the day will be able to maintain their commercial relationship. These aims translate into the potential advantages of using ADR to resolve a dispute.

ADR comes in varying forms; four of the methods are mediation, executive tribunal (also known as 'mini trial'), expert determination and early neutral evaluation, of which mediation is by far the most widely-used. Each one will be looked at in turn.

Mediation

23.02 This is a commonly used ADR procedure. Generally, all parties to the dispute must agree for their differences to be dealt with by way of mediation, as it is essentially a voluntary process. The Court of Appeal in *Halsey v Milton Keynes General NHS Trust [2004] EWCA Civ 576* affirmed this position by holding that the courts can merely encourage parties to mediate, rather than ordering them to do so, and that a party which is ultimately successful in proceedings, but which has refused mediation, will not be penalised for that refusal by any costs order unless the refusal to mediate is unreasonable. As these costs consequences can be severe, a party who is offered the opportunity to mediate should not reject that offer lightly. Mediation, however, will not be suitable in all cases. The Court of Appeal envisioned the situation in which a defendant which considers itself to have a very strong defence may not wish to mediate so as to avoid having to make any 'nuisance payment' simply to dispose of an unmeritorious claim against it.

The parties to the mediation will select a neutral party to assist them in reaching an acceptable agreement. The mediator is usually an expert in the subject matter of the dispute as well as being a trained mediator. The mediator's role is to persuade the parties to focus on their underlying concerns and differences. Although the process is not binding, it tends to operate as a concentrated period of negotiation which can lead the parties towards a binding settlement agreement, which may otherwise take much longer to achieve. As a consequence, mediation can be a cost-effective way to resolve a dispute. Talks can break down but if they do the parties can proceed to litigation or arbitration instead, although a mediation which does not provide an immediate resolution may often narrow the issues in dispute such that a settlement follows shortly after.

Executive tribunal (or 'mini trial')

23.03   This again is a voluntary procedure and is non-binding. The parties appoint a neutral expert to whom they present an abbreviated version of their case. The expert then supervises the proceedings. It is a more formal process than mediation, which involves discussion rather than presentation. At the close of a mini trial, the neutral expert gives a non-binding opinion as to his view upon the case. The purpose behind this process is that with views having been expressed as to the merits of the parties' agreements, the parties thereafter attempt to negotiate a binding settlement.

Expert determination

23.04   This is a binding form of a mini trial or executive tribunal, but only if the contract between the parties in dispute provides for dispute resolution by way of expert determination. It is the contract which gives the binding effect. It is closer in nature to an arbitration than it is to mediation or an executive tribunal. The expert is again neutral, and is either agreed upon by the parties or appointed by a third party, who has a role similar to that of a judge or arbitrator.

Early neutral evaluation

23.05   This combines elements of both mediation and expert determination. The process involves the parties in dispute engaging a neutral independent person, who has expertise in the subject matter of the dispute, at an early stage in the dispute. The independent expert reviews the merits of each party's case, and delivers an opinion on the likely outcome of the dispute.

PART 5

Specific Types of Insurance

Chapter 24
All risks insurance

- Nature of all risks insurance
- Effect of the policy being all risks

Nature of all risks insurance

24.01 Various forms of property insurance are written on an All Risks basis. Historically, goods in transit insurance and marine cargo insurance were frequently written on this basis. This trend then spread to householders' insurance, and in more recent years All Risks insurance has become the preferred type of property insurance for most large-scale commercial risks. It frequently forms the core of global property insurance programmes placed for multi-national corporations (see 18 GLOBAL INSURANCE PROGRAMMES).

The term 'All Risks' is certainly misleading as such policies do not cover all forms of loss. Most All Risks policies will exclude a number of perils as well as certain types of property.

Effect of the policy being all risks

24.02 The main advantage of an All Risks policy is to make it somewhat easier to substantiate a claim than under a specific risks policy. The insuring clause in an All Risks policy will simply specify that the policy covers the insured property for physical loss or damage during the underwriting period.

Therefore, to fall within that cover, the insured must prove that:

(*a*) the claim is in respect of insured property;

(*b*) physical loss or damage has occurred to that property; and

(*c*) the cause of the loss was fortuitous.

When the insured has overcome those hurdles, the burden of proof will then pass to the insurer to demonstrate that the peril which caused the loss was excluded from cover. This was established in *British and Foreign Marine Insurance Co Ltd Appellants v Gaunt Respondent [1921] 2 AC 41*. In *Re National Benefit Insurance Co [1933] 45 Ll L Rep 147*, it was alleged that goods in transit failed to arrive at their destination, and the court decided that it was sufficient for the insured to prove the non-arrival of the goods to satisfy its burden of proof.

In contrast, in specified perils insurance such as fire, the insuring clause will state additionally that the physical loss or damage must be caused by a particular peril (eg fire). In those circumstances, the insured has an additional hurdle to overcome, namely, the proof that the particular physical loss and damage was proximately caused by the specified peril (see 13 CAUSATION).

It should be noted that the insuring clause in the All Risks policy does not specify that the peril causing the physical loss or damage must be accidental. This is, however, a fundamental requirement of valid insurance policies and will therefore be implied into any policy.

In other words, the insured must prove that an element of risk existed during the insurance period.

The legal authorities, however, are unclear as to whether fortuity is judged from the perspective of the insured or from that of the reasonable bystander. Clearly, if the test is subjective, then the only question that needs to be asked is whether the insured knew that the physical loss or damage was likely to occur. Certainly, in *Kier Construction v Royal Insurance (UK) 30 Con LR 45*, the court appeared to consider the question of inevitability from the viewpoint of the insured. In other words, if at the time of the purchase of the cover the parties did not expect the damage to occur, then even if objectively, and with the benefit of hindsight, the loss was inevitable, it was still an insured loss.

Chapter 25
Aviation Insurance

- Introduction
- Aircraft operators' insurance
- Airport owners' and operators' liability insurance
- Spares cover
- Products liability

Introduction

25.01   The term 'aviation insurance' is generally regarded as encompassing three types of risk:

- aircraft operators' hull risks and third party liability;
- aviation manufacturers' and suppliers' products liability; and
- airport owners' and operators' liability.

Given the nature of the underlying industry and the sums involved, both in terms of liability exposure and hull values, aviation insurance is an international business. Much of it is led (either at primary or reinsurance level) in the London market where a significant number of insurers and brokers are engaged solely in, or maintain teams dedicated to, the aviation business. Many overseas insurers write the primary business but reinsure the majority – often as much as 90% – through London.

The Lloyd's market has developed a number of standard forms for aircraft operators' insurance. The Lloyd's Aviation Underwriters' Association (LAUA) publishes copies of these, as well as certain other forms developed by particular underwriters for specific risks, in its 'Blue Book'.

This chapter addresses the principal risks insured and the issues arising under conventional aircraft, airport owners' and operators' policies. It draws on the wording of various forms which are to be found in the Blue Book. For example, the commentary on aircraft operators' insurance is based substantially on Lloyd's form AVN 1C, which is the current form of the standard Lloyd's aircraft insurance policy, governing hull, third party and passenger liability. Reference is also made to the content of other Lloyd's forms, for example in relation to loss of or damage to cargo.

Aircraft operators' insurance

25.02   The principles underlying the insurance of aircraft operators' hull risks and liabilities are generally the same for an international airline as for a domestic air taxi or charter operation, or for a private aircraft policy, though the financial limits will vary enormously. The policy will insure the aircraft owner against loss or destruction of, or damage to, the aircraft named on the policy, and will indemnify the operator against liabilities to third parties arising out of the operation of the aircraft. This will include liability to passengers (whether fare-paying or not) in the event of an accident, and liability for surface damage.

Usually an airline's aircraft fleet policy will exclude liability for death or injury to crews, which will be covered under a separate employer's liability policy. The airline may additionally effect death-in-service or personal accident insurance for the benefit of its crews.

Comprehensive liability insurance for airlines is essential as the exposure is often of high value. It is not uncommon for a major international airline to carry a liability limit of US$2 billion for any one loss. Given that new large commercial aircraft often have values in excess of US$100 million, the total value of aircraft insured would often be significantly greater than the liability limit. However, the risk of total loss of the entire fleet is remote, and would probably only be a threat for war risks underwriters.

The description of cover (and exclusions from cover) which follow are based on a number of forms to be found in the Blue Book. Reference has already been made to form AVN 1C, under which insurers provide cover in respect of three categories of loss or damage:

- loss and damage to the aircraft itself;

- legal liability to passengers; and

- legal liability to third parties other than passengers.

Perhaps surprisingly, cover in respect of loss or damage to cargo is not provided for in form AVN 1C but in a separate form, referred to as LPO 359B.

Loss of or damage to aircraft

25.03   Under the standard policy wording provided in form AVN 1C, cover is provided in respect of accidental loss of, or damage to, aircraft named in the schedule to the policy. Provision is made for aircraft to be added during the term of the policy. Each aircraft named in the schedule is insured up to a maximum sum, referred to as the 'amount insured'. It is not uncommon for aircraft to be insured at an agreed value which may be considerably in excess of the market value.

Under the terms of cover, insurers have the option to repair or pay for the loss or damage. It might be argued that on the wording of form AVN 1C they also have the option to replace an aircraft with an equivalent aircraft in the event of a total loss. Provision is also made for payment by insurers of emergency expenses necessarily incurred by the insured to ensure the security of the aircraft following damage or a forced landing.

Typically insurers will exclude liability for wear and tear, deterioration, break-down, defect or failure in or of any 'unit' of the aircraft, for example an engine, unless the resulting damage is attributable to a single recorded incident. However, where wear and tear or deterioration etc in a unit results in damage being caused to some other part of the aircraft, insurers will accept liability for that separate damage.

The interests of parties other than the aircraft operator may be recognised and protected under the policy. Of course, few airlines own their aircraft outright nowadays, and often large numbers of banks or financial institutions have an interest in any given aircraft through syndication or security arrangements. Lloyd's form AVN 67B is an endorsement to the standard aircraft policy whereby third party interests may be noted on the policy; such third parties become additional insureds under the policy, thus protecting their investment in the event that the aircraft is a total loss.

Liability of operators to passengers

25.04   Insurers will be liable to indemnify the operator for, or pay on behalf of the operator, compensatory damages (including costs awarded against the insured) in respect of the following risks:

(a)   accidental bodily injury (including death) to passengers sustained on board an aircraft or sustained while embarking or disembarking an aircraft; and

(b)   loss of, or damage to, baggage and personal effects of passengers arising out of an aircraft accident.

In international carriage by air a commercial operator's liability will usually be determined by reference to an international convention system based on the *Warsaw Convention*. The detail of this system is beyond the scope of this chapter, but in brief it provides for a presumption of liability in favour of the passenger in particular circumstances, subject to a limit of liability (save in specified circumstances). Under the terms of the cover provided by form AVN 1C, the insured is obliged to take such measures as are necessary to exclude or limit liability for the types of claim outlined above, to the extent permitted by law. Such measures may include the issue of a ticket to passengers and/or baggage check, both of which are requirements of the *Warsaw Convention*. If the insured fails to comply, the insurers' legal liability will not exceed that which would have existed had there been compliance.

Exclusions

25.05   Insurers will not be liable for injury or loss sustained by:

(*a*)   a director or employee of the insured or partner in the insured's business while acting in the course of his employment with, or duties for, the insured; or

(*b*)   a member of the flight, cabin or other crew whilst engaged in the operation of the aircraft.

Liability to third parties other than passengers

25.06   Under the terms of standard policy form AVN 1C, insurers will be liable to pay compensatory damages (including costs awarded against the insured) in respect of the following risks:

(*a*)   accidental bodily injury (including death); and

(*b*)   accidental damage to property caused by the aircraft or by any person or object falling from the aircraft.

Exclusions

25.07   Insurers will not be liable for:

(*a*)   injury (including death) or loss sustained by any director or employee of the insured or partner in the insured's business whilst acting in the course of his employment or duties;

(*b*)   injury (including death) or loss sustained by any member of the flight or cabin crew whilst operating the aircraft;

(*c*)   injury (including death) or loss sustained by a passenger boarding, on board or leaving the aircraft;

(*d*)   loss of, or damage to, any property belonging to, or in the care, custody or control of, the insured; or

(*e*)   claims excluded by the noise and pollution and other perils exclusion clause.

General exclusions to cover

25.08   The wording of standard policy form AVN 1C provides that the policy (including every section) will not apply when the aircraft:

(*a*)   is used for an illegal purpose;

(*b*)   is operated outside geographical limits;

(*c*)   is piloted by a person not specified in the policy. Where the aircraft is on the ground, any competent person may operate the aircraft;

(*d*)   is transported by another conveyance, except where the aircraft is being transported following an accident giving rise to a claim;

(*e*)   takes off or lands (or attempts to do so) in an unauthorised place, except in an emergency; or

(*f*)   carries more than the permitted number of passengers.

Conditions precedent to liability under the policy

25.09   In addition to the general exclusions to cover, there are conditions precedent which apply to each of the three categories of loss or damage discussed above (hull, third party, passenger). In outline, the insured is obliged to:

(*a*)   use due diligence to avoid accidents and diminish loss; and

(*b*)   comply with all air navigation and airworthiness orders and requirements, including ensuring that the aircraft is airworthy at the beginning of every flight.

The standard conditions precedent (detailed more fully in form AVN 1C) potentially give wide scope to insurers to avoid liability under the policy.

Liability for loss of or damage to cargo

25.10   The standard form which provides cover in respect of loss or damage to cargo is form LPO 359B, which is to be found among the miscellaneous forms in the Blue Book.

Under the terms of LPO 359B, the aircraft operator will be indemnified for all monies payable up to a specified limit for loss of or damage to cargo under:

●   the *Warsaw Convention*; or

●   other conditions of carriage agreed by the underwriters.

Coverage in respect of cargo will commence at the time of issue of the air waybill or other contract of carriage, and will terminate upon delivery of the cargo by the insured or its agent at the final warehouse or upon it being handed over to the succeeding agents or carriers.

Where a through air waybill has been issued and succeeding carriers are unwilling to accept a special declaration of value made by the consignor at the point of origin, coverage will continue, under the issuing carrier's policy, through to the final destination named in the air waybill.

Standard exclusion clauses

25.11 Aircraft operators' insurance policies usually exclude liability for the following risks:

- noise and pollution;

- war, hijacking and other perils; and

- nuclear risks.

Noise and pollution (Lloyd's form AVN 46B)

25.12 Policy form AVN 1C incorporates a standard exclusionary provision, known as AVN 46B. The effect of the exclusion is that operators are not covered for claims by third parties (other than passengers) caused by the following:

- noise (including sonic boom);

- any kind of contamination or pollution;

- electrical and electromagnetic interference; or

- interference with the use of property,

unless caused by or resulting in a crash, fire, explosion or collision or a recorded in-flight emergency causing abnormal aircraft operation.

War, hijacking and other perils (Lloyd's form AVN 48B)

25.13 A standard exclusion clause, referred to as AVN 48B, is incorporated into AVN 1C. The effect is to exclude claims caused by:

(*a*)   war, invasion, acts of foreign enemies, hostilities, civil war, rebellion, revolution, insurrection, martial law, military or usurped power, or attempts at usurpation of power;

(*b*)   hostile detonation of any weapon of war employing atomic or nuclear fission and/or fusion or any similar reaction or radioactive force or matter;

(*c*)   strikes, riots, civil commotions or labour disturbances;

(*d*)   acts for political or terrorist purposes. It is irrelevant whether the loss or damage caused is accidental or intentional;

(*e*)   any malicious act or act of sabotage;

(*f*)   confiscation, nationalisation, seizure, restraint, detention, appropriation, requisition for title or use by or under the order of any government or public or local authority of the aircraft; or

(*g*)   hijacking or any unlawful seizure or wrongful exercise of control of the aircraft or crew in flight made by a person or persons on board the aircraft acting without the consent of the insured.

Cover will be suspended with immediate effect if as a result of any of the above-mentioned acts the insured loses control over the aircraft. Separate insurance is required to cover claims arising until the aircraft is restored to the control of the insured by its safe return. 'Safe return' of the aircraft will happen once the aircraft is parked with the engines shut down, under no duress, at an airfield within the geographical limits defined in the insurance policy in effect.

Specific cover for hijacking and war risks may of course be negotiated and a policy form has been drafted for this purpose by underwriters. Policy LSW 555B effectively writes back in certain risks excluded from the All Risks policy by the wording in policy AVN 48B. The endorsement extends cover to include loss or damage caused by war, strikes, riots, acts of sabotage or terrorism, confiscation, nationalisation, seizure and hijacking. The precise terms of cover can be found in form LSW 555B.

Such coverage is subject to the same warranties, terms and conditions as are otherwise contained in the insured's All Risks policy, and the policy or endorsement is itself subject to general exclusions. Thus, for example, war between certain named states (the UK, USA, France, the Russian Federation and China) which gives rise to loss is not covered by the policy.

Loss resulting from claims for repayment of landing fees, refuelling costs, wear, tear and gradual deterioration of the aircraft will be excluded from the hijacking endorsement.

In the case of *Kuwait Airways Corp v Kuwait Insurance Co SAK [1999] 1 Lloyd's Rep 803*, the House of Lords examined the interaction between war risks and all risks and the true meaning of the term 'seizure' in the context of the policy under consideration.

The Kuwait Airways Corporation insured against war risks and seizure. The spare parts cover extended to seizure but not to war risks. The policy also provided for recovery of sue and labour costs incurred by Kuwait Airways in attempting to recover the insured property; however, it provided that those costs and expenses were to be included in computing the earlier losses provided for, namely up to US$300 million in respect of ground risks, and US$150 million in respect of seizure of spare parts at any one location. In 1990, Iraq invaded Kuwait and appropriated aircraft valued at US$692 million and spares valued at around US$300 million. The war risks underwriters offered US$300 million in total settlement and the airline appealed, claiming that it was entitled to a further US$150 million in respect of spare parts under the seizure risk. It also claimed it was entitled to claim sue and labour costs incurred in attempts to recover its aircraft.

The House of Lords held firstly that the word 'seizure' was to be understood in its usual sense as referring to forcible seizure. The US$300 million ground limit applied only to aircraft and the differently defined limit in the spare parts extension provided for an additional right of recovery in respect of such parts. Secondly, the proviso required that any sue and labour expenses were to be included with the primary losses for which cover was provided in the contract.

There being a limit on the indemnity, that limit had to be applied to the aggregate of the primary loss and the sue and labour expenses. That limit had been exhausted and, accordingly, the airline's right to claim reimbursement had also been exhausted.

Nuclear risks

25.14   There is no cover available for nuclear risks. There are two standard form nuclear risk exclusion clauses: AVN 38B and AVN 71. The former is more elaborate and, unlike AVN 71, provides for cover in the event of loss or damage arising where radioactive material such as depleted uranium is being transported by air. A proviso is that the material is stored and handled in the course of carriage in accordance with ICAO technical instructions for the safe transport of dangerous goods by air.

Both standard clauses exclude loss or destruction of, or damage to, property (and any consequential losses or expenses arising there from) and any legal liability of whatsoever nature (thus including liability for injury, sickness, disease or death) resulting from the 'hazardous properties' of radioactive material. Hazardous properties include toxic or explosive properties.

Airport owners' and operators' liability insurance

25.15   This form of insurance covers the liability risks faced by airport owners and operators and various suppliers of goods and services, including ground handling agents, maintenance suppliers and air traffic controllers. Ordinarily fuel suppliers would take out a dedicated policy. This commentary is based on the Ariel form which is in widespread use for risks underwritten in the London market.

Premises liability

25.16   The risks covered under the Ariel standard form policy are:

- bodily injury to any person including death at any time resulting from the bodily injury; and

- loss or damage to the property of others,

in each case caused by accident during the policy period.

To be covered by the policy, bodily injury or property damage must be caused:

(*a*)   by the fault or negligence of the insured;

(*b*)   by the fault or negligence of any of the employees engaged in the insured's business;

(*c*)   by any defect in the insured's premises; or

(*d*)   by any defect in the insured's ways, works, machinery or plant used in the insured's business.

It will be noted that this section of the policy (premises liability) is fault-based; in contrast to standard aircraft operator's policies, the claimant must demonstrate fault on the part of the insured. It would be exceptional to make an aircraft operator's policy subject to proof on the part of the insured since the underlying legal liability regime frequently provides for strict or presumed liability.

As a starting point, the injury or damage must occur in or about the premises specified on the policy and as a direct result of the services granted by the insured. However, cover is available for incidents occurring elsewhere in the course of any work or duties carried out by the insured or employees in connection with the business or operations specified in the policy schedule.

Exclusions

25.17   The Ariel standard form of policy excludes from cover loss or damage to property:

- owned, rented, leased or occupied by;

- in the care, custody or control of; or

- being handled, serviced or maintained by

the insured or an employee of the insured. This prevents the premises cover operating as aircraft hull cover for aircraft in the insured's custody either as hangar keeper or for third party maintenance. This exclusion will not apply to vehicles that are not the property of the insured whilst on the ground at the airport.

The standard policy also excludes from cover bodily injury and/or property damage caused by any 'mechanically propelled vehicle' which the insured allows another person to use on the road in such a manner to make them responsible for their own insurance. Ground handling companies must therefore take out separate insurance for their company fleet vehicles. This will include those vehicles used to load and unload baggage from the aircraft as well as those used to transport passengers between and within terminals.

Excluded also is bodily injury and/or property damage caused by any aircraft chartered, used or operated by, or on account of, the insured. This exclusion will not apply to aircraft owned by others which are on the ground. An indemnity is granted elsewhere in the policy, under the hangar keeper's liability section.

Cover must be agreed beforehand with the underwriters for bodily injury and/or property damage arising out of:

(*a*)   any air meet, air show or stand used for spectators; or

(*b*)   construction, demolition or alterations to buildings, runways or installations by the insured or his contractors or sub-contractors (other than normal maintenance operations).

As soon as goods or products manufactured, constructed, altered, repaired, serviced, treated, sold, supplied or distributed by the insured or his employees have ceased to be in their possession or their control, the insurance policy of the insured will not apply.

Hangar keeper's liability

25.18   Section two of the Ariel standard policy provides cover in respect of liability arising from loss or damage to aircraft or aircraft equipment not owned, rented or leased by the insured while:

- on the ground in the care, custody or control of; or

- being serviced or handled or maintained by

the insured or any employee of the insured. The airport owner will be insured for damage caused to visiting aircraft or to equipment stored by another party at the airport. No cover is available for:

(*a*)   personal effects;

(*b*)   aircraft or aircraft equipment hired or leased by or loaned by the insured; and

(*c*)   loss of or damage to any aircraft while in flight.

It should be noted that this section of the policy, unlike the section providing cover for premises liability, is not fault based.

Products liability

25.19   Section three of the Ariel standard policy will indemnify the insured for liability for bodily injury or property damage arising out of the possession, use, consumption or handling of any goods or products manufactured, constructed, altered, repaired, serviced, treated, sold, supplied or distributed by the insured or his employees. Cover is restricted to goods or products which form part of, or are used in conjunction with, aircraft. Further, the damage must occur after the goods have ceased to be in the possession or under the control of the insured.

Exclusions

25.20   The policy will not extend to:

(*a*)   damage to property of the insured or to property within his care, custody or control;

(*b*)   the cost of repairing or replacing any defective products or goods manufactured, constructed, altered, repaired, serviced, treated, sold, supplied by the insured or any defective part or parts thereof;

(c)   loss arising out of improper or inadequate performance design or specification. However, this exclusion does not apply to bodily injury or property damage insured against under the policy which results from such improper or inadequate performance etc; or

(d)   loss of use of any aircraft not actually lost or damaged in an accident giving rise to a claim under the terms of an airport owners' and operators' liability insurance policy.

Exclusions applicable to all sections of the policy

25.21   There are general exclusions which apply to the policy as a whole. For example, nuclear risks, are excluded. Also excluded is liability for bodily injury to employees or agents while acting for the insured. Further general exclusions are to be found at page three of the Ariel standard policy.

General conditions

25.22   There are general conditions attaching to the policy. These include:

- prompt notification to underwriters of any claims arising;

- provision for cancellation of coverage; and

- other conditions which appear at pages four and five of the Ariel standard policy form.

Spares cover

25.23   Insurance is available for engines, spare parts and equipment ('the property') which are to be fitted to an aircraft. Underwriters have prepared a form of wording designed to provide such cover. The form appears among the miscellaneous forms in the Blue Book and is referred to as LPO 344C.

Under the terms of the standard policy, cover will apply only where the property is owned by the insured or is the property of another party for which the insured is responsible.

The insurance will have effect while the property is:

- in the care, custody or control of the insured on the ground; or

- being carried as cargo in transit by air, road, rail or other mode of transport.

Exclusions

25.24   The insurance does not cover loss or damage to the property caused:

(*a*)   by damage occurring at any time after the start of the fitting of the property to the aircraft or placing it on board the aircraft of its destination;

(*b*)   by mechanical or electrical failure;

(*c*)   by wear and tear or gradual deterioration;

(*d*)   by neglect by the insured to save and preserve the property;

(*e*)   to property temporarily detached from the aircraft;

(*f*)   by any process when the loss or damage is caused as a direct consequence of that process;

(*g*)   when that property is carried as a spare parts kit; or

(*h*)   to property carried or stored for hire or reward by the insured.

Unexplained loss or mysterious disappearance of property is also excluded.

Products liability

25.25   Aviation products liability and insurance for such liability is beyond the scope of this chapter. Many of the principles underlying products liability risk and insurance are dealt with in detail in 36 PRODUCT LIABILITY INSURANCE. Certain relevant factors that are unique to the aviation industry are mentioned in the section on products liability cover under airport owners' and operators' liability. Where a business is supplying goods or services that give rise to a product liability it is in exactly the same position, legally, as any other manufacturer or service provider supplying components, aircraft equipment or spares, or maintenance services, with the same risk in terms of magnitude of exposure.

As a general rule most of the major airframe contractors have bespoke policies, as do many of the major subassembly manufacturers (such as engines, landing gear etc). However, the insurance industry has provided certain schemes with common underwriters subscribing whereby many of the other component suppliers can obtain cover on reasonable terms. The major schemes are the Aircraft Builders' Council (ABC) scheme in the United States and the Society of British Aircraft Companies (SBAC) scheme in the United Kingdom, though the latter has now ceased to function.

One of the features of these policies is that an insured under that policy would be precluded from pursuing a recourse or indemnity claim against another insured under the same policy. This has the effect of insureds adopting a common defence to claims rather than seeking to apportion blame among themselves.

Chapter 26
Bloodstock insurance

- Veterinary certificates and declarations of health
- Common clauses
- Moral hazard and fraud

26.01 Bloodstock insurance is the insurance of horses, for example stallions, geldings, mares and foals. Livestock insurance is the insurance of animals (normally farming animals) which are kept for use or profit, and is a wider category than bloodstock. Within this area there is also the insurance of exotics, which covers insurance of more unusual animals such as ostriches and zoo animals, and aquatics insurance, which covers insurance of fish (usually commercial fish farms) or aquatic mammals such as dolphins. However, these will not be dealt with in this handbook.

Veterinary certificates and declarations of health

26.02 The owner of a horse, which it is proposed should be the subject of bloodstock insurance, will often be asked to complete a veterinary certificate or declaration of health in respect of the horse. This certificate is normally signed by the owner's vet prior to insurers accepting the animal for insurance, in very much the same way that an individual proposer for personal accident or medical insurance would complete and sign a questionnaire relating to the state of his health. As there is no guarantee that the veterinary certificate has been completed by the horse's usual vet, there is usually a policy term which states that the owner warrants that the horse is in good health and free from injury at the date of commencement of the insurance.

Common clauses

All risks mortality

26.03 All Risks Mortality (ARM) cover is the backbone of bloodstock insurance, and indemnifies the insured (the owner of the horse) for the horse's actual

227

value if it dies through accident, illness or disease during the term of the policy. This value could differ enormously from the purchase price. Intentional slaughter is excluded, as is death following a surgical operation unless necessitated by accident, disease or illness. Other exclusions would normally relate to such things as malicious injury or poisoning. A number of conditions precedent or warranties are usually imposed on the insured, such as the requirement that the horse is in sound health at inception, and that the insured will provide proper care and attention to the horse during the policy period. The insured must also not use his horse for any purpose other than that specified in the policy. Loss of use and theft cover are normally dealt with as optional 'add ons' to the ARM policy.

Loss of use

26.04   Additional cover can be sought for loss of use (LOU) of an animal. This cover would protect the insured against financial loss arising as a result of the insured animal being injured and unable to fulfil the use for which it was insured. For example, LOU cover might indemnify the owner of a stallion kept solely for entering into dressage competitions if it damaged its leg and was unable to compete. Another example is that LOU cover might respond if a stallion kept solely for breeding purposes became infertile. LOU claims can also arise if the horse is stolen, rather than injured. Most bloodstock policies which provide LOU cover require that the insured animal be economically slaughtered within 30 days after the expiry of the (usually annual) insurance policy, in order for a valid claim for LOU to be made under the policy.

Theft and unlawful removal

26.05   As with LOU clauses, if cover is required for theft of the insured animal(s), it must be specifically sought. In *O'Brien v Hughes-Gibb and Co Ltd [1995] LRLR 90*, the insured habitually asked his broker to effect theft cover. On renewal, prior to inception of the policy under which a theft claim was subsequently made, the insured forgot to instruct his broker to obtain theft cover. Insurers declined the claim as the policy did not include cover for theft. The insured sued the broker, and the court held that the habitual request was not sufficient to impose liability on the broker who had not placed theft cover for the year in question, in the absence of a specific request to do so. Care should therefore be taken when loss of use or theft cover is sought, as these are not normally included in the standard ARM policies.

Public liability

26.06   If appropriate public liability cover is not available to a horse owner through membership of an equine or related association, such cover will have to be specifically requested. The need for such cover was highlighted in the House of Lords decision in *Mirvahedy v Henley [2003] 2 AC 491*. In that case, a horse panicked and escaped from its field, through no fault on the part of its keeper, and caused an accident on a public road. The House of Lords held the keeper of a non-dangerous animal (in this instance, a horse) was strictly liable under *s 2(2)(b)* of the *Animals Act 1971* for damage or injury caused by it while behaving in a way that was normal for its breed in the particular circumstances.

Moral hazard and fraud

26.07   There is a high potential for fraud in the sphere of bloodstock insurance. For this reason, insurers are particularly concerned to ascertain in the proposal form how long the insured has owned the horse, the purchase price paid, the purpose for which the horse will be used and details of any previous losses, claims and theft – whether they were insured or not. The answers to these questions help enable insurers to assess the moral hazard of the owner.

Horses tend to change hands frequently, and insurers therefore normally insist that the insured is the sole owner of the horse at the commencement of the insurance. Policies usually specify that the insurance will cease to cover any horse immediately the insured parts with any interest in it, even temporarily. Insurers thereby seek to avoid the situation where they agree to insure a particular animal, only to discover a half share and possibly possession of the horse has been transferred to another owner about whom they have no information.

Some insurers have encountered horse sale transactions and claims being used as vehicles for money laundering. Advisers must therefore be alert to investigate cases where horses are purchased for disproportionately large sums of cash, and shortly afterwards become the subject of a mortality claim. Some unscrupulous insureds who do not have LOU cover, but are faced with the prospect of paying for the feed and upkeep of a horse that is only fit for grazing, could deliberately kill or injure their horses or put them in a situation where an 'accident' is inevitable, in order to make an ARM claim under their policy.

Chapter 27
Buildings and property insurance

- Introduction
- Types of building and property insurance
- Exclusions
- Typical conditions
- Extensions to buildings and property insurance

Introduction

27.01 This chapter is concerned with the particular features of building and property insurance, and most importantly, policies on commercial premises and dwellings and their contents. 32 GOODS IN TRANSIT INSURANCE considers goods and transit policies. Other aspects of property insurance have been considered elsewhere: in particular, insurable interest (4 INSURABLE INTEREST), policyholders' duties, which include utmost good faith, non-disclosure and misrepresentation, fraud, minimising loss and increase in risk (6 POLICYHOLDER DUTIES) and insurance contracts (1 CONTRACT OF INSURANCE).

Types of building and property insurance

27.02 There are as many types of property insurance as there are properties. The types of properties covered will vary between the simple semi-detached house in Hounslow to global programmes of property insurance covering a multi-national for damage to property throughout its offices and manufacturing centres, with values perhaps in excess of US$15 billion.

Specified perils v All Risks

27.03 Traditionally, property insurance has been provided on a specified perils basis. In other words, the insuring clause will limit cover to physical loss and damage caused by a named peril such as fire. Other specified perils might include storm or flood etc. Thus, the insured must prove the causal connection between the peril and the loss.

In contrast, All Risks cover places no limitations in the insuring clause on the type of peril and, therefore, the burden of proof rests with the insurer in proving that a particular cause of loss is an excluded peril. Over the last ten years this type of cover has become more popular, especially amongst the larger commercial insured.

It is now possible to purchase combined lines policies which provide insureds with cover, not only for property, but also employers' liability, public liability and other forms of cover. Indeed, in some larger property programmes, insureds have been provided with aggregate cross class deductibles. Also, it has become common for a wider range of property to be included in commercial property insurance, such as computers and data. Whereas boiler and machinery coverage used to be dealt with under separate and specific insurances, it has now become common for this sort of coverage to be provided under a general All Risks property programme.

Trigger of cover

27.04   Most property policies are triggered by physical loss or damage occurring during the policy period, caused by a peril occurring during the same policy period.

Disclosure of risk

27.05   The duty of utmost good faith and disclosure on the part of the insured is crucial to any insurance, but especially where buildings and property insurance is concerned. This subject is dealt with in depth in 6 POLICYHOLDER DUTIES, but some particular issues arise in respect of this class of business.

In respect of smaller commercial risks, proposal forms will be used by insurers and will, to some extent, set out the type of information sought by insurers. In the absence of a proposal form, what should the insured expect to disclose? He should disclose both the moral hazard and the physical hazard. The moral hazard to the insurers would include a criminal record or claims history, or any factor which casts doubt upon the honesty of the insured or the company, even when the circumstances cover the insureds' relationship with third parties (see *Insurance Corp of the Channel Islands and Royal Insurance (UK) v Royal Hotel Ltd [1998] Lloyd's Rep IR* 151).

As to the physical hazard, it would of course be relevant to the underwriters to know the location and the construction of the property. For example, is the property in close proximity to an area which floods regularly? It may also be relevant to insurers to know what steps have been taken in respect of fire prevention and security. Do the premises, for example, have the benefit of a sprinkler system or smoke detectors? Both security and fire prevention is often dealt specifically in the policy as either a warranty or a condition precedent.

If, however, it is the intention of insurers to incorporate such clauses as warranties and/or conditions precedent, it is important that they are drafted most precisely. For example, in the case of *Hussein v Brown [1996] 1 Lloyd's Rep 627*, the insured in the proposal form confirmed that the premises were fitted with a security alarm. In fact the alarm was fitted, but when a fire destroyed the factory in question the alarm did not work. Insurers argued that the warranty provided must be construed as an ongoing obligation to maintain the alarm system. The court determined, however, that in the absence of precise words, no such obligation could be imputed, and thus by simply installing an alarm the insured had complied with the warranty.

It should be noted that some proposal forms do turn information disclosed into warranties removing the necessity of proving materiality. Such clauses requiring an insured to warrant the truth of the description are not favoured by the Association of British Insurers.

It would of course be highly relevant to insurers to know of any peculiarities of the premises which characterise them as a high risk.

Exclusions

27.06 The number and importance of exclusions depends, to some extent, upon the type of cover. In respect of specified perils cover, some exclusions become less important because the burden of proof would be upon the insured to prove that the proximate cause of the loss is, for example, flood.

In contrast, however, properly drafted exclusion clauses are critical to the operation of an All Risks insurance policy. Such exclusion clauses are numerous and can be difficult to categorise. Generally, the exclusions, however, fall into two categories, either excluded property or excluded perils.

Certain property will usually be excluded from such policies such as land, roads, pavements and bridges. It would also be unusual for vehicles, watercraft and aircraft to be covered under a typical property policy.

Perils exclusions may also be subdivided into sub categories as set out below.

Natural peril exclusions

27.07 On occasions, flood, storm, tempest, earthquake, earth subsidence and earth movement may be excluded. It would depend to a large extent on whether underwriters consider that that an area is particularly susceptible to such a risk.

Storm, tempest and flood are standard insured perils under a buildings policy. The term 'storm' generally means high winds accompanied by rain or snow, although it has been held in one Scottish case that a heavy fall of snow, with little wind, which accumulated on the insured's roof and caused it to collapse constituted a loss by storm (*Glasgow Training Group (Motor Trade) Ltd v Lombard Continental plc 1989 SC 30 r*). 'Tempest' plainly entails high winds. The word 'flood' taken alone probably means no more than an undesired accumulation of water, but in the context of 'storm, tempest, flood' a flood requires something violent, sudden and abnormal; in *Young v Sun Alliance and London Insurance Ltd [1976] 2 Lloyd's Rep 189*, a gradual seepage of water into the insured's house, to a level of about three inches, was held not to be a flood as the ingress of water did not meet this requirement (see also *Rohan Investments Ltd v Cunningham [1999] Lloyd's Rep IR 283*).

Unlike 'storm' and 'tempest,' 'flood' can overlap with non-weather related perils. For example, in *The Board of Trustees of the Tate Gallery v Duffy Construction Ltd [2007] EWHC 361 (TCC)* Jackson J held that the discharge of a large volume of water into the Tate Gallery from a burst pipe outside (but within the boundary of the insured location) fell within both '*flood*' and '*bursting or overflowing of water tanks, apparatus or pipes*' which was another specified peril.

Industrial perils

27.08 More usually, however, certain types of perils associated with manufacturing are excluded so as to avoid underwriters becoming guarantors for products and/or workmanship. Thus, usually, faulty design and workmanship are excluded, although resulting damage not otherwise excluded, may be brought back into cover. For example, a defectively welded pipe in a manufacturing process would not itself be covered under a typical policy, but any damage caused by the escaping fluid to other machinery may well be covered under the resulting damage proviso.

Courts have distinguished between faulty design and faulty workmanship. It is generally easier to prove the former. In respect of faulty design, the courts have determined that it is not necessary to prove that the defective design was negligently drawn (see *Queensland Government Railways and Electric Power Transmission Ltd v Manufacturers Mutual Insurance Ltd [1969] 1 Lloyd's Rep 214*). In contrast, to rely upon a faulty workmanship exclusion it is necessary to prove that the workman was negligent in some way.

Other exclusions may be boiler and mechanical breakdown, although this is now more often covered under All Risks property insurance policies (see 24 ALL RISKS INSURANCE). Frequently nipple or joint leakage, failure of welds, contamination and damage caused by escape of water from tank, apparatus or pipe are also excluded.

Computer systems

27.09 Despite several years having passed since the millennium, almost all policies still contain an exclusion, which must surely be redundant, of any losses due to the failure of computer systems to recognise a calendar date.

A number of policies now exclude losses arising from the distortion or erasure of information stored on computer systems. However, the drafting of some of these makes little sense and shows the evolutionary approach to draftsmanshiip at its worst. For example, in *Tektrol Ltd (formerly Atto Power Controls Ltd) v International Insurance Co of Hanover Ltd [2005] EWCA Civ 845* the relevant exclusion had, it would seem, been combined with the wording of a 'civil commotion' exclusion so as only to apply to erasure etc of information caused by rioters, strikers, locked-out workers or malicious persons. The Court of Appeal held that this exclusion did not apply to erasure of information caused by a widely distributed computer virus, even though the author was undoubtedly a malicious person, because the references to rioters etc showed that the exclusion was only intended to apply to some sort of direct attack on the insured's premises. General malicious acts targeted at computer users at large were not within the scope of the exclusion.

War and allied perils exclusions

27.10   Most property insurance will exclude war and allied perils which would include riot. A typical example might be as follows:

> 'Damage occasioned by war, invasion, act of foreign enemy, hostilities (whether war be declared or not), civil war, rebellion, revolution, insurrection or military or usurped power, nationalisation, confiscation, requisition, seizure or destruction by government or any public authority.'

One of the key problems in relying on such an exclusion is the difficulty that insurers find in proving the causal nexus between the excluded peril and the loss. Frequently it is difficult to gather sufficient evidence in war-affected territories to prove that cause of particular damage (for example a looted supermarket) was in fact caused by the war. Insurers have attempted to improve their position by removing the proximate cause test using words such as 'contributing to' or 'indirectly' thus requiring insurers only to prove that war was a contributing factor to the loss rather than the sole or dominant cause.

Indeed, in some policies insurers have even included a reverse burden of proof clause whereby if underwriters have proved prima facie that the loss has taken place in a war-affected territory, then providing some basic evidence is available as to causation, the burden of proof will transfer to the insured to satisfy the court that the loss was not caused by war or allied perils.

One of the more comprehensive accounts on the effect of causation and description of the different types of perils covered by such clauses was provided by Mustill J (later Lord Mustill) in *Spinney's (1948 Ltd) v Royal Insurance Co Ltd [1980] 1 Lloyd's Rep 406*.

Theft and fraud exclusions

27.11   The fraud of the insured or a corporation is usually dealt with under the conditions section of a property policy. Some policies, however, will exclude specifically the fraud or theft by certain persons such as employees of the company.

Where theft is an insured peril, the term is to be given a meaning which accords with the definition of the *Theft Act 1968*, namely, appropriation of the property of another with the intention of permanently depriving that other of the property. It is possible for the property to be appropriated where the owner is deprived of it by trick. In *Dobson v General Accident Fire and Life Assurance Corp [1990] 1 QB 274*, the insured sold the insured jewellery to a purchaser who paid with a stolen cheque. The Court of Appeal held that the insured had been the victim of a 'theft'. It might be added that *s 18* of the *Sale of Goods Act 1979* provides that ownership of goods is presumed to pass to the buyer as soon as the agreement is made even though payment is deferred to a later date. It follows that the result in *Dobson* would have been different had the insured not reserved ownership of the jewellery pending his receipt of full payment, for otherwise the property would have belonged to the purchaser and it could not have been said that the purchaser had appropriated property 'belonging to another'.

Theft policies may be restricted to theft 'committed by persons present on the premises of the insured'. This wording was considered by the High Court in *Deutsche Genossenschaftsbank v Burnhope [1995] 1 WLR 1580*, in which an innocent agent collected securities from the insured bank for his employer, and the employer subsequently absconded with the securities. It was held that there was a theft, but that it had been committed not by the agent but rather by his employer. As the employer had not been physically present on the premises when the appropriation occurred the policy exclusion prevailed.

The need for a physical link to the premises is illustrated by the approach of the Court of Appeal to the rather dramatic events in *Canelhas Comercio Importacao e Exportacao Ltd v Wooldridge [2004] EWCA Civ 984*. The managing director of the insured jewellery company was kidnapped along with his family. A bomb belt was attached to his son and he was ordered to drive to his business premises and persuade his staff to hand over some emeralds. He told his staff of the threats to his family and they complied. The Court of Appeal held that his Insurers were not entitled to rely upon a terms in an all risk policy limiting their liability for 'robbery when the premises are open for business' because the reference in the clause to the premises being open for business made it clear that it only applied to theft by threats of violence made to the insured's staff *at* the insured's premises.

Policies on premises which insure against burglary frequently require theft from the premises following forcible and violent entry. These words were considered by the Court of Appeal in *Nash (t/a Dino Services Ltd)v Prudential Assurance Co Ltd [1989] 1 Lloyd's Rep 379*, where the insured's car was broken into and the keys to his premises removed, and these were subsequently used to gain access to his premises. The Court of Appeal decided that the robbery had involved the use of 'force', as physical effort – albeit nominal – had been needed to use the keys. The entry had not, however, been violent, and the claim failed.

Inevitable loss

27.12 It might be thought that inevitable loss would be implicitly excluded from an insurance policy as insurance is only intended to cover accidental loss. These types of exclusions are frequently included to either increase the effectiveness of the exclusion or point out to the insured that such loss is not covered. Typical exclusions are latent defects, gradual deterioration, inherent vice, wear and tear, corrosion, rust, wet or dry rot, evaporation and shrinkage.

Other exclusions

27.13   This 'catch all' section will vary widely from policy to policy, but it will certainly include consequential loss, and possibly goods in transit and lack of incoming utilities. On the other hand, some policies will cover such perils within the policy or by way of endorsement for additional premium.

Typical conditions

27.14   Many conditions which are to be found in building or property policies will also be found in other forms of insurance and are dealt with elsewhere in 14 CLAIMS (in particular notification of claims, fraudulent claims and proof of loss) and policyholders' duties (6 POLICYHOLDER DUTIES).

It is worth mentioning, however, that the fraud condition in this type of cover tends to be a standard form similar to the following:

> 'If a claim is fraudulent in any respect or fraudulent means are used by the insured or by anyone acting on his behalf to obtain any benefit under the policy or damage to the property insured or to the property used by the insured at the premises for the purpose of the business is caused by the wilful act or the connivance of the insured all benefit under the policy shall be forfeited.'

It should be noted that such condition covers not only self induced loss but also fraudulent claims. In *Insurance Corporation of Channel Islands Ltd and Royal Insurance Ltd v The Royal Hotel [1997] LRLR 94*, the court decided that the effect of this particular clause was to forfeit all benefit *ab initio*.

This type of insurance will also frequently include increase in hazard clauses which will attempt to prevent the insured increasing substantially the nature of the risk, and also reasonable care clauses attempting to place upon the insured an obligation to take reasonable care of the insured property. In both instances, however, the courts have proved to be remarkably creative in circumventing their effect in protecting insurers (see 6 POLICYHOLDER DUTIES).

Typical conditions specific to property policies also include the following:

- the 'non-invalidation' clause. This is often found in policies designed for landlords and provides that the cover provided shall not be prejudiced by any act or default of the tenant that increases the risk of loss or damage, provided immediate notification is given by the landlord when he becomes aware of this;

- the 'unoccupied premises' clause. There are several variations on this clause. Some provide that cover ceases altogether if the premises are left unoccupied for more than 30 consecutive days. Others provide that cover will continue (sometimes for restricted perils) but only on condition that the Insured inspects the property weekly, shuts off all services and boards up accessible windows.

Courts are more likely to uphold conditions which are specifically drafted to deal with a type of risk such as a sprinkler warranty which might require the insured to maintain sprinklers on a regular basis. Frequently, premium is clearly rated on the basis of such undertakings and courts are more likely to enforce such specific conditions or warranties. This would also apply to security requirements.

A good example of a commercially minded approach to the construction of an alarm warranty is found in *Anders & Kern UK Ltd (t/a Anders & Kern Presentation Systems) v CGU Insurance plc (t/a Norwich Union Insurance) [2007] EWCA Civ 1481.* The judge upheld a term requiring a key holder to remain at the premises in the event that the insured received notification from the alarm monitoring company that the line was down. The court refused to imply a term that the key holder would not be required to remain at the premises if it would put him in personal danger because the alarm warranty and it accompanying terms showed a clear allocation of risk such that the insurer was to be off risk if the premises were unattended unless the alarm was fully operational.

Average clauses are found in buildings and property insurance (see 19 AVERAGE). It is also quite usual to find subrogation waiver clauses in this type of cover but this is dealt with in 16 SUBROGATION.

Extensions to buildings and property insurance

Business interruption

27.15

(a) As indicated at 27.13 above, consequential loss is excluded from property insurance in respect of commercial premises, but is usually brought back in by way of business interruption extension.

(b) A policy insuring property does not, in the absence of express wording, cover financial loss accruing to the insured as a direct result of damage to the property. In *Maurice v Goldsborough Mort & Co Ltd [1939] AC 452,* a firm of wool brokers insured a quantity of wool in their possession belonging to a wool grower. The wool was destroyed, and a question arose as to how the insurance monies received by the brokers were to be allocated as between themselves and the grower. The House of Lords ruled that the brokers could retain only an amount equal to the cost of services rendered, and were unable to retain a sum representing loss of profits on warehouse charges and on resale, as these matters were not insured under the policy. Again, in *Re Wright & Pole (1834) 1 Ad & El 621,* an innkeeper who had insured his inn against fire was entitled to recover the value of the buildings but could not recover the financial cost of hiring other premises and loss of trade pending repair.

Loss of profits and other consequential business interruption losses must, therefore, be insured separately. Policies or policy extensions of this type are subject to general principles of insurance law. In particular, all material facts must be disclosed to the insurer at the inception, including the profitability or otherwise of the business (*Stavers v Mountain (1912) Times, 27 July*).

(c) Most business interruption policies include a clause requiring that it only operates in conjunction with a policy insuring the insured's interest in material damage to the said property at the same premises. Sometimes business interruption cover will simply be an extension of the material damage policy or, alternatively, there may be in existence a separate policy issued by different underwriters. Generally speaking, however, the payment under the business interruption policy in addition to its own terms of cover will be dependent upon the insured being entitled to make a claim under the material damage policy. The importance in drafting such provisos carefully was made clear in *Glengate-KG Properties Ltd v Norwich Union Fire Insurance Society Ltd [1996] All ER 487*, where insurers certainly did not draft the material damage proviso carefully enough to produce the result they intended.

Denial of access

27.16 This is a common extension in the business interruption section of a property policy and provides cover for financial loss when access to the insured premises is prevented or hindered due to damage by an insured peril to a neighbour's property. A common example of when this might apply would be a fire in a unit in a shopping centre – businesses in neighbouring units may suffer no physical damage but it may be many weeks before they can resume trading whilst the fire is investigated and the area made safe.

Debris removal

27.17

(i) This provides for removal of the debris off site and/or the temporary removal of property from premises for cleaning and renovation etc after loss. Debris removal coverage usually is dependent upon physical loss or damage to property covered under the main policy and frequently it is limited financially as a proportion of the material damage loss.

(ii) In certain types of property insurance it can be an important extension. For example, if earthworks are covered within an open pit mine, the removal of debris from site in the event of an earthworks failure could constitute a very large part of the loss.

Increased cost of construction

27.18   Cover is provided under a property policy for the cost of repairing the property or replacing it with an equivalent property in a condition equal to but not better than the property destroyed. If an old building is damaged beyond repair, the Building Regulations may not allow the insured to rebuild without making improvements to the specification, such as fitting double glazing, which will increase the cost and would otherwise be regarded as betterment and so be irrecoverable.

However, because the insured has no choice but to comply with these statutory requirements, most policies contain an extension allowing the insured to recover such costs, as long as the insured was not already required to make these improvements prior to the damage. This is also known as a public authorities extension because only improvements required by an authorised public body or required by law are covered.

Chapter 28
Construction risks insurance

- Risk issues
- Project insurance
- Insurance under the JCT construction contracts
- Issues arising from the operation of Contractors' All Risks insurance
- Latent defects insurance

Risk issues

28.01 A typical construction contract exposes all the participants to risk of different kinds. Some of the risks arise under the general law of contract and tort. For example, the owner/client (referred to as the employer in many standard form contracts such as those of the Joint Contracts Tribunal (JCT)) could incur liability as an occupier of a site for injury or damage suffered by a visitor to the site under the *Occupiers Liability Acts 1957* and *1984*. The main contractor can also incur liability as an occupier.

However, some of the risks to participants in a construction contract are created, or at least allocated, by the contract itself. The participants will wish to insure against many of those risks, and may be required to do so as part of the contractual responsibilities. Modern construction (and engineering) contracts invariably contain sophisticated insurance provisions, regulating the insurance cover that must be obtained, by whom and exceptions and extensions to the cover.

Project insurance

28.02 It would be possible for each party to take separate insurance for each of the risks to which it is exposed. However, there are good commercial reasons, especially on very large projects, for obtaining comprehensive project insurance. There should be significant savings in premiums over piecemeal cover by several parties, and administrative costs are typically reduced. This type of insurance (sometimes called 'wrap-up insurance' in North America) is attractive in traditional projects, subject to the argument that the employer ought not to transfer a burden from the contractor to himself without good reason, but is more problematic in a design and build contract, where truly comprehensive project insurance would need to include the professional indemnity cover of the designers and other consultants used by the contractor.

Even if project insurance is not obtained, there are 'composite' or 'combined' policies for contractors that include the employer's liability risk, public liability risk and loss or damage to the contract work (the part usually covered by an all risks policy).

To the advantages of economy and simplicity of project insurance can be added some certainty on the part of the employer as to the cover in place. For these reasons, the major standard form construction contracts (such as JCT) almost invariably require the contractor to take out comprehensive insurance, including the misleadingly-named 'Contractors' All Risks', but also insurance of its other potential liabilities to the employer. The contractor is also typically required to indemnify the employer against loss and to be insured in order to be able to discharge this responsibility. The indemnity provisions of a contract such as the JCT form must be read with its insurance provisions to obtain an accurate account of the position.

Insurance under the JCT construction contracts

28.03   As a general principle, it can be stated that insurance under the JCT contract is the contractor's responsibility, although the employer will often look to his consultants and advisers to ensure that the appropriate cover is in place. In *Pozzolanic Lytag Ltd v Bryan Hobson Associates [1998] 63 Con LR 81* it was held that a project manager had a duty to ensure that the insurance required by the contract to be maintained by the contractor was actually in place.

There are two categories of risk which are almost invariably covered by the insurance provisions of JCT 2005, and a third which is sometimes also included. JCT 2005 also requires the contractor to take out professional indemnity insurance as soon as possible after the contract with the employer is entered into.

Insurance against injury to persons or property

28.04   JCT 2005 requires the contractor to indemnify the employer against any third party claims for: (i) injury or death unless the employer is personally or vicariously liable (the employer will need insurance against this risk); or (ii) damage to property to the extent that the injury or damage is shown to be due to negligence, breach of statutory duty, omission or default of the contractor or any contractor's person. The contractor is not liable for loss or damage caused by specific perils to property for which insurance has been taken out by the employer. A common device to deal with this requirement is for the contractor to be instructed to insure in his and the employer's names (a joint names policy). Any claim can then be made against either party and would be covered by the policy.

Insurance against damage to the works

28.05   The works themselves, meaning the buildings or other structures being constructed under the contract, must be insured under JCT 2005 against the risk of damage, destruction and non-completion 'for the full reinstatement value of the works'. The type of insurance taken out is either 'All risks insurance' or 'Specified perils insurance'.

Insurance for employer's loss of liquidated damages

28.06   The employer can opt to require the contractor to obtain liquidated damages insurance. The insurance will cover the situation where the contractor has to be given extensions of time under the contract, thus forfeiting the employer's right to claim liquidated damages for late completion.

Issues arising from the operation of Contractors' All Risks insurance

Coverage

28.07   The basic principle is that all risks insurance covers any loss not caused by an 'excluded peril'. The benefit to the insured lies in not having to prove that the loss falls within the cover. It is enough to show that loss has occurred in order to initiate a claim under an all risks policy. To resist the claim, the insurer would have to show that the cause of the loss fell within an exclusion, the burden of proof being upon the insurer.

Risks excluded

28.08   JCT 2005 authorises the exclusion of certain risks from its definition of all risks insurance, such as property defects due to 'wear and tear, obsolescence, deterioration, rust or mildew'. There are also exclusions of loss or damage arising out of war and various other types of civil and military conflict. Perhaps the most contentious exclusion is for faulty workmanship and faulty design. The exact content of such an exclusion depends upon its wording and how it is implemented. The courts have often been called upon to deal with attempts by insurers to bring defects within exclusions of this kind, in cases such as *Kier Construction v Royal Insurance (UK) [1994] 30 Con LR 45*, where the meaning of defective workmanship was considered.

Latent defects insurance

28.09   The essential components of latent defects insurance (LDI) are as follows: it is a non-cancellable material damage insurance against specified latent defects and damage caused by them. It gives protection for a period of 10 years and is sometimes referred to as 'decennial' insurance. It is funded by a single premium paid 'up front' at the inception of the project, or in two stages, the first at preliminary design stage and the second at the date of practical completion. It is only after practical completion that the insurers are on risk. The premium is paid in principle by the developer (employer), although there is nothing to prevent him from negotiating with his design and construction team to share it.

Basic cover is limited to structure and weather shield envelope (although additional optional cover for some types of consequential loss, such as loss of rent, can be purchased). The benefit of the cover is to be transferable to successive owners and to whole-building tenants (tenants of part of the building or individual units receive an indemnity). Deductibles apply, but are set at levels designed to impose discipline on the conduct of developers and producers (ie contractors and consultants).

Sir Michael Latham in his 1994 report recommended that LDI should be compulsory in the commercial sector, the residential section being already largely covered by the National Housebuilders Council (NHBC) scheme and similar arrangements. The 1997 report of Latham's working group 10 has never been implemented but LDI is available commercially from a number of insurers in the United Kingdom, where it is often described as BUILD insurance (Builders Users' Insurance against Latent Defects).

Chapter 29
Directors and officers liability

- Nature and scope of directors and officers insurance
- Common sources of liability for directors

The nature and scope of directors and officers insurance

Background

29.01   *Section 233* of the *Companies Act 2006* expressly permits a company to purchase insurance on behalf of its directors and officers in respect of liabilities which they may incur in relation to the company. A directors and officers policy is designed to provide protection to a company's directors and officers in respect of many forms of civil liability and defence costs in relation to their activities, or arising out of their capacity as a director or officer of a company.

A typical directors and officers policy will have two insuring clauses. The first provides direct indemnification by the insurer to the director or officer. The second provides that the insurer will reimburse the company to the extent that the company has already indemnified its directors or officers. Most standard directors and officers policies do not provide any 'entity cover' to the company in respect of its own exposure to civil liability or defence costs although this type of cover may be available on payment of additional premium.

The trigger for cover under a directors and officers policy is a 'wrongful act'. This is generally widely defined to include any act, error or omission committed by a director in his capacity as such.

Most policies are written on a composite basis for the benefit of each director or officer individually rather than jointly as a group.

Permutations of cover

29.02   Cover varies considerably from policy to policy, but some general points should be borne in mind:

(*a*)   Virtually all directors and officers policies are written on a 'claims made' basis, which means that they only cover losses arising and notified during the policy period. Retired directors facing a claim in relation to their period in office may not be covered.

(*b*)   Criminal fines and penalties are generally not insurable under English law, particularly where resulting from intentional conduct. However, costs incurred defending criminal prosecutions will generally be covered, subject to fraud and dishonesty exclusions.

(*c*)   Many policies exclude claims brought or liabilities incurred in certain jurisdictions.

(*d*)   A director may be called upon to participate in a regulatory, disciplinary or criminal investigation. If no wrongful act is alleged and legal liability has not been established, the directors and officers policy may not respond. Free-standing defence costs cover to meet such a situation is available under certain policies.

(*e*)   Some directors and officers policies provide cover in respect of employment claims to the company as well as the directors. This can erode the aggregate limit of cover available to the directors in respect of claims brought against them personally. It may also have unwelcome tax consequences for directors on the basis that the Revenue may argue that any premiums paid or losses incurred under the policy as a whole do not qualify for tax relief under a statutory exemption which exists only in respect of standard directors and officers cover.

Common sources of liability for directors

Duties to the company

29.03   All directors owe a number of fiduciary duties to the company on whose board they sit. Traditionally these were a matter of common law but have now been codified in the Companies Act 2006.

Sections 171–177 set out a number of general duties with which directors must comply, summarised below. Section 170(3) states that the

> 'general duties are based on certain common law rules and equitable principles as they apply in relation to directors and have effect in place of those rules and principles as regards the duties owed to a company by a director'.

Section 170(4) goes on to provide that the

> 'general duties shall be interpreted and applied in the same way as common law rules or equitable principles, and regard shall be had to the corresponding common law rules and equitable principles in interpreting and applying the general duties'.

There will, however, be some initial uncertainty whilst the courts get to grips with how to apply the new statutory code of duties.

General duties in force from 1 October 2007:

- to exercise reasonable care, skill and diligence;

- to exercise independent judgement;

- to act in the way that they consider, in good faith, would be most likely to promote the success of the company for the benefit of its members as a whole (having regard to six specified factors);

- to act in accordance with the company's constitution and to exercise their powers for the purposes for which they are conferred;

General duties in force from 1 October 2008:

- to avoid conflicts of interest;

- not to accept benefits from third parties;

- to declare any interest in a proposed transaction or arrangement with the company.

As previously these duties are only enforceable by the company rather than by individual shareholders (see *Companies Act 2006, s 170(1)*) However the so-called 'derivative' action, to allow shareholders to bring claims in the name of the company against directors, has been expanded in scope under the Companies Act 2006. From 1 October 2007, previous restrictions on such actions no longer apply and are available in respect of all alleged breaches of duty (actual or threatened) by directors or former directors. Furthermore, the Companies Act 2006 does not require a shareholder to hold any minimum number of shares in order to have standing to bring a claim and the claim can be brought in respect of breaches of duty alleged to have occurred before the shares were purchased (*s 260(4)*). A number of important procedural safeguards have however, been included in the new regime in an attempt to prevent vexatious claims.

Duties to third parties

29.04   Following the House of Lords' decision in *Williams v Natural Life Health Foods [1998] 2 All ER 577*, the scope for third parties to bring direct claims for negligent misstatement against a company director acting in his capacity as such is limited. This case decided that in the absence of clear evidence that a director has assumed personal and direct responsibility for advice or information to an individual, the individual will not have a right of action against him.

This restriction, however, applies only to claims seeking to recover pure economic loss for negligence, and the House of Lords has recently confirmed that a director may be sued as readily as any other agent for his own fraudulent conduct (*Standard*

Chartered Bank v Pakistan National Shipping Corpn [2003] 1 AC 959). The same applies to actions against a director for his negligence if that results in property damage or personal injury.

Other statutory liabilities

29.05   Under the statutory regimes that affect directors, there are many ways in which a director can incur civil liability or liability for fines and penalties. These include:

(a)   civil liability for wrongful trading under *Insolvency Act 1986, s 214* in circumstances where a director allows a company to continue trading beyond the time at which he should reasonably have concluded that it was insolvent;

(b)   disqualification under the *Company Directors Disqualification Act 1986* on a variety of grounds, including a general provision enabling a director to be disqualified in circumstances where his conduct was such as to make him unfit to be concerned in the management of a company;

(c)   civil liability under the *Financial Services and Markets Act 2000, s 90* to any investors in a company who can show that they have suffered a loss as a result of reliance on untrue or misleading statements contained in listing particulars or as a result of the omission from the particulars of any matter required to be included by the Act.

In addition to these examples there are many other statutory provisions in respect of which directors can incur civil or criminal liability. Much will depend on the scope and sphere of the operations conducted by the company on whose board he sits.

Chapter 30
Employers' liability insurance

- Introduction

- Compulsory insurance for injuries at work

- Contents of the policy

- Liabilities faced by an employer

- Who is the employee?

- Transfer of liabilities

- Enforcement

Introduction

30.01   Accidents in the workplace are estimated to be responsible for around 40% of all recorded personal injuries. English law imposes a variety of common law and statutory duties upon employers to secure the safety of their employees. The growth of personal injury claims early in this century led to the development of employers' liability insurance. Regrettably, it proved to be the case that the least safety conscious employers were those most likely not to insure against liability, with the result that many injured employees, having substantiated a claim against their employers, found their judgments to be worthless as the employers were not backed by liability insurance. Consequently, the *Employers' Liability (Compulsory Insurance) Act 1969* (*EL(CI)A 1969*), which entered into force on 1 January 1971, made it compulsory for employers to insure against liability to employees. By *s 3* of the Act, Local Authorities are exempt from the requirement to effect insurance

It is an interesting exercise to compare the 1969 Act with the *Road Traffic Act 1988* (*RTA 1988*), which imposes an obligation upon the users of motor vehicles to insure against liability arising from use on a public road (see 35 MOTOR VEHICLE INSURANCE). *RTA 1988* is much wider in a number of important respects.

(a)   *RTA 1988* covers property damages, whereas *EL(CI)A 1969* is concerned only with death or personal injury.

(b)   Under *RTA 1988* the insurer of a motor vehicle is unable to rely upon breach of policy conditions by the insured, and upon any right to avoid the policy for the insured's duty of utmost good faith, whereas *EL(CI)A 1969* removes only a very limited range of defences from the insurer.

(c)   The victim of an insured driver (*RTA 1988*) has a direct cause of action against the insurer if the driver fails to satisfy the judgment, whereas an injured employee (*EL(CI)A 1969*) can sue his employer's insurers where the employer has failed to meet a judgment only in the case of the employer's insolvency (under the *Third Parties (Rights Against Insurers) Act 1930*).

(d)   If the employer does not carry insurance, there is no fall back compensation scheme equivalent to the Motor Insurers' Bureau (see 35 MOTOR VEHICLE INSURANCE).

Compulsory insurance for injuries at work

The obligation to insure

30.02   Every employer carrying on any business in Great Britain is required to take out and maintain insurance against liability for bodily injury or disease sustained by his employees arising out of and in the course of their employment in Great Britain (*EL(CI)A 1969, s 1(1)*). The policy must be issued by an insurer authorised to carry on insurance business of the class in question (*EL(CI)A 1969, s 1(3)(b)*; see 10 INSURANCE COMPANIES). The policy must be 'approved', that is, not narrower in scope than is required by the Act (*EL(CI)A 1969, s 1(3)(a)*). (For exceptions to the obligation to insure see 30.12 below.)

Amount of cover

30.03   The amount of cover to be procured is specified by statutory instrument made under *s 1(2)* of *EL(CI)A 1969*. The present figure is £5 million 'in respect of claims relating to any one or more of his employees arising out of any one occurrence' (*Employers' Liability (Compulsory Insurance) General Regulations 1998 (SI 1998/2573), reg 3*). The maximum figure relates not to individual injuries but rather to the occurrence which gives rise to individual injuries, and is therefore an aggregate figure. In practice, most authorised insurers provide cover of at least £10 million.

Course of employment

30.04   Compulsory insurance need not extend to injuries suffered by an employee acting outside the course of his employment. It should be noted that an employee is acting in the course of his employment even though he may be disobeying his employer's orders: the test is whether the employee was going about his employer's business at the time. An employee travelling to and from work is not acting in the course of his employment unless the job requires travelling between sites or offices (*Smith v Stages [1989] 1 All ER 833*), neither is an employee who is engaged in after-hours social activities, such as playing football for his employer's team (see *R v National Insurance Commissioner [1977] 1 WLR 109*).

To avoid the potential conflict that can arise when an employee travels in a motor vehicle and sustains injury, the *Motor Vehicles (Compulsory Insurance) Regulations 1992 (SI 1992/2036)* provided for the compulsory insurance requirements pursuant to *RTA 1988* to extend to all motor vehicle passengers, with the effect that the claim falls to be dealt with by the motor policy insurers rather than the employers' liability policy insurers (*Employers' Liability (Compulsory Insurance) Exemption (Amendment) Regulations 1992 (SI 1992/3172)*).

Contents of the policy

30.05   An employers' liability policy follows the pattern of general liability policies. However, under *reg 2(1)* of *SI 1998/2573*, four types of policy condition are prohibited from inclusion in a compulsory policy. The prohibited conditions relate to the insurer seeking to avoid liability:

(*a*)   in the event of some specified thing being done or omitted to be done after the happening of the event giving rise to a claim under the policy (eg notice of loss clauses or admissions of liability);

(*b*)   unless the policyholder takes reasonable care to protect his employees against the risk of bodily injury or disease in the course of their employment (reasonable care clauses have, independently of this provision, been given limited meaning by the courts, and have been confined to recklessness);

(*c*)   unless the policyholder complies with the requirements of any enactment for the protection of employees against the risk of bodily injury or disease in the course of their employment (so that, for example, breaches of the *Factories Act 1961* by the employer cannot provide a defence to the insurer); and

(*d*)   unless the policyholder keeps specified records or provides the insurer with or makes available to him information therefrom (a clause of this type may relate to a record of wages paid or to an accident book).

An insurer remains free to provide that the employer is to indemnify the insurer for sums required under the legislation to be paid by the insurer to an injured employee where any of the above terms has been broken by the employer (*SI 1998/2573, reg 2(2)*).

Liabilities faced by an employer

Common law liability

Direct liability

30.06   An employer owes a duty of care to his employees to take reasonable care for their safety. The leading authority is *Wilsons & Clyde Coal Co Ltd v English* .

[1938] AC 57, in which the employers of a miner killed due to the operation of an unsafe system of work were sued by the miner's family. The House of Lords rejected the employers' defence that the duty to organise working systems had been delegated to an employee, and held that the employers' duty could not be delegated. Lord Wright's speech contains the classic statement of the scope of an employer's duty, namely, to provide 'a competent staff of men, adequate material, and a proper system and effective supervision'.

The duty is not absolute, and merely requires the employer to act reasonably. In *Latimer v AEC [1953] AC 643*, for example, in which an employee was injured having fallen over on a floor made slippery by flooding, the House of Lords ruled that the employers had, in clearing up the flood, taken all reasonable care to overcome the danger, and that it was unreasonable to expect the employers to provide absolute protection by closing the factory down until the floor was completely dry. In *Dixon v London Fire and Civil Defence Authority, Times, 22 February, 1993*, a fireman was injured due to slipping on wet quarry tiles at his place of work. The Court of Appeal held that the employers had not broken their duty of care, as they had taken reasonable care to fix the leak which had caused the wetting. The Court of Appeal further held that it would have been unreasonable for the employers to install an entirely different floor surface despite the fact that the quarry tiles were not the safest possible flooring in the circumstances.

Vicarious liability

30.07   In addition to an employer's direct liability to his employees, he may also be vicariously liable for the negligent acts of fellow employees and independent contractors working on his premises. As far as vicarious liability for employees is concerned, the employer is liable for all injuries negligently inflicted by one employee on another if the negligent employee was acting in the course of his employment. The concept of 'course of employment' is a wide one, and may include the activities of an employee acting contrary to the employer's business. In *Rose v Plenty and Another [1976] 1 WLR 141*, the employers of a milkman were held to be liable for injuries to a child falling from one of their milk floats, even though the employee milkman had been specifically forbidden to carry children in this way.

Where an employer is held to be vicariously liable for the acts of an employee, the employer is entitled at common law to be indemnified by the employee by reason of an implied term to that effect in the contract of employment. The real impact of this rule is to permit the employers' liability insurers, having indemnified the employer, to exercise subrogation rights against the employee (see *Lister v Romford Ice and Cold Storage Co Ltd [1957] AC 555*, a case in which the employer's insurers were able to recoup their payment to an injured employee from the guilty employee, who happened to be the injured employee's father). This rule remains the law, but insurers agreed with the government in the wake of this case not to exercise subrogation rights against negligent employees. In a later case, *Morris v Ford Motor Co Ltd [1973] QB 792*, the Court of Appeal refused to extend the *Lister* case to injuries caused by an employee who had been borrowed from another employer.

In the case of an independent contractor, the employer's liability is personal rather than vicarious. The employer is liable only if his own conduct has been negligent, for example if he has failed to exercise reasonable care in selecting a competent independent contractor, or if he has failed adequately to supervise the independent contractor's performance of his obligations. Whether a contractor is properly to be regarded as independent or falls within the category of an employee is considered below at 30.09.

Liability arising under statute

30.08   The *Health and Safety at Work etc Act 1974* (*HSWA 1974*) established a system of administrative control and penal sanctions relating to general duties requiring safety in the workplace. However, the *HSWA 1974* does not confer any civil rights upon an employee injured in consequence of his employer's breach of any provision of the Act. The employee's civil rights are available either under the common law or by means of an action based upon other health and safety legislation for breach of statutory duty.

Over the decades the range of different statutes provided for regulation within different industries, most notably the various *Factories Acts*, mines and quarries legislation and regulations governing offices, shops and railway premises.

This industry-by-industry approach to health and safety was eventually superseded with the implementation in the United Kingdom of the *European Framework Directive*, introducing a wide-ranging series of regulations governing workplace health and safety.

Just as the *HSWA 1974* does not afford any civil remedy, the *Management of Health and Safety at Work Regulations 1992* (*SI 1992/2051*) similarly, when first introduced, did not attract civil liability. However, following the Management of Health and Safety At Work (Amendment) Regulations 2006 compensation claims can now be brought based directly on a breach of the 1992 Regulations. Claims may also be brought against employees by third parties who were affected by their work. In *Stark v The Post Office, unreported, 2000 (CA)*, the claimant was employed as a delivery postman and suffered injury during the course of his employment when the front wheel of the bicycle that he was riding locked, causing him to be thrown over the handlebars. The accident was caused by a defect in the bicycle which would not have been detected upon a thorough examination. The Court of Appeal held that *reg 6(1)* of the *Provision and Use of Work Equipment Regulations 1992* (*SI 1992/2932*) imposed an absolute obligation on the employers to maintain work equipment in efficient working order and good repair.

In *Fytche v Wincanton Logistics plc [2004] UKHL 31* the House of Lords considered whether the duty placed on an employer under the Personal Protective Equipment Regulations 1992 to keep PPE in repair extended only to the risk in relation to which the equipment was supplied or whether it extended to all possible risks.

The claimant lorry driver was provided with steel capped safety boots when collecting milk from farms – to protect him from dropping milk churns. Water got into his boots causing frostbite. The House held the obligation to keep the boots in good repair extended to keeping them free from defects relating to the risks that the boots had been provided to provide protection against.

By comparison, in *Hawkes v London Borough of Southwark, unreported, 1998 (CA)* the Court of Appeal held that a test of 'reasonable practicability' is still relevant when considering the system of work giving rise to a claim pursuant to the *Manual Handling Operation Regulations 1992 (SI 1992/2793)*. See also *Koonjul v Thameslink Healthcare Services (2000)*. The claimant was an experienced care assistant who worked at a small residential home for children with learning disabilities. In the course of making a bed she bent down and pulled the bed away from a wall, injuring her back. The bed was unusually low in case children with epilepsy fell out of bed (which was against the wall for the same reason). It was accepted that the force required to move the bed was very modest. The Court of Appeal held that the defendant was not liable: Lady Justice Hale stated:

> 'It is an employment involving a number of everyday tasks, any one of which could involve something which could be described as a manual handling operation – lifting bedding, moving beds around in order to make them, moving the chest of drawers, or moving the chair in order to make the bed. There are innumerable tasks around such a home, and the idea that the level of risk involved (which I have already said was very low) should be met by a precise evaluation of each of those tasks and precise warnings to each employee as to how each was to be carried out, seems to me to take the matter way beyond the realms of practicability.'

In addition to the European Directives, the *Employers' Liability (Defective Equipment) Act 1969* entitles an injured employee to sue his employer where he suffered injury as a result of using defective equipment that had been manufactured and supplied to the employer by an independent manufacturer. It is for the employer to sue the manufacturer for the liability that he has incurred towards his employee.

The word 'equipment' covers both 'plant' (tools and machinery to be used by the employee), and 'stock in trade' (articles produced by the use of plant). In *Knowles v Liverpool City Council (1993) Times, 15 October*, a flagstone which the employee had been employed to lay was held to be 'equipment'.

In *Wright v Romford Blinds & Shutters Ltd [2003] EWHC 1165* the claimant was standing on top of a van, loading shuttering that was being passed up to him when he lost his footing and fell. The fall was held to be directly associated with the work being undertaken. The defendant had not put up guard rails or raised edges on the roof surface. No risk assessment had been carried out. It was held that there was a breach of reg 13 of the Workplace (Health, Safety and Welfare) Regulations 1992 as the roof of the van was a 'workplace' and the defendant had failed to prevent the claimant from pulling a distance likely to cause injury.

The Work at Height Regulations 2005 which came into force on 6 April 2005 now governs, as the title suggests, all aspects of working at height and place duties upon an employer for his employee and any other person under his control.

Who is the employee?

An 'employee'

30.09 The term 'employee' is defined as meaning 'an individual who has entered into or works under a contract of service or apprenticeship with an employer whether by way of manual labour, clerical work or otherwise, whether such contract is expressed or implied, oral or in writing' (*EL(CI)A 1969, s 2(1)*). The most important distinction to be drawn here is between an employee and an independent contractor.

Over the years various tests have been developed to identify who should properly be classed as an independent contractor and therefore not an employee. The courts have gradually moved away from tests such as 'who controls and directs the work' to an assessment of the 'economic reality' of the relationship between the parties. Even where the independent contractor describes himself as such and provides his own equipment, he may well be held to be an employee when the financial reality of the relationship between the parties is considered (see *Lane v The Shire Roofing Company (Oxford) Ltd [1995] IRLR 493; Wharf v Bildwell Insulations Ltd [1999] CLY 2047*).

Residence in Great Britain

30.10 An employee must be ordinarily resident in Great Britain to obtain the benefit of the 1969 Act (*EC(CI)A 1969, s 2(2)(b)*). *SI 1998/2573* extends protection to an employee, who is not ordinarily resident in Great Britain, but who is injured in the course of his employment while present in Great Britain for a continuous period of not less than 14 days. An employee not ordinarily resident in Great Britain may, of course, be covered by employers' liability insurance on a voluntary basis, but the employer is under no common law duty of care, either to take out such insurance, or to warn the employee that they should take steps to procure first party insurance against injury incurred abroad (*Reid v Rush & Tomkins Group plc [1989] 3 All ER 228*). This does not apply to work on offshore installations, which are covered separately by *SI 1998/2573*.

Relatives

30.11 *EL(CI)A 1969* does not require insurance to be taken out in respect of an employee who falls into any of the following categories of relation to the employer: husband, wife, father, mother, grandfather, grandmother, stepfather, stepmother, son, daughter, grandson, granddaughter, stepson, stepdaughter, brother, sister, half-brother or half-sister (*EL(CI)A 1969, s 2(2)(a)*).

Specific exceptions

30.12 The compulsory insurance requirement does not apply to:

(*a*)   various categories of local authority employees (*EL(CI)A 1969, s 3(1)(a),(2)*);

(*b*)   employees of a statutory body under national ownership or control (*EL(CI)A 1969, s 3(1)(b)*);

(*c*)   employees of various bodies listed in the *Employers' Liability (Compulsory Insurance) Exemption Regulations 1971 (SI 1971/1933)*, including transport, water and judicial authorities; or

(*d*)   (with effect from 1 July 1994) an employer's liability for the death of or personal injury to an employee in a motor vehicle accident (*Employers' Liability (Compulsory Insurance) Exemption (Amendment) Regulations 1992 (SI 1992/3172)*).

Transfer of liabilities

30.13   *Regulation 5* of the *Transfer of Undertakings (Protection of Employment) Regulations 1981 (SI 1981/1794) (TUPE 1981)* provides that on the completion of a transfer of a business all the 'old' employers' rights, powers, duties and liabilities under or in connection with any such contract, shall be transferred to the 'new' employer. In addition, anything done before the transfer is completed by or in relation to the old employer, in respect of that contract, or a person employed in that undertaking or part, shall be deemed to have been done by or in relation to the transfer.

These Regulations have caused confusion in circumstances where a worker suffers a personal injury due to the employer's negligence, but then thereafter the business is transferred to a new employer. Which employer should the worker sue?

This issue has been considered by the Court of Appeal in *Bernadone v Pall Mall Services Group ; Martin v Lancashire County Council [2000] 3 All ER 544*. The Court of Appeal held that *Regulation 5* was wide enough to allow for a liability for personal injury to arise in connection with the contract, and as such it was transferred to the new employer under *TUPE 1981*. In addition, the court held that the old employers' right to recover from its insurers in respect of liability to an employee for personal injury arising under *EL(CI)A 1969* also transferred to the new employer, thereby transferring the old employers' insurance cover to the new employer.

Although the new employer will have the benefit of the old employers' insurance cover, the new employer will still be responsible for the excess or deductible under the policy.

Enforcement

Sanctions

30.14   It is a criminal offence for an employer to fail to procure the required insurance. Criminal liability, in the case of a company, may be extended to any officer of the company who was responsible for the default (*EL(CI)A 1969, s 5*). However, if the employer's default is not remedied and an employee is injured, the employee will simply be left uncompensated if the employer cannot afford to pay the damages.

Certificates

30.15   To guard against failure to insure, the 1969 Act sets up an inspection regime (*EL(CI)A 1969, s 5*). An employer taking out insurance must, within 30 days, be issued by the insurer with a certificate in the statutory form, stating the name of the policyholder, the date of the commencement of the insurance, the date of the expiry of the insurance and the name of the insurer (*SI 1998/2573, reg 5*). A copy of the certificate must be displayed at each of the employer's places of business (*SI 1998/2573, reg 6*) and must be produced for inspection to the Health and Safety Executive or an inspector appointed by the Department of Trade and Industry (*SI 1998/2573, regs 7 and 8*).

Chapter 31
Environmental insurance

- Sources of environmental liability
- Insurance against environmental liability

31.01   Greater awareness of the effects of environmental degradation has led to the development in England and Wales of environmental liability regimes. The enforcement of these regimes means that companies are no longer able to ignore environmental liabilities arising from their acts or omissions. Environmental liabilities may take the form of: liabilities to third parties for damage to their person or property; responsibility for cleaning up the environment imposed by a regulator like the Environment Agency; sanctions for criminal environmental offences; and legal costs. One way of managing these liabilities, other than fines for criminal offences which are not insurable as a matter of public policy, is to insure them.

Sources of environmental liability

31.02   Insurance may be sought against environmental liabilities arising from the common law and from statute.

Common law

31.03   The principal common law sources of environmental liability are nuisance (public and private), negligence, the rule in *Rylands v Fletcher (1868) LR 3 HL 330* and, to a much more limited extent, trespass. For the first three torts, there must be damage and that damage must be reasonably foreseeable. For the fourth tort, damage is not a pre-requisite; the claimant need only show interference with its land.

Statute

31.04   Environmental legislation imposes criminal liability on polluters and, as noted in 31.01 above, for public policy reasons, it is not possible to insure against fines. In addition, there are statutory provisions which authorise regulatory authorities to require the remediation (clean up) of polluted land and/or water. Examples include *s 161A* of the *Water Resources Act 1991* which authorises the Environment Agency to serve a notice requiring a person who caused or knowingly permitted a pollutant to enter a body of water to remediate it and, if practicable, restore the aquatic environment; and *s 78E* of the *Environmental Protection Act 1990* which, subject to certain conditions, requires a local authority, where it has identified land as contaminated, to serve a notice requiring the person who caused or knowingly permitted the contamination, or if that person cannot be found after a reasonable inquiry, the owner or occupier of the land, to remediate it.

Other statutory provisions also impose civil liability on a polluter. An example is *s 73(6)* of the *Environmental Protection Act 1990* which authorises a person who has suffered property damage or personal injury caused by an unlawful deposit of waste to bring an action for damages against the person who deposited the waste, or knowingly caused or knowingly permitted it to be deposited.

The liabilities outlined above may be covered by public liability or environmental insurance policies.

Insurance against environmental liability

Public liability policies

31.05   Public liability policies generally cover the insured in respect of damages or compensation that the insured is legally liable to pay to third parties for personal injury and property damage which takes place during the policy period and which is connected with the insured's activities. Personal injury or property damage may result, among other things, from pollutants or exposure to pollutants. Claims for such injury or damage may be made many years after the policy period has ended. A typical coverage clause might state:

> 'The insurer will indemnify the insured for all sums which the insured shall become legally liable to pay as damages [or compensation] because of bodily injury or property damage occurring during the period of insurance.'

In the United States, disputes have arisen over when an occurrence took place and whether liability to remediate a third party's land can be said to be damages within the terms of a general liability policy. Other issues include whether liability for remediating groundwater which is not owned by a landowner is covered by the policy.

English courts have been called upon to determine the extent to which public liability policies cover environmental liability less frequently than the courts in the United States. The most significant recent case is that of *Bartoline Ltd v Royal & SunAlliance Insurance plc [2006] EWHC 3598* . In this case, water pollution resulted from foams used to fight a fire at Bartoline's warehouse. Under powers contained in the *Water Resources Act 1991*, the Environment Agency took emergency measures to clean up and sent Bartoline the bill. It also ordered Bartoline to carry out further clean up works. Bartoline claimed its and the Environment Agency's costs under its public liability insurance, but the court decided that these did not constitute 'damages' and were not therefore covered.

The increase in environmental liabilities in the UK, and pollution insurance coverage claims in the US, led insurers of UK risks to restrict cover for pollution under public liability policies. Since 1990, on the recommendation of the Association of British Insurers, virtually all public liability policies exclude cover for gradual pollution.

Environmental insurance policies

31.06   The exclusion of cover for gradual pollution in public liability polices and the increase in environmental liabilities have encouraged the development of environmental insurance policies. Generally speaking, such policies:

(*a*)   are written on a claims-made – and reported basis – to trigger the cover, the insured must make a claim and report it to the insurer during the policy period or an extended reporting period;

(*b*)   are written on a site-specific basis; and

(*c*)   cover liability arising from gradual as well as sudden pollution without differentiating between them.

Environmental insurance policies are available to cover liabilities arising from pollution to third parties for bodily injury, property damage and, depending on the policy, remediation costs, defence costs and certain specified economic losses. Other environmental insurance policies cover the cost of remediating an insured's own site, remediation costs above a specified amount and errors and omissions of environmental consultants and laboratories.

An example of a coverage clause in an environmental insurance policy designed to cover third party claims is:

> 'The insurers agree to pay loss on behalf of the insured that the insured is legally liable to pay as a result of a claim first made against the insured and reported to the insurer in writing during the policy period for property damage, bodily injury or clean-up costs arising from pollution conditions on an insured site.'

Chapter 32
Goods in transit insurance

- Goods in transit insurance in context

- Goods in transit and carrier's liability distinguished

- Coverage under good in transit policies

- Exclusions and conditions

- The Marine Institute Cargo Clauses

Goods in transit insurance in context

32.01 Goods in transit insurance is the means by which a person with an interest in goods while en route from, say, a seller to a purchaser, insures against the risk of loss or damage during transit. Usually the carriage would be associated with the sale of the goods, but it is also employed where goods are conveyed to the custody of a hirer.

It is important to distinguish three separate contracts that may exist:

(*a*) a contract between vendor and purchaser for sale of the subject goods;

(*b*) a contract of carriage (usually) between vendor and carrier; and

(*c*) a contract of insurance between cargo interests or the carrier and the insurer.

Where, as may often occur, insurance is taken out by the carrier, the latter (rather than the owner) may be the named insured on the policy. As a bailee, the carrier has an insurable interest, even though he has no ownership interest in the goods. Alternatively, the carrier may take out insurance as agent for the owner. This agency relationship will extend to the claims stage where, for instance, a freight forwarder lodges a claim on behalf an owner (*Granville Oil & Chemicals Ltd v Davis Turner & Co Ltd [2003] 2 Lloyd's Rep 356*). For the avoidance of confusion, the carrier is referred to as such in this chapter, and not as 'the insured'. If ambiguity arises as to whether the policy protects the owner's full interest in the goods, or indemnifies the carrier for its legal liability, the policy will be construed as covering the value of the goods (*Hepburn Appellant v A Tomlinson (Hauliers) Ltd Respondents [1966] AC 451*).

The three contracts set out above frequently need to be analysed in conjunction with each other, in order to ascertain the rights and liabilities of the various parties. For instance, the sale contract will determine when risk (and thus insurable interest) passes from vendor to purchaser. The contract of carriage will determine the obligations of the carrier to the owner in the event of loss or damage. For instance, in international carriage by air or sea (or, between many European states, by road) the carrier is subject to a presumption of liability, which is itself usually subject to a limitation of liability.

Goods in transit insurance eliminates any inability of cargo interests to recover, in part or at all, the value of the goods from the carrier. In the event of loss or damage, cargo insurers will pay up to the full insured value of the goods. If the carrier has taken out the policy he must, after deducting any sums due to him (such as charges for carriage), account to the owner for the surplus. If the contract of carriage requires the carrier to effect insurance, he would hold those proceeds on trust, offering the owners a degree of protection in the event of the carrier's insolvency. No trust arises if there is no obligation on the carrier to insure (*Re Dibbens & Sons (In Liquidation) [1990] BCLC 577*).

Goods in transit and carrier's liability distinguished

32.02   Goods in transit insurance should be distinguished from whatever liability insurance the carrier may have, although when the carrier effects goods in transit insurance for the benefit of cargo interests (ie owners), confusion can arise between the two policies. If cargo insurers do indemnify cargo interests in respect of a loss during transit, the cargo insurers will (under most legal systems) be subrogated to the cargo interests' right to claim against the carrier.

The difference between the two situations is that, whereas cargo insurers indemnify the loss in full, their ability to recover from the carrier (or its insurers) will depend on establishing a legal liability. This may or may not be fault-based and can be important.

(*a*)   In international air carriage subject to *Montreal Additional Protocol No 4 1975* or the *Montreal Convention 1999*, the air carrier's liability is absolutely limited to 17SDR/kg (unless cargo interests have declared a higher value for carriage). In high value cargo cases, cargo insurers may only be able to recover a minute proportion of the claim.

(*b*)   The claims by cargo interests against goods in transit insurers and the recourse claim against the carrier may be subject to different laws which may lead to inconsistent results.

Coverage under goods in transit policies

Commencement and termination

32.03 The policy starts when the carriage commences. The points at which carriage begins and at which it terminates both depend on the construction of the policy.

(a) Goods in the carrier's custody awaiting loading were covered under a policy effective when the goods were 'in transit per [carrier's] vehicles' in *Crows Transport Ltd v Phoenix Assurance Co Ltd [1965] 1 WLR 383*, followed by the Court of Appeal in *Eurodale Manufacturing Ltd v Ecclessiastical Insurance Office plc [2003] EWCA Civ 203*, even in relation to goods which were only held at a warehouse and not transported during the time in which the carrier had an insurable interest in the goods.

(b) Goods in the carrier's physical possession will be insured under a policy covering goods in the carrier's 'trust' – the term is not given its literal legal meaning. Goods in the possession of the carrier's agent will be in the carrier's 'trust' even if the agent intends to abscond with them (*John Rigby (Haulage) Ltd v Reliance Marine Insurance Co Ltd [1956] 2 QB 468*).

(c) Theft by a dishonest authorised carrier is usually covered: a clause excluding 'theft by a bogus subcontractor' is only effective where goods are entrusted to someone other than the genuine subcontracted carrier at the outset (*London Tobacco Co (Overseas) Ltd v DFDS Transport Ltd and Sun Alliance and London Insurance plc (Third Party) [1994] 1 Lloyd's Rep 394*).

(d) Goods which have safely arrived at the carrier's warehouse at destination have been 'finally disposed of' by the carrier (even though the consignee has not collected them) (*Bartlett & Partners, Ltd v Meller [1961] 1 Lloyd's Rep 487*).

Transit

32.04 'Transit' refers to the passage of goods from one place to another. It does not stop because the vehicle is temporarily parked. The policy covered theft of goods while the van was parked and left unattended in *Sadler Bros Co v Meredith [1963] 2 Lloyd's Rep 293*. On the other hand, deviation may take the goods outside the scope of cover. In *SCA (Freight) Ltd v Gibson [1974] 2 Lloyd's Rep 533*, goods were damaged during an unauthorised trip to the centre of Rome after loading for carriage to Manchester. The deviation was considered a joyride and not part of the 'transit', so the goods were not covered.

Storage

32.05 Specific provision may appear in a policy covering road haulage for overnight storage in a secure location. There are many authorities on this issue, such as:

- a yard enclosed by high walls but without a roof is not a 'garage' (*Barnett & Block v National Parcels Insurance Company, Ltd (1942) 73 Ll L Rep 17*);

- nor is it a warehouse (*Leo Rapp, Ltd v McClure [1955] 1 Lloyd's Rep 292*);

- but goods in an enclosed yard and covered by tarpaulins are 'in store' (*Wulfson v Switzerland General Insurance Company, Ltd (1940) 67 Ll L Rep 190*); and

- a railway arch is not a 'public warehouse' (*Firmin & Collins, Ltd v Allied Shippers, Ltd [1967] 1 Lloyd's Rep 633*).

In *Glencore International AG v Alpina Insurance Co Ltd (No 2) [2004] 1 Lloyd's Rep 567* it was held that a request for open cover for transit and storage would not be limited by a 30-day premium-free period as that clause could not be construed (as desired by the Insurer) as a request for 30 days' cover only.

Exclusions and conditions

32.06   Typically, goods in transit insurance will not cover goods while the vehicle has been 'left unattended'. Of the many decisions based on this test, the following circumstances amounted to a vehicle being left unattended:

(a)   A driver walked 37 yards away from the vehicle in order to urinate. For part of that time he had his back to the vehicle (*Starfire Diamond Rings, Ltd v Angel [1962] 2 Lloyd's Rep 217*). The Court of Appeal expressly sought to avoid a precise definition of the phrase 'left unattended', but it is clear from the judgments of Lord Denning MR and Upjohn LJ that the driver should be in a position to see the vehicle and/or hear anything taking place, and have a reasonable prospect of preventing any interference.

(b)   A driver parked his vehicle outside a customer's premises, in his vision but not in his immediate proximity (*Ingleton of Ilford, Ltd v General Accident Fire and Life Assurance Corpn, Ltd [1967] 2 Lloyd's Rep 179*).

(c)   The driver of a vehicle visited a washroom at a motorway service station for no more than 68 seconds (the time off camera as recorded by CCTV systems) (*Sanger (t/a SA Jewels) v Beazley [1999] 1 Lloyd's Rep 424*). In that case it was accepted that if the driver entered the washroom the vehicle was no longer 'attended'; in *obiter dicta* the judge clearly regarded the driver's ability to see the vehicle as important. The test to be applied was that contained in the judgment of Lord Denning MR in *Starfire* (see (a) above).

On the other hand, the insurance was still effective where:

(i)   the driver was asleep in the cab (*Plaistow Transport, Ltd v Graham [1966] 1 Lloyd's Rep 639*);

(ii)   the vehicle was within a few feet of the carrier's representative but outside her line of vision (*Langford and Langford v Legal and General Assurance Society Ltd [1986] 2 Lloyd's Rep 103*); and

(iii)   the vehicle was parked at a petrol pump while the carrier's representative was paying for petrol (*T O'Donoghue Ltd v Brian Malcolm Harding and Edgar Hamilton & Carter Ltd [1988] 2 Lloyd's Rep 281*). Critically the vehicle was parked as close as possible to the kiosk and the driver kept a close watch on it, only diverting his attention to sign the credit card slip.

Other conditions that may be imposed include requirements that:

(A)   There must be adequate locks on the vehicle. However in *De Maurier (Jewels), Ltd v Bastion Insurance Co Ltd, and Coronet Insurance Co Ltd [1967] 2 Lloyd's Rep 550*, it was held that compliance with such a clause was not a condition precedent to insurers' liability.

(B)   The vehicle must be locked when the loss occurred and there must have been forcible entry. In *Princette Models, Ltd v Reliance Fire and Accident Insurance Corporation, Ltd [1960] 1 Lloyd's Rep 49*, evidence that the vehicle was unlocked entitled insurers to avoid the claim.

(C)   The carrier must take reasonable care of the goods. This is interpreted narrowly, and requires the carrier only to avoid acts of recklessness rather than mere negligence. A carrier's failure to check references of an employee who later absconded with the insured goods was not a failure to act with reasonable care in *W & J Lane v Spratt [1970] 2 QB 480*.

Loss

32.07   Whether a loss has occurred is a question of fact. Under an All Risks policy, all that must be proved is loss or damage in transit. Knowledge of the whereabouts of the goods does not necessarily prevent a claim – goods detained illegally by state authorities were 'lost' for the purposes of an All Risks policy in *London and Provincial Leather Processes, Ltd v Hudson [1939] 2 KB 724*.

The Marine Institute Cargo Clauses

Commencement and duration of cover

32.08   Cargo insurance written in the London market is frequently governed by the Marine Institute Cargo Clauses. Separate forms have been drafted for marine and air carriage. The current form of each is the 1 January 1982 edition. The main structure is the same under each form, and each includes the transit clause (the old 'warehouse to warehouse' clause), which determines the commencement, duration and termination of cover. The insurance:

(*a*)   starts when the goods leave the warehouse or place of storage named in the policy – the requirement to name this point eliminated disputes as to whether insurers were on risk for land journeys prior to sea or air carriage;

(*b*)   continues during the course of transit; and

(*c*)   finishes on the first of three events:

   (i)   delivery to the warehouse or place of storage at destination,

> (ii)   delivery to any other warehouse or place of storage which the carrier elects to use for storage other than in transit, or for allocation to individual purchasers, or

> (iii)   (in the marine clauses) expiry of 60 days after completion of discharge of the goods from the vessel at the final port of discharge, or

(in the air clauses) expiry of 30 days after unloading from the aircraft at the final place of discharge.

Cover will remain in place despite delay due to circumstances beyond the control of the owner, such as war or strike at the point of discharge. The interaction of the various elements of the clause and the issue of which circumstances are within the control of the owner was examined (under an earlier form of the warehouse to warehouse clause) in *Safadi v Western Assurance Co [1933] 46 Ll L Rep 140*. The owner consigned goods from Manchester to Damascus; the final port of discharge for the sea carriage was Beirut. It was said that the rail journey from Beirut to Damascus was too dangerous to convey the goods, and they remained in Beirut for more than 30 days (the limiting period in the form at the time), but were then destroyed by fire. The judge found that the owner knew of the risks in Syria, and had chosen to keep the goods in Beirut when they could have been conveyed to Damascus without undue danger. In those circumstances, the events were within the control of the owner so the extended cover did not apply.

The point in time at which cover attaches can have an important impact on the insurer's liability. Conflicting legislative and contractual provisions for the attachment of cover were considered in *Nima SARL v The Deves Insurance Public Co Ltd (The 'Prestrioka') [2002] EWCA Civ 1132*. In that case it was argued that a 'warehouse to warehouse' clause under the Institute Cargo Clauses overrode statutory provisions on attachment in the Marine Insurance Act 1906. That Act provides at s 44 that where the destination is specified in the policy, and the ship, instead of sailing for that destination, sails for any other destination, the risk does not attach. It was held that this clause does not override s 44. If on an assessment of the facts the court holds that the ship never intended to head for the named destination at the time of departure then it had never embarked on the named voyage and cover had not attached.

Scope of cover

32.09   The Marine Institute Cargo Clauses provide for three levels of cover:

- All Risks (the 'A' clauses);
- marine and loading risks (the 'B' clauses); and
- marine risks only (the 'C' clauses).

The air clauses only provide for All Risks cover. War risks are generally excluded but a separate form provides for war risks cover if required.

Under All Risks cover, cargo interests only have to show that goods were in sound condition upon despatch but damaged on arrival (*Electro Motion, Ltd v Maritime*

Insurance Company, Ltd, and Bonner [1956] 1 Lloyd's Rep 420) for insurers to be *prima facie* liable. Insurers then have the burden of proving that the loss was due to an excepted peril (*Re National Benefit Insurance Co [1933] 45 Ll L Rep 147*).

Change in the course of transit

32.10   If the goods fail to reach their destination due to an interruption in transit outside the owner's control, cover terminates unless a continuation is requested and additional premium paid if required. Cover will then continue until the first of two events occurs:

- sale at an intermediate port; or
- expiry of 60 days after arrival at an intermediate port.

The provisions encompass the carrier failing to complete the carriage, with or without cause, which may include a voluntary change of destination or the effective frustration of the voyage. In such circumstances the owner is entitled to maintain cover on premium and at conditions to be agreed, so long as immediate notice is given to insurers.

When goods are intended for transhipment, arrival of the goods in a warehouse or place of storage in the destination named in the policy does not normally end the cover. This is because the policy does not contemplate a final place of storage in the named destination and it would be impractical to require separate cover to be arranged from that point onwards (*Bayview Motors Ltd v Mitsui Marine and Fire Insurance Co Ltd [2002] EWCA Civ 1605*).

Chapter 33
Legal expenses insurance

- Forms of cover
- Relationship with conditional fee agreements
- Regulation

Forms of cover

Before the event insurance

33.01 Legal expenses insurance provides the insured with an indemnity, subject to financial limits under the policy, in the event that he becomes embroiled in legal proceedings as a litigant. Cover of this type is included in many forms of liability insurance, whereby the insurer agrees either to defend or indemnify the insured in respect of the costs of any legal proceedings brought against the insured. In relation to motor and employers' liability policies, this cover may also extend to providing an indemnity for the cost of criminal proceedings brought against the insured (eg driving offences and breaches of health and safety legislation). This insurance is provided before the event as so is known as before the event ('BTE') insurance.

Pursuant to the *Insurance Companies (Legal Expenses Insurance) Regulations 1990 (SI 1990/1159)*, such before the event insurance cover has developed so that it is now possible to obtain insurance against general litigation costs, whether such general litigation is anticipated or not. Cover is generally written on the basis of costs incurred during the year of cover granted by the policy, so that the insured is under a duty to disclose to the insurer all potential legal disputes at the date of the inception of the insurance.

Despite efforts by specialist brokers and insurers over the last 20 years, very little 'stand alone' legal expenses insurance has been sold in the UK. Nearly all UK business is part of a more general package policy, normally attached to a household or motor policy.

This contrasts in particular with the position in continental Europe where insurance packages for this type of product are highly regulated and the regulatory environment is more conducive to the selling of 'stand alone' products such as legal expenses insurance.

Consequently, in the UK there is a tendency to confuse such legal expense insurance with conditional fee arrangements when in reality the latter is more properly after the event insurance.

After the event insurance

33.02 While it is possible for a litigant to purchase legal expenses insurance cover after the event that has given rise to their potential costs exposure, such insurance cover is inevitably expensive and unattractive. This is known as after the event ('ATE') insurance. The introduction of conditional fee arrangements now overcomes many of these difficulties.

Historically, legal aid has been available to those potential litigants who satisfied certain financial and merit criteria, but in most circumstances legal aid has now been withdrawn and conditional fee agreements have been introduced instead to provide such after the event cover (*Access to Justice Act 1999*).

In purchasing ATE cover, the insured is obtaining cover in the event that he fails in his action against the third party and costs are awarded against him. The ATE insurer will have to indemnify the insured in such circumstances.

By contrast the insured who pursues a successful claim against a third party will recover both his own legal fees and also the premium he paid for the after the event policy. For conditional fee agreements entered into pre 1 November 2005 recovery is pursuant to the *Conditional Fee Agreement Regulations 2000 (SI 2000/692)*. This is now repealed by the *Conditional Fee Agreement (Revocation) Regulations (SI 2005/2905)*. Conditional fee agreements are now regulated by primary legislation eg *Access to Justice Act 1999, s 29*.

Relationship with conditional fee agreements

33.03 Where the insured has a legal expenses insurance policy and subsequently, within the term of the policy, a claim arises, the legal expenses insurer will be responsible for satisfying any order for costs (subject to policy limit) made against the insured. In addition, the insurer is responsible for discharging the insured's own legal costs on terms set out within the policy cover. These obligations do not extend to any form of contingency or conditional fee arrangement. Similarly, where the insured has the benefit of such pre-event legal expenses insurance cover then any subsequent litigation covered by the policy cannot be the subject of a separate conditional fee agreement between the insured and his conducting lawyer.

This has been the subject to recent Court of Appeal decisions. In deciding what questions should be asked by the parties' solicitors to check whether legal expense insurance cover is in place, the Court of Appeal in *Myatt v National Coal Board [2007] EWCA Civ 307* and *Garrett v Halton BC [2007] EWCA Civ 278* gave some useful guidance. The extent of the questioning will depend on the circumstances including the nature of the client – does he have a real knowledge and understanding of insurance matters?; the circumstances in which the solicitor was instructed; the nature of the claim – is it likely that the standard insurance policy will cover it?; the cost of the ATE insurance premium; and, if the claim had been referred to solicitors on a panel, the fact that the referring body has already investigated the question of the availability of legal expenses insurance.

The Court of Appeal also had to consider the reasonableness of ATE premiums in the case of *Rogers v Merthyr Tydfil CBC [2006] EWCA Civ 1134*. The fact that the ATE premium was large compared with the damages recovered did not necessarily mean that it was disproportionate. The Court of Appeal were prepared to recognise staged premiums.

Regulation

33.04   Legal expenses insurance gives rise to potential conflicts of interest affecting the legal expenses insurer itself, where it is both the legal expenses insurer of party A and property or liability insurer of party B, and A and B become involved in a dispute. The possibility that one or other of the parties may be pressurised to settle the dispute on disadvantageous terms has been recognised, and two amendments made to the *Insurance Companies Act 1982* in 1990 – the *Insurance Companies (Legal Expenses Insurance) Regulations 1990 (SI 1990/1159)* and the *Insurance Companies (Legal Expenses Insurance)(Application for Authorisation) Regulations 1990 (SI 1990/1160)* – seek to remove this possibility. The Regulations were based on the European Community's *Legal Expenses Directive 1987 (Directive 87/344/EEC)*. The combined effect of the Regulations is as follows:

(a)   Legal expenses cover must be provided in the form of an independent policy and not as part of some other form of insurance (*SI 1990/1159, reg 4*). There are some important exceptions to this, notably, marine insurance, liability insurance and travel insurance (*SI 1990/1159, reg 3*).

(b)   An insurer offering legal expenses insurance must take steps to prevent claims under a legal expenses policy from being dealt with by a person who deals with claims under other policies. The simplest way of avoiding potential conflicts of interest is by use of an independent subsidiary (*SI 1990/1159, reg 5*).

(c)   The insured under a legal expenses policy is entitled to instruct a lawyer of his choice, this right taking effect as a term of the policy (*SI 1990/1159, reg 6*).

(d)   Legal expenses insurance is a distinct class of general insurance business, and authorisation to carry on legal expenses insurance business must be obtained from the Secretary of State application for authorisation is to be in accordance with Financial Services and Markets Act 2000 (*SI 2001/544*).

(e)   Any dispute between the insured and the legal expenses insurer must be resolved by arbitration if the insured so wishes (*SI 1990/1159, reg 8*).

Chapter 34
Marine Insurance

- Marine insurance defined
- General principles
- Types of marine policy
- The premium
- Warranties
- Currency of the voyage
- Marine risks: hulls and freight policies
- Marine risks: cargo policies
- Exclusions from marine cover
- Marine losses
- Measure of indemnity
- Rights of insurers

Marine insurance defined

The Marine Insurance Act 1906

34.01   Marine insurance is governed by a statutory code, the Marine Insurance Act 1906 (MIA 1906). The Act was not an attempt to change the law as it stood at the time, but rather sought to codify 18th and 19th century decisions on marine insurance. The rules of the common law including the law merchant are preserved, save insofar as they are inconsistent with the Act (MIA 1906, s 91(2)). When reading the Act's provisions, care should be taken, as much of the Act lays down presumptions which operate only if no contrary intention is shown in the contract of insurance.

Marine insurance is generally written in London on the basis of standard conditions which are incorporated into the insurance contract. Whilst London Underwriters may agree to provide cover based on a number of different sets of

275

conditions, the standard clauses are those now issued by the International Underwriting Association of London, known as 'Institute clauses'. Institute clauses exist for policies covering hull and machinery (time and voyage), freight (time and voyage), cargo , war and strikes (hulls, cargo and freight), and the interests of mortgagee banks. This is not an exhaustive list. The Institute clauses set out the risks covered together with other terms relevant to the scope of cover provided and the obligations on the insured. The clauses amend and supplement certain provisions in the Act.

This chapter looks at those aspects of insurance law unique to marine insurance. However, many of the principles contained in the Act also apply to non marine insurance and these are considered elsewhere in their relevant chapters.

Nature of marine insurance

34.02   A policy of marine insurance indemnifies the insured against 'marine losses, that is to say, the losses incident to a marine adventure' (MIA 1906, s 1). A marine adventure involves the exposure to 'maritime perils' of a vessel, cargo or freight earned by a vessel, as well as the risk that the owner of (or other person interested in or responsible for) insurable property may incur liability (MIA 1906, s 3). A maritime peril means any peril consequent on or incidental to the navigation of the sea, including perils of the seas, fire, war and piracy (MIA 1906, s 3). Marine insurance is widely defined and includes a policy taken out by the mortgagee of a vessel (*Continental Illinios National Bank & Trust Co of Chicago v Bathurst (The 'Captain Panagos DP') [1985] 1 Lloyd's Rep 625*).

Policies covering mixed sea and land risks

34.03   A contract of marine insurance may cover both land and sea risks (*MIA 1906, s 2*)The most common illustration of this is the standard cargo cover written in the London Market (Institute Cargo Clauses A, B and C, cl 8) which provide cover on a 'warehouse-to-warehouse' basis.

A policy covering the construction of a vessel is also a marine policy (*MIA 1906, s 2(2)*). Such types of policy may be stated to terminate either when the vessel is delivered to the purchaser or when the vessel is launched. Port risks policies can be issued to cover the risks of a vessel laid up in port.

General principles

The duty of good faith

34.04   Contracts of marine insurance are contracts of the utmost good faith (*MIA 1906, s 17*). An insured and the insured's agents must, therefore, disclose all material circumstances to the insurer before the contract is concluded (*MIA 1906, s 18–19*) and must ensure that all material representations are true (*MIA 1906, s 20*) (see 6 POLICYHOLDER DUTIES).

Insurable interest

34.05   An insured must have an insurable interest in the subject-matter of the insurance (as defined by *MIA 1906, s 5*). The insured need not have an insurable interest when it takes out the policy but must have such an interest at the time of loss (*MIA 1906, s 6*). (See also *MIA 1906, ss 7–14 and 4* INSURABLE INTEREST.)

Contracts of marine insurance entered into prior to 1 September 2007 by way of gaming or wagering are void (*MIA 1906, s 4(1)*). Such contracts include policies where the insured has no expectation of obtaining an insurable interest and where the policy is written on 'policy proof of interest' terms (defined by *MIA 1906, s 4(2)(b)*). Whilst PPI policies are void, they are still common in the London market particularly in respect of insurances covering increased value hull risks and loss of hire/freight. In practice, PPI policies are honoured and treated as legally binding by insurers, although there is a risk that liquidators of insolvent insurers may defend a claim on grounds that the policy is void.

Assignment

34.06   A marine policy is freely assignable, unless the policy itself provides otherwise (*MIA 1906, s 50(1)*). The ability to assign marine policies is commercially essential both in respect of hull and cargo insurance. Claims under hull policies are routinely assigned by owners of vessels to their mortgagee banks. Cargo policies are assigned by the seller to the buyer of goods under CIF and related sales. Where insured property is sold, there will not be an automatic assignment of rights under the insurance to the buyer and there needs to be a separate agreement to this effect (*MIA 1906, s 15*) (see 3 DURATION OF INSURANCE CONTRACTS).

The policy

34.07   A contract of marine insurance is deemed to be concluded when the proposal of the insured is accepted by the insurer, whether a policy is issued at the same time or not (*MIA 1906, s 21*). Where marine insurance is placed at Lloyd's, the contract is usually concluded when the slip is signed or 'scratched' by the Underwriter (see 11 LLOYD'S).

A contract of marine insurance is inadmissible in evidence unless it is embodied in a marine policy in accordance with the Act (*MIA 1906, s 22*). The only requirements for a marine policy are that the policy must contain the name of the insured or the person effecting the policy on his behalf (*MIA 1906, s 23*), must be signed by or on behalf of the insurer (*MIA 1906, s 24*) and must designate the subject-matter insured with reasonable certainty (*MIA 1906, s 26*).

Types of marine policy

Voyage and time policies

34.08   A marine policy may insure a particular voyage or it may last for a stated duration (*MIA 1906, s 25*). There can also be a 'mixed policy' covering both voyage and time elements. For example, a policy can be for a stated voyage, with the insured being covered for a period of days following the safe arrival of the vessel.

The distinction between time and voyage policies can be important because of the following differences:

(a)   Under a voyage policy, whether on hull, cargo or freight, the insured warrants the seaworthiness of the vessel at various stages, including the commencement of the voyage (*MIA 1906, s 39(1)–(4)*) although the application of the warranty is generally limited for cargo insurance by cl 5 of the Institute clauses. Under a time policy, there is no implied warranty of seaworthiness (*MIA 1906, s 39(5)*). For unseaworthiness of the vessel to provide insurers with a defence in respect of resulting loss or damage, they must prove that the vessel was sent to sea in an unseaworthy condition with the privity of the assured (*MIA 1906, s 39(5)*). The test for privity was recently considered by the Court of Appeal in *Manifest Shipping Co Ltd v Uni-Polaris Insurance Co Ltd [2003] 1 AC 469*.

(b)   There are strict rules in *ss 42 to 49 of MIA 1906* concerning voyage policies which by definition do not apply to time policies. The insured voyage must commence within a reasonable time otherwise the insurer may avoid the contract (*MIA 1906, s 42*). If the voyage commences from a different location to the one agreed in the insurance contract or if the vessel sails for an alternative destination, the risk does not attach (*MIA 1906, ss 43 and 44*). Changes of voyage, deviation and delay may also discharge insurers from liability (*MIA 1906, ss 45, 46 and 48*). Certain deviations and delays are excused, such as where caused by circumstances beyond the master's control or where necessary to save the vessel or human life (*MIA 1906, s 49*). In addition, the Institute clauses covering hull and cargo risks contain held covered clauses maintaining the cover under the insurance in the event of delay, provided the insured gives notice immediately upon becoming aware of the change and amended terms and premium are agreed.

Valued and unvalued policies

34.09   Under *s 27 of MIA 1906*, a policy of marine insurance may be either valued or unvalued. A policy is valued if it specifies the agreed value of the subject matter insured. All other types of policy are unvalued. The principal significance of the distinction relates to the amount recoverable following a loss:

(a)   if a policy is valued, then in the absence of fraud, the value agreed by the parties is conclusive (*MIA 1906, s 27(3)*). The measure of indemnity will either be the agreed value in the event of total loss or a proportion of the agreed value in the event of partial loss;

(b)   if a policy is unvalued, the measure of indemnity is determined by reference to the market value of the subject matter insured calculated at the date of commencement of the risk plus certain charges and expenses (*MIA 1906, s 16*).

An insured may therefore insure marine property for a sum in excess of its true value and this is a departure from the true indemnity principle which underlines insurance. However, there are advantages for both sides. The insured is buying certainty and can take into account the costs of purchasing replacement property. For the insurer, the higher the agreed value, the higher the premium. Further, for hull insurers, a high agreed value reduces the prospect of a constructive total loss as under the Institute clauses the cost of repairs must exceed the insured value not the market value for such a claim to arise.

An agreed value may be set aside in the event of fraud. Insurers may also allege that an overvaluation is a breach of the duty of good faith entitling the insurers to avoid the policy; see recently *Strive Shipping Corpn v Hellenic Mutual War Risks Association (The 'Grecia Express') [2002] Lloyd's Rep IR 669, paras 445–490*.

It is therefore important to distinguish between an agreed value (denoting a valued policy) and a sum insured (denoting an unvalued policy), where the sum insured fixes the maximum indemnity of the insurer, leaving the insured to prove its loss by reference to the insurable value of the property (*MIA 1906, s 16*). This is a question of policy interpretation.

There have been a number of recent cases illustrating the principles the courts will apply in considering whether a policy is valued or unvalued; *Kyzuna Investments Ltdv Ocean Marine Insurance Association (Europe) [2000] Lloyd's Rep IR 513* (yacht insurance) and *Thor Navigation Inc v Ingosstrakh Insurance [2005] 1 Lloyd's Rep 547* (hull insurance). Whilst yacht and hull insurance is usually placed on an agreed value basis and whilst both polices incorporated the Institute clauses which are drafted for use with valued policies, it was held that the use of the words 'sum insured' meant that both polices were unvalued.

Floating policies and open covers

34.10   A floating policy describes cover provided by the insurer in general terms, leaving the name of the ship or ships and other particulars to be defined by subsequent declaration (*MIA 1906, s 29(1)*). The insured is obliged to declare all risks falling within the terms of the cover and the insurer is bound to accept all such declarations (*MIA 1906, s 29(3)*).

The maximum aggregate amount that can be insured in respect of all of the declarations will usually be set out in the floating policy. Each declaration will, therefore, reduce the amount of further cover available to the insured under the facility.

An open cover policy fulfils a similar function by allowing the insured to make declarations in respect of risks falling within the terms of the cover. In an open cover, however, there is generally no aggregate limit as found in a floating policy, rather there is a limit for each declaration. Open covers may fall within the statutory definition of floating policies; see the discussion in *Glencore International AG v Ryan (The 'Beursgracht') (No 2) [2001] 2 Lloyd's Rep 608.*

There are also covers used in the marine market which fall outside the definition of floating policies. Under some facilities, the insured can elect whether to declare a particular risk, but, if he does, the insurer is bound to accept. With this type of cover, the insurer runs the risk that the insured will be selective in the risks which are declared. Under other types of facility, each declaration must be agreed by the insurer.

The premium

34.11   There are three important differences between the rules relating to marine and non-marine payment of premium (see 5 PREMIUMS).

(*a*)   in marine insurance there will frequently be a policy term allowing the insured to obtain additional cover subject to the payment of additional premium. There is a statutory mechanism allowing an additional premium to be fixed (*MIA 1906, s 31*);

(*b*)   unless otherwise agreed in the policy, where a marine policy has been arranged through a broker, the broker bears personal responsibility to the insurer for payment of the premium (*MIA 1906, ss 52–54*);

(*c*)   marine insurance law is marginally more generous than general insurance law as to when the insured is entitled to a return of his premium in the event that the risk fails to attach or terminates early (*MIA 1906, ss 82–84*). The Institute clauses and International hull clauses also permit a return of premium to the insured in certain circumstances.

Terms relating to the payment of premium will be set out in the LMP slip.

Warranties

What is a warranty?

34.12   A warranty is a contractual promise by which the insured undertakes that some particular thing shall or shall not be done, that some particular condition will be fulfilled or that a particular state of facts is or is not true (*MIA 1906, s 33(1)*). If the warranty is not complied with, the insurer is discharged from liability from the date of breach, regardless of whether the breach of warranty caused the loss (*MIA 1906, s 33(3)*). (See also *The Bank of Nova Scotia v Hellenic Mutual War Risks Association (Bermuda) Ltd (The 'Good Luck') [1991] 2 Lloyd's Rep 191.*)

Breach of warranty is excused in certain circumstances (*MIA 1906, s34*).

Marine insurance warranties

34.13   In addition to any express warranties contained in the policy, certain warranties are implied into contracts of marine insurance.

Implied warranty of seaworthiness for vessels

34.14   The implied terms relating to seaworthiness vary depending on whether the policy covers a voyage or is for a specified time (*MIA 1906, s 39*).

Voyage policies

34.15   There is an implied warranty that at the start of the voyage the ship is seaworthy for the purpose of the particular voyage insured (*MIA 1906, s 39(1)*). A ship is seaworthy if she is reasonably fit to withstand the ordinary perils of the sea for the insured voyage (*MIA 1906, s 39(4)*). The requirement of seaworthiness embraces the condition of the vessel, the competence of the crew and the stowage of the cargo. Where the policy attaches while the ship is in port, the ship must also be reasonably fit to meet the 'ordinary perils' of the port (*MIA 1906, s 39(2)*).

If a voyage involves different stages, the ship must be seaworthy at the start of each stage for that particular stage (*MIA 1906, s 39(3)*). For example, if the voyage is first on a canal, and then at sea, the ship must be seaworthy for the voyage through the canal at the commencement of the voyage through the canal, and then must be seaworthy for the voyage at sea at the commencement of the sea voyage, even if work is required to be done after the ship has transited the canal in order to make her seaworthy for the sea voyage.

Time policies

34.16   There is no implied warranty of seaworthiness at any stage in a time policy. Instead, the insurer is not liable for any loss attributable to unseaworthiness, if the ship was sent to sea in an unseaworthy state with the 'privity' of the insured (*MIA 1906, s 39(5)*).

34.17   To be privy to unseaworthiness, , the insured must have knowledge of the defects in the ship and that these defects made the ship unseaworthy. Knowledge for these purposes includes 'blind eye knowledge'. (*Compania Maritima San Basilio SA v The Oceanus Mutual Underwriting Association (Bermuda) Ltd (The 'Eurysthenes')* [1976] 2 Lloyd's Rep 171; *Manifest Shipping & Co Ltd v Uni-Polaris Insurance Co Ltd and la Réunion Européene (The 'Star Sea')* [2003] 1 AC 469; [1997] 1 Lloyd's Rep 360).

Seaworthiness of goods

34.18   There is no warranty that the cargo must be seaworthy (*MIA 1906, s 40(1)*). However, for a voyage policy on goods, there is an implied warranty that at the commencement of the voyage the ship is not only seaworthy as a ship but is also reasonably fit to carry the cargo to the destination contemplated by the insurance (*MIA 1906, s 40(2)*).

Warranty of legality

34.19   There is an implied warranty that the adventure insured is a lawful one , and that, so far as the insured can control the matter, the adventure shall be carried out in a lawful manner (*MIA 1906, s 41*). The question of legality is determined as a matter of English law.

Accordingly, if the adventure is illegal from the outset, the policy is void. However, not every act of illegality will make the contract itself illegal; instead the illegal act must go to the core of the adventure (*Euro-Diam Ltd v Bathurst [1988] 2 All ER 23*; *Royal Boskalis Westminster NV v Mountain [1997] 2 All ER 929*).

If the adventure is legal at the outset, but then becomes illegal, insurers are discharged from the point of illegality. There is a distinction between an illegal venture and a venture which is legal but is performed unlawfully. The implied warranty of legality will usually only apply to the former.

Warranty of neutrality

34.20   In time of war, a term is sometimes included in the policy warranting that the ship or her cargo is neutral. This warranty is in an attempt to protect against the property being seized by belligerent countries.

If insurable property is expressly warranted neutral, then the insured property must have a neutral character at the commencement of the risk (*MIA 1906, s 36(1)*). In addition, so far as the insured can control it, the neutral character of the property must be preserved for the period of the policy. If a ship is expressly warranted neutral, *s 36(2)* of *MIA 1906* implies a further condition that the ship shall carry the necessary papers to establish her neutrality, so far as the insured can control this.

Warranty of nationality

34.21   There is no implied warranty as to the nationality of a ship, or that her nationality will not be changed during the period of the policy (*MIA 1906, s 37*). However, under the Institute clauses, a change of the vessel's flag will terminate the insurance cover unless insurers agree to the contrary in writing..

Warranty of good safety

34.22   Where the subject-matter insured is warranted 'well' or 'in good safety' on a particular day, it is sufficient if the property is safe at any time during that day (*MIA 1906, s 38*)).

Currency of the voyage

34.23   Under a voyage policy, the insured risk is defined by the voyage to be performed and any changes in the voyage may therefore fundamentally alter the risk. Under time policies on ships, there are fewer restrictions as insurers have agreed to cover all voyages during the period in question. There are however some restrictions on voyages under time policies, where for example the vessel sails outside Institute Warranty or Navigating limits (hull risks) or into additional premium areas (war risks).

The *MIA 1906* lays down certain rules specific to voyage policies.

Commencement of risk

34.24   Voyage policies normally provide for the cover to start 'from' a particular port, or 'at and from' a particular port. If the voyage is insured 'at and from' a port, the cover commences as soon as the ship arrives at that port in good safety. It is not necessary for the ship to be at the port when the contract is concluded, but there is an implied condition that the insured adventure will commence within a reasonable time. If the voyage is insured 'from' a port, the cover commences as soon as the vessel sets sail from that port, again subject to an implied condition that the risk will commence within a reasonable time (*MIA 1906, s 42(1)*). A breach of this implied condition gives the insurer the right to avoid the insurance contract.

Breach of the implied condition concerning delay will not provide insurers with a defence to claims if the delay was due to circumstances known to the insurer before the contract was concluded or if he waived the condition (*MIA 1906, s 42(2)*).

Where the place of departure is specified in the policy, and the ship sails from somewhere else, the risk does not attach (*MIA 1906, s 43*). Similarly, where the destination is specified in the policy and the ship sails for another destination, again the risk does not attach (*MIA 1906, s 44*).

The performance of the voyage

34.25   After the insured risk has commenced, the insurer may have defences to claims where there the voyage is not performed as agreed, or there is a change of voyage, delay or deviation.

Change of voyage

34.26   If the insured voluntarily changes the destination of the vessel, then this constitutes a change of voyage and, unless the policy provides otherwise, the insurer is discharged from liability from the time of change (*MIA 1906, s 45*). The insurer comes off risk as soon as the decision to change the voyage is manifested. It does not matter whether the ship has in fact changed course (*MIA 1906, s 45(2)*).

The change of voyage must be voluntary. If a change is required by law, or imposed by some external authority, then there is no change of voyage within the meaning of *MIA 1906* (*Rickards Appellant v Forestal Land, Timber and Railways Co Ltd Respondents [1942] AC 50*).

Delay and deviation

34.27   If, under a voyage policy, the insured does not prosecute the voyage with reasonable dispatch, the insurer is discharged from liability as from the time when the delay became unreasonable (*MIA 1906, s 48*).

A deviation occurs if the ship departs from the insured route, but still intends to sail to the agreed destination. The route to be followed can be agreed with the insurer. If there is no agreement, it will be the customary route for that particular voyage (*MIA 1906, s 46*). If there are several ports of discharge, the insured must follow the agreed order, or if there is no agreement, call at the ports in geographical order (*MIA 1906, s 47*). Once there has been an actual deviation, rather than the mere intention to deviate, the insurer is automatically discharged from liability (*MIA 1906, s 46(1)–(3)*). It is immaterial that the ship may have regained the insured route before the loss occurs.

The insurer is still liable if there has been a lawful excuse for delaying or deviating. The possible lawful excuses are listed in *s 49* of *MIA 1906*, and are as follows:

(*a*)   where authorised by the terms of the policy;

(*b*)   where caused by circumstances beyond the control of the master or owners of the vessel (eg bad weather, outbreak of war);

(*c*)   where reasonably necessary to comply with a policy warranty(eg re-equipping a vessel in order to make her seaworthy for the next stage of the voyage);

(*d*)   where reasonably necessary for the safety of the ship or insured subject matter;

(*e*)   in order to save human life or aid a ship in distress where human life may be in danger;

(*f*)   where reasonably necessary to obtain medical or surgical aid for any person on board the vessel; and (*g*)   where caused by the barratrous conduct (see 34.36 below) of the master or crew, if barratry is an insured peril under the policy.

In addition, the Institute clauses covering hull and cargo risks contain held covered clauses maintaining the cover under the insurance in the event of delay, provided the insured gives notice immediately upon becoming aware of the change and amended terms and premium are agreed.

Marine risks: hulls and freight policies

General considerations

34.28

(*a*)   The Institute Hulls Clauses 1/10/83 and 1/11/95 offer a standard form of cover against a wide range of marine perils. There are also a separate set of hull clauses, being the International Hull Clauses 2002 and 2003. References below are to the Institute Hull Clauses 1/11/95 as the Institute Freight clauses were revised at the same time, although the Institute Clauses 1/10/83 remain in more common use.

(*c*)   Clause 6 of the Institute Clauses divides the insured perils into two groups. The second group (cl 6.2) provide cover provided that the loss or damage has not resulted from want of due diligence by the insured.

(*d*)   In this context, 'the insured' includes owners, managers, superintendents and onshore management, although the reference to superintendents and onshore management is often deleted by agreement.

(*e*)   The Institute Clauses also cover certain liability risks (collision, general average and salvage). Other liability risks facing owners are generally insured through membership of a mutual protection and indemnity (P&I) club.

Summary of cover

34.29   Hulls and freight policies usually provide cover for:

(*a*)   loss or damage caused by:

>   (i) perils of the seas, rivers, lakes or other navigable waters (see 34.31 below),
>
>   (ii) fire, explosion (see 27 BUILDINGS AND PROPERTY INSURANCE),
>
>   (iii) violent theft by persons from outside the vessel (a degree of force is necessary, even if only against property, and theft by passengers or crew is not covered – *MIA 1906, Sch 1, para 9*),
>
>   (iv) jettison,
>
>   (v) piracy (see 34.34 below),

      (vi) contact with land conveyance, dock or harbour equipment or installation,

    (vii) earthquake, volcanic eruption or lightning,

  (viii) accidents in loading, discharging or shifting cargo or fuel (previously subject to the due diligence provision).

(b) subject to the due diligence provision, loss or damage caused by:

      (i) bursting of boilers, breakage of shafts or any latent defect in the machinery or hull (see 34.35 below),

    (ii) negligence of master, officers, crew or pilots (see 34.37 below),

  (iii) negligence of repairers or charterers, provided such repairers or charterers are not an insured under the policy,

  (iv) barratry of master, officers or crew (see 34.36 below),

   (v) contact with aircraft, helicopters or similar objects or objects falling therefrom .

(c) pollution hazard:

      (i) loss of or damage to the vessel caused by a governmental authority acting to prevent or mitigate damage to the environment or a real or threatened pollution hazard,

    (ii) resulting directly from damage to the vessel for which insurers are liable under the insurance provided that the actions of the governmental authority have not resulted from a want of due diligence by the insured.

(d) collision liability:

      (i) 75% of any sums payable by the insured to third parties in respect of legal liabilities arising from a collision,

    (ii) excluding sums paid in respect of removal of wrecks; loss of life, personal injury or illness; and pollution, contamination or damage to the environment.

(e) salvage and general average

(f) sue and labour

Perils of the seas

Definition

34.30 Perils of the seas refers only to fortuitous accidents or casualties of the seas, excluding the ordinary actions of the winds and waves (MIA 1906, Sch 1, para 7). It is not a peril of the seas where the vessel sinks simply due to old age or decay.

The most common peril of the seas is heavy weather. There is no need for the weather to be unforeseeable or exceptional to constitute a peril of the seas (see J J Lloyd Instruments Ltd v Northern Star Insurance Co Ltd (The 'Miss Jay Jay') [1985] 1 Lloyd's Rep 264). On the other hand, a peril which is inevitable will not satisfy the requirement of fortuity.

A peril of the seas must be 'of the seas'. Machinery breakdown is excluded from cover under this heading , as the event must be one that can happen only at sea (The Thames and Mersey Marine Insurance Co Ltd v Hamilton, Fraser, & Co (1887) LR 12 App Cas 484.

Burden of proof and causation

34.31   The burden of proving that a loss was fortuitous and caused by a peril of the seas is on the insured. So, if a vessel sinks in unexplained circumstances, there is no presumption that the loss was caused by an insured peril (Rhesa Shipping Co SA v Herbert David Edmunds [1985] 2 All ER 712; National Justice Compania Naviera SA v Prudential Assurance Co Ltd ('The Ikarian Reefer') [1993] 2 Lloyd's Rep 68). However, where the insured can prove that the vessel was seaworthy when she set out, there is no evidence from the crew as to the cause of loss and the vessel has never been seen again, there may be a presumption that the vessel sank due to perils of the seas (Lamb Head Shipping Co Ltd v Jennings (The 'Marel') [1992] 1 Lloyd's Rep 402; affirmed on appeal [1994] 1 Lloyd's Rep 624).

It is important to bear in mind that the entry of seawater into a vessel is not of itself a peril of the seas.

Unseaworthy vessels

34.32   If a loss results from a combination of unseaworthiness and adverse sea conditions, the position is as follows.

(a)   Under a voyage policy, the insured has impliedly warranted the seaworthiness of the vessel for the particular voyage, and the insurer can rely upon breach of warranty (MIA 1906, s 39(1)). The application of the warranty of seaworthiness is generally limited for cargo insurance by cl 5 of the Institute clauses.

(b)   Under a time policy, there is no warranty of seaworthiness, but the insured cannot recover if he was privy to the unseaworthy state of the vessel when it set sail and the loss was attributable to unseaworthiness (MIA 1906, s 39(5); see The Star Sea at 34.18 above).

(c)   If the insurer cannot rely upon the defences above (for example, because the insured under a time policy was not aware of the unseaworthiness), the insured will still need to demonstrate that a proximate cause of the loss was perils of the seas.

Piracy

34.33   Piracy includes passengers who mutiny and rioters who attack the ship from the shore (*MIA 1906, Sch 1, para 8*). Violence, or the threat of force, is necessary, as 'piracy is not committed by stealth' (*Athens Maritime Enterprises Corporation v Hellenic Mutual War Risks Association (Bermuda) Ltd (The 'Andreas Lemos')* [1982] 2 Lloyd's Rep 483). Piracy is not restricted to the high seas, but may occur in territorial waters. Pirates must be acting for personal gain and not for some wider public or political motive (*Republic of Bolivia v Indemnity Mutual Marine Assurance Co Ltd [1909] 1 KB 785*).

Machinery damage

34.34   Failure of machinery is not a peril of the sea, as machinery can fail whether or not a vessel is at sea (see *The Inchmaree* at 34.31 above). Lack of cover for this type of loss was remedied by the '*Inchmaree*' clause, which covers loss or damage caused by bursting of boilers, breaking of shafts or any latent defect in the machinery or hull of the vessel, subject to the insured complying with the due diligence provision. This clause does not, however, extend to the cost of repairing the defect itself (*Scindia Steamships (London) Ltd v London Assurance [1937] 3 All ER 895*). See also *Promet Engineering (Singapore) Pte. Ltd v Sturge (The 'Nukila') [1997] 2 Lloyd's Rep 146*. Clause 41 of the International Hull Clauses does provide some cover for the cost of repairing the defect which caused the damage.

Barratry

34.35   Barratry includes 'every wrongful act wilfully committed by the master and crew to the prejudice of the owner' (*MIA 1906, Sch 1, para 11*). The essence of barratry is a breach of duty by the master or crew, which causes loss to the owner. It does not matter that the master or crew were in fact disobedient in an attempt to further the owner's interests, as in *Earle v Rowcroft [1803–1813] All ER Rep 166*, where the vessel was seized in an enemy port after the crew had entered the port in an attempt to obtain a higher price for the cargo. Other common examples of barratry include:

(a)   smuggling by the crew, breach of customs regulations or illegal trading;

(b)   deviation by the crew in order to use the vessel for their own purposes;

(c)   deliberate scuttling of the vessel by the crew, perhaps in an attempt to hide the fact that the cargo has been sold by the crew and the proceeds retained, as in the case of *Shell International Petroleum Co Ltd Appellants v Gibbs Respondent [1983] 2 AC 375*.

An owner can succeed in a plea of barratry only if he had no connection with the conduct of the master or crew, and the burden of proving that he was implicated so as to defeat a claim for barratry is borne by the insurers. Indications of an insured's involvement will include any motive which he may have had for sinking the vessel and whether there was good opportunity for communication between the insured and the crew (see *The Ikarian Reefer* at 34.32 above). Moreover, the insured must have exercised due diligence in his supervision of the crew. An insured who turns a blind eye to the crew's conduct, or who is aware of previous breaches of instructions by them but takes no steps to remedy the problem, may l be unable to recover if the vessel is lost as a result of barratry (*Pipon v Cope (1808) 1 Camp 434*).

Negligence

34.36   Cover is provided for loss or damage caused by the negligence of the master or crew, the insurer remains on risk (cl 6.2 of the Institute clauses and *MIA 1906, s 55(2)(a)*). The cover for negligence is subject to the due diligence provision.

Marine risks: cargo policies

Summary of cover

34.37

(*a*)   Standard form cover is provided by the Institute cargo clauses.

(*b*)   Three different classes of cover are available:

   (i)   all risks (Institute Cargo clauses (A));

   (ii)   limited risks, including: fire or explosion, vessel being stranded or sunk , overturning or derailment of land conveyance, collision, discharge of cargo at a port of distress, earthquake, jettison, washing overboard and entry of sea water; (Institute Cargo clauses (B))and

   (iii)   more limited risks, covering the risks set out immediately above except excluding earthquake, washing overboard and entry of sea water (Institute Cargo clauses (C)).

Exclusions from marine cover

War and strikes risks

34.38   The Institute Hulls, Freight and Cargo clauses covering marine risks all exclude losses caused by war, strikes and related risks. War and strikes cover can be obtained separately under the Institute War and Strikes clauses (see 24 SPECIFIC TYPES OF INSURANCE).

Wilful misconduct

34.39   The insurer is not liable for any loss attributable to the wilful misconduct of the insured (*MIA 1906, s 55(2)(a)*). This reflects the common law principle that insurance covers fortuitous events, and not losses brought about by the insured's own deliberate conduct. There is, however, a fine line between deliberately caused losses and thoughtless conduct giving rise to an unintentional loss: only the former is excluded. An insured who fails to take reasonable care to avoid a loss is not, under this principle, debarred from recovering under the policy unless it provides to the contrary.

The burden of proof is on insurers to prove fraud. The standard of proof is the civil test of the balance of probabilities but account is taken of the gravity of the allegations (*Brownsville Holdings Ltd v Adamjee Insurance Co Ltd (The 'Milasan')* [2000] 2 Lloyd's Rep 458; *Strive Shipping Corpn v Hellenic Mutual War Risks Association (The 'Grecia Express')* [2002] Lloyd's Rep IR 669).

Delay

34.40   The Institute Hulls and Cargo Clauses exclude loss or damage caused by delay, reflecting *s 55(2)(c)* of *MIA 1906*. The 'time charter' clause of the Institute Freight Clauses excludes 'any claim consequent on the loss of time whether arising from a peril of the sea or otherwise', although there is no statutory exclusion similar to that relating to hulls and cargo policies.

Inherent vice and related perils

34.41   Unless the policy provides otherwise, loss or damage caused by 'ordinary wear and tear, ordinary leakage and breakage, inherent vice or nature of the subject matter insured' is excluded (*MIA 1906, s 55(2)(c)*). The Institute clauses reflect this and also exclude insufficiency of packing or preparation of the subject-matter insured.

Inherent vice involves a loss arising due to the condition of the subject-matter insured, without the operation of any external factors, as for example where the natural sweating of leather gloves caused condensation which in turn caused damage to the gloves (*T M Noten BV v Paul Charles Harding* [1990] 2 Lloyd's Rep 283). The meaning of inherent vice was recently considered in *Mayban General Assurance Bhd v Alstom Power Plants Ltd* [2004] 2 Lloyd's Rep 609.

Section 55(2)(c) makes it clear that loss or damage caused by inherent vice can be covered. This is a question of construction of the policy, as in *Soya GMBH Mainz Kommanditgesellschaft v White* [1983] 1 Lloyd's Rep 122, where a policy on a cargo of soya beans, covering 'the risks of heat, sweat and spontaneous combustion', was held to cover natural sweating of the beans.

Marine losses

Forms of loss

34.42   Four forms of loss are recognised by marine insurance law:

- actual total loss

- constructive total loss

- partial loss (particular average)

- general average

An actual total loss requires destruction of the subject-matter insured or for the insured to be irretrievably deprived of possession of the subject-matter. A partial loss usually refers to damage. A constructive total loss is an intermediate claim, and is concerned with a loss which, while not amounting to an actual total loss, is in effect a total loss in an economic sense. General average arises where one party to a shared adventure incurs a loss, in the form of sacrifice or expenditure, to assist the other parties in time of general peril. General average losses are adjusted between the interested parties, for example owners and cargo interests.

Policies may cover either partial loss and/or total loss (*MIA 1906, s 56*). A policy on total loss will be presumed to include both actual and constructive total loss (*MIA 1906, s 56(3)*). If total loss only is covered, the policy may be warranted to be 'fpa' (free of particular average – *MIA 1906, s 76*).

Actual total loss

34.43   An actual total loss takes place where the subject matter insured is:

(a)   destroyed or so damaged as to cease to be a thing of the kind insured, or where the insured is irretrievably deprived of the subject matter (*MIA 1906, s 57*) (see for example *Fraser Shipping Ltd v Colton [1997] 1 Lloyd's Rep 586*); or

(b)   in the case of a ship, where she has been missing for a reasonable time (*MIA 1906, s 58*).

Constructive total loss

Definition

34.44   A constructive total loss is a loss which does not amount to an actual total loss but is, in effect, a total loss in the economic sense. Such a loss occurs in any one of six situations:

(a)   where the subject matter is reasonably abandoned on account of an actual total loss appearing to be inevitable (*MIA 1906, s 60(1)*);

(b)   where the subject matter is reasonably abandoned because it could not be preserved without an expenditure which would exceed the value of the preserved subject matter (*MIA 1906, s 60(1)*);

(c)   where the insured is deprived of the possession of his ship or goods by an insured peril and it is unlikely that he can recover them within a reasonable time (*MIA 1906, s 60(2)(i)(a)* (*The "Bamburi" [1982] 1 Lloyd's Rep 312*);

(d)   where the insured is deprived of the possession of his ship or goods by an insured peril and the cost of recovering them would exceed their value when recovered (*MIA 1906, s 60(2)(i)(b)*);

(e)   where a ship is damaged and the cost of repair would exceed the repaired value (*MIA 1906, s 60(2)(ii)*). Under the Institute clauses, the test is whether the expenditure would exceed the insured value of the vessel;

(f)   where goods are damaged and the cost of repair and forwarding the goods to their destination would exceed their value on arrival (*MIA 1906, s 60(2)(iii)*).

Effect of constructive total loss

34.45   If there is a constructive total loss, the insured has the option to claim from the insurer an indemnity based either on a total loss or on a partial loss (*MIA 1906, s 61*). In most circumstances, the insured will wish to recover for a total loss, as the full insured value of the vessel is then payable and any increased value policy will be triggered.

Notice of abandonment

34.46   To recover for a constructive total loss, the insured must usually serve on the insurer a 'notice of abandonment' (MIA 1906, s 62(1)). Service of the notice does not alter the nature of the insured's loss, but merely the amount recoverable (*Bank of America National Trust and Savings Association v Chrismas (The 'Kyriaki')* [1993] 1 Lloyd's Rep 137). For service of the notice to be valid it may be oral or written (*MIA 1906, s 62(2)*), and must be given with reasonable diligence after the insured has received reliable information or after a reasonable time for enquiries if the information is doubtful (*MIA 1906, s 62(3)*). Notice must be given to the insurer direct or to a person authorised by him to accept it and not, for instance, to the insured's own agent (*Vacuum Oil Co v Union Insurance Society of Canton (1926) 25 Ll L Rep 546*).

If the notice is accepted, which can be done expressly or impliedly through conduct of the insurer – but not through mere silence (*MIA 1906, s 62(5)*) – it is binding on the insurer (*MIA 1906, s 62(6)*). This does not, however, deprive the insurer of the right to rely upon defences of which he was unaware when the notice was accepted (*Norwich Union Fire Insurance Society, Ltd Appellants v WMH Price, Ltd Respondents [1934] AC 455*, a case in which the loss had, unknown to the insurer, been caused by an uninsured peril).

Service of a notice of abandonment is unnecessary in the case of an actual total loss (*MIA 1906, s 57(2)*); the effect of service is merely to allow an insured who has suffered a constructive total loss to recover on the basis of a total loss rather than partial loss. A notice of abandonment can be dispensed with even in the case of constructive total loss where the insurer has waived service, or where service would serve no useful purpose (*MIA 1906, s 62(7)(8)*). The insurer is not obliged to accept notice of abandonment.

The requirement for a notice of abandonment was recently considered in *Kastor Navigation Co Ltd v Axa Global Risks (UK) Ltd [2004] 2 Lloyd's Rep 277.*

Abandonment

34.47 If the insured has suffered an actual total loss, or a constructive total loss where a notice of abandonment has been served, then:

(a)   the insured is entitled to be paid the full insured value of the insured subject matter, and

(b)   the insurer has the right to take what remains of the insured subject matter by way of salvage. (*MIA 1906, s 63(1)*). If a ship is abandoned, the insurer is entitled to take any freight which is in the course of being earned by the ship (*MIA 1906, s 63(2)*), although under the Institute Clauses the hull insurer will waive the right to freight in favour of the freight insurers.

Partial loss

34.48 Marine policies cover 'particular average', which consists of two elements:

(a)   *partial loss*, which arises where the subject matter has sustained damage which can be repaired at a cost less than the repaired value (*MIA 1906, s 64*); and

(b)   *salvage charges*, which are charges payable by the insured under maritime law to a person who has attempted to avert the insured peril or minimise its consequences. (*MIA 1906, s 65*).

Charges incurred under contract with a salvor – 'particular charges' – do not fall within the definition of particular average, but may be recovered by the insured under a separate 'sue and labour' clause (see 34.56 below).

General average

34.49 A general average loss is a loss caused by or directly consequential on a 'general average act'; it includes expenditure and sacrifice (*MIA 1906, s 66(1)*). There is a general average act where such expenditure or sacrifice is reasonably and voluntarily made at time of great peril by one person for the benefit of others (*MIA 1906, s 61(2)*). An illustration of a general average act is the jettisoning of cargo from a vessel which is shipping water, in an attempt to preserve the vessel and the remaining cargo on board.

An insured who performs a general average act is entitled to recover from his insurers (*MIA 1906, s 66(4)*). He also has the common law right, which will vest in his insurers by way of subrogation, to claim a rateable contribution from the other persons interested in the adventure who have benefited from the general average act (*MIA 1906, s 66(3)*). General average contributions are insured under the Institute clauses (*MIA 1906, ss 66(5), 73*).

Normally general average contributions are settled between the insurers of the various interests represented in the adventure. The situations in which a general average loss takes place, and the principles governing the settlement between insurers, are laid out in the *York-Antwerp Rules 1974*, as amended in 1990, 1994 and 2004.

Measure of indemnity

General introduction

34.50   The amount which the insured can recover under a marine policy – the 'measure of indemnity' (*MIA 1906, s 67*) – depends upon whether the policy is valued or unvalued (see 34.09 above).

(*a*)   In the case of a valued policy, the value of the subject matter agreed by the parties at the outset is, in the absence of fraud by the insured, conclusive as between the parties (*MIA 1906, s 27(3)*). The amount which the insured recovers is, therefore, based upon the agreed value.

(*b*)   If the policy is unvalued, which is comparatively rare in marine insurance, the basis of the measure of indemnity is the 'insurable value', calculated in accordance with *s 16* of *MIA 1906*. The insurable value is normally the value of the subject matter at the date of the commencement of the risk (compare non-marine insurance, where the insurable value is assessed at the time immediately prior to the loss). Unvalued marine policies are subject to average, the insured being deemed to be his own insurer for any uninsured sum (*MIA 1906, s 81*). Thus, if the insured is covered for 90% of the actual value of the subject matter, and suffers a partial loss of, say 50%, the insurer and the insured will bear the loss in the proportions 90:10, so that the insured will recover only 45% of the total insurable value from the insurer and must bear the remainder himself.

Loss of or damage to the vessel

34.51   If the vessel has been totally lost, the insured recovers:

(*a*)   under a valued policy the full sum agreed (*MIA 1906, s 68(1)*);

(*b*)   under an unvalued policy, the full insurable value, determined as of the date of the commencement of the risk (*MIA 1906, s 68(2)*).

If the vessel has been damaged, the agreed value is disregarded, and the insured recovers under both a valued and an unvalued policy in accordance with the following principles:

(*a*)   where the vessel has been repaired, the insured recovers the reasonable cost of repairs (*MIA 1906, s 69(1)*) – under the Act recovery is limited to two-thirds of this figure, but this restriction is ousted by the Institute Clauses and the International Hull Clauses;

(b) where the vessel has been only partially repaired, the insured recovers the reasonable cost of the repair effected plus depreciation (the diminution is value of the vessel due to her partially repaired state), subject to the ceiling of the reasonable cost of full repair (*MIA 1906, s 69(2)*);

(c) where the vessel has not been repaired and has not been sold, the insured recovers depreciation arising from the unrepaired damage, subject to a limit of the reasonable cost of repair (*MIA 1906, s 69(3)*);

(d) where the vessel has not been repaired and has been sold, the insured recovers the difference between the market value of the vessel immediately prior to the loss and the sum for which she was sold (*Pitman v The Universal Marine Insurance Co (1881–82) LR 9 QBD 192*).

Loss of or damage to cargo

34.52 If the cargo has been totally destroyed, the insured recovers:

(a) under a valued policy, the full sum agreed (*MIA 1906, s 68(1)*);

(b) under an unvalued policy, the full insurable value, determined by the invoice price of the goods when purchased by the insured (*MIA 1906, s 68(2)*).

If the cargo is a partial loss, the insured recovers:

(i) under a valued policy, a proportion of the agreed value representing the degree of damage (*MIA 1906, s 71(1)*);

(ii) under an unvalued policy, a proportion of the insurable value representing the degree of damage (*MIA 1906, s 71(2)*).

If the cargo has been delivered to its port or final destination, and is there found to be damaged, the insured recovers:

(A) under a valued policy, a proportion of the agreed value representing the diminution of the actual market price at the place of arrival (*MIA 1906, s 71(3)*);

(B) under an unvalued policy, the difference between the undamaged and the damaged market price of the goods at the place of arrival (*MIA 1906, s 71(4)*).

Loss of freight

34.53 If an insured peril deprives the insured of his ability to recover the costs of carriage of cargo, or of the hire of his vessel, the insured will recover:

(a) under a valued policy, the full agreed value or a proportion of the agreed value representing the degree of loss (*MIA 1906, s 70*);

(b)   under an unvalued policy, the full insurable value or a proportion of the insurable value representing the degree of loss (*MIA 1906, s 70*).

Suing and labouring

Nature

34.54   The suing and labouring clause is invariably found in English marine insurance policies on property – for instance cl 13 of the Institute Time Clauses. Where the policy contains such a clause, the sue and labour cover is deemed to be a separate agreement to the agreement found in the contract of insurance.

The duty

34.55   It is the duty of the insured, and his agents, under a marine policy to take all reasonable measures to avert or minimise a loss (*MIA 1906, s 78(4)*). Under the Institute Time clauses, if such measures are taken by the insured, then they can recover an additional sum up to the amount insured under the policy.

The duty to sue and labour is not absolute. The insured must take all reasonable measures to avert or minimise a loss. Therefore, an insured who fails to summon assistance in the belief that the vessel is in no immediate danger, and who also fails to take steps, which would be known only to a skilled engineer, to stem an ingress of water, is not in breach of duty (*AP Stephen v Scottish Boatowners Mutual Insurance Association (The 'Talisman')* [1989] 1 Lloyd's Rep 535). Further, an insured who fails to institute proceedings against a third party is not in breach of the duty if the proceedings are unlikely to result in a recovery from the third party (*Bayview Motors Ltd v Mitsui Marine and Fire Insurance Co Ltd* [2002] 1 Lloyd's Rep 652.

A failure on the part of the insured to sue and labour may provide insurers with a defence to the claim on grounds that the loss has been caused by the insured's failure to act rather than an insured peril (*National Oilwell (UK) Ltd v Davy Offshore Ltd* [1993] 2 Lloyd's Rep 582; *State of the Netherlands (Represented by the Minister of Defence) v Youell and Hayward* [1997] 2 Lloyd's Rep 440, [1998] 1 Lloyd's Rep 236. If the insured fails to mitigate a loss, for example by pursuing a recovery action, the insurer may have a claim in damages to the extent he has been prejudiced (*Noble Resources Ltd and Unirise Development Ltd v George Albert Greenwood (The 'Vasso')* [1993] 2 Lloyd's Rep 309. The duty of the insured to sue and labour is reciprocated by the insurer's duty to indemnify the insured for the costs of suing and labouring, although this duty is contractual rather than statutory (*MIA 1906, s 78(1)*). Indemnification is only required if the insured's action has been taken to avoid a loss by a peril insured under the policy (*MIA 1906, s 78(3)*), although the Court of Appeal has held that the insured can make a claim on the insurer if the insured had good grounds for believing that the peril faced by his property was covered under the policy (*Integrated Container Service Inc v British Traders Insurance Co Ltd* [1984] 1 Lloyd's Rep 154).

Loss or damage caused by the negligence of the master and crew is expressly covered under the Institute clauses and by reference to *s 55(2)(a)* of *MIA 1906*. If a negligent failure on the part of the master or crew to sue and labour were to provide insurers with a defence to a claim, this would restrict the cover otherwise available to the insured for negligence. It is submitted that where loss or damage is caused by an insured peril (whether negligence or otherwise) and the master or crew fails to take steps to minimise the damage, the resulting claim will still be covered unless there is a clear break in the chain of causation.

Costs recoverable

34.56   The costs recoverable are laid down by the Institute clauses and International Hull clauses, which extend to:

(*a*)   salvage charges incurred under contract (but not salvage charges incurred under maritime law, in the absence of contract – *MIA 1906, ss 65, 78(2)*) – in practice most salvage is conducted under contract, by means of the Lloyd's Open Form;

(*b*)   other costs reasonably and properly incurred, and this may include costs which are incurred in an unsuccessful attempt to avert the loss.

The insured can only recover reasonable expenditure, that is those expenses a reasonable person would incur to preserve his property if he had no insurance (see the *Integrated Container Service* case at 34.56 above).

The amount recoverable under the suing and labouring clause is additional to the policy moneys themselves, as the clause is regarded in law as a totally distinct contract. However, under the Institute clauses, the sue and labour indemnity is limited to the amount insured. Further, if the insured is under insured and is only able to recover a proportion of his loss. then he may only recover the same proportion of his suing and labouring costs. Under the 2003 version of the International Hull Clauses, this reduction for under-insurance has been abolished.

Rights of insurers

34.57   The rules in *MIA 1906* relating to the rights of insurers following payment are identical to those applicable in non-marine insurance:

(*a*)   ss 32 and 80 of *MIA 1906* (see 18 DOUBLE INSURANCE AND CONTRIBUTION); and

(*b*)   s 32 of *MIA 1906* (see 16 SUBROGATION).

In addition, as discussed earlier, where an insurer pays a total loss he is entitled to take over what remains of the insured property.

Chapter 35
Motor vehicle insurance

- Nature of motor vehicle insurance
- The contract
- First party cover
- Compulsory insurance scheme
- Motor Insurers' Bureau

Nature of motor vehicle insurance

35.01 Two forms of risk may be covered by a motor policy:

(a) *First party motor vehicle insurance.* The minimum third party cover is for fire and theft, although comprehensive cover, including injury to the insured himself or damage to his property, is generally available.

(b) *Compulsory insurance scheme.* This covers the driver's liability to any third party including any passenger, and includes personal injury and property damage inflicted by the insured on a third party.

Where the third party suffers loss following the negligent driving of a person who is either uninsured or who cannot be identified, the third party is protected by the fall back Motor Insurers' Bureau scheme.

The contract

Utmost good faith

35.02 The proposer for a motor policy must answer truthfully all questions put to him, and must disclose all material facts to the insurer (see 6 POLICYHOLDER DUTIES). An insurer is obliged to meet any judgements obtained by the third party against the insured. However, the insurer may have a common law right to avoid the motor policy for non-disclosure or for misrepresentation, provided that the misrepresentation or non-disclosure was material, and that it actually induced the insurer to make the policy (*Pan Atlantic Co Ltd v Pinetop Insurance Co Ltd [1994] 3 All ER 58*).

Material facts in relation to a motor policy have been held by the courts to include:

(*a*)   the age of the vehicle (*Santer v Poland [1924] 19 Ll L Rep 29*);

(*b*)   the price paid for the vehicle or its current market value;

(*c*)   the nature of the insured's interest in the vehicle, for example, whether the insured is the owner or hirer of the vehicle (*Guardian Assurance Co Ltd v Sutherland [1939] 63 Ll L Rep 220*);

(*d*)   the location of the vehicle and whether or not it is to be kept garaged;

(*e*)   the age of the driver (*Broad v Waland [1942] 73 Ll L Rep 263*);

(*f*)   the driving experience of the driver (*Corcos v De Rougemont [1925] 23 Ll L Rep 164*);

(*g*)   the persons who will be driving the vehicle (*Magee v Pennine Insurance Co [1969] 2 QB 507*);

(*h*)   the driving record of the insured, including criminal convictions (*Dent v Blackmore [1927-1929] 29 Ll L Rep 9*); and

(*j*)   the previous claims record of the insured (*Farra v Hetherington [1931] 40 Ll L Rep 132*).

Warranties

35.03   The insured's answers to express questions on the proposal form are commonly converted into warranties by the 'basis of the contract' clause at the bottom of the proposal (see 3 DURATION OF INSURANCE CONTRACTS). At common law, a warranty must be complied with exactly, and in the event of breach the insurer is discharged from liability whether or not the warranty was material to the risk or had any causative impact on the loss. Motor warranties may be taken on a variety of matters, including the price paid for the vehicle, the uses to which it is to be put and the insured's criminal convictions (see, for example, *Provincial Insurance Co Ltd v Morgan & Foxon [1933] AC 240*).

Policy conditions

35.04   Motor policies contain a range of conditions limiting the insured's use of the insured vehicle and requiring its maintenance. Motor policies will also lay down conditions dealing with the making of claims, and prohibiting the insured from admitting liability to any third person in the event of an accident. It is also normal for the policy to contain a 'reasonable care' clause, requiring the insured to take all reasonable steps to avoid loss (see *Hayward v Norwich Union Insurance Ltd [2001] EWCA Civ 243*). Where the condition is framed as a condition precedent to the liability of an insurer, an insured in breach will have no right to claim under the policy; where, by contrast, the condition is not stated to be a condition precedent, the insurer will have to pay any loss, but will be entitled to claim damages from the insured representing any loss caused to the insurer for breach (see 2 TERMS IN INSURANCE CONTRACTS).

In the case of a liability claim against the insured by a third party, the insurer is unable, under *s 148* of the *Road Traffic Act 1988* (*RTA 1988*), to rely upon the vast majority of policy conditions in order to defeat the claim, although the conditions can be relied upon as regards any first party claim. If the insurer is required to make payment under this provision, in circumstances in which he would otherwise have had a defence, the insurer can seek an indemnity from the insured himself (*RTA 1988, s 148(3)–(5)*). The subject matter of the conditions which cannot be relied upon by the insurer is as follows (*RTA 1988, s 148(1)–(2),(5)*).

(*a*)   The age, or physical or mental condition, of persons driving the vehicle. There are often clauses which limit cover where the insured is under the influence of alcohol or drugs (see, for example, *National Farmers Union Mutual Insurance Society Ltd v Dawson [1941] 2 KB 424* and *Louden v British Merchants Insurance [1961] Lloyd's Rep 154*). However, in *Criminal Proceedings against Bernaldez C-129/94 [1996] All ER (EC) 741*, the European Court of Justice held that any contract term restricting liability of insurers for third party risks was void.

(*b*)   The condition of the vehicle. A term which requires the insured to maintain the vehicle in good condition is broken only if the insured knew or ought to have known of the defect. Thus the insured would not be able to recover if his vehicle has no brakes, or has bald tyres, but will be able to recover if the defects in the brakes were not readily apparent (see *Conn v Westminster Motor Insurance [1966] 1 Lloyd's Rep 407* and *Amey Properties Limited v Cornhill Insurance plc [1996] LRLR 259*). Some policies are more general and require the vehicle to be kept 'roadworthy' – this seems to mean only that the vehicle must be roadworthy when it sets out, and the insurer is not exempted if the vehicle develops a defect during the course of a journey which causes an accident (*Barrett v London General Insurance Co [1935] 50 Ll L Rep 99*; *Trickett v Queensland Insurance Co Ltd [1936] 53 Ll L Rep 225*).

(*c*)   The number of persons that the vehicle carries. In *Clarke v National Insurance [1964] 1 Q.B. 199*, the insurer was able to deny liability in respect of a vehicle designed for four persons but actually carrying eight. A condition which prohibits overloading will not, however, be construed as referring to the number of passengers (*Houghton v Trafalgar Insurance Co Ltd [1953] 2 Lloyd's Rep 503*).

(*d*)   The weight or physical characteristics of the goods that the vehicle carries. Overloading clauses are probably caught by this provision.

(*e*)   The time at which or the areas in which the vehicle is used. The most common clause restricting use – the 'social, domestic or pleasure (sdp)' limitation – would seem to fall outside this category. There is a good deal of authority on the 'sdp' limitation, and it has been held that driving for mixed business and pleasure purposes, or driving an injured employee from his place of work to receive medical attention, is not use of the vehicle for 'sdp' purposes (*Passmore v Vulcan Boiler and General Insurance Co Ltd [1936] 54 Ll L Rep 92*).

(*f*)   The horsepower or cylinder capacity or value of the vehicle.

(*g*)   The carrying on the vehicle of any particular apparatus.

(*h*)   The carrying on the vehicle of any particular means of identification other than any means of identification required to be carried by or under the *Vehicle (Excise) Act 1971*.

(*j*)   Any condition which removes the liability of the insurer in the event of some specified thing being done or omitted to be done by the insured after the happening of the insured event, for example, late claims and admissions of liability by the insured (*Alfred McAlpine plc v BAI (Run-Off) [2000] 1 Lloyd's Rep 437*).

Driver extension clauses

Other drivers

35.05   Many policies permit the vehicle to be driven by other identified persons or by any person driving with the insured's consent. In the event that liability to a third party is incurred, any person who is authorised to drive the vehicle is given a direct cause of action against the insurers (*RTA 1988, s 148(7)*).

The question of what constitutes consent by the insured to another person is important for determining:

(*a*)   whether the insurer is liable under the policy; and

(*b*)   whether the driver has committed a criminal offence by driving the vehicle while uninsured (*RTA 1988, s 143*).

Other vehicles

35.06   It is also common for the policy to allow the insured to drive any other vehicle. Such cover is however, merely ancillary to the primary cover and if the insured's own vehicle is sold, the policy lapses and the insured is no longer insured under his own policy to drive any other vehicle (*Rogerson v Scottish Automobile & General Insurance Co Ltd [1931] 41 Ll L Rep 1; Tattersall v Drysdale [1935] 52 Ll L Rep 21*).

First party cover

35.07   A motor policy covering first party risks, will simply extend to the following forms of protection:

(a) personal injury suffered by the insured. Cover may be restricted to 'accidental injury caused by violent, external and visible means'; and

(b) property damage inflicted upon the insured's property, in particular his vehicle.

Compulsory insurance scheme

Compulsory insurance requirement

35.08   *Section 143* of *RTA 1988* (as amended by the *Motor Vehicles (Compulsory Insurance) Regulations 2000 (SI 2000/726)*) lays down two criminal offences:

(a) using a motor vehicle on a road or other public place, when there is not in force a policy covering statutory liability; and

(b) causing or permitting the use of a motor vehicle on the road or other public place when there is not in force a motor policy covering statutory liabilities.

A 'motor vehicle' is a mechanically propelled vehicle (other than an invalid carriage) intended or adapted for use on roads (whether or not fit to do so), and a 'road' is any highway to which the public has access (*RTA 1988, ss 185, 192*) (see *Cutter v Eagle Star Insurance Company Limited, Clarke v Kato [1998] 4 All ER 417*).

Failure to insure

35.09   Failure to insure is not only a criminal offence, but also amounts to a civil wrong. The victim of an uninsured driver may, therefore, bring an action for breach of statutory duty against him and against a person who caused or permitted him to use the vehicle without insurance (*Monk v Warbey [1935] 1 KB 75*). This is likely to be of little significance for the victim himself, as he will have a remedy against the Motor Insurer's Bureau in such a case (*Norman v Aziz [2000] Lloyd's Rep IR 52*). However the Bureau can, by use of subrogation, sue the tortfeasor and seek to recover its payment accordingly.

Using a motor vehicle

35.10   The user of the vehicle is the person who has control over it at all times; this will generally be the driver, although a person in a parked car may nevertheless be the user of it. A passenger in a vehicle cannot normally be said to be using it (see *Hatton v Hall [1997] RTR 212*). However a passenger may be regarded as 'user' if he is the vehicle's owner (*Cobb v Williams [1973] RTR 113*), if he has helped to steal the vehicle (*Leathley v Tatton [1980] RTR 21*), or if he has allowed himself to be carried in pursuance of a joint enterprise (*O'Mahoney v Joliffe [1999] RTR 245*).

Causing or permitting use

35.11   A criminal offence is permitted by the person in control of the vehicle (who is normally but not necessarily the insured) only where use by an uninsured person is authorised by him. If the insured allows another person to use his vehicle only on condition that that person produces his own insurance, uninsured use by that person does not amount to an offence on the insured's part (*Newbury v Davis [1974] RTR 367*). The position is otherwise if the insured simply takes the user's word that he is insured (*Baugh v Crago [1975] RTR 453*).

Exemptions

35.12   Exemption from the compulsory insurance requirement is given to various public service vehicles, for example local authority, police, air force and health service.

Scope of the compulsory insurance

35.13   The policy must be issued by a UK-authorised insurer or by an insurer established and authorised elsewhere in the EU, as long as he has a claims representative in the UK. In all cases, the insurer must belong to the Motor Insurers' Bureau (*RTA 1988, s 145(2),(5)–(6)*).

The policy will provide cover in respect of:

(a)   *Personal injury.* The policy must cover such persons specified in the policy in respect of liability for the death or personal injury to any person caused by or arising out of the use of the vehicle on a road or other public place. In *Dunthorne v Bentley [1996] PIQR P323,* where the driver ran across the road into the path of an oncoming vehicle, her reason for being in the road was held to have arisen from the use of her vehicle.

The driver's liability for the cost of emergency treatment (under *RTA 1988, ss 157–159,* which covers in-patient and out-patient treatment) must also be covered. The collection of NHS hospital charges in road traffic accident cases where compensation is paid is now centralised. The *Road Traffic (NHS) Charges Act 1999* provides a national administrative system to ensure that all cases in which recoupment of NHS charges are possible, are identified and that the charges are collected and passed on to the hospitals which provided the treatment. Private hospitals remain within *RTA 1988.*

(b)   *Property damage.* The policy must cover the insured and such persons within the policy in respect of liability which may be incurred for damage to property (*RTA 1988, s 145(3)(a)*).

(c)   *EEC risks.* A policy must cover the insured and other drivers in respect of any liability which may be incurred in any EEC state other than Great Britain (*RTA 1988, s 143(3)(b)*).

(d)   *The protection of passengers.* The compulsory insurance requirement extends to passengers in the insured's vehicle, including the insured when he is a passenger or person driving the vehicle with his consent. However, although an agreement between the insured and the passenger may be binding at common law, it is void under *s 149* of *RTA 1988*.

Obligation for insurer

Authorised drivers

35.14 A victim has the right to bring an action against the insurers, irrespective of any right which the insurer might have to avoid the policy or to deny liability (*RTA 1988, s 151*).

A number of conditions must be met before the direct action may be brought.

(*a*) The insurer must have delivered to the insured a certificate of insurance (*RTA 1988 s 151(1)*) (see *Motor & General Insurance Co v Cox [1991] 1 WLR 1443*).

(*b*) The victim must have obtained judgment against the driver.

(*c*) The victim must have given the insurer notice within seven days of commencement of proceedings (*RTA 1988, s 152(1)(a)*). No special form of words is required and the onus is on the insurer to prove that they did not have the necessary notice or warning (*Desouza v Waterlow [1999] RTR 71*).

Unauthorised drivers

35.15 *Section 151(2)(b)* of *RTA 1988*, implementing EU legislation, provides that if there is a motor policy in force covering the insured, the insurer under the policy will be liable to meet judgments against unauthorised drivers, including a thief. The amount and the conditions for liability are the same as for insured or authorised drivers, subject to one exception. The insurer is not liable to a victim who has suffered physical injury or property damage or who has been carried in a stolen vehicle, unless either the passenger was unaware that the vehicle was stolen, or he could not reasonably have been expected to alight from it (*RTA 1988, s 151(4)*).

Provision of information

35.16 The driver of a motor vehicle who is involved in an accident which causes physical injury or damage to property is under a statutory duty to give his name and address and to produce his insurance documents. Failure to comply with this section is a criminal offence (*RTA 1988, s 170*). In *DPP v McCarthy [1999] RTR 323*, the driver was permitted to give his name and the address of a third party (ie his solicitor's address).

The victim's direct action against the insurer

35.17   Following the introduction of *the European Communities (Rights against Insurers) Regulation 2002* there is a direct claim against insurers. A victim has the right to bring a direct action against the insurers, irrespective of any right which the insurer might have to avoid the policy or to deny. The conditions for liability are the same as for insurers obligations to meet judgment for authorised drivers, This applies to accidents that occurred after 19 January 2003.

Motor Insurers' Bureau

35.18   The statutory scheme for compulsory liability insurance for motor vehicles, which had existed in the UK from 1930, proved from its inception to have two weaknesses:

- the negligent driver may have been uninsured; and

- the negligent driver may not have been traceable ('hit and run cases').

In both these cases, there was no insurance fund against which the victim could claim. The Motor Insurers' Bureau (MIB) was established in 1946 to provide a fund. The MIB, which consisted of all authorised motor insurers, entered into an agreement with the Government, under which the MIB was to accept liability for the victims of uninsured drivers. In 1969, this was extended to cover victims of untraced drivers.

Compensation of victims of uninsured drivers

35.19   The role of the MIB under this agreement is to provide a safety net for innocent victims of drivers, who have been identified but are uninsured. The date of the relevant accident is important for determining which of the Uninsured Drivers Agreements is applicable.

(*a*)   Claims arising in respect of an incident occurring between 1 December 1972 and 30 December 1988 are governed by the agreement between the Secretary of State and the Bureau dated 22 November 1972.

(*b*)   Claims arising in respect of an incident occurring between 31 December 1988 and 30 September 1999, are governed by the agreement between the Secretary of State and the Bureau dated 21 December 1998.

(*c*)   Claims arising on or after 1 October 1999 are governed by the agreement between the Secretary of State for the Environment, Transport and the Regions and the Bureau dated 13 August 1999.

MIB's obligation to satisfy compensation claims

35.20   The MIB's basic obligation is to satisfy judgments which fall within the terms of the agreement and which, because the defendant to the proceedings is not insured, are not satisfied.

Exceptions

35.21 The MIB is not liable under the agreement in the case of a claim:

(*a*) in respect of loss or damage caused by the use of a vehicle owned by or in the possession of the Crown, unless the responsibility for motor insurance has been undertaken by someone else, or the vehicle is in fact insured;

(*b*) made against any person who is not required to insure, by virtue of *s 144* of *RTA 1988*.

(*c*) a claim (commonly called 'subrogated') made in the name of a person suffering damage or injury, which is in fact wholly or partly for the benefit of another who has indemnified or is liable to indemnify that person;

(*d*) a claim in respect of damage to a motor vehicle or losses arising from such damage, where the use of the damaged vehicle was itself not covered by a contract of insurance, as is required by *Part VI* of *RTA 1988* and the claimant knew or ought to have known that was the case; and

(*e*) a claim made by a passenger in a vehicle where the loss or damage has been caused by the user of the vehicle, if the user of the vehicle was not covered by a contract of insurance and the claimant knew or ought to have known that the vehicle was being used without insurance, had been stolen or unlawfully taken or was being used in connection with a crime.

Conditions precedent to the MIB's obligation

35.22 The claimant must take reasonable steps to establish whether there is any insurance covering the use of the vehicle which caused the injury or damage. If enquiries show that there is an insurer then, even though the relevant liability may not be covered by the policy in question, the claim should be pursued with such insurer. If there is no insurance governing the use of the vehicle, or the insurer cannot be identified, or the insurer asserts that it is not obliged to handle the claim, or if for any other reason the insurer will not satisfy any judgment, the claim should be directed to the MIB.

The MIB does not have to wait for judgment to be obtained before intervening, and a claimant may apply to the MIB before the commencement of proceedings. Claims should be made using the MIB's application form and accompanied by supporting documents as soon as possible and sent by facsimile transmission, registered or recorded delivery post to the MIB's registered office.

The claimant must give the MIB notice in writing within 14 days of commencement of legal proceedings and the notice must have with it a copy of the sealed claim form or writ, any documents required by the relevant rules of procedure, and the Particulars of Claim, whether or not endorsed on the claim form.

Subject to which MIB agreement applies, different rules are then laid down by which the claimant must notify the MIB of procedural developments in his case.

Limitations on MIB's liability

35.23 *Property Damage Compensation*. The MIB is not liable for the specified excess of any loss (this may be £175 or £300 depending upon which agreement is applicable to the particular claim) and its ceiling on liability for property damage is £250,000.

Compensation received from other sources. The MIB may deduct from the relevant sum, an amount equal to any compensation from, for example, the Policyholders Protection Board, an insurer, etc.

Untraced drivers

35.24 Where the owner or driver of a vehicle cannot be identified, application may be made to the MIB under the relevant Untraced Drivers' Agreement. The date of the accident is relevant in order to determine which agreement is applicable. Accidents occurring on or after 1 July 1996 are covered by the Agreement between the Secretary of State for Transport and the Bureau dated 14 June 1996. For accident after 14 February 2003 the Untraced Drivers' Agreement 2003 applies.

These agreements provide, subject to specified conditions, for the payment of compensation for death or personal injury. Damage in respect of damage to property caused by an identified vehicle is only covered under the later agreement, and is subject to a £300 excess and limit of £250,000.

Both agreements do not apply to a case in which:

(*a*)   the death or bodily injury was caused or arose out of the use of a motor vehicle which was owned by or in the possession of the Crown;

(*b*)   at the time of the accident, the person suffering death or bodily injury was allowing himself to be carried in a vehicle and either before or after the commencement of his journey, he could reasonably have been expected to have alighted from the vehicle, if he knew or had reason to believe that the vehicle was stolen or unlawfully taken, was being used without insurance, was being used in connection with a crime or was being used as a means of escape from or avoidance of lawful apprehension.

The MIB shall not be under any liability in respect of the relevant death or injury, if the applicant is entitled to receive compensation from the MIB under any agreement providing for the compensation of victims of uninsured drivers. Where it is unclear whether the owner or driver of a vehicle has been correctly identified, it is sensible for the claimant to register a claim under both the Untraced Driver's Agreement and the Uninsured Drivers Agreement, following which the MIB will advise which agreement will, in its view, apply in the circumstances of a particular case.

Chapter 36
Product liability insurance

- Introduction
- The risk insured
- Claims occurring or claims made
- Exclusions
- Conditions

Introduction

36.01   Whilst product liability insurance is not compulsory, unlike for example motor insurance or certain types of professional indemnity insurance, it is a vital protection for any company engaged in manufacturing or supplying goods to a third party. The policy provides cover for legal liability in respect of personal injury or damage to property arising from the sale or supply of products specified in the policy. The policy customarily also covers legal costs. Damages awards and the costs of litigation can be both substantial and difficult to predict, and insurance against exposure to such risks is essential for any business.

Product liability insurance can take the form of a specific policy, but it is more often included in a general liability policy which also covers public and sometimes employers' liability. However, for the purposes of this chapter, the product liability provisions will be dealt with in isolation.

The risk insured

36.02   The wording of the operative clause will vary, but in general terms the policy provides an indemnity for sums which the insured becomes legally liable to pay by way of compensation or damages, in respect of accidental bodily injury or loss of, or damage to, property caused by products sold or supplied by the insured.

Compensation or damages

36.03   Policy wordings vary as to whether they refer to 'compensation' or to 'damages'. For the most part, any such variation will not matter and there will be no difference in the level of cover available.

However, the distinction will be important in some instances. Some product liability policies exclude liability arising from litigation in the United States because of the magnitude of damages awards and costs in that jurisdiction. For those which do not contain such an exclusion, an award of punitive damages, which is not uncommon in the US, can vastly increase the amount payable under the policy. If the operative clause refers to 'damages', the policy will cover the full amount awarded (subject to any limits of liability). If, on the other hand, the operative clause provides an indemnity for 'compensation', the indemnity will not extend to any award of punitive damages, as such damages are not compensatory in nature. The punitive element will be excluded from insurers' liability under the policy and will be solely for the account of the insured.

Financial loss

36.04   The cover is against sums awarded in respect of 'bodily injury' and 'loss of or damage to property'. It does not indemnify the insured against liability for pure financial loss which is not a direct consequence of the physical damage. For example, where sugar supplied by the Insured to A for incorporation into mincemeat was contaminated, rendering the mincemeat unfit for use, the Insured's liability for the cost of replacing the mincemeat was covered by its product liability policy; but A's loss of profits resulting from the loss of a contract with B and the enforced renegotiation of a contract with C were not a direct consequence of the damage to the mincemeat caused by the incorporation of contaminated sugar and were therefore not covered.

It is possible to obtain an extension to the policy to cover pure financial loss. However, such extensions of course require an additional premium and contain a number of exclusions.

Accidental injury and damage

36.05   In order to be covered under the policy, the injury and/or property damage must be 'accidental'. This may be dealt with by using 'accidental' in the operative clause, or by way of an exclusion which provides that there is no indemnity if the circumstances giving rise to the claim resulted from the deliberate act or omission of the insured. So, for example, if a car manufacturer knew there to be a dangerous defect arising from the manufacturing process for the car's braking system but continued selling the cars whilst investigating the position, any injury to a customer resulting from the failure of the braking system would not be covered by the policy as such injury would not be accidental. However, if the existence of a defect in the braking system was not known to the manufacturer, any customer injuries which resulted would be covered.

Territorial and jurisdiction restrictions

36.06 The policy will specify the territory within which the injury or damage must occur in order to be covered. Although it is possible to restrict the geographical area in this way, many businesses are international and, even if they do not overtly have an overseas operation, it is perfectly feasible for their products to be sold or transported anywhere in the world without their knowledge or involvement. It is impossible for an insured to predict where its products might cause damage, and many policies, therefore, provide cover for injury or damage occurring anywhere in the world.

It is less common for the policy to contain a restriction as to the jurisdictions in relation to which the insurance will respond to a claim. However, such restrictions can be provided for. The insurer may, for example, wish to restrict its liability to claims brought within its resident jurisdiction – this would enable a more educated assessment as to the likely quantum of a claim, the amount of legal costs and the length of time litigation will take. Mindful of US damages levels, some policies exclude claims brought in North America. Given that the *Product Liability Directive 1985 (85/374/EEC)* has been inconsistently implemented within the EU member states, forum shopping is not uncommon and a product liability insurance policy can take this into account by use of jurisdictional restrictions.

Use of such jurisdictional restrictions is not particularly common. It is more usual, however, for a policy to require that coverage disputes be dealt with in a specified jurisdiction.

Claims occurring or claims made

36.07 There are two means of dealing with the question of which policy is the relevant one for the purpose of paying out on a claim: 'claims occurring' and 'claims made' forms. The 'claims made' policy is now far more common in product liability policies.

Claims occurring

36.08 Historically, this form was in general use. The insurers were on risk for claims in respect of injury or damage which occurred during the policy period. Policies are normally renewed every year, commonly with different underwriters on risk in each year. The policy against which the claim was to be applied was that current when the damage giving rise to the claim occurred. This can lead to uncertainty for insurers. For example, some forms of bodily injury, such as asbestosis, might have occurred many years before manifesting themselves and resulting in a claim under the product liability insurance. However, those insurers named on the policy year when the injury occurred, which could be decades earlier, would still be on risk. Claims occurring policies are still used, but their significant drawback is that the insurers can never know with confidence when they are no longer on risk.

Claims made

36.09   This form of policy fixes the insurers' exposure to claims made during the period of the policy. It represents a considerable improvement for insurers over the claims occurring policy in that it provides certainty as to when they are on and off risk. It also avoids what can be an extremely difficult assessment, for which expert assistance may well be required, as to when an injury might have occurred. Claims relating to tobacco litigation and asbestosis, where the injury to a plaintiff might occur over a number of years with the cumulative effect of smoking or with each exposure to asbestos are obvious examples of when it might be difficult to pinpoint when the injury occurred. In the context of employers' liability the UK court has addressed that difficulty by holding that two different employers were each liable for the claimant's asbetosis given that he was exposed to asbestos during his employment with each of them.

A disadvantage of the 'claims made' policy might, however, be perceived to be the risk of numerous onerous claims being made in just one or a few policy years in respect of events occurring many years previously. This is the converse of the 'longtail' problems inherent in claims occurring policies as illustrated by the asbestosis claims. That risk can be alleviated from insurers' point of view by the use of liability limits which can either set a maximum liability for any policy year and/or a maximum aggregate per claim.

There could clearly be a risk of insurers refusing renewal of a policy in circumstances where there has been an occurrence which has not yet resulted in claims. A hybrid claims made and occurrence provision can be included in the policy. If there has been an occurrence which has been notified within the policy period, the policy might provide that claims subsequently notified will be covered. Alternatively, it is possible for the insured to obtain an extension to the policy which affords the insured an additional specified period in which to make a claim, provided that the occurrence giving rise to the claim was during the policy period.

Exclusions

36.10   Exclusions will obviously vary from policy to policy but the most common are dealt with below.

Injury to insured's employee and damage to insured's property

36.11   This reinforces the fact that the policy covers the liability of the insured to third parties, and not injury or damage suffered by the insured itself. There are other policies available by which the insured can protect itself from the risk of injury to its employees or damage to its property.

Contractual liability assumed by insured

36.12   The essence of this exclusion is that insurers cannot know the full extent of the contractual relationships to which the insured is committed. The insured might enter into a contractual commitment which could significantly extend insurers' liability. Such commitments are excluded, and the insurers will not pay out unless the insured would have been found liable in any event, even if the contract in question had not been entered into. This exclusion may be of limited application given that most additional contractual commitments assumed by the insured are likely, if breached, to result in liability for financial loss which is not in any event covered by the policy.

Damage to a product, lack of fitness for purpose, repair, replacement, recall and disposal of defective goods

36.13   The rationale for this exclusion is that the policy is intended to cover liability in respect of injury and property damage to third parties and will not therefore respond when the insured is found liable for claims which attach to the product itself. Some of these claims, such as those relating to fitness for purpose, product recall or disposal, are likely to comprise financial loss rather than property damage or bodily injury and would for that reason generally not be covered by the policy in any event.

Disputes can arise if the policy does not make clear whether this exclusion applies to a product in its entirety or only to a defective component part. Generally the insurer will intend to exclude liability for defects in the product as a whole. If this is not made expressly clear in the policy, the insured may attempt to limit the application of the exclusion only to the particular component that has proved defective.

Although there are circumstances in which the insured will have a both statutory and common law obligation to recall a product in relation to which a defect is discovered, the expenses involved in that exercise are not covered by a product liability policy unless the insured has obtained an extension to the policy.

The giving of advice, design and specification for a fee

36.14   This exclusion normally applies where such services are supplied without a product resulting. Liability in connection with some of these activities, such as the giving of advice, is excluded as insurance protection can be obtained by way of a professional indemnity policy.

It is possible for a slightly different and more problematic exclusion to apply where a product is supplied which excludes claims for liability arising from the failure of a product to perform the purpose for which it was supplied due to design or specification defects. Assessing whether the malfunctioning of a product is due to a design defect (which would not be covered) or some other cause, such as a fault in the manufacturing process (which would be covered), will not always be a straightforward assessment and may require a great deal of expensive expert analysis.

Other exclusions

36.15 There are a number of other exclusions often found in policies: radioactive/nuclear contamination, war, pollution (particularly if there is a risk of claims being brought in the US or Canada); deliberate acts of the insured; products supplied for incorporation into aviation products and product tampering; contamination; and extortion (rare but, where required, the subject of a separate policy).

Conditions

36.16 The conditions which appear in product liability policies are fairly standard and generally unremarkable.

The insured is normally required to give immediate written notice of circumstances which may give rise to a claim. The insured must not admit liability or enter into any negotiations without insurers' consent. The insurers have full discretion in the conduct and settlement of claims. The policy will normally provide for cancellation on notice to the insured.

Reasonable precautions

36.17 Most policies will require the insured to take reasonable precautions at its own expense to prevent circumstances which might give rise to a claim under the policy and to rectify any defects which might give rise to a claim as soon as possible after they come to its notice. Compliance with this condition may well include instituting at its own expense a product recall. We have already seen that the cost of such an exercise will be excluded from the indemnity provided by the policy. This condition makes clear that failure to institute a recall could also allow the insurers to avoid liability entirely under the policy.

Chapter 37
Professional indemnity insurance

- Sources of professional liability
- Compulsion to insure
- Basis of cover
- Scope of cover
- Extensions to the basic insuring agreement
- Exclusions
- Conditions
- Dispute resolution

Sources of professional liability

37.01 Professionals' liability can arise from several sources: an undertaking to achieve a desired result; a contractual duty to exercise reasonable skill and care (either expressly provided for in the professional's terms of engagement or implied by law: *Supply of Goods and Services Act 1982, ss 13, 16*); a concurrent duty of care owed to the client in tort (*Henderson v Merrett [1995] 2 AC 145*); or a duty of care owed to a third party who is not a client (*Hedley Byrne & Co Ltd v Heller & Partners Ltd [1964] AC 465*; *Caparo v Dickman [1990] 2 AC 605*; *White v Jones [1995] 2 AC 207*).

Compulsion to insure

37.02 Certain professionals are required by statute or the rules of their professional bodies to provide satisfactory evidence of professional indemnity insurance cover before they are permitted to practise. The governing body of a profession may impose requirements as to minimum limits and terms of cover, and may stipulate an approved minimum wording. It may also designate approved insurers.

Basis of cover

37.03   Professional indemnity policies written in the London market are generally 'claims made' policies, rather than 'occurrence basis' policies. Under an
occurrence basis policy, the insurer agrees to indemnify the insured for loss
arising out of a defined event which must occur within the policy period,
irrespective of when damage arises. A considerable period of time may elapse
between the occurrence of the insured event and loss arising from it.

Under a claims made policy, the insurer agrees to provide indemnity for any claim
made against the insured during the policy period, irrespective of when the event
giving rise to the claim occurred. The insurer must be notified of claims prior to
the expiry of the policy period. Problems can arise if proceedings are issued but
the insured is not made aware of them until after expiry of the policy period
(*Robert Irving & Burns v Stone [1998] Lloyd's Rep IR 258*). The court will avoid
'excessive formality' in considering whether or not a claim has been made against
the insured (*J Rothschild Assurance plc v Collyear [1999] Lloyd's Rep IR 6*).

The insured may have the right (or obligation) to notify 'circumstances which may
give rise to a claim'. If a claim is made after the end of a policy period during
which circumstances were notified, cover may still be available provided the claim
arises out of the circumstances notified.

Scope of cover

37.04   Although breaches of contract and acts of negligence may, in some cases,
be illegal, illegality will not by itself deprive insured professionals of cover where
they are in breach of duty, in spite of the *ex turpi causa* principle of public policy (a
person may not enforce rights under a contract of any kind if it is tainted by
illegality: see *Tinsley v Milligan [1994] 1 AC 340*).

Similarly, although the definition of insurance suggests that the event insured must
be uncertain (ie it is uncertain whether the event insured will ever happen, or as
to the time at which it will happen) (*Prudential Insurance Co v Inland Revenue Comrs
[1904] 2 KB 658*) an intentional act or omission will not necessarily fall outside
the scope of cover even though, in one sense, it does not depend upon a fortuitous
event outside the intention of either the insurer or the insured.

The operative clause of a professional indemnity insurance policy may restrict
cover to negligent acts, errors, omissions etc; alternatively, cover may be widely
drawn in respect of 'any act, error, omission, breach of contract or duty, or
allegation thereof'. In *Total Graphics Ltd v AGF Insurance Ltd [1997] 1 Lloyd's Rep
599*, a failure to place insurance as instructed was not proved to be a negligent
act, error or omission within the terms of the policy.

Some professional indemnity policies define the nature of the insured's business
and seek to limit the indemnity available by reference to the professional's
business activities. Indemnity may, nevertheless, be available for work performed
gratuitously.

Whatever the terms of the operative clause, it is necessary to look at the cause of a loss to determine whether indemnity will be available. A judgment of a court is likely to be determinative of indemnification. However, where a claim is compromised short of judgment it is not enough to rely upon the manner in which the claim was formulated against the insured; it is necessary to ascertain the real basis on which the claim was compromised (*MDIS Ltd (formerly McDonnell Information Systems Ltd) v Swinbank [1999] 2 All ER (Comm) 722*; and *West Wake Price & Co v Ching [1957] 1 WLR 45*).

Extensions to the basic insuring agreement

37.05 Indemnity will usually be available against the costs of defending any claim covered by the policy; it may extend to the costs of enquiries or investigations (such as regulatory or disciplinary proceedings) which are connected to or arise out of covered claims or circumstances. Special provisions usually apply to the costs of defending criminal proceedings (see 37.06 below). Defence costs may be included within the limit of indemnity or be payable in addition. Indemnity may also be extended to cover the following situations:

(*a*) where partners and employees have left an insured firm but were with it at the date of the act or omission, or have performed work after retirement in the name of, or on behalf of, the insured firm;

(*b*) where an insured firm acquires or merges with another firm; and

(*c*) where partners or employees act in various capacities in the course of their professional duties but the insured firm itself has no legal liability arising out of an individual's appointment.

Exclusions

37.06 Indemnity will usually be excluded in respect of:

(*a*) claims for which the insured firm is entitled to indemnity under a previous policy or under other existing policies under which payment is actually made;

(*b*) any fines, penalties, punitive or exemplary damages;

(*c*) awards of multiple damages (save as to the compensatory amount);

(*d*) claims where there is adjudged to have been fraud or dishonesty by an insured, committed with actual fraudulent or dishonest purpose and intent (save that innocent partners may still be covered in respect of any liability and indemnity may be available for costs of defending criminal proceedings, if the accused is acquitted);

(*e*) trading losses or liabilities incurred by a business managed or carried on by the insured (although cover will generally be available for claims against receivers, liquidators or administrators acting in their normal capacity);

(*f*) losses arising from guarantees of investment performance or warranties or guarantees;

(*g*) claims made in the USA and Canada, on the grounds that these can lead to higher awards of damages; and

(*h*) liabilities for personal injuries and property damage (though there may be indemnity in respect of loss of documents: for example, where solicitors hold important and valuable documents such as title deeds on behalf of clients).

Conditions

37.07 Professional indemnity insurance policies commonly include the following conditions:

(*a*) a requirement of prompt written notice of any claim and provision of such information as insurers may reasonably require;

(*b*) a specified limit to insurers' liability and a retention of risk by the insured;

(*c*) aggregation of claims arising out of the same or related acts or omissions;

(*d*) a requirement that the insured should not admit liability for or settle any claim, nor incur any costs or expenses without insurers' written consent. This may be coupled with a right for insurers to take over conduct of the defence or settlement of a claim, subject to a 'QC clause' (see 37.08 below);

(*e*) where a professional governing body has imposed minimum terms of cover, there may be a special condition providing that insurers will waive their rights to avoid cover for non-disclosure or misrepresentation, late notification or breach of condition, provided that the insured establishes to the insurers' satisfaction that such conduct was innocent and free of fraudulent conduct or intent to deceive. Where insurers suffer prejudice in consequence of such conduct, the indemnity available may be reduced by an amount reflecting the degree of prejudice suffered by insurers.

Dispute resolution

37.08 Where insurers are entitled to take over conduct of the defence or settlement of any claim in the name of an insured, the insured is usually protected against being required to contest proceedings by the inclusion of a 'QC clause'. This provides that insurers and insured shall agree upon counsel who shall advise whether proceedings should be contested or pursued. Solicitors and counsel instructed to advise in such circumstances must have regard to the insured's interests amongst other matters. (See also PART 4 DISPUTE RESOLUTION).

Chapter 38
Reinsurance

- Nature of reinsurance
- Formation of reinsurance agreements
- Reinsurance pools
- Misrepresentation and non-disclosure
- Terms of reinsurance agreements

Nature of reinsurance

38.01 Although the principles discussed in this chapter apply to all forms of reinsurance, most of the problematic issues are taken from non-marine reinsurance for the simple reason that this is the class of business which seems to have given rise to most of the judicial consideration, particularly in the more modern cases. In a handbook of this nature, particularly when reinsurance is dealt with in a single chapter, there is hardly any room to mention, let alone discuss fully, disputes which can arise in particular sectors of the reinsurance market (eg marine reinsurance placed on a 'total loss only' (TLO) basis where the original policy provided cover against All Risks). One particular specialist area which does not deserve complete omission but which cannot be examined in any depth is life reinsurance. This class of reinsurance is exceptional because, unlike every other form of reinsurance (see 38.02 below), it may include elements which are not, strictly speaking, indemnities against liability of the reinsured. With the exception of certain group life contracts, life reinsurance is generally written on a proportional basis (see 38.04 below) and will be written either on the same terms as the original policies, or on what is known as a 'risk premium' basis. In the latter type of reinsurance, the only risk reinsured is that of premature death: the reinsurer does not reinsure any endowment element of the original policy. The reinsurance premium, which is payable annually, will tend to rise during the first few years of the contract and will then reduce gradually as the policy reserve builds up.

Reinsurance is now regulated in a very similar way to insurance under the terms of the *Financial Services and Markets Act 2000* (*FSMA 2000*) and subordinate legislation (see 12 INSURANCE COMPANIES). Although reinsurance business is not explicitly defined as a regulated activity requiring authorisation under the *FSMA 2000*, it is reasonably clear from the number of references to reinsurance business within the Act that reinsurers are intended to be just as much subject to the provisions of the *FSMA 2000* as insurers who write direct insurance business.

General definition

38.02   A contract of reinsurance was defined by Mansfield CJ in *Delver v Barnes (1807) 1 Taunt 48* as:

> '... a new insurance effected by a new policy on the same risk which was before insured in order to indemnify the underwriters from their previous subscriptions; and both policies are to be in existence at the same time.'

Reinsurance is, therefore, indemnity insurance taken out by an insurer to cover his own exposure to the underlying risk. It is a separate contract with terms which may – and often do – differ from those in the original insurance contract. The definition in *Delver v Barnes* indicates that a reinsurance contract is a fresh policy issued by the reinsurer on the original subject matter. The more modern view, however, is to regard reinsurance of all types exclusively as a form of liability insurance, covering the insurer's liability to the original insured rather than replicating the insurer's exposure to the original risk. See *Wasa International Insurance Co Ltd and AGF Insurance Co Ltd v Lexington Insurance Co [2008] EWCA 896 Civ.*)

Separate contract

38.03   The *Delver v Barnes* definition also makes it clear that reinsurance is a separate contract with terms which may differ from those in the underlying insurance policy. There seems to be a general presumption in English law that facultative reinsurance (see 38.04 below) is to be construed as being 'back-to-back' with the underlying insurance, so that the insurer's liability is more or less mirrored in the reinsurance agreement (see *Forsikringsaktieselskapet Vesta First Respondents (Plaintiffs) v Butcher Appellant (First Defendant) [1989] AC 852*; *Groupama Navigation et Transports v Catatumbo CA Seguros [2000] 2 Lloyd's Rep 350*). The position is wholly different with a reinsurance treaty (see 38.05 below) which covers the whole account, or a section of the whole account, of the reinsured (see *AXA Reinsurance (UK) plc v Field [1996] 2 Lloyd's Rep 233*).

The contract between the insured and the insurer is a separate one from the contract between the insurer and the reinsurer (*Meadows Indemnity Co Ltd v The Insurance Corporation of Ireland plc and International Commercial Bank plc [1989] 2 Lloyd's Rep 298*). Ordinarily, therefore, the operation of the principle of privity of contract means that the insured has no ability to claim against the reinsurer in the event that the insurer neglects to pay under the original policy. This point is affirmed by s 9(2) of the *Marine Insurance Act 1906*, which provides that the original insured has no right or interest in respect of any reinsurance arranged by the insurer. The insured's right of recourse, therefore, is against his own insurer alone, or, in the event of the insurer's insolvency, he may be entitled to compensation from the Financial Services Compensation Scheme provided that the policy is provided by a 'relevant person' as defined by the *FSMA 2000*.

Some reinsurance agreements nevertheless provide that, in the event of the reinsured's insolvency, the insured has a direct claim against the reinsurer for sums owing by the reinsurer to the reinsured in respect of the original insured's claim. Until recently, any such 'cut-through' clause would have been ineffective as a matter of English law, as the insured was not a party to the reinsurance agreement and could not enforce the clause against the reinsurer. The *Contracts (Rights of Third Parties) Act 1999* makes provision, however, for the possibility of a third party to enforce a term in a contract which expressly confers such a right upon the third party. While the Act is unlikely to be of much effect in relation to treaty reinsurance, it is possible that facultative contracts could be worded so as to allow the original insured to make a claim directly against the reinsurer. Whether such provisions will be effective against the liquidator of an insolvent reinsured must, however, be doubtful because application of a cut-through could diminish the assets available for distribution to the reinsured's other creditors and could offend against the principle that such assets must be distributed *pari passu* (ie in equal proportions) to creditors of the same class. Further discussion of this complex topic is beyond the scope of this book.

Forms of reinsurance

38.04   Reinsurance may take one of two forms:

(*a*)   *facultative reinsurance*, which is the reinsurance of a single risk by means of a specific reinsurance policy; or

(*b*)   *treaty reinsurance*, by virtue of which the reinsurer makes a standing offer to the reinsured that all risks fitting a given description and within given financial limits accepted by the reinsured are covered by the treaty. Treaties are either obligatory (the usual form), in that the reinsurer has no right to refuse individual liabilities accepted by the reinsured, or facultative/ obligatory, in which case the reinsured is permitted to pick and choose the risks to be ceded to the reinsurer.

Both facultative and treaty reinsurance may be either proportional or non-proportional.

Under a proportional reinsurance contract, the risk is shared between the reinsured and the reinsurer in fixed proportions. Such contracts may be either:

(i)   *quota share*, in which the reinsurer participates in the reinsured's original business on substantively the same terms as the reinsured for its proportion of the risk; or

(ii)   *surplus*, in which the reinsured retains part of the original risk and cedes the surplus, generally in amounts representing exact multiples of the amount retained (called the reinsured's 'line').

Under a non-proportional reinsurance contract, the liability is layered: the reinsured bears a retention and the sum in excess of the retention is accepted by the reinsurer.

(*a*)   *Excess of loss reinsurance* is the most common form of non-proportional reinsurance under which the reinsurer covers part of each loss sustained by the reinsured in excess of the reinsured's retention and subject to the limit of indemnity of the reinsurance contract.

(*b*)   *Stop loss reinsurance* is a variant under which the reinsurer's liability begins once the aggregate of the reinsured's losses reach a given financial limit. An illustration of stop loss reinsurance is that procured by Lloyd's Names to cover their potential underwriting liabilities (see 11 LLOYD'S).

Reinsurance is commonly arranged in excess layers, and it is possible to find more than one form of reinsurance involved in respect of a single risk. For example, the reinsured may bear the first £25,000 of loss itself, reinsure the next £100,000 under a quota share arrangement, and arrange excess of loss cover with another reinsurer for all losses exceeding £125,000 but subject to a limit of £500,000.

Reinsurance treaties will often be evidenced by lengthy and complex documents. By contrast, facultative reinsurance may be created by a 'slip policy', which specifies only the nature and basic terms of the contract.

Formation of reinsurance agreements

Reinsurance in advance of insurance

38.05   The definition of reinsurance in *Delver v Barnes* (see 38.02 above) contemplates that the insurer will reinsure only after the underlying insurance policy is in place. Market practice, particularly in the case of large risks, is to the contrary: frequently, a broker instructed to place insurance will seek reinsurance first, thereby making it easier to find original insurers prepared to accept the primary risk, since they will have the knowledge that a substantial proportion of their liability can be passed on to reinsurers. This practice can lead to legal difficulties in relation to the duty of care owed by the broker placing the reinsurance since the reinsured, to whom that duty is normally owed, may not have been ascertained when the reinsurance was placed (see *General Accident Fire and Life Assurance Corpn v Peter William Tanter v Peter William Tanter (The 'Zephyr')* [1985] 2 Lloyd's Rep 529; *Youell v Bland Welch & Co Ltd (The 'Superhulls Cover' Case) (No 2)* [1990] 2 Lloyd's Rep 431)

Reinsurance pools

38.06   Large risks and treaties are generally underwritten by groups of reinsurers rather than by one reinsurer individually. Reinsurers may, for this purpose, enter into pooling arrangements whereby the pool members agree that each of them will accept a given proportion of the risks underwritten by the pool. A pool will often be represented by an underwriting agent, who is given authority either to underwrite at his discretion, or to receive and pass on risks for consideration by the pool members themselves. The pool will sometimes be represented by one of its number, acting as a 'fronting' company, which will accept the risk in its entirety. The fronting company will then enter into retrocession agreements (ie reinsurance of reinsurance contracts) with the other pool members, with the result that the fronting company retains its agreed proportion of the risk, while the retrocessionaires (ie the companies agreeing to the retrocession contract) have their individual agreed proportions of the risk ceded to them. Fronting may produce administrative savings and overcome problems where only the fronting company is authorised to carry on reinsurance business in the territory in which the pool is operating. Fronting can, however, also give rise to problems, particularly if one of the retrocessionaires becomes insolvent and cannot indemnify the fronting company for the retrocessionaire's agreed proportion of the original risk.

The role of the underwriting agent acting for the pool is discussed in 10 UNDERWRITING AGENCIES.

Misrepresentation and non-disclosure

Facultative agreements

38.07   Facultative reinsurance agreements are contracts of liability insurance and are thus subject to the usual duty of utmost good faith. The reinsured may be in breach of its duty in one of two ways:

(*a*)   If there is a false statement in, or a material omission from, the proposal form for the original policy, and this has been incorporated by reference into the reinsurance agreement, the reinsurer has the right to set aside the reinsurance agreement (*Lambert & Co-Operative Insurance Society Ltd [1975] 2 Lloyd's Rep 485*).

(*b*)   If there is a false statement or a material omission in the negotiations between the insurer and the reinsurer, the reinsurer has the usual right to avoid the agreement for breach of duty by the reinsured.

A material false statement made to the insurer, but not repeated to the reinsurer, renders the original policy, but not the reinsurance agreement, voidable. If the insurer chooses not to rely upon the misrepresentation defence and pays the claim, the reinsurer may have a defence to the reinsured's claim on the basis that the reinsured has not made a *bona fide* settlement of the underlying loss (see 38.21 below).

Treaties

38.08   Reinsurance by treaty has two distinct stages: the making of the treaty, and the declaration of individual risks to the treaty. Although the treaty is not, strictly speaking, a contract of reinsurance, but rather a framework agreement, it is nevertheless clear that a full duty of utmost good faith operates at the stage of placement of the treaty, requiring the reinsured to disclose all material facts about risks which will be allotted to the treaty (see *Glasgow Assurance v Symondson (1911) 104 LT 254*). The position under a line slip, which requires separate consideration of each risk bound, is different. A line slip is a contract *for* insurance which is not itself a contract of utmost good faith, whereas individually the declarations to the line slip are contracts *of* insurance and therefore of utmost good faith: see *HIH Casualty and General Insurance Ltd v Chase Manhattan Bank [2001] Lloyd's Rep IR 191*, confirmed by the Court of Appeal on this point at *[2001] Lloyd's Rep IR 703*.

Some difficulty surrounds the question whether full disclosure is required when each individual risk accepted by the insurer is ceded to the reinsurer under the treaty. The reinsured may be under a contractual duty to submit particulars to the reinsurer by way of lists of risks, called *bordereaux*. Probably, however, no additional duty of disclosure arises at this stage. While it is the case that each individual cession under a treaty takes effect as a separate contract of reinsurance in its own right (*Citadel Insurance Co v Atlantic Union Insurance Co SA [1982] 2 Lloyd's Rep 543*), most reinsurance agreements are construed as obligatory, so that the reinsurer cannot refuse to accept the ceded risk. Indeed, in some cases, the issuing of a policy by the insurer operates as an automatic cession of liability to the reinsurance treaty. A duty of disclosure would, therefore, appear to be superfluous.

The reinsurer's protection in the case of facultative obligatory treaty reinsurance arguably stems not from the doctrine of utmost good faith, but from an implied term in the reinsurance contract under which the reinsured agrees to exercise reasonable care in the carrying on of its business. The implied duties were set out in *Phoenix General Insurance Co of Greece SA v Halvanon Insurance Co Ltd [1985] 2 Lloyd's Rep 599*. (in which they were not regarded as controversial by the parties). Under the formulation adopted there, the reinsured is required to conduct its business in accordance with the ordinary practice of the market and to exercise due care and skill in the conduct of all business applicable to the treaty. In particular, the reinsured impliedly agrees to:

(*a*)   keep full and proper records of all risks accepted, premiums received and claims against it;

(*b*)   investigate all claims to ensure that they fall within the cover of the policy before paying them;

(*c*)   properly investigate proposed risks before acceptance;

(*d*)   keep full, proper and accurate accounts showing the amounts due and payable by the reinsurer to the reinsured;

(*e*)   ensure that all amounts payable to the reinsured are collected promptly; and

(*f*)   ensure that all documents are available for inspection by the reinsurer.

Although this case probably remains good law in relation to facultative/obligatory (or other proportional) contracts, the Court of Appeal in *Bonner v Cox [2006] 2 Lloyd's Rep 152* held that a reinsured owes no such implied duty of care to a reinsurer in excess of loss business.

What is 'material'?

38.09   There are only a few cases in which the issue of what constitutes a material fact for the purposes of a reinsurance agreement has arisen squarely for decision, although the following facts are clearly material.

The amount of the reinsured's retention

38.10   The retention is the primary protection available to the reinsurer, so that any intention on the part of the reinsured to reinsure this retention elsewhere will be material (*Traill v Baring (1864) 33 LJ Ch 521*). This principle has, however, been diluted in two more modern authorities.

(*a*)   In *Société Anonyme d'Intermediaries Luxembourgeois v Farex Gie [1995] LRLR 116*, although it was accepted that the cedant's retention would be a matter of great concern to a reinsurer, nevertheless, unless the reinsurer is told, or is entitled to assume from a previous course of dealing, that there is or is not a significant retention on each risk which he is being asked to accept, it is up to the reinsurer to ask what the position is.

(*b*)   In *Kingscroft Insurance Co Ltd v Nissan Fire & Marine Insurance Co Ltd [1999] Lloyd's Rep IR 603*, it was held that a whole account quota share reinsurer was not entitled to avoid its contract on the grounds that the reinsured had sought excess of loss reinsurance for its retained line under the quota share contract, since the obtaining of such reinsurance was a common practice in the London market, and the whole account quota share reinsurers ought to have known that the reinsured might choose to purchase excess of loss protection in respect of its retention.

The reinsured's previous losses and claims history

38.11   This is clearly a most important factor which a reinsurer will wish to take into account (see *Pan Atlantic Insurance Co Ltd v Pine Top Insurance Co Ltd [1994] 2 Lloyd's Rep 427*). It should be noted, however, that claims experience in recent years is unlikely to be a reliable guide, as losses may take some time to become manifest, particularly in relation to third party liability (also referred to – particularly in the USA – as 'casualty') business.

The extent of the reinsured's liability under the original policy

38.12   If the original policy commits the reinsured to liability in cases which the reinsurer would normally expect to find excluded, the reinsured must disclose the existence of the exceptional liability: see *Property Insurance v National Protector Insurance [1913] 108 LT 104* (winter cover for marine risks on the Great Lakes); *Sumitomo Marine & Fire Insurance Company v Cologne Reinsurance Company, 552 NYS 2d 891 [1990]* (acceptance of liability for risks of nuclear damage).

Remedies for misrepresentation or non-disclosure

38.13   A reinsurance contract is voidable for breach of the reinsured's duty of utmost good faith prior to placement. If the breach consists of a misrepresentation, the court will not excuse the misrepresentation by applying *s 2(2)* of the *Misrepresentation Act 1967* and awarding damages to the reinsurer in lieu of its right to avoid (see *Highlands Insurance Co v Continental Insurance Co [1987] 1 Lloyd's Rep 109*). Many reinsurance treaties contain an 'errors and omissions' clause, which provides (in effect) that the reinsurer must meet any claim despite an error or omission by the reinsured in operating the agreement. A clause of this type is, however, intended only to rectify clerical errors in the supply of information during the currency of the agreement and was held, in *Pan Atlantic Insurance* (see 38.11 above), not to excuse any breach of the duty of utmost good faith on the part of the reinsured.

Terms of reinsurance agreements

Duration

38.14   There is probably a presumption that a facultative reinsurance contract is to commence and terminate on the same days as the underlying policy, and ambiguous wording in the reinsurance contract will be construed accordingly (see *Commercial Union Assurance Co plc v Sun Alliance Insurance Group plc and Guardian Royal Exchange plc [1992] 1 Lloyd's Rep 475*), but such a back-to-back construction may not always be possible (see *Youell v Bland Welch* at 38.05 above). There is no presumption of symmetry of duration between the original policy and the reinsurance agreement in the case of treaty reinsurance. Indeed, it is quite common for a reinsurance treaty to be placed on a 'risks attaching' basis, that is, where the period of the reinsurance is (say) 1 January to 31 December 2000, it will cover losses under any original policies issued by the reinsured during that period. It is possible, in such circumstances, for the reinsured to issue a 12-month policy in November 2000 under which a loss occurs in October 2001. Notwithstanding that the period of the reinsurance contract will have expired some ten months earlier, this loss would still be covered by the reinsurance.

Incorporation by reference

38.15   Facultative reinsurances may consist of little more than a single page slip policy referring to standard market terms and appended to the original policy. The reinsurance may attempt to incorporate the terms of the original policy by wordings such as 'all terms and conditions as original' or simply 'as original'. It is settled that this form of wording has an incorporating effect, but only in respect of such terms in the original policy as are appropriate to a contract of reinsurance (see *Home Insurance Company of New York v Victoria-Montreal Fire Insurance Company [1907] AC 59*; and *Pine Top Insurance Co Ltd v Unione Italiana Anglo Saxon Reinsurance Co Ltd [1987] 1 Lloyd's Rep 476*). Attempts at incorporation by reference have given rise to considerable uncertainty in a number of reported reinsurance cases, and were criticised by the House of Lords in *Forsikringsaktieselskapet Vesta* (see 38.03 above).

Inspection of records clauses

38.16 Reinsurers are, generally speaking, not given detailed information about the underwriting of the original account which they have agreed to protect, nor about the claims arising under that account which are presented to them for settlement. In substitution for the provision of detailed information of this nature, the parties to reinsurance treaties usually agree to confer on the reinsurer a right to inspect the books and records of the reinsured. An example of an inspection of records clause found in a London market reinsurance treaty reads as follows:

> 'No further particulars shall be required by the reinsurer, but the books of the reinsured, so far as they concern the policies and/or contracts falling within the scope of this agreement, shall be open to inspection by an authorised representative of the reinsurer at any reasonable time during the continuance of this agreement or any liability thereunder.'

Even in the absence of an express clause such as this, a right of inspection is probably to be necessarily implied into a reinsurance treaty. Such a term was agreed by the parties to be implied into the facultative/obligatory contact in *Phoenix General Insurance* (see 38.08 above). While *Bonner v Cox* disapproved the implication of some of these terms into excess of loss contracts (see 38.08 above), the issue of an implied right of inspection did not arise there. Some doubt has, however, been cast on a reinsurer's right of inspection in the absence of an express inspection of records clause by the following remarks of Hoffmann LJ in *SAIL v Farex Gie* (see 38.10 above).

> 'Reinsurers are free to stipulate for whatever rights of inspection they please ... If they are not entitled to inspection as a matter of contractual right and a dispute arises, English law gives them no procedural means of inspection unless they are first able to raise a triable issue on the material otherwise available to them. This may mean that reinsurers are unable to uncover defences which greater rights of inspection would have revealed, but this is a commercial risk which they accept at the time when the contract is made.'

It may be, however, that Hoffmann LJ's comments should be confined to cases where a reinsurer with no readily apparent defence to the reinsured's claims is attempting to embark upon a 'fishing expedition' in the hope that a viable defence will emerge from the inspection.

If a reinsurer is already in possession of information entitling it to avoid the contract on grounds of misrepresentation or non-disclosure, the exercise by the reinsurer of a contractual right of inspection may be disadvantageous, as the reinsured may be able to argue that the reinsurer has waived its right of avoidance by asserting a contractual right such as inspection (see *Iron Trades Mutual Insurance Co Ltd v Companhia de Seguros Imperio [1991] 1 Re LR 213*). In *Strive Shipping Corpn v Hellenic Mutual War Risks Association (The 'Grecia Express') [2002] 2 Lloyd's Rep 88*, however, it was suggested that exercising a right to inspect should not be regarded as an affirmation of the contract because an inspection of records provision should be seen as an ancillary but independent provision in the reinsurance, similar in effect to an arbitration clause. In order to avoid any risk of suggestion that the reinsurer has affirmed the contract, however, an inspection in these circumstances should be carried out only under a clear reservation of rights.

If, on the other hand, a reinsurer does not have evidence which will entitle it to avoid the contract, but suspects that such evidence exists, inspection should be demanded without delay. In *Trinity Insurance Co Ltd v Overseas Union Insurance Ltd [1996] LRLR 156*, the reinsured applied for summary judgment against the reinsurer in respect of unpaid claims, and the reinsurer was refused leave to defend the action when its request for inspection of the reinsured's records was made only after the summary judgment application.

Arbitration clauses

38.17   Most reinsurance treaties contain arbitration clauses. In some older reinsurance treaties (ie contracts concluded in the 1970s or earlier), the arbitration clauses are often in 'honourable engagement' or 'equity' form. A typical wording is as follows:

> 'The arbitrators shall interpret this reinsurance as an honourable engagement and they shall make their award with a view to effecting the general purpose of this reinsurance in a reasonable manner rather than in accordance with a literal interpretation of the language.'

The older authorities are uniformly hostile to honourable engagement clauses. In *Maritime Insurance Company, Ltd v Assecuranz-Union Von 1865 (1935) 52 Ll L Rep 16*, it was held that, depending upon its wording, such a clause runs the risk of invalidating the entire reinsurance agreement, on the basis that the parties did not intend to create legal relations. Alternatively, a court might construe the arbitration clause as void for attempting to oust the supervisory jurisdiction of the English courts, so that the reinsurance agreement as a whole would be held to be valid, but the obligation to arbitrate would be unenforceable (see *Orion Compania Espanola de Seguros v Belfort Maatschappij voor Algemene Verzekgringeen [1962] 2 Lloyd's Rep 257*). The modern view of honourable engagement clauses is more lenient. In *Home & Overseas Insurance Co Ltd v Mentor Insurance Co Ltd (UK) [1989] 1 Lloyd's Rep 473*, the Court of Appeal held that the wording quoted above was effective to create a binding obligation to arbitrate, and that the arbitrator was merely relieved from the duty to apply a literal construction to the words of the reinsurance contract. The clause could not, however, excuse the arbitrators from applying the ordinary principles of the law governing the reinsurance agreement, so that, for example, a refusal to apply the rules of utmost good faith could not be justified by an honourable engagement clause. It was further held in *Hiscox v Outhwaite (No 3) [1991] 2 Lloyd's Rep 524*, that the High Court, when exercising its power to hear an appeal against an arbitral award on a point of law, should recognise the wider discretion conferred by an honourable engagement clause, and should thus be less willing to overturn the arbitrator's award on a point of construction.

The cases cited above were all decided prior to the coming into force of the *Arbitration Act 1996 (AA 1996)*. *Section 46(1)(b)* of the *AA 1996* empowers the tribunal to decide the dispute 'in accordance with such other considerations as are agreed by' the parties. A wide interpretation of this provision could confer an almost limitless discretion on the arbitrators as to what considerations they may take into account in deciding the issues in dispute. Section *46(1)(b)* does not, however, apply where the dispute arises under an arbitration agreement made prior to 31 January 1997, when the Act came into force. Arbitral proceedings (even if commenced after 31 January 1997) under an arbitration agreement entered into before that date will, therefore, continue to be governed by the pre-1996 Act cases.

Losses and claims

Accrual of reinsured's right to indemnity

38.18   In liability insurance there is a general presumption that the insurer's obligation to indemnify the insured arises on proof of the insured's liability and not on discharge of that liability, ie actual payment to the third party by the insured. The same principle applies to reinsurance contracts. The point is likely to be of particular significance when the reinsured has become insolvent and is unable to make payment to its original insureds. The explanation for the decisions reached in some noteworthy reinsurance cases may be that this presumption is sufficiently strong to override what appears to be express language to the contrary. For example, in *Home & Overseas Insurance Company* (see 38.17 above), the reinsurer's obligation, as expressed in the 'ultimate net loss' clause of the contract, was to indemnify the reinsured for losses which the reinsured ' actually paid'. The Court of Appeal held that the meaning of that phrase was sufficiently uncertain to merit an arbitration hearing as to whether the reinsurer came under any liability before actual payment had been made by the reinsured. The same approach was adopted *In Re A Company No 0013734 of 1991 [1992] 2 Lloyd's Rep 415*, and in what is now the leading case on this issue, *Charter Reinsurance Co Ltd v Fagan [1996] 2 Lloyd's Rep 113*, the House of Lords held, in the context of a claim by an insurance company in provisional liquidation against its reinsurers for an indemnity, that the words 'actually paid' in the ultimate net loss clause in the relevant reinsurance contract had, in effect, to be construed as 'liable to be paid'.

Loss settlements clauses

38.19   A persistent difficulty in reinsurance law has proved to be the development of contract language under which the reinsurer is liable to indemnify the reinsured for genuine settlements reached with the original insured, even though it might subsequently prove to be the case that the reinsured was not liable to the original insured as a matter of law. In *Hill v Mercantile and General Reinsurance Co plc [1996] 1 WLR 1239*, Lord Mustill recognised that there is an inherent tension in reinsurance between, on the one hand, the need to avoid investigating the same issues twice, and, on the other, the need to ensure that the integrity of the reinsurer's bargain is not eroded by a settlement over which he has no control. In the resolution of this conflict, there are only two rules, both of them obvious: the first is that the reinsurer cannot be held liable unless the loss falls both within the cover of the policy reinsured and within the cover created by the reinsurance; the second is that the parties are free to agree on ways of proving whether these requirements have been satisfied.

Early wordings

38.20   The earliest attempt to resolve this 'tension of reinsurance' was the phrase 'pay as may be paid thereon', which was used in the late 19th century. A line of cases, however, beginning with *Chippendale v Holt [1895] 1 Com Cas 197*, held that these words did not have the desired effect and meant instead that the reinsurer was liable to the reinsured only if the reinsured was actually liable to the original insured; a *bona fide* settlement of the original claim did not, therefore, suffice.

Follow the settlements

38.21   The setback (from the reinsured's point of view) of *Chippendale v Holt* (see 38.20 above) led to the adoption of a number of fresh formulations, including 'follow the settlements'. This wording was tested before the Court of Appeal in *The Insurance Co of Africa v SCOR (UK) Reinsurance Co Ltd [1985] 1 Lloyd's Rep 312*. The Court of Appeal held in this case that the 'follow the settlements' clause had the effect of reversing *Chippendale v Holt*, with the result that reinsurers who agreed to follow their reinsureds' settlements were obliged to indemnify reinsureds whose liability had been established by judgment or arbitration award, or who had 'acted honestly and … taken all proper and businesslike steps in making their settlement'. Reinsurers were not entitled to re-open a genuine settlement and seek to prove that there was no legal liability on the part of the reinsured. Pure *ex gratia* payments (in the sense of payments made in the absence of liability) are, however, probably not included in this formulation; neither should a term be implied that any costs incurred by the reinsured in defending the original insured's claim are to be indemnified by reinsurers.

It was subsequently held in *John Robert Charman v Guardian Royal Exchange Assurance plc [1992] 2 Lloyd's Rep 607* that the burden of proving that the reinsured has not acted in a proper and businesslike fashion is borne by the reinsurer. This case also decided that a reinsured acts properly in investigating a loss by appointing a reputable loss adjuster, taking reasonable steps to ascertain that the loss adjuster's report has been fairly reached, and negotiating with the insured in a businesslike fashion on receiving the report.

Alternative formulations

38.22   Some reinsurance wordings require reinsurers to follow the reinsured's settlements, including any *ex gratia* payments. The validity of such clauses has yet to be tested, but they are arguably binding on the basis that '*ex gratia*' should not be interpreted as meaning 'in the absence of liability', but only 'without admission of liability' (see *Edwards v Skyways Ltd [1964] 1 WLR 349*). *Ex gratia* can however also be construed in a wider sense as covering settlements which are made on the basis that there is no liability to indemnify: see *Assicurazioni Generali SpA v CGU International Insurance plc [2003] Lloyd's Rep IR 725*. This judgment was upheld by the Court of Appeal (*[2004] EWCA Civ 429*) but without further consideration of the meaning of 'ex gratia'. In *Charman v Guardian Royal Exchange* (see 38.21 above), the clause in question obliged the reinsurer to follow the settlements of the reinsured 'liable or not liable'. The court held that these additional words did not extend the reinsurer's liability to *ex gratia* payments (in the sense of payments made in the knowledge that there was no liability) and that the words were, in effect, meaningless. Other clauses require that the settlement of the original claim falls within the terms both of the original policy and the reinsurance contract: see *Hill v Mercantile & General Reinsurance Co plc [1996] 1 WLR 1239*.

In the USA, the formula 'follow the fortunes' has long been used. The only reported English decision on 'follow the fortunes' (*Hayter v Nelson and Home Insurance Co [1990] 2 Lloyd's Rep 265*) held that there was no authority on the meaning of the phrase and considerable uncertainty over what it meant. The judge refused to accept that a 'follow the fortunes clause' was an express provision obliging the retrocessionaire to be bound automatically by judgments or awards against the reinsurer. 'Follow the fortunes' is nevertheless generally regarded as having at least the same effect as 'follow the settlements', so that the reinsured is entitled to be indemnified for genuine settlements but cannot seek recovery for *ex gratia* payments.

Claims co-operation and control provisions

38.23   The wide liability accepted by reinsurers under some follow settlements and follow fortunes clauses is restricted by other policy terms. Under a claims co-operation clause, the reinsured is obliged to keep the reinsurer informed of the progress of negotiations with the insured and not to reach any settlement unless the reinsurer has approved it. Under a claims control clause, the reinsured is obliged to relinquish to the reinsurer the control of all negotiations with the original insured.

It was decided in *Insurance Company of Africa v SCOR* (see 38.21 above) that the reinsurer's obligation to follow the reinsured's settlements is overridden by a claims co-operation or control clause. A claims co-operation clause in ICA's reinsurance contract did not, however, affect the actual result in this case, as the reinsured was held to have proved its liability to the original insured, so that the reinsurers were obliged to provide an indemnity. It is important to note that if the claims co-operation or control clause is expressed as a condition precedent, any failure to co-operate will deprive the reinsured of the right to indemnity, notwithstanding the possibility of proof of the reinsured's underlying liability (*Gan Insurance Co Ltd v Tai Ping Insurance Co Ltd [2001] Lloyd's Rep IR 291*).

Choice of law problems

38.24 One consequence of the fact that the contracts between the insured and insurer on the one hand and the insurer and the reinsurer on the other are separate contracts (see 38.02 above) is that each is capable of being governed by a different law (for more on choice of law see 2 TERMS IN INSURANCE CONTRACTS). This may entail that even though the wordings of the insurance and reinsurance agreements are identical, different meanings are to be ascribed to the words used under their respective governing laws (see *St Paul Fire and Marine Insurance Co v Morice (1906) 11 Com Cas 153, 22 TLR 449*; *Forsikringsaktieselskapet Vesta*; and *Groupama Navigation* (see 38.03 above). However, see also *Wasa International Insurance Co Ltd and AGF Insurance Co Ltd v Lexington Insurance Co [2008] EWCA 896 Civ*).

Chapter 39
Space insurance

- Introduction
- Terminology
- General
- The risks
- The legal framework
- Industry practice
- Types of coverage
- And finally ...

Introduction

39.01   Compared to other areas of insurance, space insurance is a relatively new area – the first policy was written in 1965 for Intelsat I – and is continuously developing. Whereas states and governmental organisations were instrumental in pioneering space exploration, in recent years the commercial exploitation of space has increased at a rapid rate. Space tourism is no longer in the realms of science fiction and will result in new insurance products being developed.

Hitherto space insurance has been primarily concerned with the launch of commercial satellites. Typically, the launch of a satellite involves a satellite operator and a satellite manufacturer (usually separate organisations) one of whom procures launch of the satellite by contracting with a launch services provider. In recent years there has been an increasing tendency for satellite manufacture contracts to provide for delivery of the satellite to the satellite operator in orbit. This development has resulted in manufacturers having responsibility to negotiate with the launch provider and insure risks until the satellite is delivered in the in-orbit phase and the risk passes to the operator. Insurance of space objects is concerned with the protection of value of the space object as an asset on the ground during four phases of its life: during manufacture, during pre-launch whilst it is travelling to the launch site, during launch, and whilst in-orbit. Insurance may also cover the risks of liabilities amongst the parties involved and to third parties both in space and on the ground.

Terminology

39.02 Whilst detailed examination of the various types of space object are outside the scope of this chapter, it may assist to provide a brief explanation of certain terms used.

(a)   *Launch vehicle.* The vehicle that launches a satellite (or other space object) into orbit. It can either be an expendable rocket (ELV) such as Ariane or a reusable vehicle (RLV) such as the space shuttle.

(b)   *Satellite.* There are various types of satellite – commercial communications satellites (which can be used for telecommunications, broadcasting or data transfer), meteorological satellites, remote sensing satellites that observe the Earth from space, and scientific satellites.

(c)   *Transponder.* That component which sends and receives radio signals to and from a satellite. It is thus one of the key components of a satellite.

General

39.03   Insurance of space objects is a unique area of insurance for the following reasons:

- few risks are placed each year compared to other types of insurance such as aviation and marine;

- policies are written and negotiated on an individual basis for each space object;

- because of the technical complexity (and often in the case of a satellite's uniqueness) of the items insured, detailed presentations as to the technical specifications and nature of the satellite and the launch vehicle to be used are provided to underwriters (however, some countries like the United States impose restrictions on non-US citizens receiving detailed technical information and underwriters may face information restrictions);

- since it is difficult to repair objects in space, relatively minor damage or malfunctions may result in a total loss; and

- when losses occur the sums involved may be extremely large.

The risks

39.04   The two main risks are as follows:

(a)   damage to the space object itself, including partial losses such as degradation in performance or reduction of expected life; or total loss of the space object. In addition to total destruction of the space object (for example in an explosion on launch) total loss may also encompass failure to achieve the desired orbit, or serious loss of life expectancy or loss/failure of a certain number of transponders; and

(*b*)   third party liability.

The legal framework

39.05   The main instruments governing the use of outer space and the liability regime are considered in outline below. Not all states are parties to these Conventions.

Treaty on Principles Governing the Activities of States in the Exploration and Use of Outer Space, Including the Moon and Other Celestial Bodies

39.06   This treaty sets out the principle that all states may explore and use outer space on an equal basis for the benefit of all countries, and in accordance with international law, including the UN Charter. States bear international responsibility for national activities carried out in outer space and keep jurisdiction and control over launched space objects.

The treaty does not define what is meant by 'outer space'.

The Convention on International Liability for Damage Caused by Space Objects 1972 ('the Liability Convention')

39.07   This is the main instrument setting out the liability framework for damage caused by space objects. 'Space objects' includes component parts of the space object as well as its launch vehicle and parts of the launch vehicle. It does not include natural objects such as meteorites.

Damage is defined as 'loss of life, personal injury or other impairment of health; or loss of or damage to property of states or of persons, natural or juridicial, or property of intergovernmental organizations'.

(*a*)   the following are liable for damage caused by space objects:

    (i)   the state that actually launches the space object;

    (ii)   the state that procures the launch of a space object;

    (iii)   the state from whose territory the space object is launched;

(*b*)   the state on behalf of the victim can hold any of the above liable for the damage;

(*c*)   the applicable standard of liability depends on the type of damage caused;

(*d*) in respect of damage caused by a space object on the Earth's surface or to an aircraft in flight, liability is absolute; and

(*e*) in respect of damage elsewhere (such as in damage occurring in space) liability is fault based.

If two or more states participate in a joint launch they will be jointly liable.

A state can only avoid absolute liability if it can prove that:

● the damage resulted from the gross negligence or an act or omission done with intent to cause damage on the part of the claimant state (or the persons it represents); and

● it complied with the requirements of international law.

There are no limits to compensation recoverable. Compensation is determined in accordance with international law and the principles of equity and justice, on the basis that the person on whose behalf the claim is presented is restored to his pre-damage position. Nor is there any limit in respect of nuclear damage.

Damage to nationals of the launching state or foreign nationals (whilst they are participating in the operation of a space object or within the immediate vicinity of a planned launching state) is excluded.

Claims are presented by states utilising diplomatic channels and must be brought within one year of the damage occurring or the identification of the state liable. If the claim is not settled, either party can request that a three-member claims commission be established (with a member appointed by each state, and the chairman appointed by those members).

Industry practice

39.08 When considering liability among the various parties involved in a satellite launch, note that it is common to find provisions for cross-waivers of liability in the contracts for manufacture of satellites and launch vehicles and provision of launch services, with the aim that each manufacturer or launch service provider bears their own risk. Such clauses have been upheld in cases in the United States.

Types of coverage

Loss or damage to the space object

39.09 Coverage for damage to the space object itself is generally provided by reference to the stage of the space object's life.

(a)   *Manufacture.* Space objects can be insured for damage during the manufacturing process, in a similar manner to other items insured against loss or damage during the manufacturing process.

(b)   *Pre-launch.* Coverage is available for risks associated with damage to a satellite or launch vehicle on the ground, including whilst in storage and in transit to the launch site, and during the pre-launch assembly, testing and inspection phases. Coverage usually commences from acceptance of the satellite from the manufacturer and terminates when the launch vehicle is intentionally ignited or at lift-off or release of hold-down clamps.

(c)   *Launch.* These policies usually begin from intentional ignition of the launch vehicle and end following separation of the satellite from the launch vehicle and completion of initial functional testing to check that the satellite is working correctly. Coverage is for the risk of the satellite being damaged or lost in the launch phases, or failing to achieve the anticipated orbit. Coverage can be for just the launch phase or include the commissioning phase (usually 180 days) or for longer periods – sometimes up to a year after launch. However, in recent years the distinction between launch and in-orbit insurance has become blurred with some policies offering coverage for launch plus five years. Some satellite manufacturers offer 'turnkey' or in-orbit delivery to the satellite operator. As a result, manufacturers may now need to purchase manufacture, pre-launch and launch cover.

(d)   *In-orbit.* These policies usually commence after functional testing has been completed and are renewed generally on an annual basis. Generally, satellites have a life-expectancy of around 10 years or until the onboard fuel expires, although the lifespan is increasing with the advance of technology. Prior to renewal, underwriters will expect to receive a health report, indicating that the satellite is functioning as it should.

Whilst launch and in-orbit policies are usually written on an asset value basis (ie on the basis of the space object's value as an asset rather than its income-producing capabilities), it is possible for policies to cover temporary service interruption or loss or profits or revenue and expenses (such as altering ground equipment) that may be incurred if it becomes necessary to use a different satellite.

Partial loss

39.10   Coverage is usually provided for total loss of the satellite and for partial loss of the satellite's capability. Partial loss may be defined to occur on several bases such as:

(a)   *Loss of propellant.* This is the station-keeping fuel which a satellite needs to keep in its correct orbital position. If this is lost the satellite's life is reduced.

(b)   *Loss of electrical power.* If a satellite loses electrical power then it may not be possible for it to operate all transponders.

(c)   *Transponder failure.* A transponder may fail, thus reducing the satellite's revenue-earning capacity.

Policies often provide formulae to calculate the amount due in respect of a partial loss.

Liability

39.11   Liabilities to third parties can arise under the Liability Convention outlined at 39.07 above. Policies are available that cover the risks of death/personal injury, property damage, damage to the launch facility, and consequential losses to third parties such as loss of revenue and service interruption.

Transponder coverage

39.12   Satellite users (eg a television company) may lease transponders from the satellite operator, and policies are available to protect them (and/or the satellite operator) in the event that one or more transponders become inoperable. Such coverage can include loss of revenue or the costs of obtaining alternative transponder capacity on another satellite.

Service interruption coverage is also available, covering incurred production and transmission costs.

Delay

39.13   Policies are available to cover losses arising from launch delay such as contractual penalties, loss of profits, expenses arising from a need to change the launch vehicle or source alternative satellite capacity.

Political risks

39.14   Policies are available providing coverage against various risks, including the risk that export licences may be revoked by a government for satellites intended to be launched on launch vehicles provided by other states. Confiscation of a satellite by the launching state or termination of the launch contract following civil unrest in the launching state may also be covered.

Re-launch guarantee

39.15   Some launch providers – for example Arianespace – have introduced launch risk guarantees that provide for a free replacement launch vehicle in the event that the satellite is lost due to a launch vehicle failure. Launch providers can obtain insurance similar to launch coverage to cover the terms of their guarantee.

And finally ...

39.16 Policies have been drafted that purport to indemnify the policyholder if abducted by aliens. Caution should be exercised if claims are presented under such policies, which are probably intended to be novelties rather than real insurance.

Chapter 40
War risks and related perils

- The insurability of war risks
- Particular war risks
- Proximate cause
- Perils related to war risks
- Strikes
- Terrorism and political risks

The insurability of war risks

The market

40.01   Insurers have always been cautious in writing insurance against the perils of war, due to the potentially devastating consequences of war. In times of peace, insurance for mainland risks will generally include war cover. However, as far as transport policies are concerned, particularly those on vessels and aircraft, there is a heightened danger of the insured subject matter encountering war conditions in other regions, and the practice is for insurers to exclude liability for losses consequent upon war, but to provide separate cover at an increased premium.

Commercial insurance in time of war

40.02   In time of war it is necessary for vital industries and transport to be maintained. Commercial war risks insurance may, however, be unobtainable. For this reason, various government schemes have been introduced to ensure that those involved in commerce can contribute to the war effort. The schemes involve the government acting as either reinsurer of, or co-insurer with, commercial insurers.

(a)   The *War Risks Insurance Act 1939* and the *War Damage Act 1943* (both now repealed) allowed the government to operate compulsory commodity insurance schemes to protect stocks of commodities against enemy action or measures taken in anticipation of enemy action, and

(b)   The *Marine and Aviation Insurance (War Risks) Act 1952* authorises the government to enter into reinsurance agreements covering war risks affecting ships, aircraft and cargo.

Particular war risks

40.03   The following risks are those usually excluded from general policies and included in war risks cover. The peril of piracy is, exceptionally, treated as a marine peril rather than a war risks peril.

War

40.04   The word 'war' has been the subject of numerous court decisions. It has been held to include not just full war between nations but also localised conflicts over the ownership of territory (*Kawasaki Kisen Kabushiki Kaisha of Kobe v Bantham Steamship Co Ltd [1939] 2 KB 544* – the Chino-Japanese dispute) and civil war (*Curtis & Sons v Mathews [1918] 2 KB 825* – the Irish Easter rising). In determining whether a war exists, the English courts are not concerned with formal declarations of war or even whether the British Government has recognised, for diplomatic purposes, that a state of war exists.

Civil war

40.05   In addition to being a subdivision of war, civil war is an insurable peril in its own right. The meaning of this phrase was considered at length by Mustill J in *Spinney's (1948) Ltd, Spinney's Centres SAL and Michel Doumet, Joseph Doumet and Distributors and Agencies SAL v Royal Insurance Co Ltd [1980] 1 Lloyd's Rep 406*, a case which concerned destruction of commercial assets in Beirut in 1976 during fighting between various Lebanese religious groups. The judge held that the existence or otherwise of a civil war had to be determined by reference to three matters.

(a)   Are there identifiable opposing sides? This test excludes fighting between purely disparate groups, but the mere fact that each side is made up of factions does not prevent a finding of civil war. Some degree of polarisation is required.

(b)   Do the opposing sides have coherent objectives? The most likely objective is territorial, although the obtaining of political concessions may be sufficient.

(c)   Is the scale of the dispute sufficient to amount to civil war? Relevant factors include the number of combatants and casualties, the size of the territories occupied by the protagonists, the degree and duration of the conflict and the extent to which ordinary life has been disrupted.

In the *Spinney's* case, Mustill J ruled that none of these elements of civil war had been satisfied on the facts.

342

Rebellion and revolution

40.06 A rebellion was defined by Mustill J in the *Spinney's* case (see 40.05 above) as 'organised resistance to the ruler or government of a state, intended to supplant their authority over all or a part of the state'. As the *Spinney's* case itself demonstrates, if those responsible for the fighting do not have the co-ordinated intention of the overthrow of authority, there cannot be a rebellion. The word 'revolution' has never been defined in an insurance case, but would seem to bear much the same meaning as 'rebellion'.

Insurrection

40.07 An insurrection, like a rebellion, requires some intent on the part of those opposing authority to supplant that authority in all or a part of that state, but it is satisfied by a lesser degree of co-ordination than that necessary for a rebellion. If the co-ordination is present, it is irrelevant that there has been coercion on the part of the insurrectionists to obtain popular support (*National Oil Co of Zimbabwe (Private) Ltd v Nicholas Collwyn Sturge [1991] 2 Lloyd's Rep 281* – uprising in Mozambique). However, in the absence of any intention to overthrow the government, there cannot be insurrection (see the *Spinney's* case at 40.05 above). The necessary evidence of intention can be ascertained from literature issued by the opposing force, as in the *National Oil Company of Zimbabwe* case.

Civil commotion

40.08 Civil commotion is a state of affairs something short of civil war, and consists of violent internal disorder which is co-ordinated but not necessarily aimed at the overthrow of a government (see the *Spinney's* case at 40.05 above). The limits of civil commotion are illustrated by *London and Manchester Plate Glass Co Ltd v Heath [1913] 3 KB 411*, where suffragette movement supporters simultaneously (and without threat of personal violence) broke shop windows in various parts of London. The Court of Appeal held that there was no civil commotion, as the acts were not sufficiently proximate to each other to amount to co-ordinated violence, and in any event, violence was not involved in the damage itself but rather in protests following the arrest of the movement's supporters; such protests not having been co-ordinated.

Riot

40.09 The term 'riot' was given a statutory meaning by *s 1* of the *Public Order Act 1986*. The criminal offence of riot (which applies equally to insurance contracts – *Public Order Act 1986, s 10(2)*, amending the definitions in the *Schedule* to the *Marine Insurance Act 1906*) takes place, in accordance with *s 1(1)*:

> '... where twelve or more persons who are present together use or threaten unlawful violence for a common purpose and the conduct of them (taken together) is such as would cause a person of reasonable firmness present at the scene to fear for his personal safety.'

Riot can be committed in private as well as in public, the 12 persons need not use or threaten violence simultaneously and the common purpose can be ascertained from the behaviour of the participants (*Public Order Act 1986, s 1(2)–(5)*). It is also perfectly possible to have riot by silence, if the necessary threats are implicit by conduct. There cannot, however, be riot if violence is used not in furtherance of the participants' main objective, but rather in their attempts to effect an escape (*Athens Maritime Enterprises Corpn v Hellenic Mutual War Risks Association (Bermuda) Ltd (The 'Andreas Lemos') [1983] 1 All ER 590* – escape from scene of robbery).

The introduction in 1986 of a figure of 12 participants has significantly narrowed the scope of riot, as at common law the required minimum number of participants was three. The former width of riot is illustrated by *London and Lancashire Fire Insurance Co Ltd Appellants v Bolands, Ltd Respondents [1924] AC 836*, in which an armed robbery of a bakery by a group of four men was held to fall within the definition of riot. The overlap between ordinary risks and war risks has, in effect, been removed by the change effected by the 1986 Act.

Hostile acts by or against a belligerent power

40.10   This phrase is found in marine policies, and is aimed at the case in which a merchant vessel assisting in the war effort has been lost as a result of its activities. The wording indicates that the loss must be caused either by an attack by an enemy or by an attack on the enemy. There are many old cases in which a merchant vessel has been lost by means of collision with a friendly warship or when taking evasive action from a hostile vessel. Under previous war risks wordings ('hostilities and warlike operations'), such risks were treated as war risks, but this has ceased to be the case since the adoption of new wordings in 1983.

Derelict weapons of war

40.11   Loss caused by abandoned or derelict weapons of war is treated as a war risk by the marine clauses. The clauses were altered to this effect in 1982, following the decision of the High Court in *Costain-Blankevoort (UK) Dredging Co Ltd v Davenport (The 'Nassau Bay') [1979] 1 Lloyd's Rep 395*, in which it was held that a dredging vessel which was lost after having sucked up live shells abandoned after the Second World War had not been the victim of hostilities, on the ground that the dumping of ammunition was a peaceable and not a hostile act.

Proximate cause

40.12   Where damage to property results directly from conflict, the need for loss to be proximately caused by war is easily satisfied. More difficult issues arise where losses occur as an indirect result of war. The following situations have arisen in the cases.

Perils related to war risks

40.13

(*a*)   Loss has occurred in the course of preparation for war, eg in the training of troops or in the course of evacuation. It is unlikely that such losses can be regarded as proximately caused by war. Nevertheless, there are cases, largely concerned with the Irish troubles in the first quarter of the last century, in which it has been held that the theft of vehicles to be used in bombing and other terrorist raids are losses proximately caused by civil war. For example, the case of *Thomas Boggan v The Motor Union Insurance Co (1923) 16 Ll L Rep 64*, in which a domestic car was hijacked apparently for terrorist use, illustrates this line of authority.

(*b*)   The loss inflicted is of an economic rather than a military nature, with the intention of undermining the economy of the state. This was the case in *National Oil Company of Zimbabwe* case (see 40.07 above), in which an oil pipeline was destroyed by rebels for this very purpose. The High Court ruled that the loss was one caused by insurrection.

(*c*)   The loss has occurred in a place far distant from the forum of the dispute. It has been held in the United States that the hijacking of an American aircraft in Europe, and its subsequent destruction by hijackers, could not be proximately caused by the Middle Eastern conflict in respect of which the terrorists purported to act (*Pan American World Airways Inc v The Aetna Casualty & Surety Co [1975] 1 Lloyd's Rep 77*).

(*d*)   A ceasefire has been agreed, but a loss occurs due to the refusal of a particular faction to accept the validity of the ceasefire. There are no English authorities on this, but the American courts have ruled that such a loss is not attributable to war.

Other causation tests

40.14   The doctrine of proximate cause is often excluded in relation to war risks, and is replaced by other forms of wording. Where a policy excludes war risks it may exclude all direct and indirect consequences of war. In such a way the proximate cause test will be displaced and thus the insurer will be able to rely upon the war exclusion even if it can only prove that war, or an associated peril, is merely a contributing cause of the loss.

For example, a civil war may result in a supermarket being left without any security which, in turn, results in looting. If the insurers had to prove that the war or civil war was the proximate or dominant cause of the looting they may have some difficulty in making the causal connection. On the other hand, if they only have to prove that war contributed to the cause of the loss, then they would probably succeed in relying upon the exclusion.

Indeed, some property policies incorporate a reverse burden of proof clause in the war exclusion. By this means, in the event that the insurer can show, prima facie, the state of war or allied peril in a particular territory, the burden of proof transfers to the insured to prove that the loss is not caused by that peril.

In contrast, a war policy may require that a loss is caused solely by a war or allied peril risk before cover is provided.

Strikes

40.15   Cover against loss caused by strikes is frequently excluded from policies on commercial goods, and such an exclusion is standard in marine and aviation policies. In the marine market, strikes insurance is nevertheless available under the Institute strikes clauses. The losses in question are those caused by strikers, locked out workmen, or persons taking part in labour disturbances. Clearly these phrases cover physical damage to goods, but it is important to distinguish such direct losses from the financial consequences of delay flowing from strikes. Whether the strikes wording incorporates losses caused by delay is a matter of construction of the wording in question, but the general presumption is that loss by delay is not proximately caused by a strike.

Terrorism and political risks

Political risks exclusions

40.16   Marine and aviation policies commonly exclude loss caused by terrorists and persons acting from a political motive. There is no English case law on the meaning of these terms, and one question which remains to be decided is whether the phrase 'political motive' has to be assessed in accordance with the intention of the person causing the loss, or whether its meaning is objective. Similar, and largely unresolved, problems have been encountered in extradition law, the general effect of which is to prevent the extradition of persons for crimes of a political nature. There are a number of UK statutory definitions of 'terrorism'.

Terrorism risks and commercial buildings

40.17   At the end of 1992 the insurance market determined, in the light of the St Mary Axe bomb in April 1992, to withdraw terrorism cover from commercial and industrial properties; a move forced upon insurers by an earlier decision of the reinsurance market to withdraw reinsurance cover for such risks. Following expressions of concern, both by the operators of commercial buildings and by institutional investors, the Government agreed to provide the necessary reinsurance cover itself in order to allow insurance to be reinstated. The reinsurance scheme subsequently agreed between the market and the Government was given the force of law by the *Reinsurance (Acts of Terrorism) Act 1993*. In the light of the events of 11 September 2001 terrorism cover has been significantly restricted for domestic premises in the UK.

Under the 1993 Act, insurers continue to withdraw insurance cover in excess of £100,000 (£2,500,000 in respect of blocks of flats) for terrorist risks. Those insurers wishing to participate in the scheme reinstate terrorism cover for sums in excess of this figure, at premiums based on commercial rates. Reinsurance is provided by Pool Re, a company formed for this specific purpose by participating insurers. Pool Re is funded by premiums, by investments and, if necessary, by a levy on its members. Pool Re's risk is retroceded to the government in consideration for a premium, and on usual reinsurance terms. By acting as insurer of last resort, the government has ensured the continuation of terrorism cover. The scheme does not prevent insurers from seeking reinsurance on the open market. It will be seen that the scheme does not provide insurance cover against terrorism to all operators of commercial buildings, but rather only to those operators who are prepared to pay a commercial premium for such cover.

The scheme covers 'acts of terrorism', a phrase defined as meaning 'acts of persons acting on behalf of, or in connection with, any organisation which carries out activities directed towards the overthrowing or influencing, by force or violence, of Her Majesty's Government in the United Kingdom or any other government *de jure* or *de facto* (*Reinsurance (Acts of Terrorism) Act 1993, s 2(3)*). This definition makes it clear that the scheme applies only to organised terrorism rather than to isolated acts of vandalism. Subtly different definitions are often employed in domestic motor or buildings and contents insurance.

PART 6

Regulatory Matters

Chapter 41
Regulation of sales of insurance products

- Regulation of insurance intermediaries
- What insurance mediation activities are regulated?
- Authorisation and ongoing supervision

Regulation of insurance intermediaries

41.01 The sale of insurance contracts in the UK is regulated by the Financial Services Authority (FSA). The FSA is responsible for the authorisation and supervision of firms involved in the sale of insurance products. The sale of contracts of long-term insurance with an investment element has long been subject to regulation by the FSA. On 14 January 2005 the scope of regulation was extended to include general insurance contracts (eg motor, property and liability insurance) and pure protection contracts (critical illness, private medical insurance and income protection). The regulatory regime applicable to the sale of non-investment insurance contracts is less onerous than that which applies to those involved in the sale of *qualifying contracts of insurance* (see 41.04 below for definition). See 18.03 for a description of the classification of contracts of general insurance and contracts of long-term insurance.

The extension in scope of FSA regulation resulted from the implementation in the UK of the *Insurance Mediation Directive (IMD)*. The UK's approach to implementing the IMD by domestic legislation was, in part, through secondary legislation amending the *Financial Services and Markets Acts 2000 (Regulated Activities) Order 2001 (SI 2001/544) (RAO)* which describes the activities the FSA regulates.

Implementation of the IMD

41.02 The *IMD* was approved by the European Parliament on 30 September 2002. The *IMD* seeks to provide for common minimum standards for the regulation of insurance intermediaries and facilitate a single market in insurance mediation.

These minimum requirements on insurance intermediaries can broadly be summarised as:

(*a*)   possessing appropriate knowledge and ability;

(*b*)   being of good repute;

(*c*)   carrying professional indemnity insurance of at least EUR 1 million any one claim and EUR 1.5 million any one period of insurance;

(*d*)   measures to protect customers against the inability of the insurance intermediary to transfer the premium to the insurance company or to transfer the amount of claims or return premiums to the insured – the IMD gives member states four options to choose from to achieve that end.

Although the *IMD* only applies to insurance intermediaries (including reinsurance intermediaries), in the UK the government has extended the scope of regulation beyond the *IMD* to mediation activities carried on by insurers.

The FSA regulation of general insurance sales and administration replaced the system of self-regulation operated by the General Insurance Standards Council (GISC).

What insurance intermediation activities are regulated?

41.03   The following insurance mediation activities, if carried on by way of business, will require regulation from the FSA unless the person conducting such activities falls within an exemption, or has its head office in another EEA state other than the UK and has obtained appropriate authority from its home state regulator to conduct the relevant business in the UK:

(*a*)   *Introducing/arranging the purchase of contracts of insurance, including making arrangements with a view to such a contract.*

   This covers a range of activities, for example, introducing a customer to an insurer or insurance broker, or helping someone fill in an application form and sending a customer's form to an insurer.

(*b*)   *Arranging transactions in connection with lending on the security of insurance policies.*

(*c*)   *Advising a person on a contract of insurance.*

   This includes recommending a specific insurance policy to a customer.

(*d*)   *Dealing in contracts of insurance as an agent.*

   This includes entering into a contract of insurance with a customer on behalf of an insurer and/or an insured.

(*e*)   *Assisting in the administration and performance of a contract of insurance.*

   This includes activities post-contract, for example notifying an insurance claim to the insurer and negotiating settlement of the claim on behalf of the customer.

Claims management on behalf of an insurer is not a regulated activity. Simply providing information to a claimant or insurer in connection with the assessment of a claim is also not a regulated activity. Expert appraisal and loss adjusting (insofar as loss adjusting is carried out on behalf of an insurer) are not regarded as activities which require regulation insofar as they amount to assisting in the administration and performance of a contract of insurance.

See 18.03–18.05 for a discussion of how a contract of insurance may be defined.

Qualifying contracts of insurance

41.04   The above activities, when carried out in relation to *qualifying contracts of insurance*, have been matters which have been subject to regulation by the FSA and its predecessors. A *qualifying contract of insurance* is now defined as a contract of long-term insurance which is not:

(*a*)   a reinsurance contract; or

(*b*)   a contract in respect of which the following conditions are met:

   (i)   the benefits under the contract are payable only on death or in respect of incapacity due to injury, sickness or infirmity;

   (ii)   the contract has no surrender value, or the consideration consists of a single premium and any surrender value does not exceed that premium; and

   (iii)   the contract makes no provision for its conversion or extension in a manner which would result in its ceasing to comply with any of the above conditions.

Qualifying contracts of insurance therefore effectively means those kinds of life policy which have some form of investment element. The regulatory regime which is already in place as regards the selling of such products is generally more onerous than the regime which will be applicable to the mediation of other contracts of insurance as a result of the implementation of the *IMD*.

Other insurance mediation activities (which are not regulated in the case of contracts of general insurance) insofar as they relate to qualifying contracts of insurance (for instance, the managing of such contracts on behalf of another person in circumstances involving the exercise of discretion and also the activity of safeguarding and administering such qualifying contracts of insurance), are also subject to FSA regulation.

By way of business

41.05   The insurance mediation activity must be carried on by way of business for it to be subject to regulation. Activities carried on otherwise than for remuneration cannot be 'by way of business'. For example an employer who offers a health insurance package to its employees but does not receive a commission or any other commercial benefit as a result of this activity will not generally be carrying on insurance mediation by way of business. However, the remuneration test is significant. Remuneration covers monetary and non-monetary payments and does not have to be provided separately from remuneration for other services. For example, in some cases insurance policies are advertised as being 'free' to customers, for example, because customers who buy a product also get insurance for that product free of charge. A firm which offers insurance of this kind to customers still needs to consider whether it is carrying on regulated activities by way of business since the business may still be receiving a financial benefit from selling insurance this way.

Exclusions

41.06   If a person is carrying on a regulated activity as set out above, there are some exclusions which may be applicable. For example, two important exclusions are:

(*a*)   *Provision of information on an incidental basis.*

This exclusion is available (in relation to the activities of arranging and assisting in the administration and performance of a contract) provided the provision of information is in relation to a contract of insurance which is not a contract of long-term insurance, and is incidental to the profession or business carried on by the information provider, whose business does not otherwise carry on any regulated activities. For example, a dentist would be able to rely on this exclusion to provide information about specific kinds of dental insurance to his customers or give his customers the details of providers of dental insurance without needing to become authorised. However, this exclusion would not be applicable if the person does more than introduce the customers to insurers or brokers, for example by providing advice in the form of a recommendation to buy a specific policy or filling out an application form on behalf of a customer.

(*b*)   *'Connected contracts of insurance'.*

This exclusion is relevant to retailers of goods (other than motor vehicles) or travel agents selling insurance policies or helping customers make claims under them.

Retailers and travel agents can benefit from this exclusion where their activities are limited to general insurance policies relating to non-motor goods ('connected contracts of insurance') which:

(i)   are for five years or less (including renewals by right);

(ii)   have an annual premium of EUR 500 or less;

(iii)   cover the risk of breakdown, loss of, or damage to the goods supplied by the retailer; or, in the case of travel, cover the risk of damage to, or loss of baggage and other risks limited to the travel booked with the travel agent;

(iv)   do not cover liability risks (ie liability of the insured to third parties) except, in the case of travel risks, where this cover is ancillary to the main cover provided by the contract;

(v)   are complementary to the non-motor goods or the services supplied by the retailer; and

(vi)   are in standard form.

The exemption for travel insurance sold with a holiday is likely to cease to be available from 2009.

Mediation activities in relation to certain classes of general insurance business (so-called large risks) are exempt provided the risk or commitment covered by the contract is not situated in an EEA state. The relevant classes and other conditions which may be applicable can be found in *Article 72D Financial Services and Markets Act 2000 (Regulated Activities) Order 2001 (SI 2001/544)* (as amended).

Appointed representatives

41.07   A person who is carrying on insurance mediation activities can avoid the need to become regulated by the FSA if they are able to persuade one or more authorised insurers or insurance intermediaries to appoint them as their appointed representative. Appointed representatives are not directly regulated by the FSA but instead the person appointing them takes regulatory responsibility as principal for the activities of their appointed representative. A written contract needs to be in place as any principal must accept responsibility in writing for the activities of the appointed representative.

Authorisation and ongoing supervision

41.08   Many of the provisions referred to in 18.6 and 18.7 in the context of insurance companies are also relevant to insurance intermediaries who become subject to FSA authorisation. In the case of insurance intermediaries who do not provide insurance mediation services in respect of long-term contracts of insurance with an investment element there are some minor relaxations to some of the requirements.

Insurance: Conduct of Business Sourcebook (ICOB)

41.09   The *ICOB* rules came into force on 14 January 2005 . The *ICOB* rules apply to:

(*a*)   insurance intermediaries, including insurers, carrying on insurance mediation activities in relation to a non-investment insurance contract for any customer or a distance non-investment mediation contract with a retail customer. However, where there is a chain of insurance intermediaries between the insurer and the customer, *ICOB* only applies to the insurance intermediary in contact with the customer. A distance contract is a contract concluded by any means which does not involve the simultaneous physical presence of the parties;

(b) insurers when selling directly in relation to non-investment insurance contracts;

(c) a firm when it manages the underwriting capacity of a Lloyd's syndicate as a managing agent at Lloyd's in relation to a non-investment insurance contract;

(d) a firm which communicates or approves a non-investment financial promotion;

(e) a motor vehicle liability insurer; and

(f) Lloyd's in relation to motor vehicle liability insurance business.

The *ICOB* rules do not apply to reinsurance contracts or transactions involving large risks where the risk is located outside the EEA. There are exemptions from many of the rules for authorised professional firms and for service companies and in respect of large risks located in the EEA.

Different rules apply depending on whether the firm is dealing with a retail customer (a policyholder acting outside their business or profession) or a commercial customer. All chapters are relevant where a firm deals with a retail customer. The rules are less stringent in relation to dealings with a commercial customer. If it is not clear whether a person is a retail customer or not, he must be treated as a retail customer.

A separate FSA sourcebook (COBS) applies to insurance intermediaries who are involved in the selling or administration of investment insurance contracts. Those rules contain provisions which are more extensive in scope than the *ICOB* rules.

In part, *ICOB* implements provisions contained in a number of EC Directives: the *IMD* (in respect of non-investment insurance contracts), the *Distance Marketing Directive* (in respect of non-investment insurance contracts and distance non-investment mediation contracts), the *Consolidated Life Directive* (in respect of cancellation rights and information requirements relating to non-investment insurance contracts which are pure protection contracts), the *Third Non-Life Directive* (in respect of information requirements relating to general insurance contracts) and the *Fourth Motor Insurance Directive* (in respect of claims made by an EEA resident arising from a motor accident in the EEA but outside his country of residence).

General Rules

41.10 *ICOB 2* sets out rules relating to communication, unfair inducements and record keeping. Any communication with customers must be clear, fair and not misleading. The rules on inducements provide that a firm should not offer or accept an inducement if it is likely to conflict with a duty it, or the recipient firm, owes to its customers. An additional requirement for distance contracts with retail customers is that firms must provide a paper copy of the contract terms and conditions if requested. The records required by *ICOB* must be readily accessible (ie available for inspection by the FSA within two business days).

Financial promotion

41.11   *ICOB 3* contains rules on the communication and approval of financial promotions, for example product brochures, advertising by email, in magazines, websites or television. There are certain exemptions but any firm needs to show they have taken reasonable steps to ensure every promotion is clear, fair and not misleading, eg comparisons must be made with contracts which meet the same needs or which are intended for the same purpose, and must be objective and must not discredit or denigrate the activities of a competitor.

Advising and selling standards

41.12   The purpose of the rules in *ICOB 4* which relate to advising and selling standards are to ensure that:

(*a*)   customers are adequately informed about the nature of the service they have received;

(*b*)   any personal recommendation is suitable for the customer's demands and needs; and

(*c*)   charges imposed on retail customers are not excessive, and that commercial customers can on request obtain details of commission earned.

The rules apply mainly to advising and arranging; they have limited application to introducing.

Status disclosure

41.13   Various disclosures must be made at certain points in the sales process. Annexes to *ICOB 4* prescribe forms which can be used for this purpose. Information to be provided includes the name and address of the firm and, where relevant, the appointed representative; the firm's statutory status (eg authorised and regulated by the FSA); the range of products; procedure for complaints; whether or not compensation may be available from the Financial Services Compensation Scheme (FSCS); and whether advice has or will be provided on the basis of a fair analysis of the market, from a limited number of insurance undertakings, or from a single insurance undertaking.

Generally, the required information must be provided in durable medium before conclusion of the contract, although information may be provided orally if the customer so requests or requires immediate cover. If information is provided orally before conclusion of the contract, it must be provided in a durable medium immediately afterwards.

ICOB 4 also sets out status disclosure requirements for insurance intermediaries when introducing the customer to another insurance intermediary including suitability and record keeping requirements where a personal recommendation has been made. In the case of retail customers, a 'Statement of demands and needs' must be provided (including on renewal) in a 'durable medium' setting out the demands and needs of the customer, confirming whether the insurance intermediary has personally recommended the contract and, if so, explaining the reason for the personal recommendation.

Product disclosure

41.14 The purpose of the rules relating to product disclosure (contained in *ICOB 5*) are to ensure that customers have the necessary information to make an informed choice about whether to buy the insurance and its suitability. There are a number of stages in disclosure:

(*a*) Pre-commitment – key policy information and a policy summary document must be produced;

(*b*) Post-application – full policy documentation must be produced;

(*c*) Renewal – certain information and an updated policy summary must be produced;

(*d*) Post-sales – eg annually renewable contracts, where details of premium changes and annual reminders of the need to update cover if the contract term exceeds one year must be produced.

ICOB 5 sets out what information must be provided to customers and when, depending on whether the policy is a distance contract, including the form and content of:

(i) the policy summary;

(ii) the statement of price;

(iii) directive required information;

(iv) the policy document and when they should be provided.

Cancellation

41.15 Prescribed periods of cancellation are set out for different types of contracts; generally, 30 days for pure protection contracts and 14 days for a general insurance contract.

Specified information must be disclosed to the customer relating to how to cancel, any conditions and the duration of the cancellation period. If the customer had requested coverage to commence before the cancellation period ends then the insurer can generally retain a proportionate part of the premium.

Claims handling

41.16   Rules (in *ICOB* 7) relating to claims handling require fair and prompt handling of claims. Retail customers must be given guidance on their claim and kept informed, with an explanation as to why a claim is refused. Insurance intermediaries are required to disclose and manage any conflicts of interest which may exist.

Specific rules in connection with distance non-investment mediation contracts with retail customers

41.17   *ICOB 8* sets out rules specific to such contracts. The FSA expects the requirements set out in *ICOB 8* to be relevant only in a small minority of cases.

The ICOB Review

41.18   At the time of writing this chapter, the FSA are consulting on proposed changes to ICOB. In relation to general insurance contracts (other than Payment Protection Insurance) the FSA has put forward plans to remove many of the detailed rules and replace them with high-level principles. For pure protection and PPI contracts the FSA is proposing additional rules to address market failure identified in relation to those products. Subject to feedback from the consultation, the FSA intend to make final rules in December 2007.

Chapter 42

Insurance Business Transfers under the Financial Services and Markets Act 2000

- Introduction
- Use of insurance business transfers
- Law and practice
- Meaning of 'transfer'
- The court's jurisdiction
- Procedure
- Effect of court's order
- UK taxation

Introduction

42.01 Where parties wish to transfer the assets and liabilities of a general or life insurance business to another party, subject to limited exceptions, a court-approved insurance business transfer (a *Part VII Transfer*) under Part VII of the Financial Services and Markets Act 2000 (*FMSA 2000*) is the only means of doing this in the United Kingdom.

A Part VII Transfer permits the transfer of insurance business without the need for individual novations of insurance policies. The process also provides a number of protections for policyholders, including:

(*a*) the appointment of an independent expert to review and report on the transfer;

(*b*) the approval of the court, which considers whether policyholders are being treated fairly; and

(c)   the right of any person who may be adversely affected by the Part VII Transfer to object at the final court hearing.

The FSA will also review the Part VII Transfer and, if relevant, will liaise with its fellow EU regulators. It also has the right to attend and to be heard on the scheme in court.

Schemes will generally take at least six months to put together and obtain court approval. The process requires co-ordination between the FSA, the firms and their advisers (legal, actuarial and tax), other EU regulators as well as in some cases the Revenue authorities for clearance purposes.

Use of insurance business transfers

42.02   Subject to the limits of s 105 of the FSMA (see 42.05 below) a Part VII Transfer can be used by life and general insurers in a wide variety of ways. These include:

(a)   intra group reorganisations;

(b)   'domestication' of an overseas branch;

(c)   sale of an insurance business;

(d)   demutualisation of a mutual insurance company; and

(e)   fund restructuring, including the reattribution of the inherited estate of a life company.

The Part VII process can be used to transfer assets and liabilities allocated to both a shareholders fund as well as a long-term fund of an insurance company.

Law and practice

42.03   Insurance business transfers were previously governed by *Sch 2C* to the *Insurance Companies Act 1982* that set out different requirements for general and long-term business transfers. Very broadly, long-term business transfers required an order of the court, and the production of a report by an independent actuary on the effect of the scheme as well as the notification of policyholders. General business transfers required only the approval of the FSA.

The procedure for life and general insurance business transfers has now been unified under *Part VII of the FSMA 2000* and both now require court approval and the production of an expert's report. The specific provisions relevant to Part VII Transfers are:

(a)   *Part VII of and Sch 12 to the FSMA 2000*;

(b)   The *Financial Services and Markets Act 2000 (Control of Business Transfers)(Requirements on Applicants) Regulations 2001 (SI 2001/3625) (2001 Regulations)*; and (*c*)   Chapter 18 of the FSA's Supervision Manual forming part of the FSA Handbook (SUP 18).

Meaning of 'transfer'

42.04   The starting point, when looking at any proposed 'transfer' from the legal point of view, is that under the general English law, although it is possible to transfer contractual rights without the consent of the counterparty, it is not possible to transfer contractual obligations without consent.

The expression 'transfer' when used in the context of insurance business means an arrangement under which liability for the insurance policies forming part of the business transferred passes from the transferor to the transferee. The transferor ceases to be liable and, for practical purposes, the policyholders are treated as if their contracts had always been with the transferee. The process is a coercive one.

A transfer is therefore to be distinguished from reinsurance; even though reinsurance can, as between transferor and transferee, pass economic responsibility in relation to the underlying contracts, legal liability to the policyholder remains with the transferor.

SUP 18 contains FSA guidance on what may constitute a transfer. Firstly, the FSA takes the view that a novation or series of novations (ie individual agreements under which the policyholder agrees to the contract moving to the new insurer) can be capable of constituting a Part VII Transfer if their number and effect is equivalent to a transfer of part of a company's insurance business. By contrast, neither the 'reinsurance-to-close' process at Lloyd's nor a mere transfer of renewal rights constitutes a transfer for the purposes of the legislation, as in neither case does legal liability to a policyholder under an existing contract pass.

The court's jurisdiction

42.05   *Section 105 FSMA 2000* limits the application of Part VII Transfers in broad terms to the following:

- insurance and reinsurance business carried on in the United Kingdom and the rest of the EEA by UK persons who have permission to carry on insurance business in the United Kingdom;

- reinsurance business carried on in the United Kingdom by EEA firms permitted to carry on insurance business in the UK (under the passporting regime); and

- insurance and reinsurance business carried on in the United Kingdom by persons with permission to carry on insurance business in the United Kingdom that are not UK authorised persons or EEA firms.

Additionally, a Part VII Transfer must result in the transferred business being carried on from the transferee's establishment in an EEA member state.

The meaning of 'carrying on insurance business in the UK' is not straightforward and has been the subject of considerable judicial interpretation. In broad terms, however, issues such as where underwriting decisions are made and policy administration is undertaken will be relevant. *Section 418 of the FSMA 2000*, which sets out the requirements for carrying on regulated activities in the United Kingdom, is also relevant.

Procedure

42.06   The court procedure that is described below applies in England and Wales. There is a slightly different procedure in Scotland.

As an overriding comment on process, it is worth bearing in mind when planning an insurance business transfer that, even for a straightforward scheme, it is likely to take at least six months from start to finish. The reasons for this include:

(*a*)   the three-month objection period for EEA regulators where policyholders have their 'habitual residence' in EEA member states;

(*b*)   the period of not less than six weeks recommended by the FSA in its guidance between sending notices to policyholders and the final court hearing;

(*c*)   if applicable, the need for the transferee to obtain FSA authorisation or vary its Part IV permission; and

(*d*)   due diligence, which will need to focus on material contracts, foreign law governed contracts and contracts with subsidiaries of the transferor.

The role of the Financial Services Authority

42.07   The FSA is currently the UK regulator of the insurance industry.

The involvement of the FSA is required at an early stage in the process as *s 109 of the FSMA 2000* requires its approval for the identity of the independent expert and the form of his report.

Although the FSA does not need to approve a transfer scheme formally, in practical terms the parties are highly unlikely to proceed with a Part VII Transfer without the support of the FSA. This is usually given in the form of a letter of non-objection issued by the FSA prior to the court hearing. The FSA also has a statutory right to attend the court hearing and make representations about the transfer (*FSMA 2000, s 110*).

During the process, the FSA will review key documents such as the scheme, policyholder notices and the report of the independent expert. The FSA also provides various certificates (*Part I of and Sch 12 to, FSMA 2000*) – first, as to the regulatory capacity of the transferee to continue the transferred business, second, as to the solvency of the transferee and, third, where EEA state regulators are consulted, as to their consent or non-objection to the proposed scheme – see below at 42.08).

Finally, the transferor is required by *reg 3(4) of the 2001 Regulations* to provide the FSA with copies of the application to court, the independent expert's report and the statement to policyholders at least 21 days before the court hearing.

Policyholders in EEA states

42.08　If the 'state of commitment' of a policy to be transferred under a Part VII Transfer is an EEA member state (other than the United Kingdom), *Sch 12, FSMA 2000* gives the regulator of that member state a three-month period to object to the transfer. The court cannot make an order sanctioning the scheme unless the FSA certifies that the supervisory authority in the relevant state has either has consented to the transfer or has not objected to it.

Schedule 12 defines the 'state of commitment' as:

(*a*)　where a policyholder is an individual, the EEA state in which he had his 'habitual residence' at the date the policy was taken out; and

(*b*)　where the policyholder is not an individual, the EEA state in which the policyholder was established or situated on the date the policy was taken out.

For a transfer of general business, *para 6(3) of Sch 12* provides a means of identifying the EEA member state 'where the risk is situate'. This will depend on the nature of the insurance – a motor risk, for example, is situate where the vehicle is registered.

The meaning of 'habitual residence' is more problematic. The term derives from EU social security law and there is no single test which can be applied. General indicators include the location of the policyholders employment, permanent residence and future intentions. This is clearly not the sort of information retained by insurance companies at the time the policyholder takes out his or her policy. This is recognised by the FSA and the courts who are prepared to be pragmatic. Generally therefore insurance companies take the following approach:

(*a*)　first, they consult their computer records to establish the number of policyholders whose current address is within an EEA member state;

(*b*)　second, they examine the original paper files of those policyholders to establish, where possible, whether any of them were resident in that EEA state on the date the policy was taken out.

It is worth emphasising that the requirement for consultation in *Sch 12* is triggered by a single policy. Accordingly, companies tend to err on the side of caution and consult where there is any indication that an EEA member state was the state of commitment of a transferring policy. Furthermore, the practice has also developed of including in the scheme document wording that excludes from the Part VII Transfer any policy in respect of which the FSA is unable to give a certificate. These 'excluded policies' are then reinsured from the transferring company to the transferee in order to achieve an 'economic' transfer of these policies.

Independent expert and scheme report

42.09   Under the Part VII regime, for both long-term and general business, there must be an independent expert appointed and they must make a report on the terms of the scheme. *Section 109* of the *FSMA 2000* specifies that the FSA must approve both the identity of the independent expert and the form of his report. The FSA's agreement to the identity of the independent expert should be sought at an early stage of the process.

The FSA's guidance indicates that the expert should be an actuary for transfers of long-term business, but need not be an actuary where he reports on a transfer of general business. The suitability of a particular individual will depend on the nature of the scheme, the business being transferred and the companies concerned. The FSA will also verify the expert's independence from the companies involved.

The FSA guidance also sets out the matters with which a scheme report should deal. In practice, the independent expert's report is one of the most important documents that will be prepared, and will be relied upon heavily by the judge. Indeed, the court may well look to the expert for assistance in understanding some of the provisions of the scheme. For this reason he/she should always attend the court hearing.

Policyholders will see a summary of the report if a circular is to be sent (this is dealt with below). The Regulations also provide that any person may obtain a copy of the report, together with a summary of the terms of the scheme, free of charge on request. The practice has developed of including this information on the website of at least one of the companies involved.

Notification to policyholders and others, and access to documentation

42.10   *Regulation 3 of the 2001 Regulations* sets out the following notification requirements for policyholders:

(a)   a notice stating that an application for a Part VII Transfer has been made must be sent to every policyholder of the transferor and transferee;

(b)   the notice must also be advertised in the London, Belfast and Edinburgh Gazettes, two UK newspapers and any EEA states which is a 'state of commitment'; and

(c)   a copy of the independent expert's report, a statement setting out the terms of the scheme and a summary of the independent expert's report must be made available to policyholders.

Compliance with the notification requirement in (a) can be particularly difficult in view of the breadth of the term 'policyholder' and the reliance on policyholder records of the transferor and transferee. However, the courts are prepared to take a pragmatic approach and, provided that the transferee and transferor companies show that all reasonable and practicable steps have been taken to overcome deficiencies in policyholder records, the court is prepared to grant dispensations in respect of, for example, policyholders whose names and current address are not on the company's records. An application for dispensation must be made by way of affidavit to the court prior to the directions hearing describing the areas in which the strict requirements of the 2001 Regulations cannot be complied with and the steps the company is taking to overcome deficiencies in its policyholder records. Dispensations are also frequently obtained in relation to EEA advertising.

As referred to in paragraph (c), the parties are also required to make available to policyholders a statement setting out the terms of the scheme and a summary of the independent expert's report. The statement does not have to be sent to policyholders, it only has to be made available to them – this is confirmed in FSA guidance in SUP 18 that states that the internet can be used for these purposes (usually via the transferor and transferee's websites). However, a copy of the independent expert's report and the statement must given free of charge to any person that requests it.

It is worth noting that, as a practical matter, it is now the FSA, rather than the court that decides what information is sent to policyholders. In its guidance in SUP 18, the FSA also states that the statement should be clear and concise and inform policyholders in broad terms of how the scheme is likely to affect him. In preparing the statement, consideration should also be given to whether any other legal requirements might apply (eg the prospectus rules) and local law requirements in other jurisdictions into which the statement is being sent.

The court application

42.11   Once the proposal is agreed between the parties and with the FSA and fully documented, the court process is started by an application to the Companies Court of the Chancery Division, submitting a Part 8 claim form, to which the scheme is annexed, together with a fee.

The first court hearing on the application takes place before a Registrar. The hearing will cover the requirements which the court will wish to see imposed for the notification of policyholders and others. The court will give directions at this stage. Following this hearing, the companies will post formal notice of the transfer which, according to the FSA's guidance, should occur at least six weeks before the court hearing to approve the transfer.

An affidavit in support of the application and claim form will cover the company's authority to transfer the business, the reasons for the transfer and, importantly, the proposals that the parties are making to notify transferring policyholders and, where appropriate, the policyholders of the transferee company and relevant dispensations sought from the court.

Final hearing

42.12   A full hearing will then be held before a judge at which he is asked to sanction the scheme. The FSA has a right to attend at this hearing, as does any person who alleges that he would be adversely affected by the carrying out of the scheme.

The leading decision on whether anyone would be 'adversely affected' was made by Hoffmann J in the unreported case of *Re London Life Association* in 1989. Hoffmann J's key principles were summarised by Evans Lombe J in his decision on *Axa Equity & Law Life Assurance Society plc v Axa Sun Life plc [2001] 1 All ER (Comm) 1010*. They are as follows:

(a)   First, the Act confers an absolute discretion on the court whether or not to sanction a scheme, but this is a discretion that must be exercised by giving due recognition to the commercial judgment entrusted by the company's constitution to its directors.

(b)   The court is concerned with whether a policyholder, employee or other interested person, or any group of them, will be adversely affected by the scheme.

(c)   This is primarily a matter of actuarial judgment involving a comparison of the security and reasonable expectations of policyholders without the scheme with what would be the result if the scheme were implemented. For the purpose of this comparison, the Act assigns an important role to the independent expert, to whose report the court will give close attention.

(d)   The FSA, by reason of its regulatory powers, can also be expected to have the necessary material and expertise to express an informed opinion on whether policyholders are likely to be adversely affected. Again, the court will pay close attention to any views expressed by the FSA.

(e)   The fact that individual policyholders, or groups of policyholders, may be adversely affected does not mean that the scheme has to be rejected by the court. The fundamental question is whether the scheme as a whole is fair as between the interests of the different classes of persons affected.

(f)   It is not the function of the court to produce what, in its view, is the best possible scheme. As between different schemes, all of which the court may deem fair, it is the company's directors' choice which to pursue.

(g)   Under the same principle, the details of the scheme are not a matter for the court provided that the scheme as a whole is found to be fair. Thus, the court will not amend the scheme because it thinks that individual provisions could be improved upon.

(*h*)   The court, in arriving at its conclusion, should first determine what the contractual rights and reasonable expectations of policyholders were before the scheme was promulgated and then compare those with the likely effect on the rights and expectations of the policyholders if the scheme is implemented.

There are further principles that can be extrapolated from the cases as follows:

● When considering the question set out at (*e*), it is acceptable to take into account the advantages and disadvantages which would be secured by particular classes of persons by the implementation of the scheme. A balancing exercise is required, and this was made clear from both the decision in *Re Refuge Assurance plc (10 December 2000, unreported)* and from para 2.3.2 of the FSA's feedback on CP110.

● In relation to (*g*), in *Re London Life Association* Hoffman J suggested that if the court viewed that the scheme was unfair, it could opine that the unfairness lay in a particular term and that a fresh scheme not containing the offending term would be likely to be acceptable.

● Although the judge in *AXA Equity & Law* referred to policyholders, the court will apply the same tests to objections raised by any other category of objector claiming to be adversely affected.

● In *AXA Equity & Law* it was stated that in any actuarial matter which is in dispute, the court's approach should be to accept the views of the independent expert and the FSA over those of the companies and any objectors. If the views of the independent expert conflict with those of the FSA, the court is likely to prefer those of the FSA.

Effect of court's order

42.13   The scope within which a court order may be given is set out in *s 112* of *FSMA 2000*. Typically it will have the following effects:

(*a*)   first, policy rights and liabilities will transfer without any requirement for consent by the relevant policyholder so that the transferee becomes directly liable to the policyholder and the transferor ceases to be liable for them – this is of course the principal objective of the order;

(*b*)   all other assets, rights, contracts and liabilities within the terms of the order will also transfer. The court also has the power to override contractual rights, such as prohibitions on the assignment of contracts, in connection with a transfer of insurance business (this is explained below);

(*c*)   the court order is the only instrument needed to effect the transfer although, where registration is needed to perfect a transfer, for example real property and shares, the registration requirement is not dispensed with;

(*d*)   the transaction is a transfer by operation of law as a result of the court's order, of the assets and liabilities within the scope of the court order. It is not a transaction of assignment nor of novation; and

(e)   because the authority is given by statute, it does not extend to foreign assets or liabilities that an order of a UK court cannot transfer as it has no jurisdiction – foreign assets or liabilities will need to be transferred by separate documents in accordance with local laws.

One particular area of interest is *s 112(2)(a)* of *FSMA 2000*, which gives the court power to order the transfer of assets or contracts even if the transferor does not otherwise have the capacity to transfer them, eg if they are explicitly or by their nature incapable of transfer without consent. A recent decision of the court on the same legislation in a banking transfer case – in *Re Cater Allen Ltd [2002] EWHC 3147 (Ch)* – confirms that this language does give the court power, where it considers in all the circumstances that this is justified, to order the transfer of assets or liabilities even where they might otherwise be non-transferable, for example because of express contractual provision. This has particular relevance to reinsurance contracts relating to the transferring insurance business. However, to date, we are not aware of the courts exercising such powers and as a matter of good business practice, the transferor is likely to approach the reinsurers for consent in any event.

UK taxation

42.14   This chapter does not cover the tax position in any detail and expert advice should always be sought. However, excluding the UK tax effect of portfolio transfers of long-term business the specific reliefs and exemptions available on transfers of long-term business do not apply.

All general insurance business carried on by a company is a trade, and the transfer of general insurance business is governed by general tax principles applicable to any disposal of a trade. Thought will need to be given, however, where business run-off is transferred as the Revenue will need to be convinced that the 'trade' is still being carried on.

VAT is not generally a problem as the transfer will usually constitute a transfer of a business as a going concern, even if it is not wholly within a VAT group.

Index

A

acceptance of offers 1.14
ADR SEE alternative dispute
  resolution
agents
  disclosure 6.06
  fraud 6.31
aircraft operators' insurance
  25.02–14
alien abduction 39.16
all risks
  insurance 14.07, 24.01–02,
    27.03, 28.07–08
  mortality (ARM) 26.03
  war risks 25.13
alternative dispute resolution
  (ADR) 23.01–05
  early neutral evaluation 23.05
  executive tribunals 23.03
  expert determination 23.04
  mediation 23.02
  mini trials 23.03
arbitration 21.01
  agreements 20.02
  appeals 21.07
  clauses 20.02
    reinsurance treaties 38.17
  confidentiality 21.05
  honourable engagement
    clauses 21.06
  procedure 21.04
  proceedings 20.07
  scope of 20.03
  severability 20.02
ARM (all risks mortality) 26.03
assigned policies 14.13
assignment 16.20
  policies 16.21–29
    consequences 16.29
    formalities 16.23
    insurer's consent 16.22
    life policies 16.25–28
    marine insurance 16.24,
      34.06
    prohibition 16.21
  proceeds of policies 16.30–31
    sale of land 16.31

assignment 16.20 – *contd*
  subrogation 16.03
ATE insurance SEE legal
  expenses insurance, after the
  event (ATE)
average
  first condition of 19.01
  general average losses 34.49
  particular average 34.48
  policies subject to 19.02
  valued policies 15.08–09
aviation insurance 25.01–25
  aircraft, loss or damage 25.03
  aircraft operators' insurance
    25.02–14
    conditions precedent 25.09
    exclusions 25.05, 25.07–08,
      25.11–14
  airport owners' and operators'
    insurance 25.15–22
    exclusions 25.17, 25.20–21
    products liability 25.19–20
  Ariel form 25.15–22
  cargo 25.10
  hangarkeeper's liability 25.18
  hijacking 25.13
  Lloyd's Aviation Underwriters'
    Association (LAUA) 25.01
  noise 25.12
  nuclear risks 25.14
  passengers 25.04–05
  pollution 25.12
  premises liability 25.16–17
  products liability 25.25
  spares cover 25.23–24
  third parties 25.06–07
  war 25.13

B

barratry 34.35
'basis of the contract'
  clauses 1.08, 6.23, 6.35
benefits 1.03
betterment 15.19
bloodstock insurance 26.01–07
  all risks mortality (ARM) 26.03
  declarations of health 26.02

bloodstock insurance 26.01–07 – *contd*
fraud 26.07
loss of use (LOU) 26.04
money laundering 26.07
moral hazard 26.07
public liability 26.06
theft 26.05
unlawful removal 26.05
veterinary certificates 26.02
bordereaux **38.08**
breach of contract 15.17
brokers
advice, suitability of 9.09
agency law 9.01–03
authority of 9.03
cancellation 9.18
claims 9.33–34
claims handling 9.19–20
commercial customers 9.15
commission 9.26
disclosure 9.11
competence 9.24
complaints handling 9.23
cover notes 1.13
damages, measures of 9.37
disclosure 6.05, 6.06
distance non-investment
mediation contracts 9.21
duties 9.28–34
duty of care 9.35
excessive charges 9.11
financial promotion 9.07
group policies 9.16
independence of 9.02
Insurance Conduct of Business
Rules (ICOB) 9.05–21
liabilities 9.35–38
liens 9.27
limitation of actions 9.36
Lloyd's 11.01
policies 5.09
marine policies 5.09
payment of the loss 9.34
persons to whom duties are
owed 9.38
post-formation duties 9.32
premiums 5.07–09
payment of 9.31
proposal forms 9.30
recovery of payments 9.34
regulation 9.04–25
reinsurance 9.02
retail customers 9.14
rights 9.26–27
statements of demands and
needs 9.10
status disclosure 9.08

brokers – *contd*
sub-brokers, duty of care 9.35
third parties 9.38
tort 9.35
training 9.24
underwriters 9.02
unsolicited services 9.12
utmost good faith, duty of 9.02
white labelling 9.17
BTE insurance SEE **legal**
expenses insurance, before
the event (BTE)
buildings
insurable interest 4.12
unvalued policies 15.11
buildings insurance 27.01–18
All Risks cover 27.03
average 19.02
business interruption 27.15
claims
following termination of
cover 3.5
limitation 14.10
computer systems 27.09
conditions 27.14
debris removal 27.17
denial of access 27.16
disclosure of risk 27.05
exclusions 27.06–13
extensions to 27.17–18
increased cost of construction
27.18
industrial perils 27.08
inevitable loss 27.12
natural peril exclusions 27.07
specified perils 27.03
theft 27.11
trigger of cover 27.04
types of 27.02–05
war perils 27.10
business relationships
insurable interest 4.05

C
captive insurers 8.03–04
causation SEE **loss, causes of**
children
insurable interest 4.05
civil commotion, meaning of
40.08
Civil Procedure Rules 22.01–09
civil war, meaning of 40.05
claims
all risks insurance 14.07
assigned policies 14.13
brokers 9.33–34
burden of proof 14.05

claims – *contd*
 contractual limitation 14.11
 cover notes 1.13
 fraudulent 6.30, 14.08–09
 handling 9.19–20
 insured perils 14.06
 limitation 14.10–14
 notification 14.01–02
 payment
  assigned policies 14.13
  insurer's obligation 14.12
  policies under trust 14.14
 policies under trust 14.14
 proof of loss 14.03–07
 standard of proof 14.05
 Statutory Declarations of loss
  14.03
 successive 15.23
 termination of cover 3.5
 third party claimants 9.20
 time for giving notice 14.02
 valuation 7.03
 waiver for breach of condition
  14.04
claims management 41.03
co-insurance 17.01–08
 subrogation 17.07
**commencement of cover 1.14,
 3.1**
 marine policies 5.03
**commercial buildings,
 reinsurance 40.17**
commercial policies
 average 19.02
 war risks 40.02
**commercial property policies,
 average 19.02**
commission, brokers 9.11, 9.26
composite insurance 17.03–06
compulsory insurance
 employers' liability insurance
  30.12
 Financial Services
  Compensation Scheme
  (FSCS) 7.07
 motor vehicles 35.08–17
**conditional fee agreements
 33.03**
conditions 1.21
 mere 2.05
 suspensive 2.03
conditions precedent 2.02
conditions subsequent 2.02
consequential loss 15.15
consideration 1.16

**construction risks insurance
 28.01–09**
 all risks cover 28.07–08
 damage to the works 28.05
 Joint Contracts Tribunal (JCT)
  contract 28.03–06
 latent defects insurance (LDI)
  28.09
 liquidated damages insurance
  28.06
 project insurance 28.02
 right of disclosure 3.3
 risks 28.01
 third party claims 28.04
contingency insurance 1.04
**continuing warranties 1.08,
 6.23, 6.35**
contra proferentem **rule 2.14,
 6.24**
contract certainty 1.22
contracts
 ambiguity 2.14
 breach of 15.17
 business-like interpretation 2.13
 commencement of cover 1.14
 construction 2.16
 context of words 2.11–12
 contra proferentem rule 2.14
 eiusdem generis rule 2.12
 extrinsic evidence 2.16
 formation 1.05, 1.17–18
 implied terms 2.15
 of insurance 12.03–04
 interpretation 2.16
 negotiation 1.05
 oral 1.05
 parol evidence rule 2.16
 parties' intention 2.08
 personal lines 1.08
 surrounding words 2.12
 technical meanings 2.10
 terms
  construction of 2.07–16
  implied 2.15
 tort 9.35
 trade meanings 2.10
 unauthorised insurers 10.02
 void for mistake 5.14
 words, meaning of 2.09–12
contribution
 amount of 18.07–09
 conditions for 18.06
 definition 18.05
 double insurance 18.04–09
 independent liability 18.08
 maximum liability 18.09

contributory negligence,
   damages 9.37
counter-offers 1.06
   acceptance of offers 1.14
   variation of terms 1.14
counter-proposals 1.06
court proceedings 22.01–09
   allocation 22.05
   case management 22.03
   disclosure 22.07
   expert evidence 22.08
   fast track 22.05
   multi-track 22.05
   overriding objective 22.02
   part 36 offers 22.06
   pre-action protocols 22.04
   settlement before trial 22.06
   small claims track 22.05
cover
   commencement 1.14, 3.1
   'difference in conditions' 8.05
   expiry 3.2
   renewal 3.3
   termination 3.2–5
      claims 3.5
      early 3.4
cover notes 1.13
creditors
   life insurance 4.05
criminal liability
   fraud 6.32
   unauthorised insurers 10.02

D
damages
   breach of contract 15.17
   brokers 9.37
   contributory negligence 9.37
   disclosure, breach of duty 6.21
   misrepresentation 6.21, 6.25
deceit, utmost good faith, duty
   of 6.25
declarations of health 26.02
deposits, repayment 1.13
'difference in conditions' cover
   8.05
directors and officers insurance
   29.01–05
   disqualification 29.05
   duties to the company 29.03
   duties to third parties 29.04
   statutory liabilities 29.05
disclosure 1.14, 6.03–21
   agents 6.06
   ambiguous questions 6.24
   breach of duty
      awareness of 6.18

disclosure 1.14, 6.03–21 – *contd*
   breach of duty – *contd*
      insurer's remedies 6.21
   brokers 6.05, 6.06
   construction of statements 6.24
   court proceedings 22.07
   criminality 6.11
   definition 6.04
   delay 6.17
   duration of duty 6.19
   'fair presentation' of risk 6.04
   fraud 6.30–38
   immaterial facts 6.12–14
   increase in hazard clauses 6.34
   innocent non-disclosure 6.05
   insurer's remedies 6.21
   limitations 6.12–14
   material facts 6.10–11
   misrepresentation 6.23–25
   presumption of inducement
      6.08
   right of 3.3
   risk increase 6.33–37
   superfluous circumstances 6.20
   waivers 6.15–16
discovery extension
   clauses 11.07
dispute resolution 21.01–07
   alternative 23.01–05
   professional indemnity
      insurance 37.08
distance non-investment
   mediation contracts 9.21
domestic property policies,
   average 19.02
double insurance 18.01–09
   contribution 18.04–09
   independent liability 18.08
   maximum liability 18.09
   rateable proportion
      clauses 18.04
duty of care
   brokers 9.35
   emergency services 16.16
   sub-brokers 9.35

E
early neutral evaluation 23.05
early termination of cover 3.4
eiusdem generis **rule 2.12**
emergency services, duty of care
   16.16
employees
   definition 30.09
   exceptions to compulsory
      insurance requirement
      30.12

employees – *contd*
  relatives as 30.11
  residence in Great Britain 30.10
employers
  life insurance 4.05
employers' liability insurance
  30.01–15
  certificates 30.15
  common law liabilities
    30.06–07
  compulsory insurance,
    exceptions 30.12
  course of employment 30.04,
    30.07
  cover, amount of 30.03
  direct liability 30.06
  employees 30.09–12
    definition 30.09
    exceptions to compulsory
      insurance requirement
      30.12
    relatives as 30.11
    residence in Great Britain
      30.10
  enforcement 30.14–15
  independent contractors 30.07,
    30.09
  liabilities 30.06–08
    transfer of 30.13
  obligation to insure 30.02
  offshore installations 30.10
  policy conditions, prohibited
    30.05
  sanctions 30.14
  statutory liabilities 30.08
  transfer of liabilities 30.13
  vicarious liability 30.07
enforcement
  employers' liability insurance
    30.14–15
  Financial Services Authority
    (FSA) 9.25
environmental insurance
  31.01–06
  common law liability 31.03
  policies 31.06
  public liability policies 31.05
  statutory liability 31.04
Equitas 11.01
equity, assignment 16.23
  life policies 16.28
ex gratia **payments 38.21, 38.22**
excess clauses 15.20
exclusion clauses 2.04
executive tribunals 23.03
expert determination 23.04
expiry of cover 3.2

express conditions 1.21

F
facultative reinsurance 38.04,
  38.07
  duration of contracts 38.14
'fair presentation' of risk 6.04
Financial Services Authority
  (FSA) 9.04
  authorisation 10.02, 12.06
  enforcement 9.25
  supervision 12.07
  transfers of insurance
    businesses 42.07
  underwriting agents 10.02
Financial Services
  Compensation Scheme
  (FSCS) 7.01–14
  amounts payable 7.06–13
  compulsory insurances 7.07
  exclusions 7.06
  funding 7.05
  general insurance 7.08
  insurance intermediaries
    7.10–13
  levies 7.05
  long-term policies 7.09
  powers 7.04
  protected risks 7.06
fire policies, average 19.02
fire protection clauses 6.37
first condition of average 19.01
franchise clauses 15.21
fraud 6.30–38
  agents 6.31
  bloodstock insurance 26.07
  claims 6.30, 14.08–09
  criminal liability 6.32
  loss 15.02
  proof of 14.09
  risk increase 6.33–37
  utmost good faith 6.02
FSA SEE **Financial Services**
  Authority
FSCS SEE **Financial Services**
  Compensation Scheme

G
global insurance programmes
  8.01–12
  captive insurers 8.03–04
    insolvency 8.11
  choice of law 8.07
  controlling claims 8.09
  'difference in conditions' cover
    8.05
  inconsistencies 8.08, 8.10

global insurance programmes 8.01–12 –
  contd
  jurisdiction 8.07
  retaining risk 8.03
  vertical contractual chains 8.04
goods in transit insurance
  32.01–10
  carriers
    liability 32.01, 32.02
    obligation to insure 32.01
  commencement 32.03
  conditions 32.06
  contracts 32.01
  exclusions 32.06
  loss 32.07
  Marine Institute Cargo
    Clauses 32.08–10
  storage 32.05
  termination 32.03
  transit 32.04
group policies 9.16

H
hazard SEE **risk**
health, declarations of 26.02
hijacking 25.13
honourable engagement
  clauses 21.06

I
ICOB SEE **Insurance Conduct**
  of Business Rules
IMD (Insurance Mediation
  Directive) 9.04, 41.01–02
implied conditions 1.21
Inchmaree **clause 34.34**
increase in hazard clauses 6.34
indemnity 15.04
indemnity insurance 1.04 SEE
  ALSO **non-indemnity**
  insurance
  insurable interest 4.04,
    4.06–4.13
  premiums 5.06
  renewal of cover 3.3
  right of disclosure 3.3
indemnity principle
  insurable interest 4.14
innominate terms 2.06
insurable interest 4.01–14
  buildings 4.12
  business relationships 4.05
  carriers 32.01
  children 4.05
  definition 4.02
  indemnity insurance 4.04,
    4.06–4.13

insurable interest 4.01–14 – *contd*
  indemnity principle 4.14
  lack of 5.12
  life insurance 4.05
  marine insurance 4.07, 34.05
  non-indemnity insurance
    4.04–4.05
  non-life insurance 4.05
  parents 4.05
  property owner 4.11
  property possession 4.13
  relatives 4.05
  requirement to show 4.03–4.04
  siblings 4.05
  spouses 4.05
  wagers 4.01, 4.03
insurance, definition 1.01–04
insurance business
  transfers SEE transfers of
    insurance businesses
  unauthorised 12.05
insurance companies 12.01–07
  authorisation requirement
    12.01, 12.06
  regulated activities 12.02
  supervision 12.07
  unauthorised insurance business
    12.05
  winding-up 7.03
Insurance Conduct of Business
  Rules (ICOB) 6.03
  advice, suitability of 9.09
  cancellation 9.18
  claims handling 9.19–20
  commercial customers 9.15
  commission disclosure 9.11
  distance non-investment
    mediation contracts 9.21
  excessive charges 9.11
  financial promotion 9.07
  general rules 9.06
  group policies 9.16
  ICOB 1 9.05
  ICOB 2 9.06, 41.10
  ICOB 3 9.07, 41.11
  ICOB 4 9.08–12, 41.12–13
  ICOB 5 9.13–17, 41.14
  ICOB 6 9.18
  ICOB 7 9.19–20, 41.16
  ICOB 8 9.21, 41.17
  insurance intermediaries
    41.08–18
  personal lines contracts 1.08
  regulated activities 10.02
  retail customers 9.14
  review 41.18

Insurance Conduct of Business Rules (ICOB) 6.03 – *contd*
statements of demands and
needs 9.10
status disclosure 9.08
third party claimants 9.20
unsolicited services 9.12
white labelling 9.17
insurance contracts 12.03–04
insurance intermediaries
advising standards 41.12
appointed representatives 41.07
'by way of business' activities
41.05
cancellation 41.15
claims handling 41.16
connected contracts of
insurance 41.06
distance non-investment
mediation contracts 41.17
exclusions from
regulation 41.06
financial promotion 41.11
Financial Services
Compensation Scheme
(FSCS) 7.10–13
ICOB 2 41.10
ICOB 3 41.11
ICOB 4 41.12–13
ICOB 5 41.14
ICOB 7 41.16
ICOB 8 41.17
Insurance Conduct of Business
Rules (ICOB) 41.08–18
product disclosure 41.14
qualifying contracts of
insurance 41.04
regulation 41.01–07
exclusions 41.06
selling standards 41.12
status disclosure 41.13
Insurance Mediation Directive
***(IMD)* 9.04, 41.01–02**
insurrection, meaning of 40.07
interest on late payments 15.17

J
Joint Contracts Tribunal (JCT)
contract 28.03–06
joint insurance 17.02

L
land
sale of, assignment of proceeds
of policies 16.31
latent defects insurance (LDI)
28.09

launch vehicles 39.02
LDI (latent defects insurance)
28.09
legal expenses insurance
33.01–04
after the event (ATE) 33.02
conditional fee agreements
33.03
before the event (BTE) 33.01
regulation 33.04
legal relations, intention to
create 1.15
liability insurance
claims
following termination of
cover 3.5
limitation 14.10, 20.07
liens, brokers 9.27
life insurance
assignment 16.25–28
claims, limitation 14.10
creditors 4.05
employers 4.05
insurable interest 4.05
letters of acceptance 1.06
premiums 5.05
proof of title 14.03
renewal of cover 3.3
subrogation 16.04
life reinsurance 38.01
'risk premium' basis 38.01
livestock insurance 26.01
Lloyd's
brokers 5.09, 11.01
contract formation 1.17–18,
11.05
disciplinary proceedings 11.03
discover extension
clauses 11.07
Equitas 11.01
forms
AVN 1C 25.01, 25.03
AVN 38B 25.14
AVN 46B 25.12
AVN 48B 25.13
AVN 67B 25.03
AVN 71 25.14
LPO 344C 25.23
LPO 359B 25.02, 25.10
LSW 555B 25.13
Franchise Board 11.01
history 11.01
losses 11.09
managing agents 11.01
Names 11.01
oversubscription 11.06

Lloyd's – *contd*
policies 1.21
average 19.02
composite nature 11.07
disputes as to meaning 11.07
inconsistent with slip 11.07
premiums 11.08
regulation 11.02–03
'reinsurance-to-close' process
42.04
slips 1.05, 1.17, 11.04–07
inconsistent with policies
11.07
Society of 11.01
structure 11.01
syndicates 11.01
underwriting agents 10.03
authorisation 10.02
regulated activities 10.02
utmost good faith, duty of
11.05
Lloyd's Aviation Underwriters'
Association (LAUA) 25.01
London Market Principles
(LMP) slips 1.18
loss
animals, of use (LOU) 26.04
broken chain of events 13.04
brokers, payment of 9.34
causes of 13.01–09
common cause 15.24
concurrent causes 13.06
exclusions from indemnity
13.09
fraud 15.02
insured's negligence 13.08
linked events 13.05
meaning of 15.01
minimisation of 6.33–37
mitigation 13.07
negligence 13.08
of possession of property 15.02
proof of 14.03–07
proximate cause 13.01
sequential causes 13.02–05
series of 15.22–24
Statutory Declarations of 14.03
unbroken chain of events 13.03
unconnected 15.22
unvalued policies 15.13
loss adjusters 38.21
loss of use (LOU) of an animal
26.04
LOU (loss of use of an animal)
26.04

M
Mareva injunctions,
subrogation 16.13
Marine Institute Cargo
Clauses 32.08–10
marine insurance 34.01–57
abandonment 34.47
notice of 34.46
actual total loss 34.43
assignment 16.24, 34.06
average 19.02
barratry 34.35
brokers 5.09
cargo, loss or damage 34.52
cargo policies 34.37
claims, limitation 14.10
commencement of cover 5.03
constructive total loss 34.44–47
contract formation 34.07
costs recoverable 34.56
definition 34.01–03
delay 34.40
early termination 3.4
exclusions 34.38–41
floating policies 34.10
freight, loss of 34.53
general average losses 34.49
goods, seaworthiness of 34.18
'held covered' clauses 3.3, 5.02
hulls and freight policies
34.28–36
cover, summary of 34.29
Inchmaree clause 34.34
indemnity, measure of
34.50–56
inherent vice 34.41
insurable interest 4.07,
4.09–10, 34.05
land risks 34.03
losses 34.42–49
actual total loss 34.43
constructive total loss
34.44–47
forms of 34.42
general average 34.49
partial 34.48
'lost or not lost' policies 4.09
machinery damage 34.34
measure of indemnity 34.50–56
negligence 34.36
open cover 34.10
partial losses 34.48
particular average 34.48
perils of the sea 34.30–32
burden of proof 34.31
causation 34.31
definition 34.30

marine insurance 34.01–57 – *contd*
  perils of the sea 34.30–32 – *contd*
    unseaworthy vessels 34.32
  piracy 34.33
  policies, types of 34.08–10
  premiums 5.02, 5.03, 34.11
  right of disclosure 3.3
  rights of insurers 34.57
  salvage charges 34.48, 34.56
  seaworthiness warranty
    34.13–18
  suing and labouring 34.54–56
  time policies 34.08, 34.16–17
  unvalued policies 34.09, 34.50
  utmost good faith 34.04
  valued policies 34.09, 34.50
  vessels, loss or damage 34.51
  voyage policies 34.08, 34.15
  voyages
    changes of 34.26
    commencement 34.24
    currency of 34.23–27
    delays 34.27
    deviations 34.27
    performance of 34.25–27
  war risks 34.38
  warranties 34.12–17
    of good safety 34.22
    of legality 34.19
    of nationality 34.21
    of neutrality 34.20
    seaworthiness 34.14–18
    seaworthiness of goods 34.18
  wilful misconduct 34.39
**Marine Insurance Act 1906
  34.01**
**Market Reform Contract
  (MRC) 1.18**
Market Reform (MR) slips 1.18
market value 15.11
material facts SEE ALSO
  disclosure
  assessment of 6.05
  meaning 6.04
  misrepresentation 6.23
  moral hazard 6.11
  physical hazard 6.10
  reinsurance 38.09–12
  test of materiality 6.07
  warranties 6.23
mediation 23.02
mere conditions 2.05
MIB SEE **Motor Insurers'
  Bureau**
mini trials 23.03
misrepresentation 1.08, 1.14
  ambiguous questions 6.24

misrepresentation 1.08, 1.14 – *contd*
  construction of statements 6.24
  damages 6.21, 6.25
  disclosure 6.23–25
  innocent 6.05
  insurer's remedies 6.25
  material facts 6.23
  reinsurance 38.07–08
    remedies 38.13
  repayment of premiums 5.15
modern equivalent cost 15.11
**money laundering, bloodstock
  insurance 26.07**
**Motor Insurers' Bureau
  35.18–24**
  compensation 35.19–21
  conditions precedent 35.22
  exceptions 35.21
  limitations on liability 35.23
  obligations 35.20–21
  uninsured drivers 35.19
  untraced drivers 35.24
**motor vehicle insurance
  35.01–24**
  authorised drivers 35.14
  causing or permitting use 35.11
  compulsory insurance 35.08–11
    exemptions 35.12
    scope 35.13
  direct claims against insurers
    35.17
  failure to insure 35.09
  first party cover 35.07
  insurer obligations 35.14–16
  Motor Insurers' Bureau
    35.18–24
    compensation 35.19–21
    conditions precedent 35.22
    exceptions 35.21
    limitations on liability 35.23
    obligations 35.20–21
    uninsured drivers 35.19
    untraced drivers 35.24
  other drivers 35.05
  other vehicles 35.06
  policy conditions 35.04
  provision of information 35.16
  unauthorised drivers 35.15
  using a motor vehicle 35.10
  utmost good faith 35.02
  warranties 35.03
**MRC(Market Reform Contract)
  1.18**
MR(Market Reform) slips 1.18
mutual insurance 1.02
  premiums 5.01, 5.02

N

non-disclosure SEE
  misrepresentation
non-indemnity insurance
  insurable interest 4.04–4.05
  life insurance 4.05
**non-proportional reinsurance
  38.04**
novations 42.04
nuclear risks 25.14

O

offers 1.06, 1.14
over-insurance 5.18, 6.11

P

parents
  insurable interest 4.05
parol evidence rule 2.16
perils of the sea 34.30–32
  burden of proof 34.31
  causation 34.31
  definition 34.30
  unseaworthy vessels 34.32
**personal accident policies,
  subrogation 16.04**
personal lines contracts 1.08
piracy 34.33
policies
  assignment 16.21–29
  conditions 1.21
  forfeiture 5.03
  group 9.16
  insurance company 1.20
  Lloyd's 1.21
  scheduled 1.20
  slips 1.21
  terms and conditions, cover
    notes 1.13
  under trust 14.14
political risks exclusions 40.16
Pool Re 40.17
post, acceptance of offers 1.14
pre-action protocols 22.04
premiums 1.02
  amount of 5.02
  brokers 5.07–09
  definition 5.01
  divisibility of risk 5.16
  forfeiture 6.21, 6.25
  Lloyd's policies 1.21, 11.08
  marine insurance 34.11
  misrepresentation 5.15
  non-payment 5.03, 5.04
  over-insurance 5.18
  payment of 5.03, 9.31
  renewal 5.04–06

premiums 1.02 – *contd*
  repayment 1.13, 3.4, 5.10–18,
    6.21, 6.25, 7.03
  variation 1.14
  warranties, breach of 5.17
**product liability insurance
  36.01–17**
  accidental injury 36.05
  advice, giving of 36.14
  claims 36.07–09
    made 36.09
    occurring 36.08
  compensation 36.03
  conditions 36.16–17
  contractual liabilities 36.12
  damages 36.03
  design defects 36.14
  employees 36.11
  exclusions 36.10–15
  financial loss 36.04
  fitness for purpose 36.13
  insured's property 36.11
  jurisdictional restrictions 36.06
  product recalls 36.13
  property damage 36.05
  reasonable precautions 36.17
  risks 36.02–06
  services 36.14
  specification defects 36.14
  territorial restrictions 36.06
**professional indemnity
  insurance 37.01–08**
  basis of cover 37.03
  compulsion to insure 37.02
  dispute resolution 37.08
  exclusions 37.06
  extensions of indemnity 37.05
  policy conditions 37.07
  QC clauses 37.08
  scope of cover 37.04
  sources of liability 37.01
project insurance 28.02
promised lines 1.17
property insurance 27.01–18
  All Risks cover 27.03
  average 19.02
  business interruption 27.15
  claims
    following termination of
      cover 3.5
    limitation 14.10
  computer systems 27.09
  conditions 27.14
  debris removal 27.17
  denial of access 27.16
  disclosure of risk 27.05
  exclusions 27.06–13

property insurance 27.01–18 – *contd*
  extensions to 27.17–18
  increased cost of construction
    27.18
  industrial perils 27.08
  inevitable loss 27.12
  natural peril exclusions 27.07
  specified perils 27.03
  subrogation 16.04
  theft 27.11
  trigger of cover 27.04
  types of 27.02–05
  war perils 27.10
proportional reinsurance 38.04
proposal forms 1.07–08
  'basis of the contract'
    clauses 1.08, 6.23
  brokers 9.30
  further enquiries 1.12
  questions, failure to ask 1.11
  utmost good faith 1.10
  waivers of information 1.09–12
proximate cause of loss 13.01
public liability policies,
  environmental insurance
  31.05

Q
QC clauses 37.08
qualifying contracts of
  insurance 41.04
quotation slips 1.17

R
rateable proportion
  clauses 18.04
reasonable care clauses 6.36
rebellion, meaning of 40.06
recovery, restrictions on
  15.19–28
regulated activities 10.02
reinstatement 15.30–34
  availability 15.31
  cost greater than anticipated
    15.33
  definition 15.30
  obligation 15.32
  option frustrated 15.33
  statutory 15.34
reinstatement cost 15.11
reinstatement insurance 15.16
reinsurance 38.01–24
  in advance of insurance 38.05
  agreements
    formation of 38.05
    terms 38.14–24
  arbitration clauses 38.17

reinsurance 38.01–24 – *contd*
  bordereaux 38.08
  brokers 9.02
  claims co-operation 38.23
  claims control clauses 38.23
  claims history 38.11
  commercial buildings 40.17
  damages, contributory
    negligence 9.37
  definition 38.02
  duration of contracts 38.14
  ex gratia payments 38.21,
    38.22
  exceptional liability 38.12
  excess of loss contracts 38.04
  facultative 38.04, 38.07, 38.14
  'follow the fortunes' 38.22
  'follow the settlements' 38.21
  forms of 38.04
  incorporation of terms by
    reference 38.15
  inspection of records
    clauses 38.16
  law, choice of 38.24
  life 38.01
  loss adjusters 38.21
  loss settlement clauses 38.19–
    20
  material facts 38.09–12
  misrepresentation 38.07–08
    remedies 38.13
  non-proportional 38.04
  Pool Re 40.17
  pools 38.06
    underwriting agents 10.04
  previous losses 38.11
  proportional 38.04
  quota share contracts 38.04
  regulation 38.01
  reinsured's right to indemnity
    38.18
  retention 38.10
  'risk premium' basis 38.01
  as a separate contract 38.03
  stop loss contracts 38.04
  surplus contracts 38.04
  terms of agreements 38.14–24
  transfers of insurance
    businesses 42.04
  treaties 38.03, 38.04, 38.08,
    38.14
relatives
  insurable interest 4.05
revolution, meaning of 40.06
riot, meaning of 40.09
risk
  attachment of 5.10, 5.13

risk – *contd*
divisibility of 5.16
'fair presentation' 6.04
increased 6.33–37
minimisation of loss 6.33–37
retaining 8.03
Road Traffic Act 1988 30.01

S
salvage, insurer's right 15.29
satellites 39.02
scheduled policies 1.20
settlements
binding 15.25
misrepresentation 15.27
mistakes 15.26
unfair 15.28
**SGIP (Statement of General
Insurance Practice) 6.03**
siblings
insurable interest 4.05
slips
Lloyd's 1.17, 11.04–07
London Market Principles 1.18
Market Reform 1.18
policies 1.21
Society of Lloyd's 11.01
space insurance 39.01–16
alien abduction 39.16
coverage 39.09
delay 39.13
launch vehicles 39.02
liability 39.11
partial loss 39.10
political risks 39.14
re-launch guarantee 39.15
satellites 39.02
transponder coverage 39.12
transponders 39.02
spouses
insurable interest 4.05
standard terms 1.14
**Statement of General Insurance
Practice (SGIP) 6.03**
**Statutory Declarations of loss
14.03**
strikes 40.15
sub-brokers, duty of care 9.35
subrogation 16.01–19
allocation of sums recovered
16.19
assignment 16.03
cause of action 16.05–09
co-insurance 17.07
emergency services, actions
against 16.16
ex gratia payments 16.12

subrogation 16.01–19 – *contd*
indemnification of the insured
16.11–15
indemnity contracts 16.04
life insurance 16.04
loss exceeding the sum insured
16.14
Mareva injunctions 16.13
operation of 16.02
personal accident policies 16.04
procedural aspects 16.17
property insurance 16.04
rights prior to payment 16.13
role of 16.01
sale of land 16.31
scope of 16.04–10
sums recovered 16.18–19
unnamed insureds 17.08
waiver of rights 16.10
wrongdoers
as beneficiaries of the policy
16.07
exempt from liability by
contract 16.08
as party to the policy 16.06
suspensive conditions 2.03

T
temporary cover 1.13
termination of cover 3.2–5
terrorism
acts of, meaning 40.17
risks 40.16–17
theft
bloodstock insurance 26.05
buildings insurance 27.11
property insurance 27.11
**Third Parties (Rights Against
Insurers) Act 1930 20.01–10**
agreements between the insurer
and the insured 20.06
compliance with policy terms
20.05
dissolved companies 20.04
insolvency 20.02
limitation periods 20.07
problems with operation of
20.09
proof of liability 20.03
reform proposals 20.10
right to information 20.08
third party claimants 9.20
tort 9.35
**transfers of insurance
businesses 42.01–14**
approval 42.01
court application 42.11

transfers of insurance businesses 42.01–14 – *contd*
court order 42.13
final hearing 42.12
Financial Services Authority
(FSA) 42.07
habitual residence 42.08
independent experts 42.09
reports 42.10
jurisdiction 42.05
law 42.03
notifications 42.10
novations 42.04
policyholder protection 42.01
policyholders in EEA states
42.08
procedure 42.03, 42.06
reinsurance 42.04
scheme reports 42.09
scheme statements 42.10
'state of commitment' 42.08
taxation 42.14
transfer, meaning of 42.04
use of 42.02
transponders 39.02
**treaty reinsurance 38.03, 38.04,
38.08**
duration of contracts 38.14

U
uberrima fides SEE **utmost good
faith**
uncertain events 1.04
underwriters
brokers 9.02
Lloyd's policies 1.21
underwriting agents
authorisation 10.02
authority 10.05
definition 10.01
duties 10.06
Lloyd's 10.03
overseas insurers 10.02
regulated activities 10.02
reinsurance pools 10.04
unnamed insureds 17.08
unvalued policies 15.10–15
buildings 15.11
consequential loss 15.15
damage to part of a property
15.14
goods 15.12
loss, general measure of 15.13
market value 15.11
modern equivalent cost 15.11
partial loss 15.13–14
reinstatement cost 15.11

unvalued policies 15.10–15 – *contd*
total loss 15.11–12
valuation 15.10–12
utmost good faith
breach of duty 6.02
damages 6.25
brokers 9.02
continuing duty 6.02
deceit 6.25
disclosure of material facts
1.14, 6.03–21
duty of 6.01–02
fraud 6.02
insurers 6.38
litigation 6.02
Lloyd's 11.05
marine insurance 34.09
motor vehicle insurance 35.02
proposal forms 1.10

V
valued policies 15.05–09
average
not subject to 15.08
subject to 15.09
partial loss 15.07
total loss 15.06
valuation 15.05
vertical contractual chains 8.04
veterinary certificates 26.02

W
wagers
insurable interest 4.01, 4.03
waivers of information 1.09–12
war
aviation insurance 25.13
civil 40.05
meaning of 40.04
war risks 40.01–14
all risks 25.13
buildings insurance 27.10
causation tests 40.14
civil commotion 40.08
civil war 40.05
commercial insurance 40.02
derelict weapons of war 40.11
hostile acts by or against a
belligerent power 40.10
insurrection 40.07
marine insurance 34.38
property insurance 27.10
proximate cause 40.12–13
rebellion 40.06
related perils 40.12–13
revolution 40.06
riot 40.09

war risks 40.01–14 – *contd*
  war 40.04
warranties 2.01
  assignment of proceeds of
    policies 16.30
  breach of 5.17
  continuing SEE 'basis of the
    contract' clauses

warranties 2.01 – *contd*
  definition 34.12
  marine insurance 34.12–17
  material facts 6.23
  motor vehicle insurance 35.03
white labelling 9.17
**winding-up of insurance
  companies 7.03**